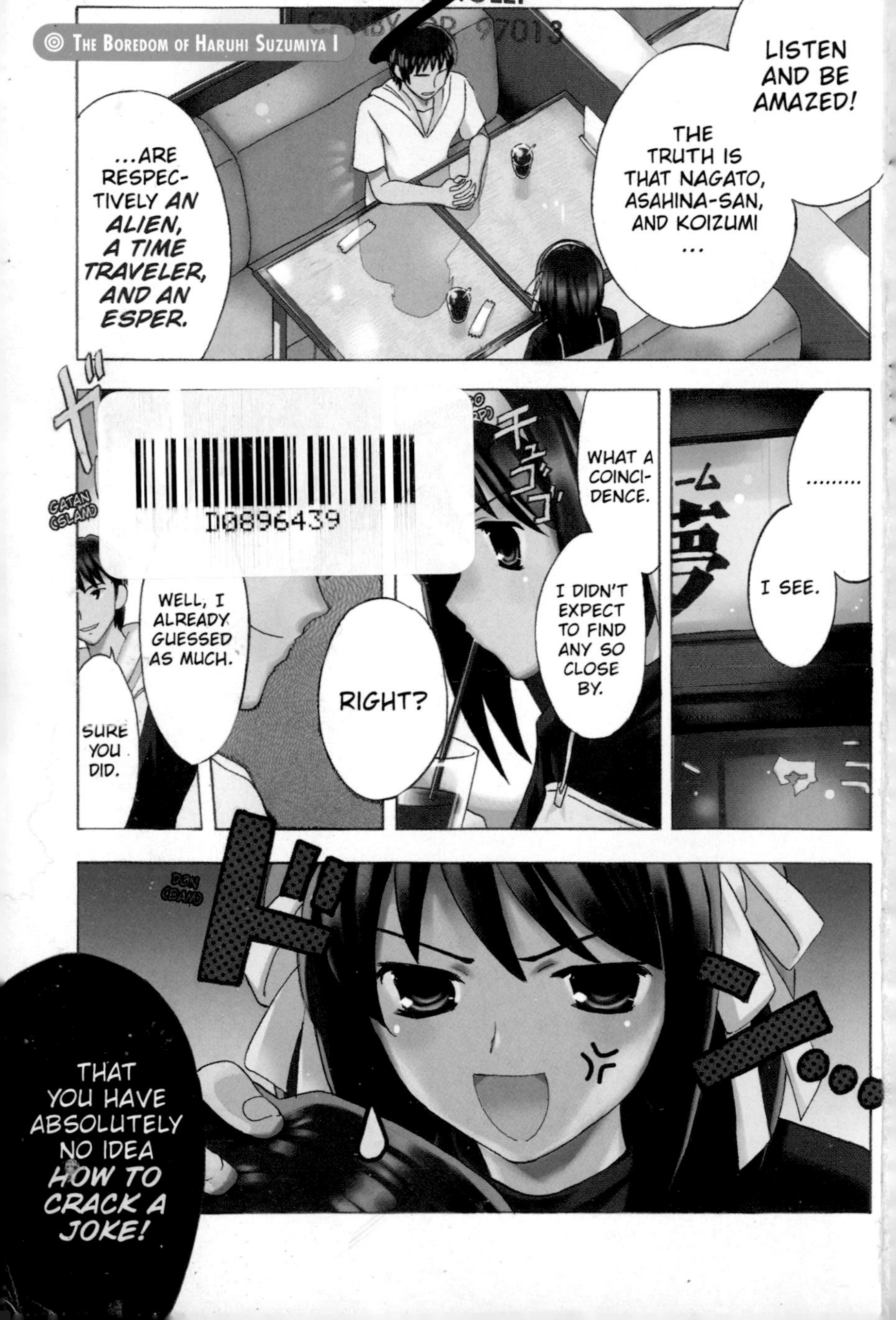
LISTEN AND BE AMAZED!
THE TRUTH IS THAT NAGATO, ASAHINA-SAN, AND KOIZUMI ...
...ARE RESPECTIVELY AN ALIEN, A TIME TRAVELER, AND AN ESPER.
....
I SEE.
WHAT A COINCIDENCE.
I DIDN'T EXPECT TO FIND ANY SO CLOSE BY.
RIGHT?
GATAN
WELL, I ALREADY GUESSED AS MUCH.
SURE YOU DID.
DGN
THAT YOU HAVE ABSOLUTELY NO IDEA HOW TO CRACK A JOKE!

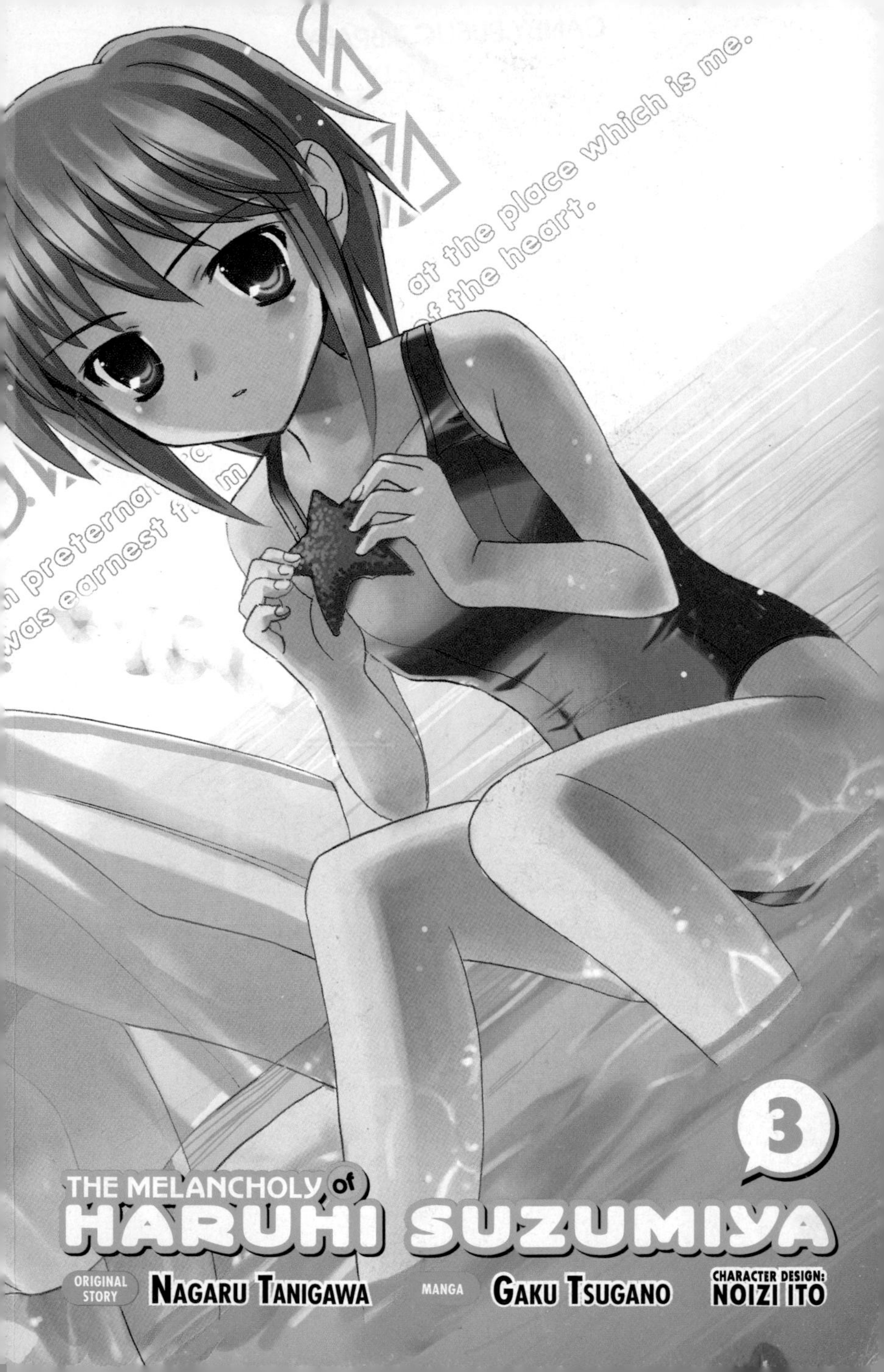
at the place which is me.
3
THE MELANCHOLY of
HARUHI SUZUMIYA
ORIGINAL STORY
NAGARU TANIGAWA
MANGA
GAKU TSUGANO
CHARACTER DESIGN:
NOIZI ITO

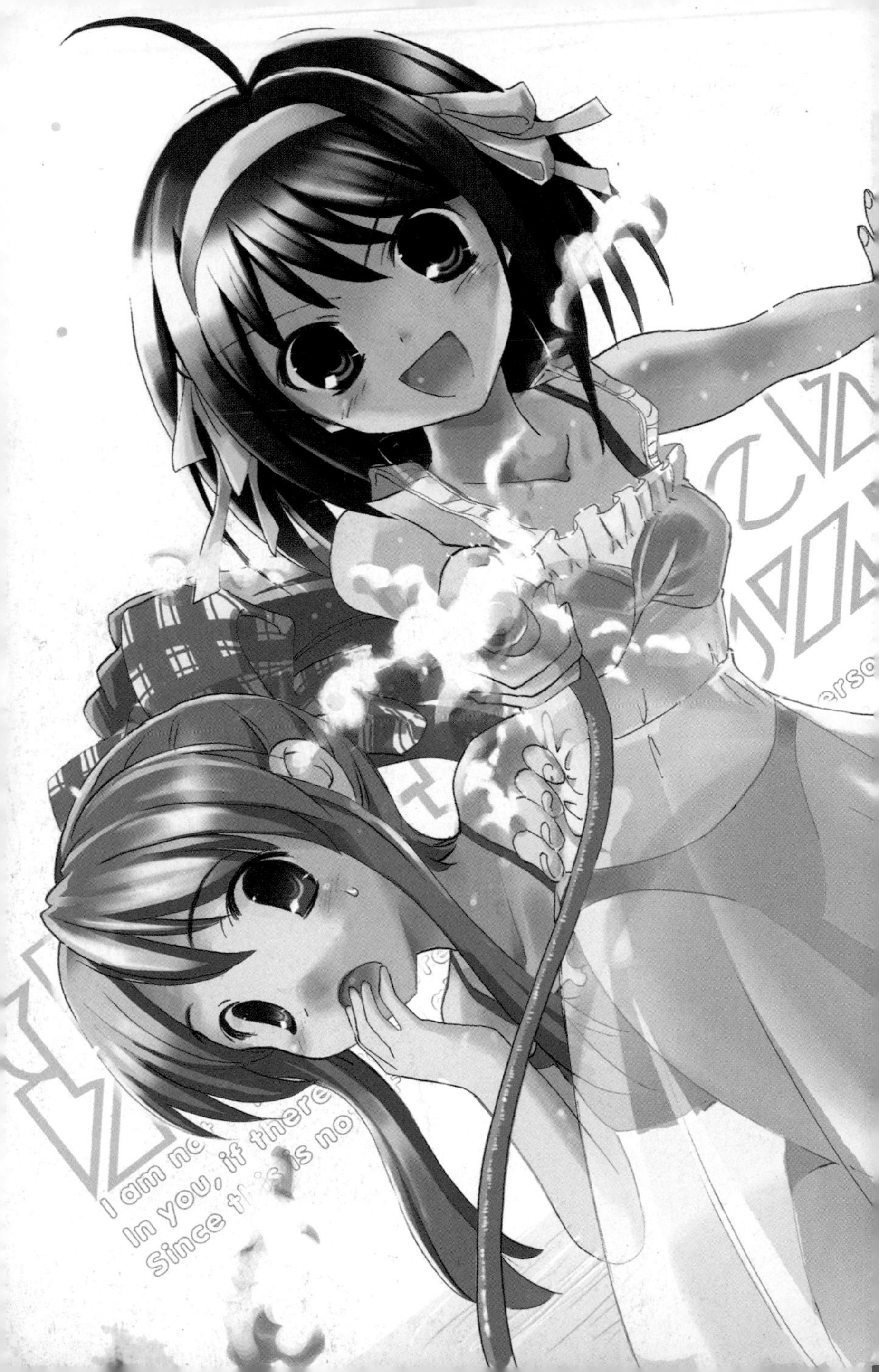
I am no
In you, if there
Since th

CONTENTS

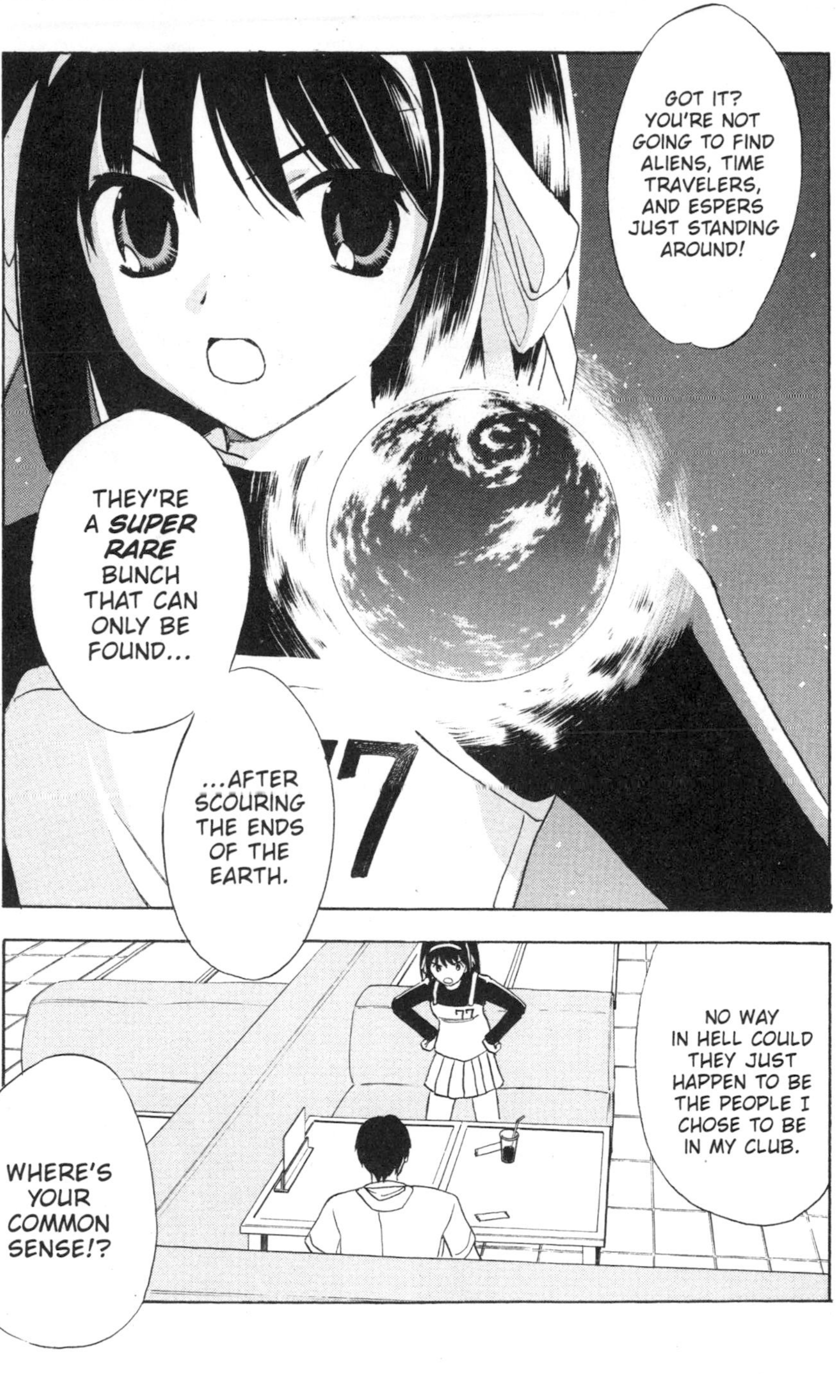
GOT IT? YOU'RE NOT GOING TO FIND ALIENS, TIME TRAVELERS, AND ESPERS JUST STANDING AROUND!
THEY'RE A SUPER RARE BUNCH THAT CAN ONLY BE FOUND...
...AFTER SCOURING THE ENDS OF THE EARTH.
NO WAY IN HELL COULD THEY JUST HAPPEN TO BE THE PEOPLE I CHOSE TO BE IN MY CLUB.
WHERE'S YOUR COMMON SENSE!?

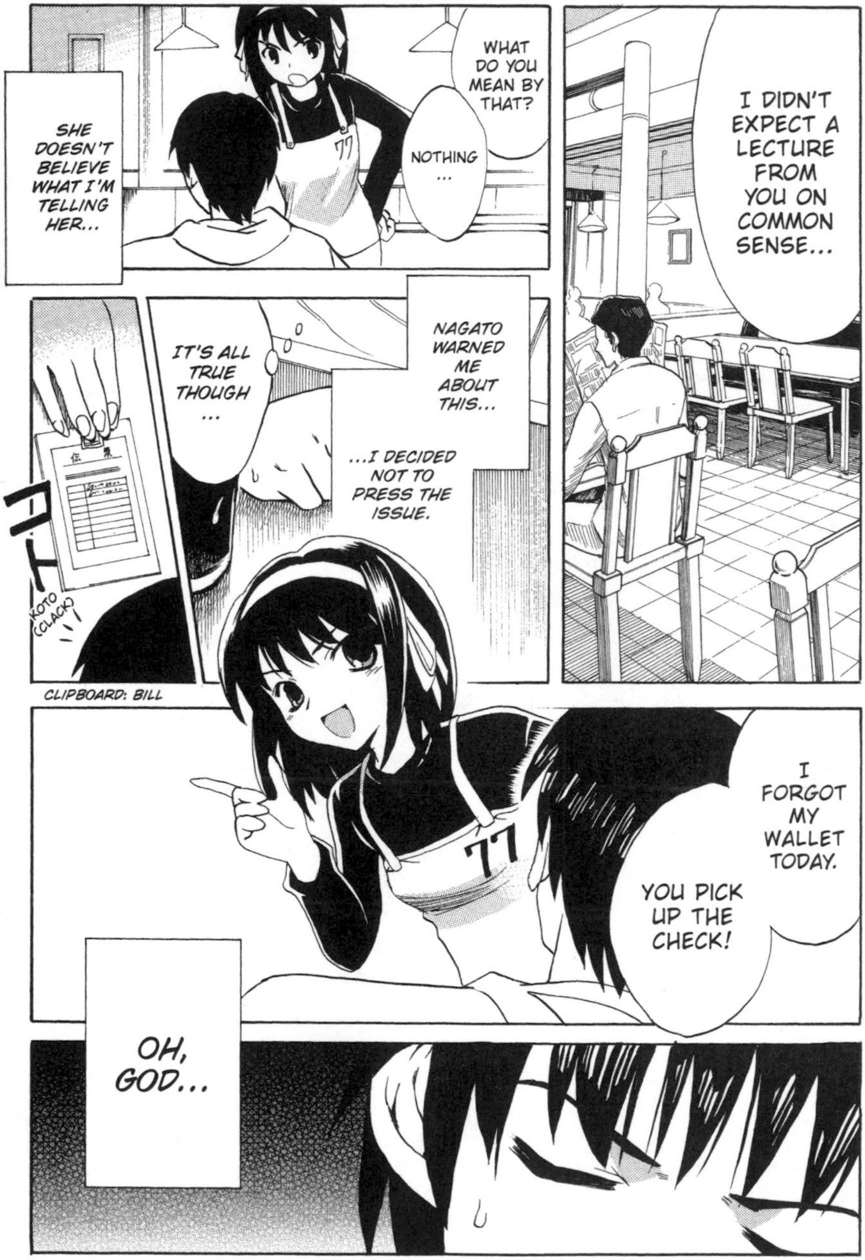
I DIDN'T EXPECT A LECTURE FROM YOU ON COMMON SENSE...
WHAT DO YOU MEAN BY THAT?
NOTHING ...
SHE DOESN'T BELIEVE WHAT I'M TELLING HER...
NAGATO WARNED ME ABOUT THIS...
...I DECIDED NOT TO PRESS THE ISSUE.
IT'S ALL TRUE THOUGH ...
KOTO (CLACK)
CLIPBOARD: BILL
I FORGOT MY WALLET TODAY.
YOU PICK UP THE CHECK!
OH, GOD...

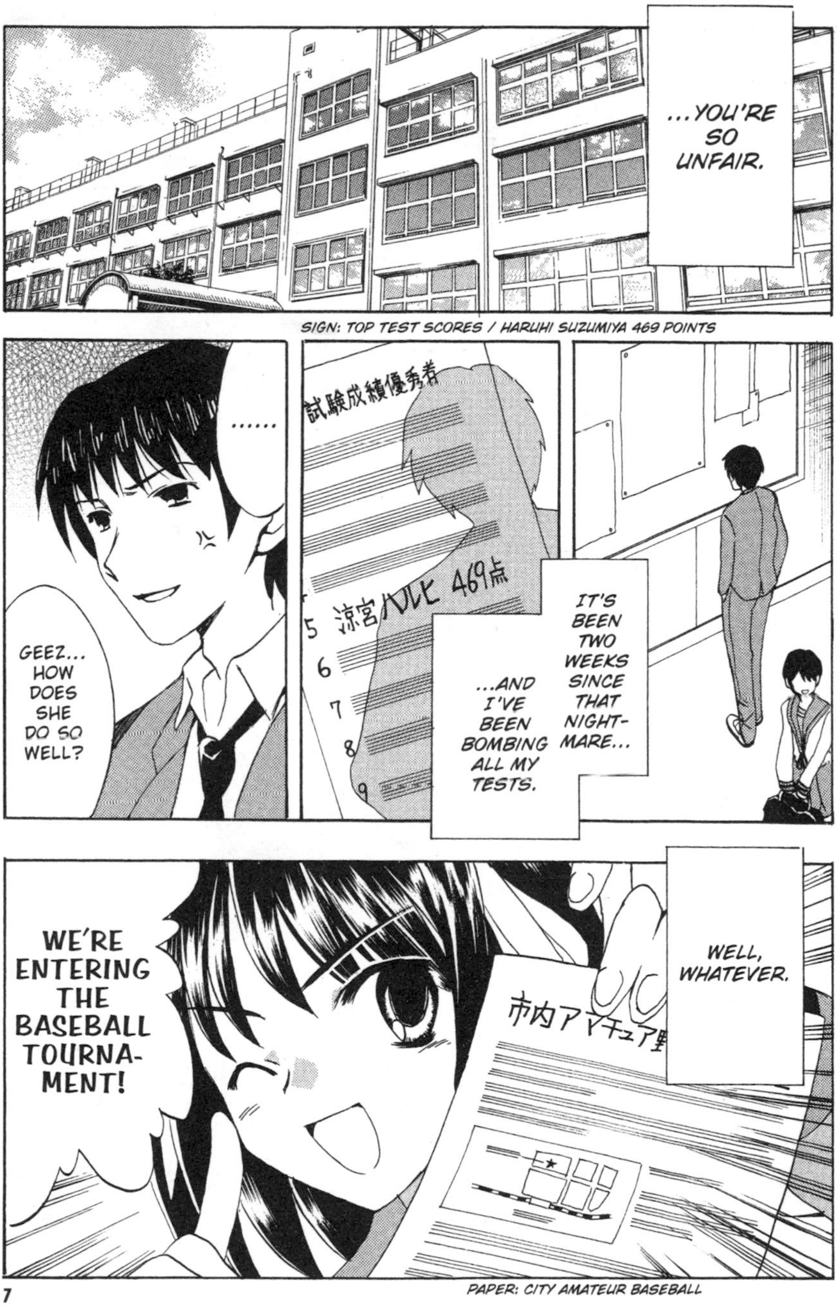
...YOU'RE SO UNFAIR.
IT'S BEEN TWO WEEKS SINCE THAT NIGHTMARE...
...AND I'VE BEEN BOMBING ALL MY TESTS.
試験成績優秀者
5 涼宮ハルヒ 469点
......
GEEZ... HOW DOES SHE DO SO WELL?
WELL, WHATEVER.
WE'RE ENTERING THE BASEBALL TOURNAMENT!
市内アマチュア

SIGN: TOP TEST SCORES / HARUHI SUZUMIYA 469 POINTS

PAPER: CITY AMATEUR BASEBALL

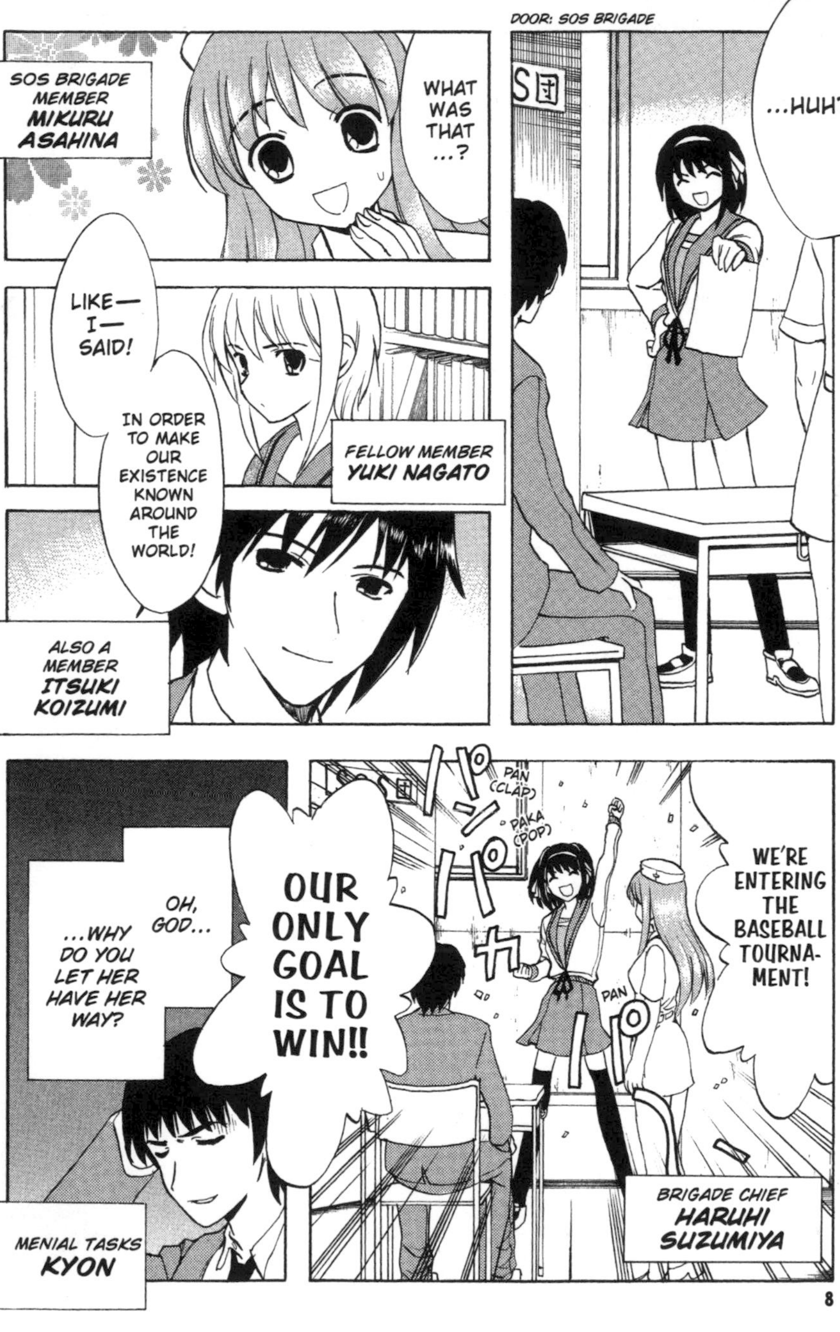
DOOR: SOS BRIGADE
...HUH?
SOS BRIGADE MEMBER MIKURU ASAHINA
WHAT WAS THAT ...?
LIKE—I—SAID!
IN ORDER TO MAKE OUR EXISTENCE KNOWN AROUND THE WORLD!
FELLOW MEMBER YUKI NAGATO
ALSO A MEMBER ITSUKI KOIZUMI
WE'RE ENTERING THE BASEBALL TOURNA-MENT!
PAN (CLAP)
PAKA (POP)
PAN
OUR ONLY GOAL IS TO WIN!!
BRIGADE CHIEF HARUHI SUZUMIYA
OH, GOD...
...WHY DO YOU LET HER HAVE HER WAY?
MENIAL TASKS KYON

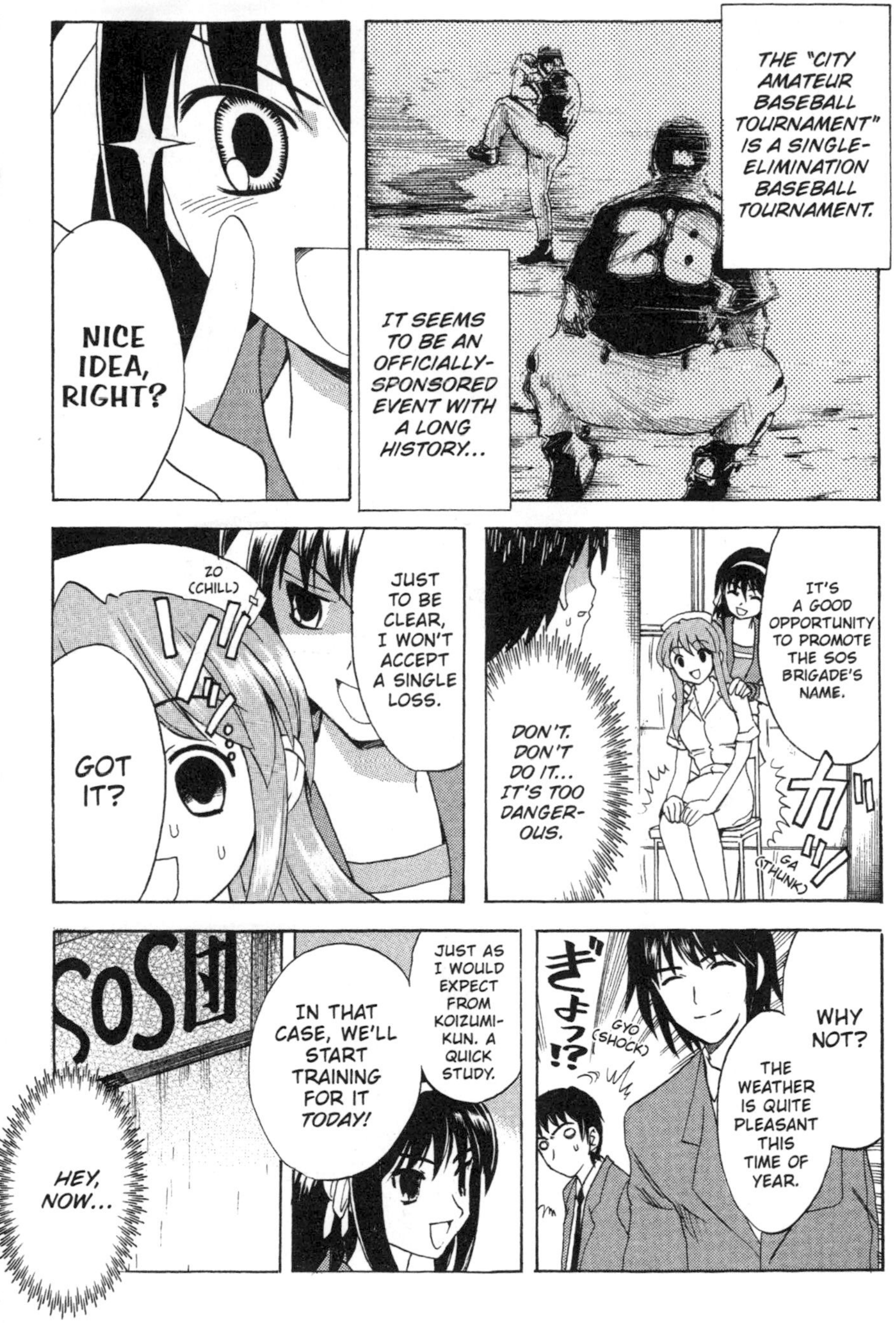
THE "CITY AMATEUR BASEBALL TOURNAMENT" IS A SINGLE-ELIMINATION BASEBALL TOURNAMENT.
IT SEEMS TO BE AN OFFICIALLY-SPONSORED EVENT WITH A LONG HISTORY...
NICE IDEA, RIGHT?
IT'S A GOOD OPPORTUNITY TO PROMOTE THE SOS BRIGADE'S NAME.
DON'T. DON'T DO IT... IT'S TOO DANGER-OUS.
GA (THUNK)
JUST TO BE CLEAR, I WON'T ACCEPT A SINGLE LOSS.
ZO (CHILL)
GOT IT?
WHY NOT?
THE WEATHER IS QUITE PLEASANT THIS TIME OF YEAR.
GYO (SHOCK)
JUST AS I WOULD EXPECT FROM KOIZUMI-KUN. A QUICK STUDY.
IN THAT CASE, WE'LL START TRAINING FOR IT TODAY!
SOS団
HEY, NOW...

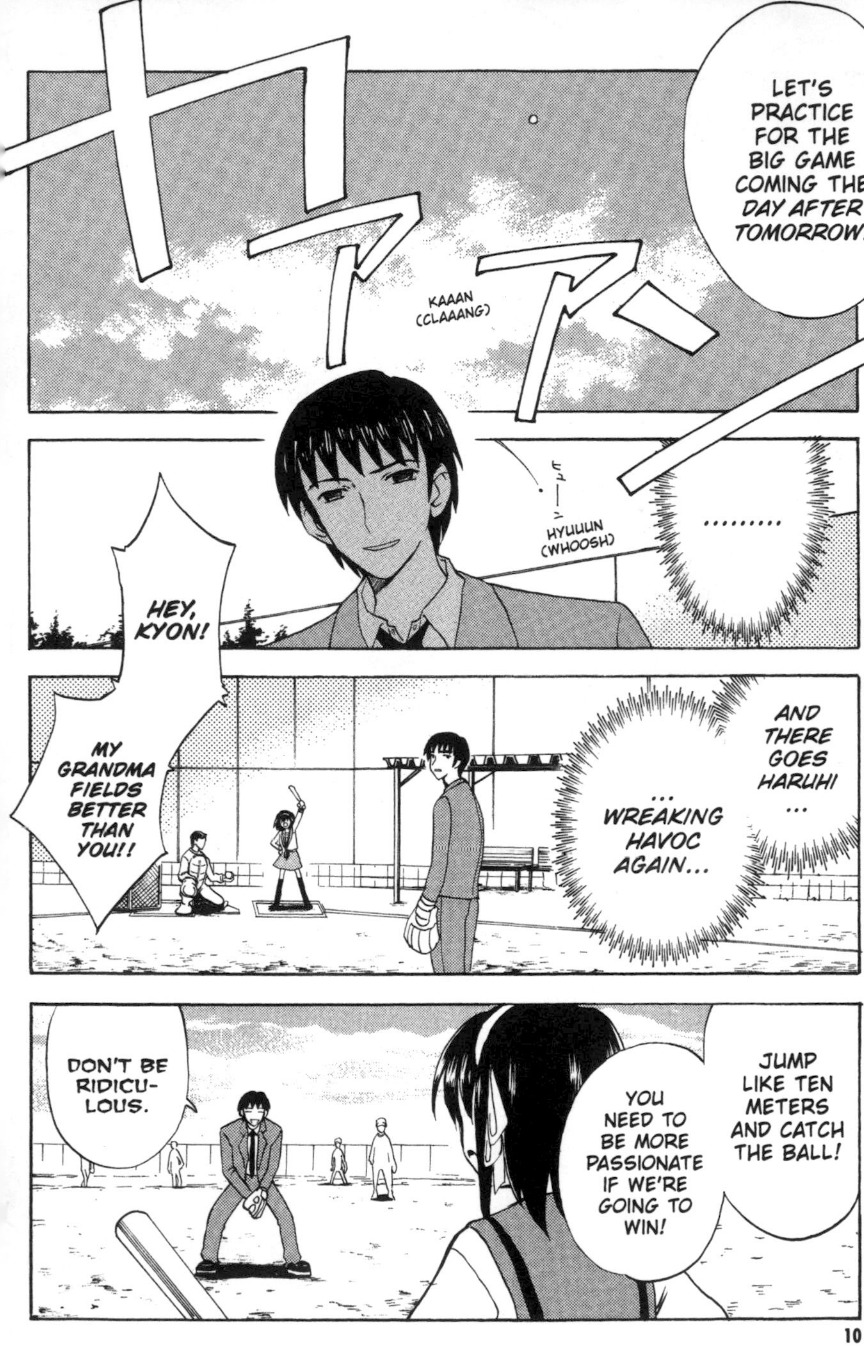
LET'S PRACTICE FOR THE BIG GAME COMING THE DAY AFTER TOMORROW!
KAAAN (CLAAANG)
....
HYUUUN (WHOOSH)
HEY, KYON!
AND THERE GOES HARUHI...
...WREAKING HAVOC AGAIN...
MY GRANDMA FIELDS BETTER THAN YOU!!
JUMP LIKE TEN METERS AND CATCH THE BALL!
YOU NEED TO BE MORE PASSIONATE IF WE'RE GOING TO WIN!
DON'T BE RIDICULOUS.

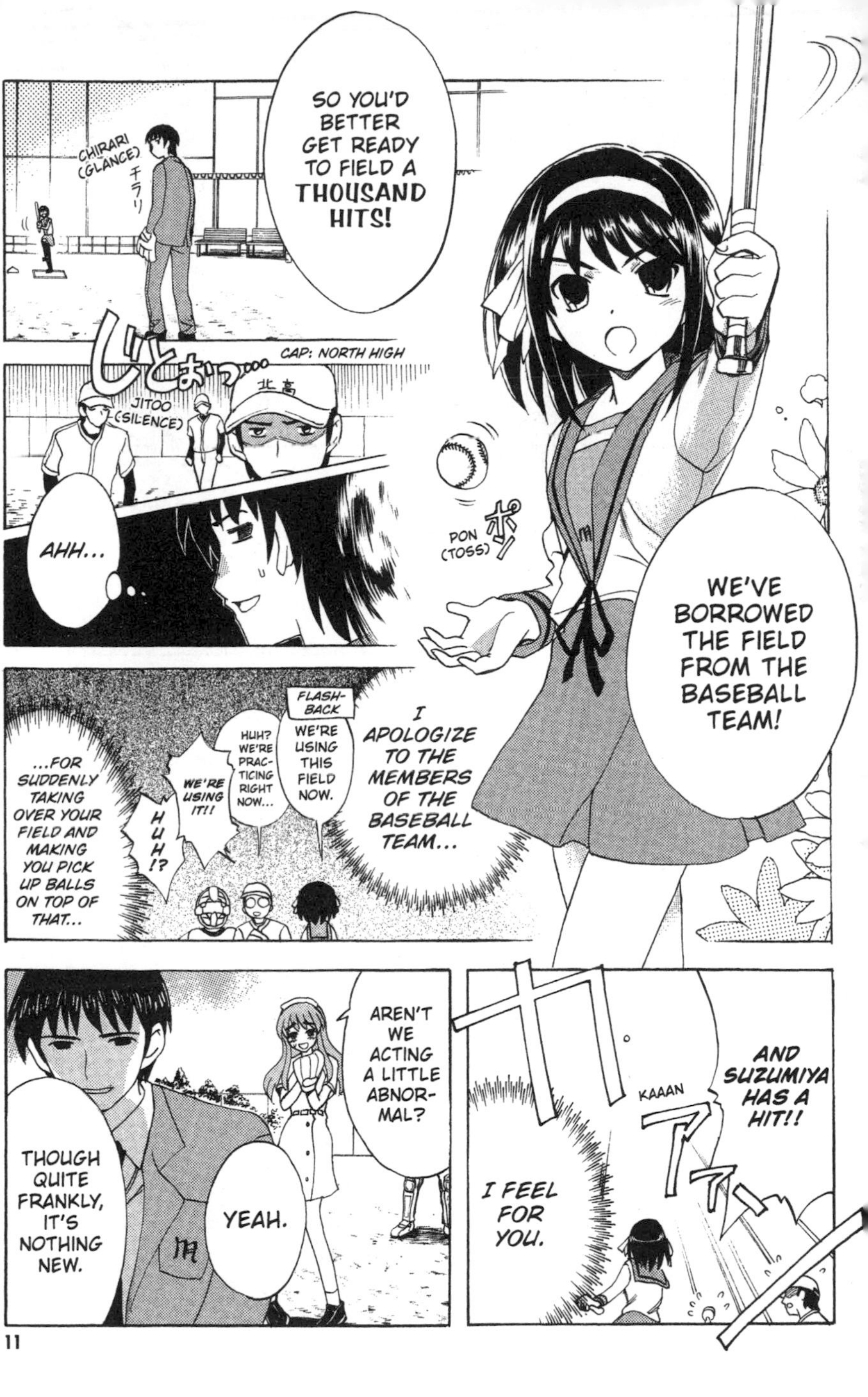
SO YOU'D BETTER GET READY TO FIELD A THOUSAND HITS!
PON (TOSS)
WE'VE BORROWED THE FIELD FROM THE BASEBALL TEAM!
CHIRARI (GLANCE)
チラリ
JITOO (SILENCE)
CAP: NORTH HIGH
AHH...
FLASH-BACK
I APOLOGIZE TO THE MEMBERS OF THE BASEBALL TEAM...
WE'RE USING THIS FIELD NOW.
HUH? WE'RE PRAC-TICING RIGHT NOW...
WE'RE USING IT!!
HUH!?
...FOR SUDDENLY TAKING OVER YOUR FIELD AND MAKING YOU PICK UP BALLS ON TOP OF THAT...
AND SUZUMIYA HAS A HIT!!
KAAAN
I FEEL FOR YOU.
AREN'T WE ACTING A LITTLE ABNOR-MAL?
YEAH.
THOUGH QUITE FRANKLY, IT'S NOTHING NEW.

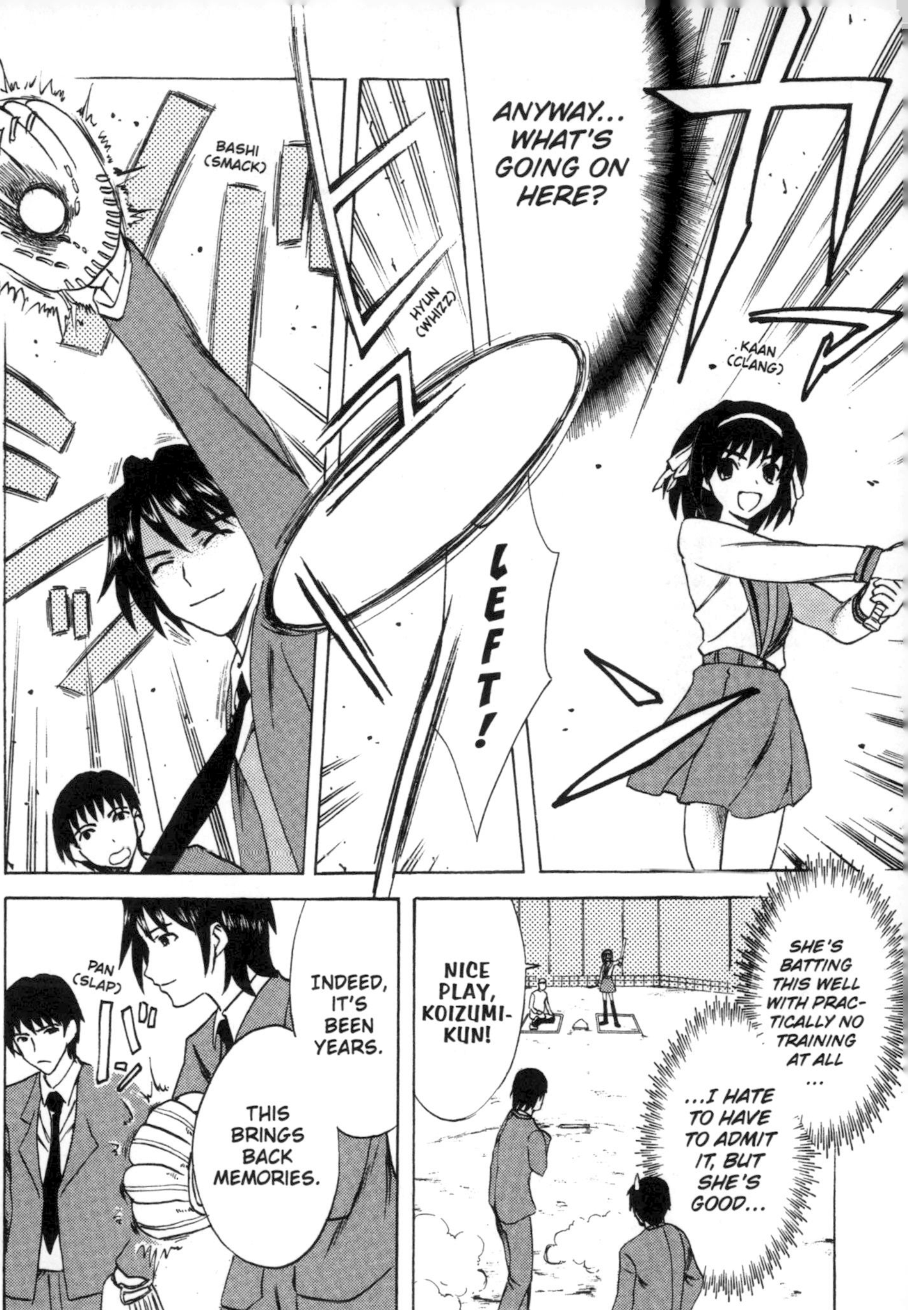
ANYWAY... WHAT'S GOING ON HERE?
KAAN (CLANG)
LEFT!
HYUN (WHIZZ)
BASHI (SMACK)
SHE'S BATTING THIS WELL WITH PRACTICALLY NO TRAINING AT ALL ...
...I HATE TO HAVE TO ADMIT IT, BUT SHE'S GOOD...
NICE PLAY, KOIZUMI-KUN!
INDEED, IT'S BEEN YEARS.
THIS BRINGS BACK MEMORIES.
PAN (SLAP)

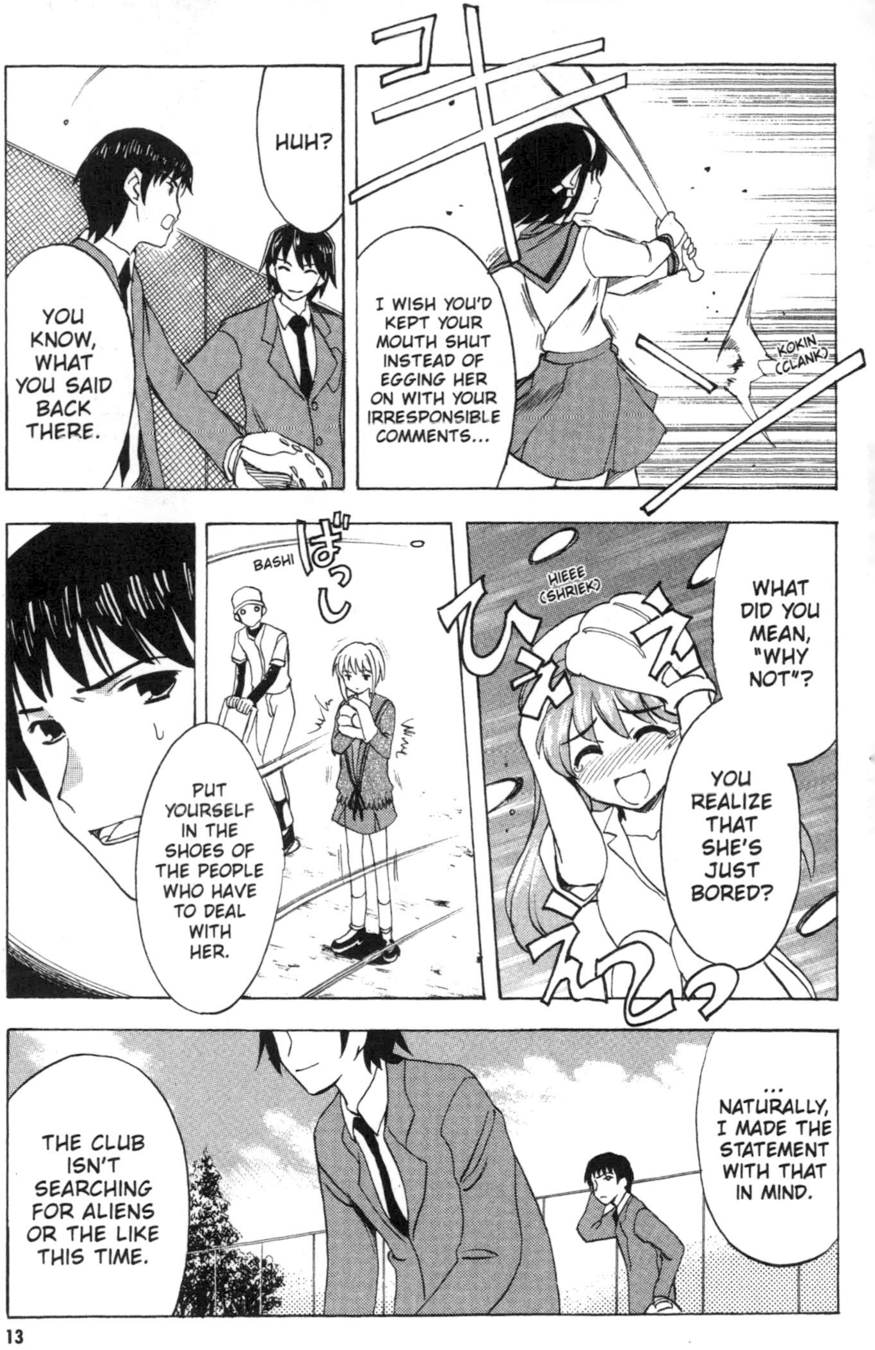
I WISH YOU'D KEPT YOUR MOUTH SHUT INSTEAD OF EGGING HER ON WITH YOUR IRRESPONSIBLE COMMENTS...
KOKIN (CLANK)
HUH?
YOU KNOW, WHAT YOU SAID BACK THERE.
WHAT DID YOU MEAN, "WHY NOT"?
YOU REALIZE THAT SHE'S JUST BORED?
HIEEE (SHRIEK)
BASHI
PUT YOURSELF IN THE SHOES OF THE PEOPLE WHO HAVE TO DEAL WITH HER.
... NATURALLY, I MADE THE STATEMENT WITH THAT IN MIND.
THE CLUB ISN'T SEARCHING FOR ALIENS OR THE LIKE THIS TIME.

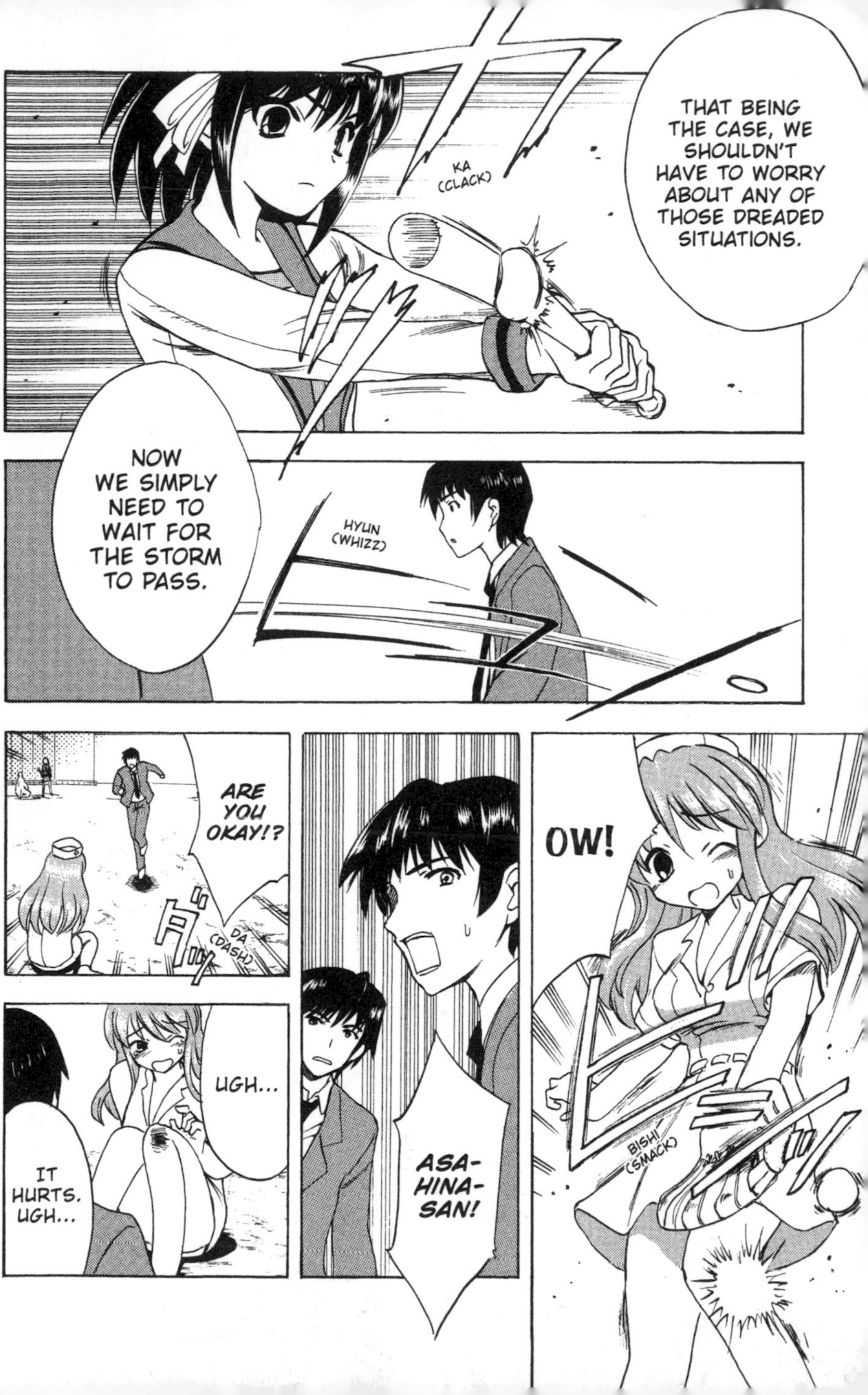
THAT BEING THE CASE, WE SHOULDN'T HAVE TO WORRY ABOUT ANY OF THOSE DREADED SITUATIONS.
KA (CLACK)
NOW WE SIMPLY NEED TO WAIT FOR THE STORM TO PASS.
HYUN (WHIZZ)
OW!
BISHI (SMACK)
ASA-HINA-SAN!
ARE YOU OKAY!?
DA (DASH)
UGH...
IT HURTS. UGH...

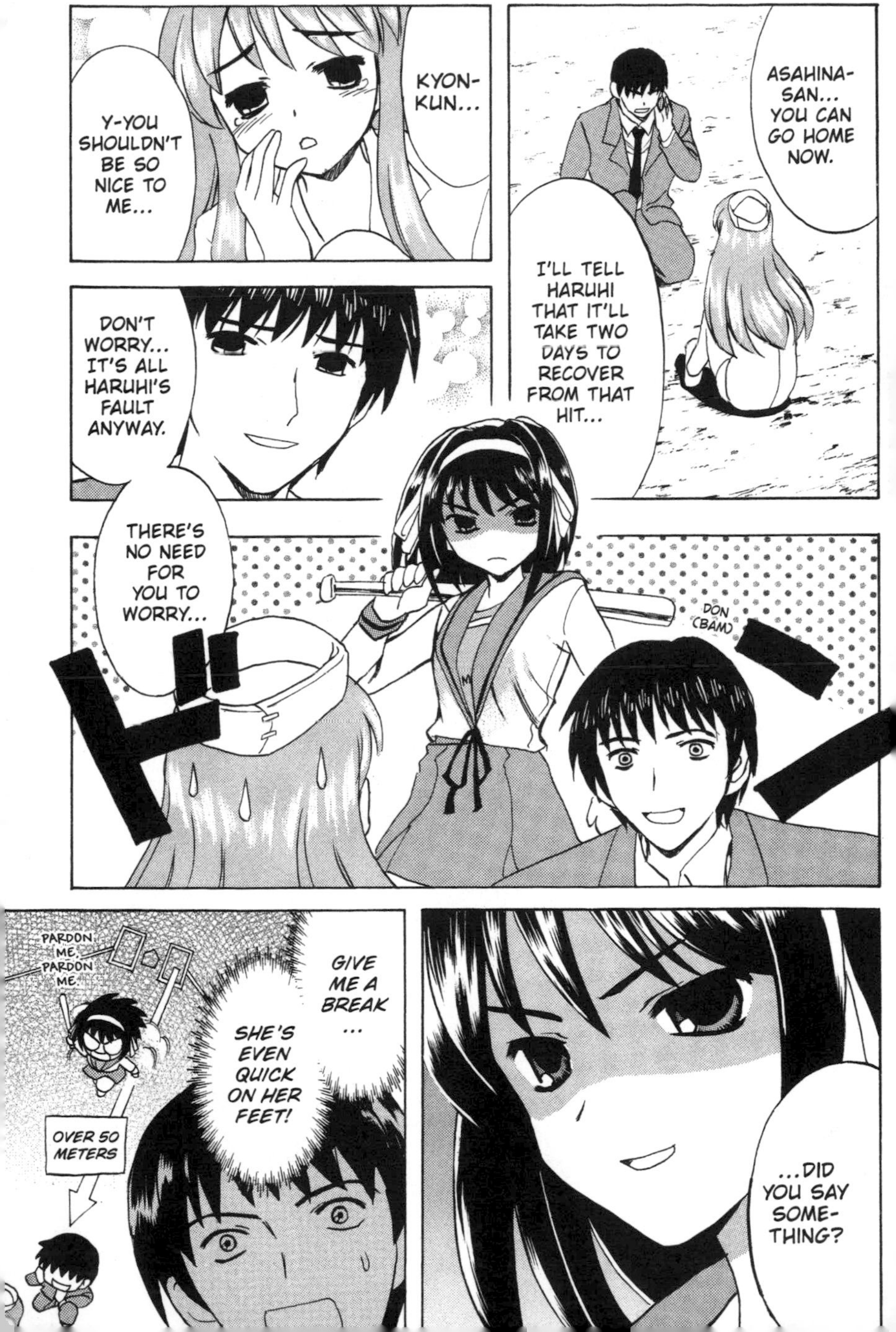
ASAHINA-SAN... YOU CAN GO HOME NOW.
I'LL TELL HARUHI THAT IT'LL TAKE TWO DAYS TO RECOVER FROM THAT HIT...
KYON-KUN...
Y-YOU SHOULDN'T BE SO NICE TO ME...
DON'T WORRY... IT'S ALL HARUHI'S FAULT ANYWAY.
THERE'S NO NEED FOR YOU TO WORRY...
DON (BAM)
...DID YOU SAY SOMETHING?
GIVE ME A BREAK ...
SHE'S EVEN QUICK ON HER FEET!
PARDON ME, PARDON ME.
OVER 50 METERS

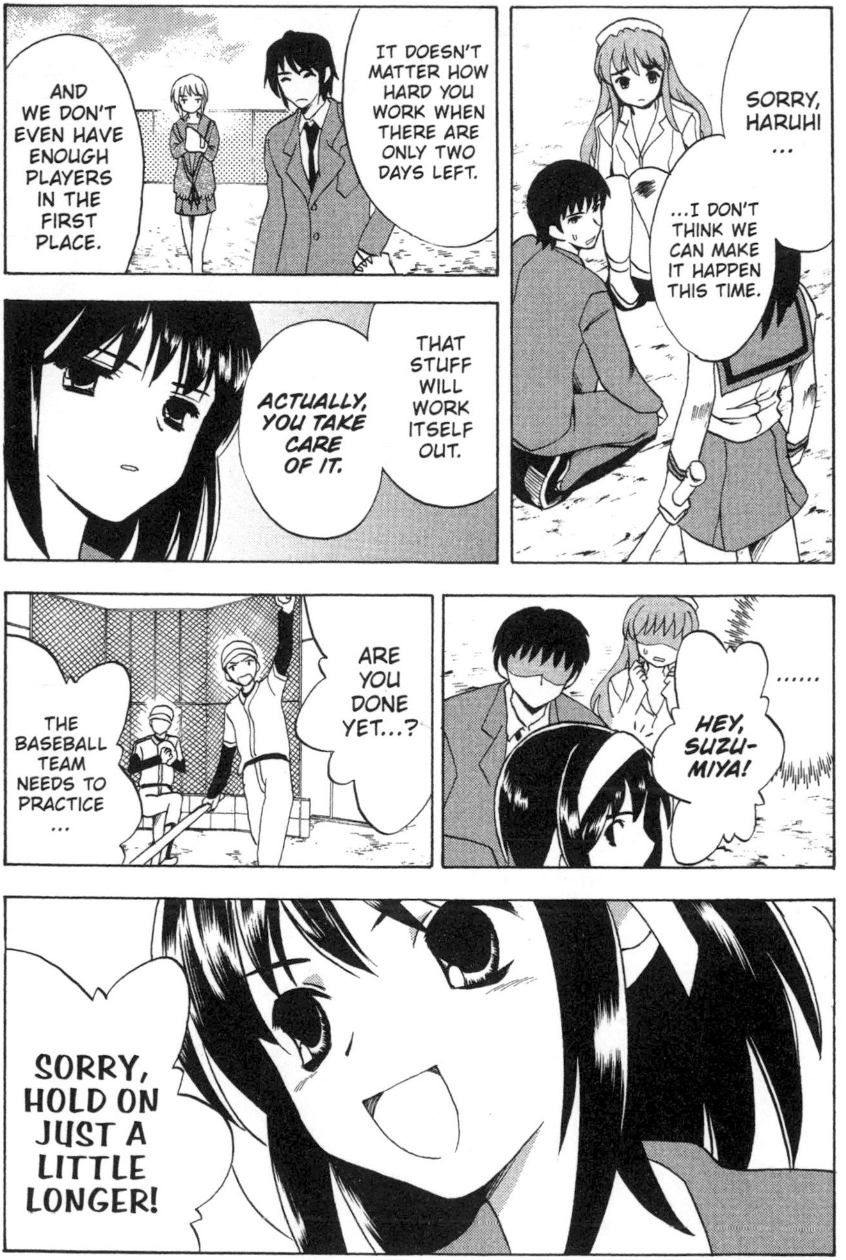
SORRY, HARUHI...
...I DON'T THINK WE CAN MAKE IT HAPPEN THIS TIME.
IT DOESN'T MATTER HOW HARD YOU WORK WHEN THERE ARE ONLY TWO DAYS LEFT.
AND WE DON'T EVEN HAVE ENOUGH PLAYERS IN THE FIRST PLACE.
THAT STUFF WILL WORK ITSELF OUT.
ACTUALLY, YOU TAKE CARE OF IT.
......
HEY, SUZUMIYA!
ARE YOU DONE YET...?
THE BASEBALL TEAM NEEDS TO PRACTICE...
SORRY, HOLD ON JUST A LITTLE LONGER!

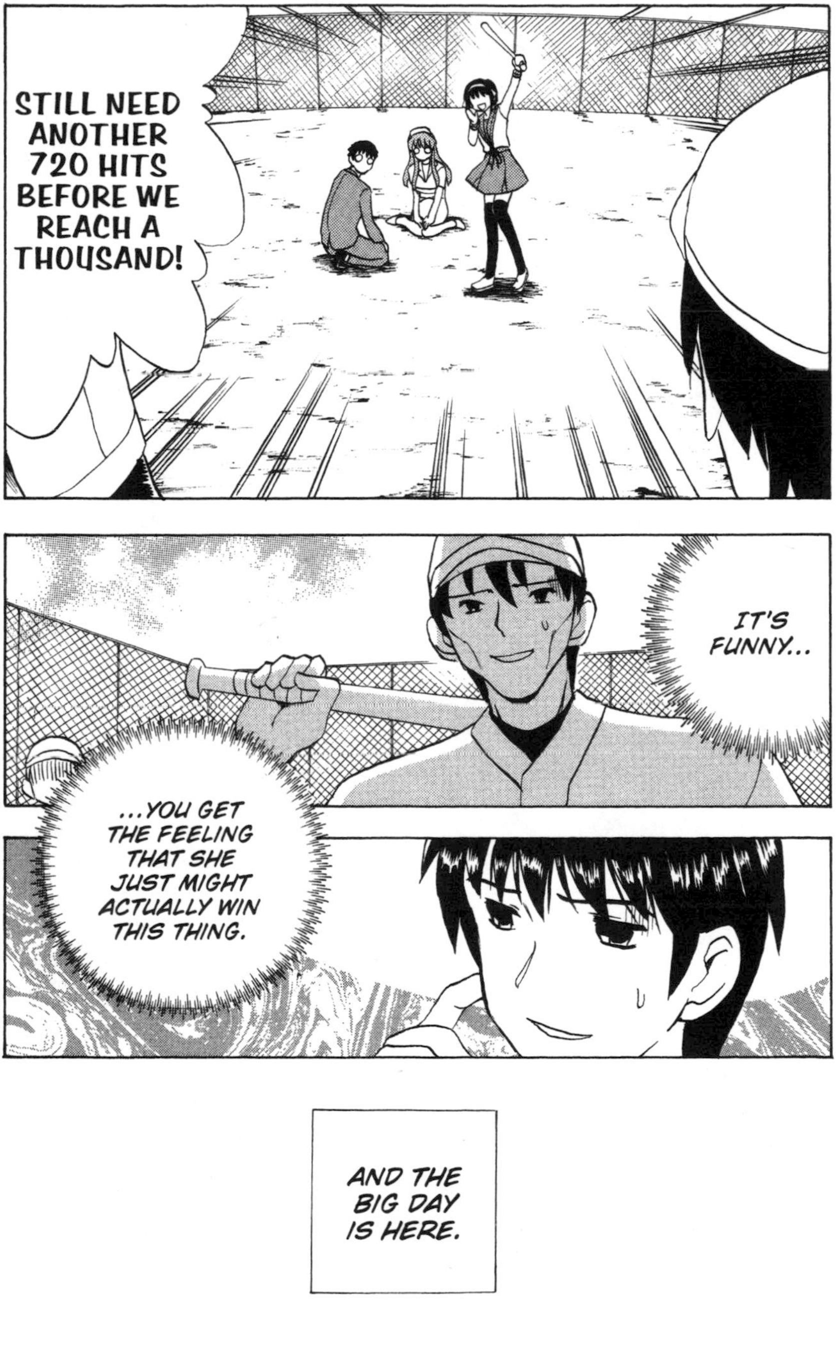
STILL NEED ANOTHER 720 HITS BEFORE WE REACH A THOUSAND!
IT'S FUNNY...
...YOU GET THE FEELING THAT SHE JUST MIGHT ACTUALLY WIN THIS THING.
AND THE BIG DAY IS HERE.

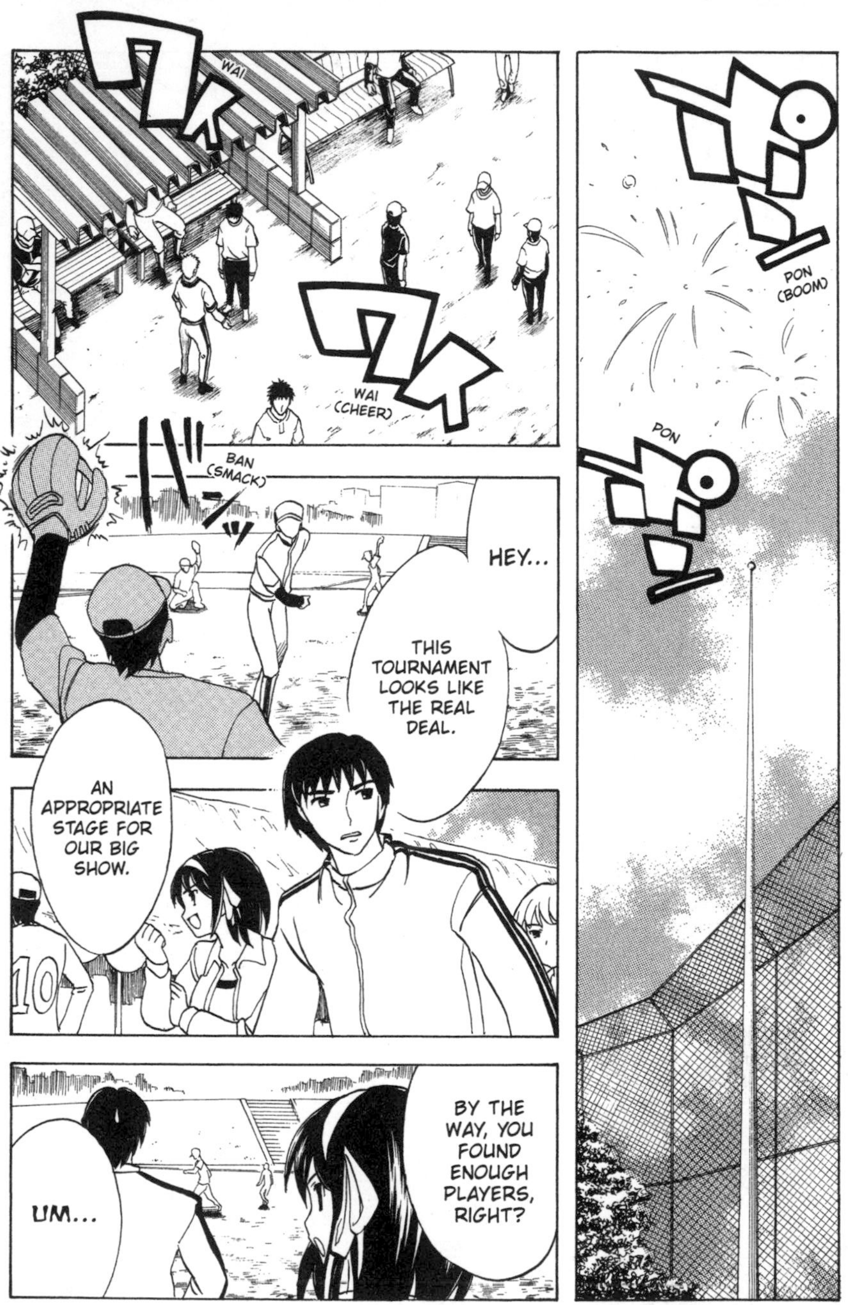
PON (BOOM)
PON
WAI
WAI (CHEER)
BAN (SMACK)
HEY...
THIS TOURNAMENT LOOKS LIKE THE REAL DEAL.
AN APPROPRIATE STAGE FOR OUR BIG SHOW.
BY THE WAY, YOU FOUND ENOUGH PLAYERS, RIGHT?
UM...

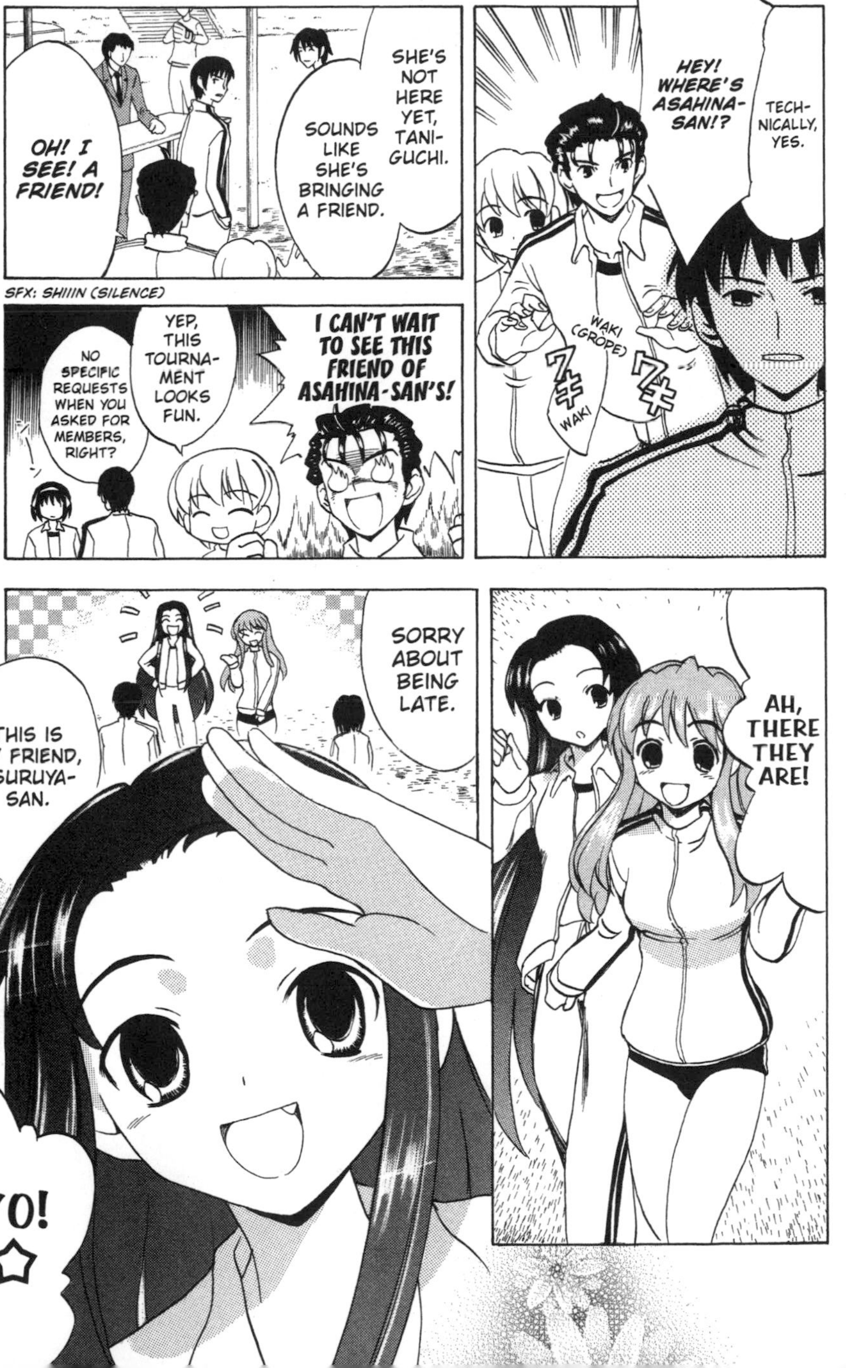
HEY! WHERE'S ASAHINA-SAN!?
TECHNICALLY, YES.
WAKI (GROPE)
WAKI
SHE'S NOT HERE YET, TANIGUCHI.
SOUNDS LIKE SHE'S BRINGING A FRIEND.
OH! I SEE! A FRIEND!
SFX: SHIIIN (SILENCE)
I CAN'T WAIT TO SEE THIS FRIEND OF ASAHINA-SAN'S!
YEP, THIS TOURNAMENT LOOKS FUN.
NO SPECIFIC REQUESTS WHEN YOU ASKED FOR MEMBERS, RIGHT?
AH, THERE THEY ARE!
SORRY ABOUT BEING LATE.
THIS IS MY FRIEND, TSURUYA-SAN.
YO! ☆

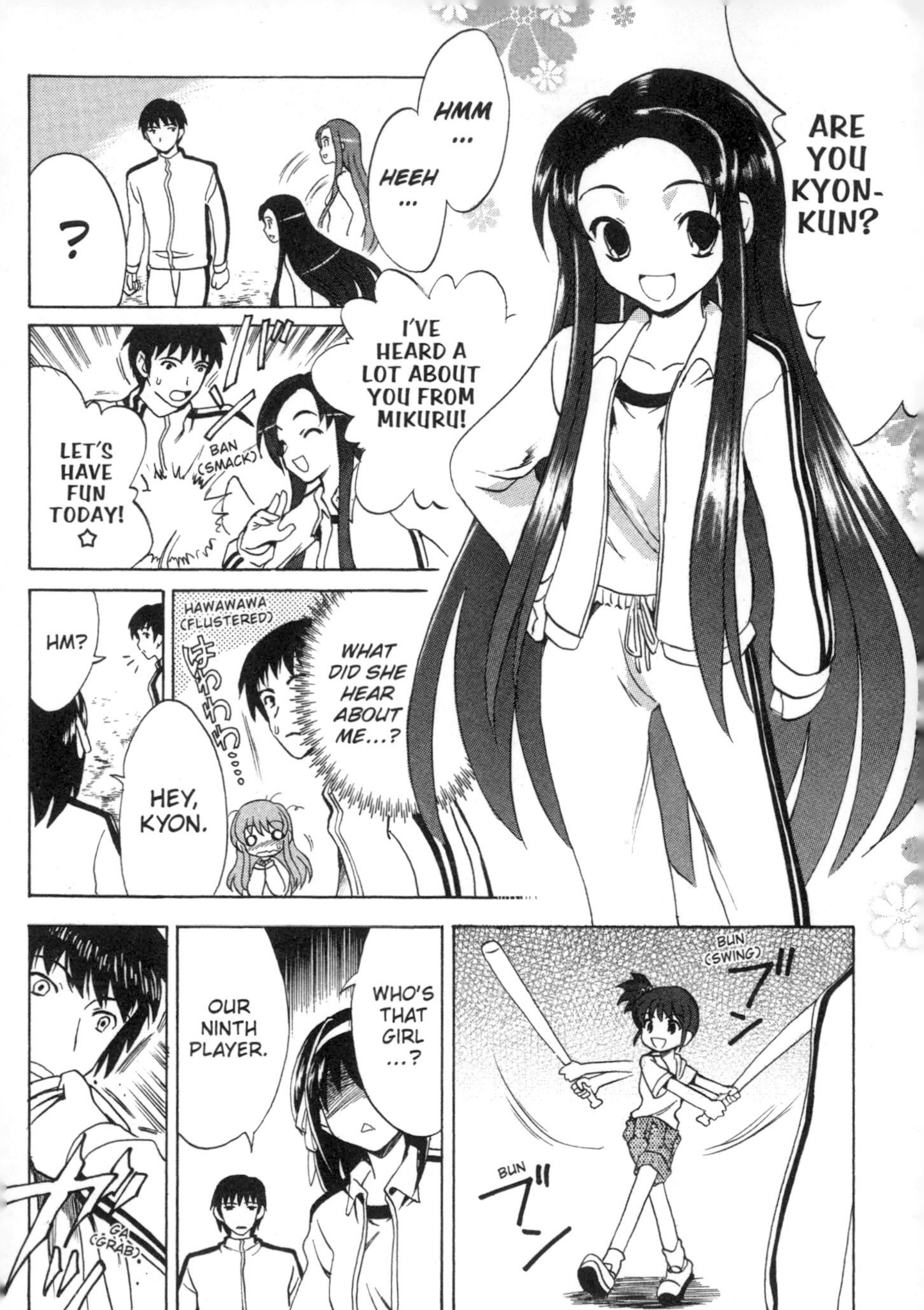
ARE YOU KYON-KUN?
I'VE HEARD A LOT ABOUT YOU FROM MIKURU!
HMM ... HEEH ...
?
BAN (SMACK)
LET'S HAVE FUN TODAY! ☆
HAWAWAWA (FLUSTERED)
WHAT DID SHE HEAR ABOUT ME...?
HEY, KYON.
HM?
BUN (SWING)
BUN
WHO'S THAT GIRL ...?
OUR NINTH PLAYER.
GA (GRAB)

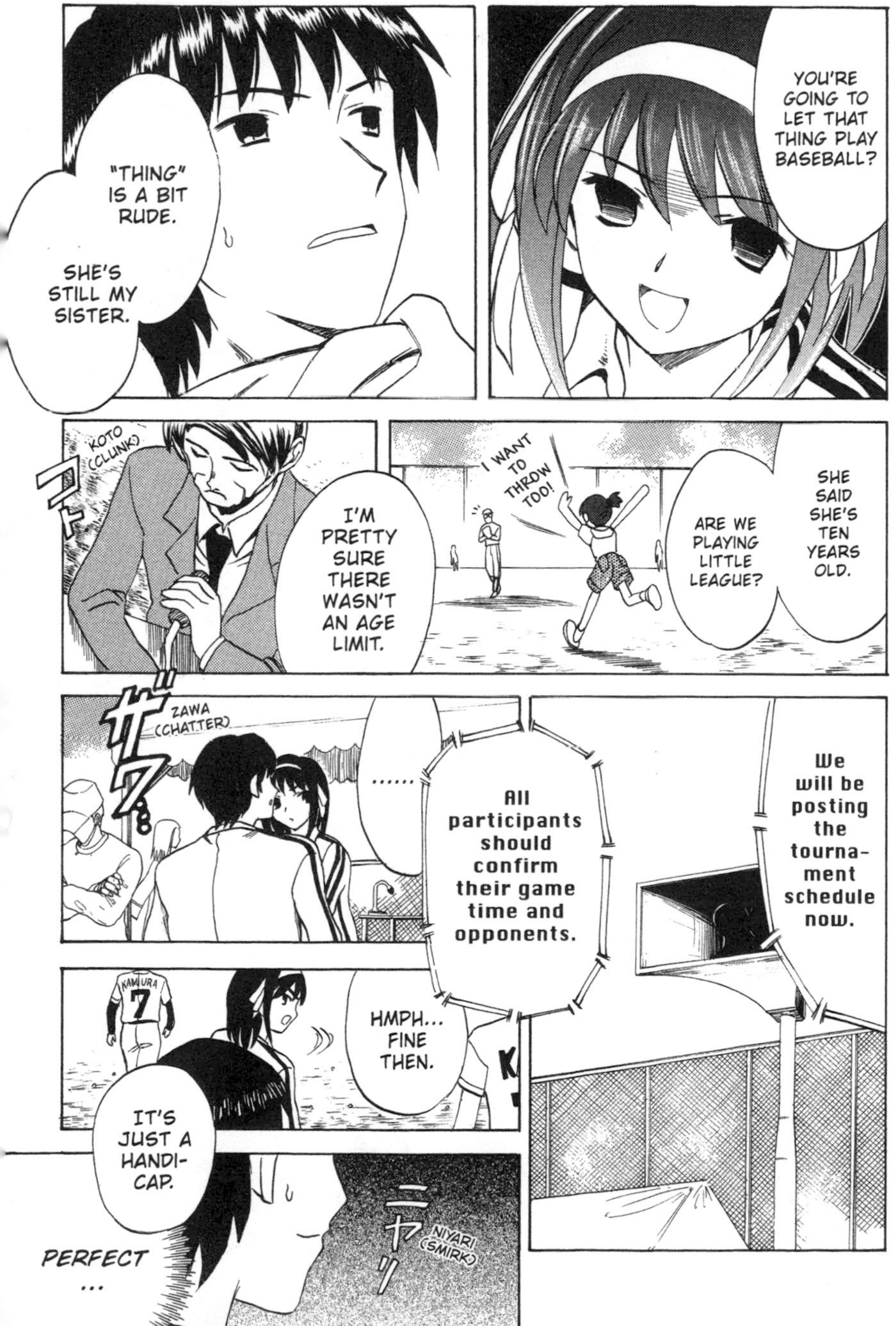
YOU'RE GOING TO LET THAT THING PLAY BASEBALL?
"THING" IS A BIT RUDE.
SHE'S STILL MY SISTER.
SHE SAID SHE'S TEN YEARS OLD.
ARE WE PLAYING LITTLE LEAGUE?
I WANT TO THROW TOO!
I'M PRETTY SURE THERE WASN'T AN AGE LIMIT.
KOTO (CLUNK)
We will be posting the tourna-ment schedule now.
All participants should confirm their game time and opponents.
......
ZAWA (CHATTER)
HMPH... FINE THEN.
IT'S JUST A HANDI-CAP.
NIYARI (SMIRK)
PERFECT ...

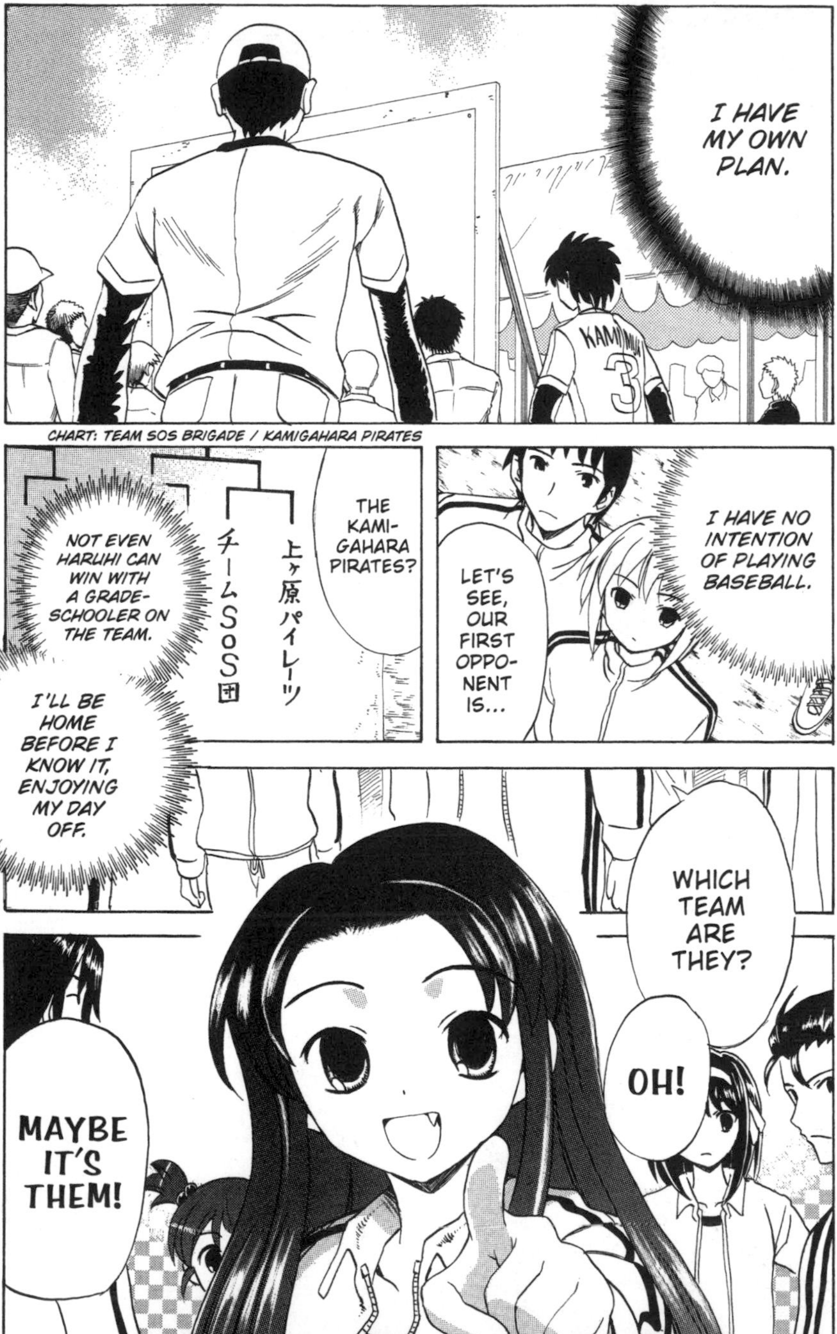
I HAVE MY OWN PLAN.
CHART: TEAM SOS BRIGADE / KAMIGAHARA PIRATES
I HAVE NO INTENTION OF PLAYING BASEBALL.
LET'S SEE, OUR FIRST OPPONENT IS...
THE KAMI-GAHARA PIRATES?
上ヶ原パイレーツ
チームSOS団
NOT EVEN HARUHI CAN WIN WITH A GRADE-SCHOOLER ON THE TEAM.
I'LL BE HOME BEFORE I KNOW IT, ENJOYING MY DAY OFF.
WHICH TEAM ARE THEY?
OH!
MAYBE IT'S THEM!

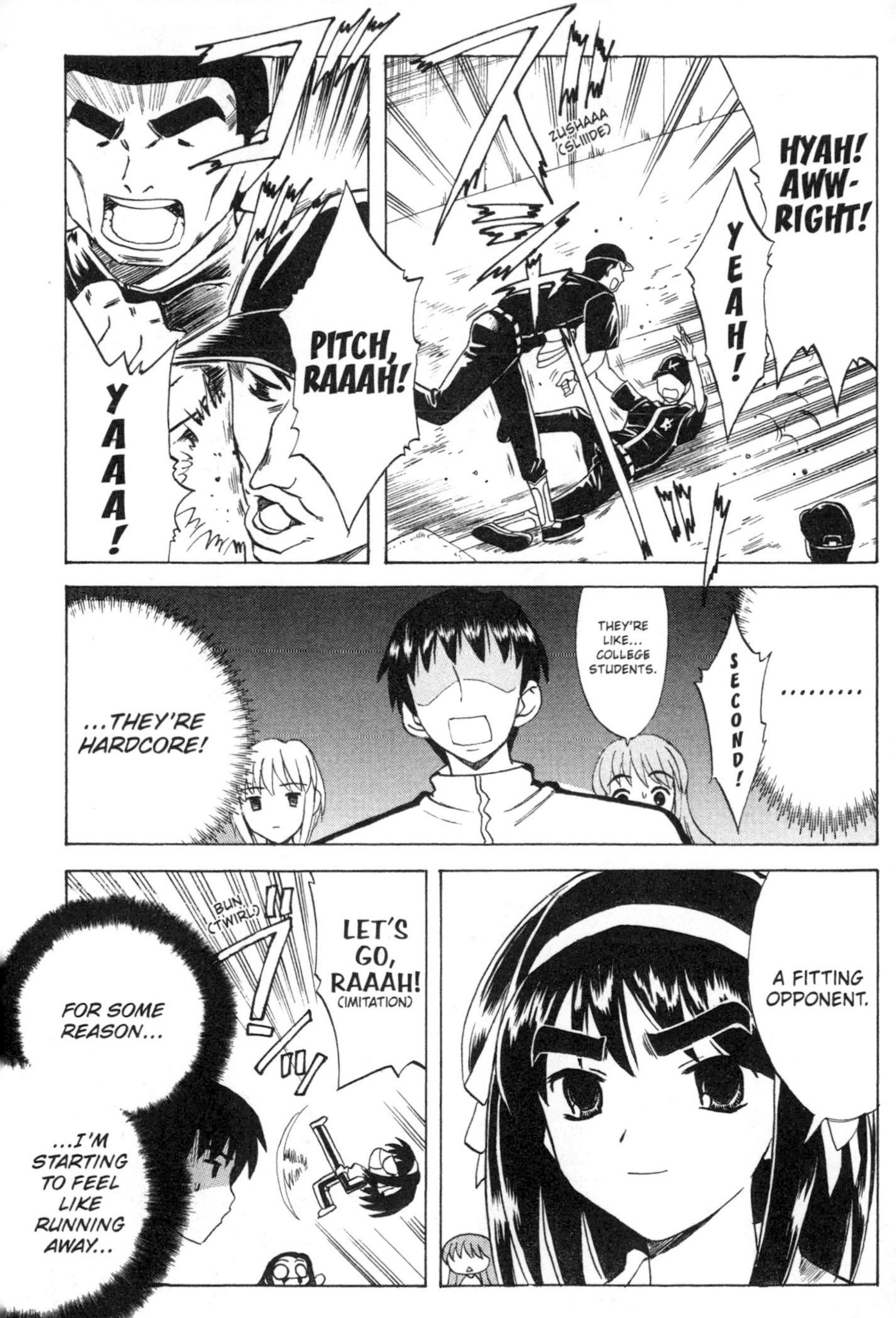
HYAH! AWW-RIGHT!
YEAH!
ZUSHAAA (SLIIIDE)
PITCH, RAAAH!
YAAAA!
....
SECOND!
THEY'RE LIKE... COLLEGE STUDENTS.
...THEY'RE HARDCORE!
A FITTING OPPONENT.
LET'S GO, RAAAH! (IMITATION)
BUN (TWIRL)
FOR SOME REASON...
...I'M STARTING TO FEEL LIKE RUNNING AWAY...

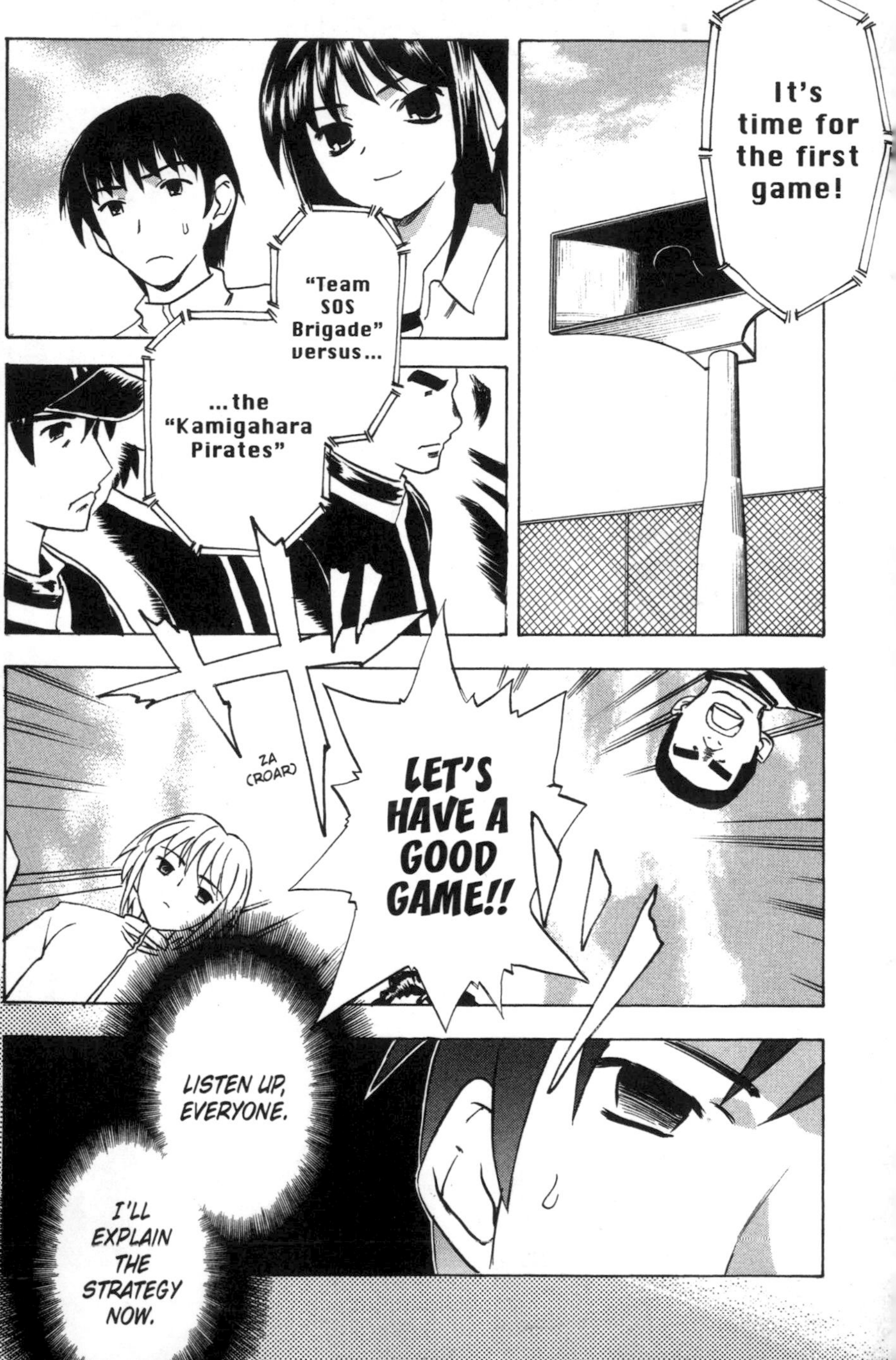
It's time for the first game!
"Team SOS Brigade" versus...
...the "Kamigahara Pirates"
LET'S HAVE A GOOD GAME!!
ZA (ROAR)
LISTEN UP, EVERYONE.
I'LL EXPLAIN THE STRATEGY NOW.

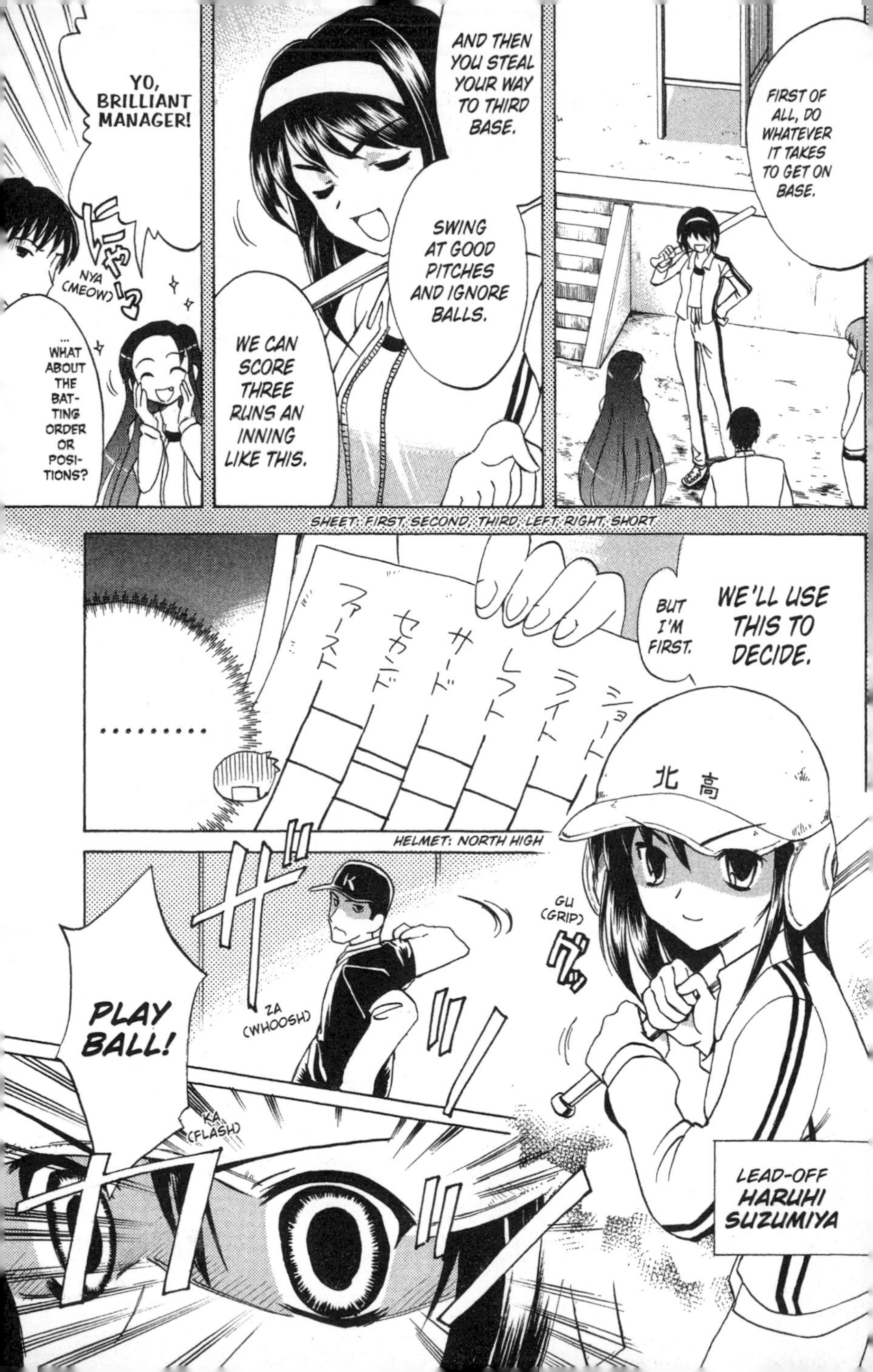
FIRST OF ALL, DO WHATEVER IT TAKES TO GET ON BASE.
AND THEN YOU STEAL YOUR WAY TO THIRD BASE.
SWING AT GOOD PITCHES AND IGNORE BALLS.
WE CAN SCORE THREE RUNS AN INNING LIKE THIS.
YO, BRILLIANT MANAGER!
NYA (MEOW)
...WHAT ABOUT THE BATTING ORDER OR POSITIONS?
SHEET: FIRST, SECOND, THIRD, LEFT, RIGHT, SHORT
WE'LL USE THIS TO DECIDE.
BUT I'M FIRST.
ショート
ライト
レフト
サード
セカンド
ファースト
....
HELMET: NORTH HIGH
北高
LEAD-OFF HARUHI SUZUMIYA
GU (GRIP)
ZA (WHOOSH)
PLAY BALL!
KA (FLASH)

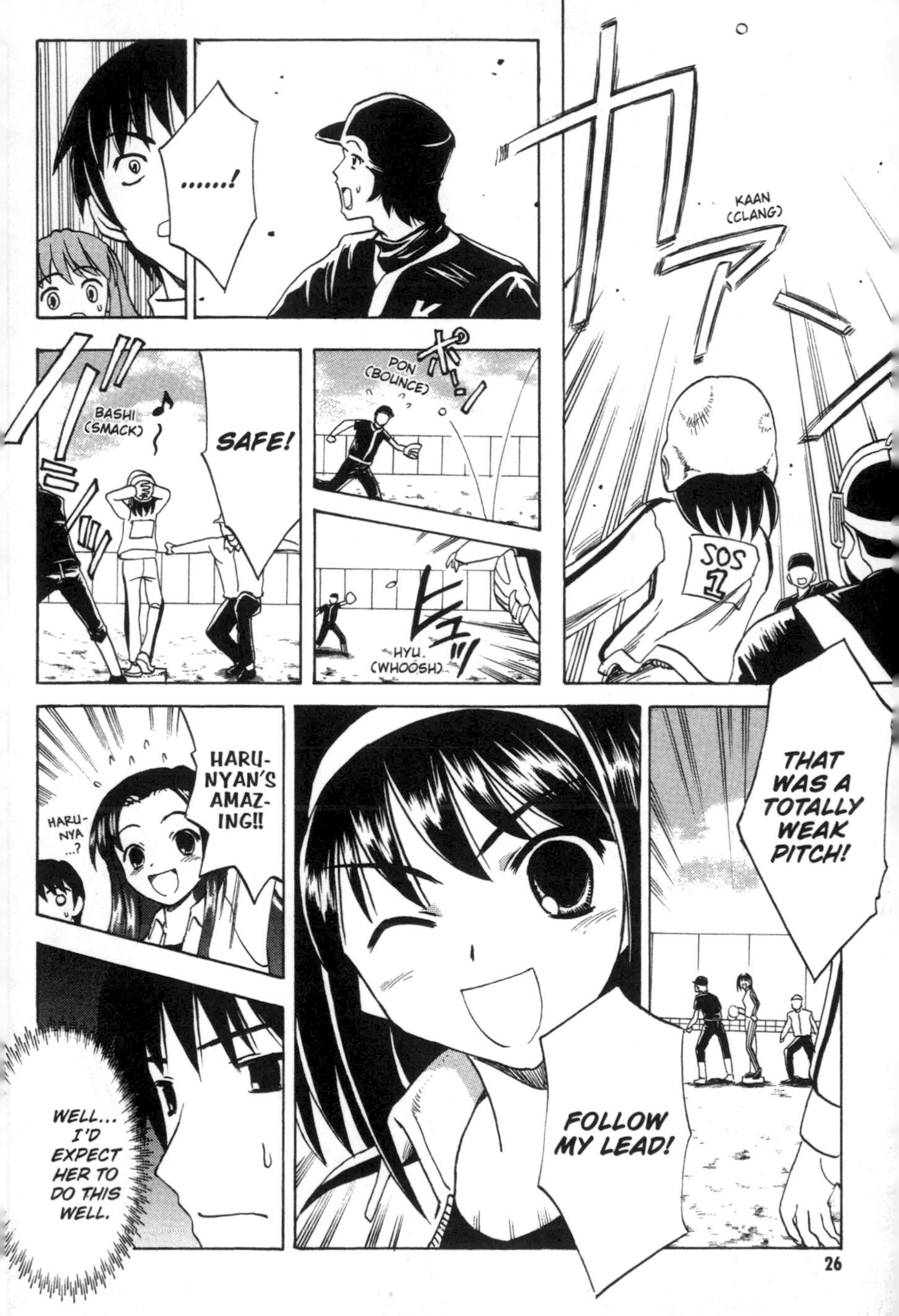
KAAN (CLANG)
......!
PON (BOUNCE)
HYU (WHOOSH)
SAFE!
BASHI (SMACK)
THAT WAS A TOTALLY WEAK PITCH!
FOLLOW MY LEAD!
HARU-NYAN'S AMAZ-ING!!
HARU-NYA ...?
WELL... I'D EXPECT HER TO DO THIS WELL.

1: SUZUMIYA / NADA, 2: ASAHINA / MUTOH,
3: NAGATO / HIRAI, 4: KYON / OSHIMA,
5: SISTER / KITADA, 6: KOIZUMI / KAWASHIMA

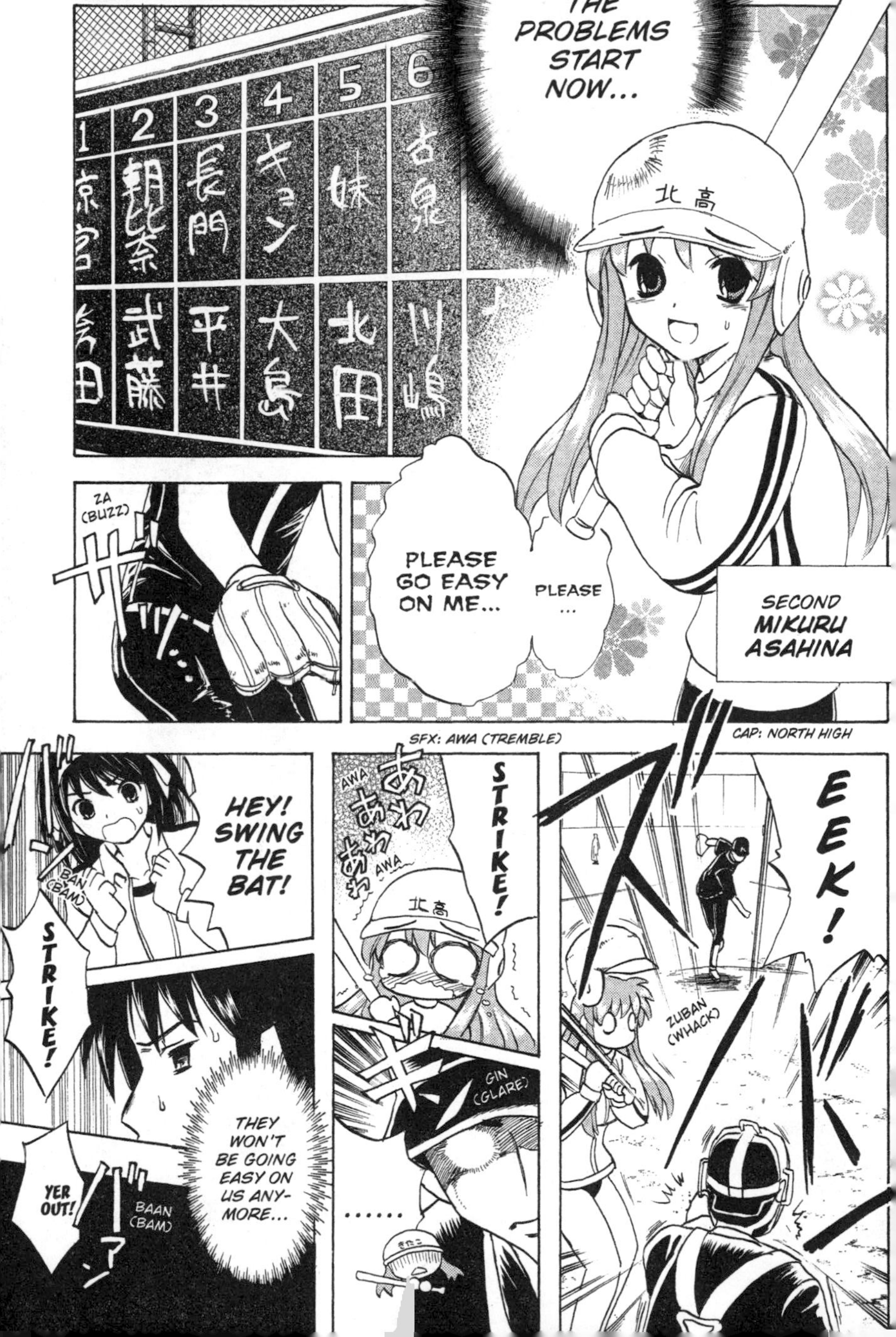
THE PROBLEMS START NOW...
SECOND MIKURU ASAHINA
PLEASE GO EASY ON ME...
PLEASE ...
CAP: NORTH HIGH
1 涼宮
2 朝比奈 武藤
3 長門 平井
4 キョン 大島
5 妹 北田
6 古泉 川嶋
ZA (BUZZ)
SFX: AWA (TREMBLE)
EEK!
ZUBAN (WHACK)
STRIKE!
あわあわあわ
AWA
AWA
北高
GIN (GLARE)
......
HEY! SWING THE BAT!
BAN (BAM)
STRIKE!
THEY WON'T BE GOING EASY ON US ANY-MORE...
YER OUT!
BAAN (BAM)

HELMET: NORTH HIGH

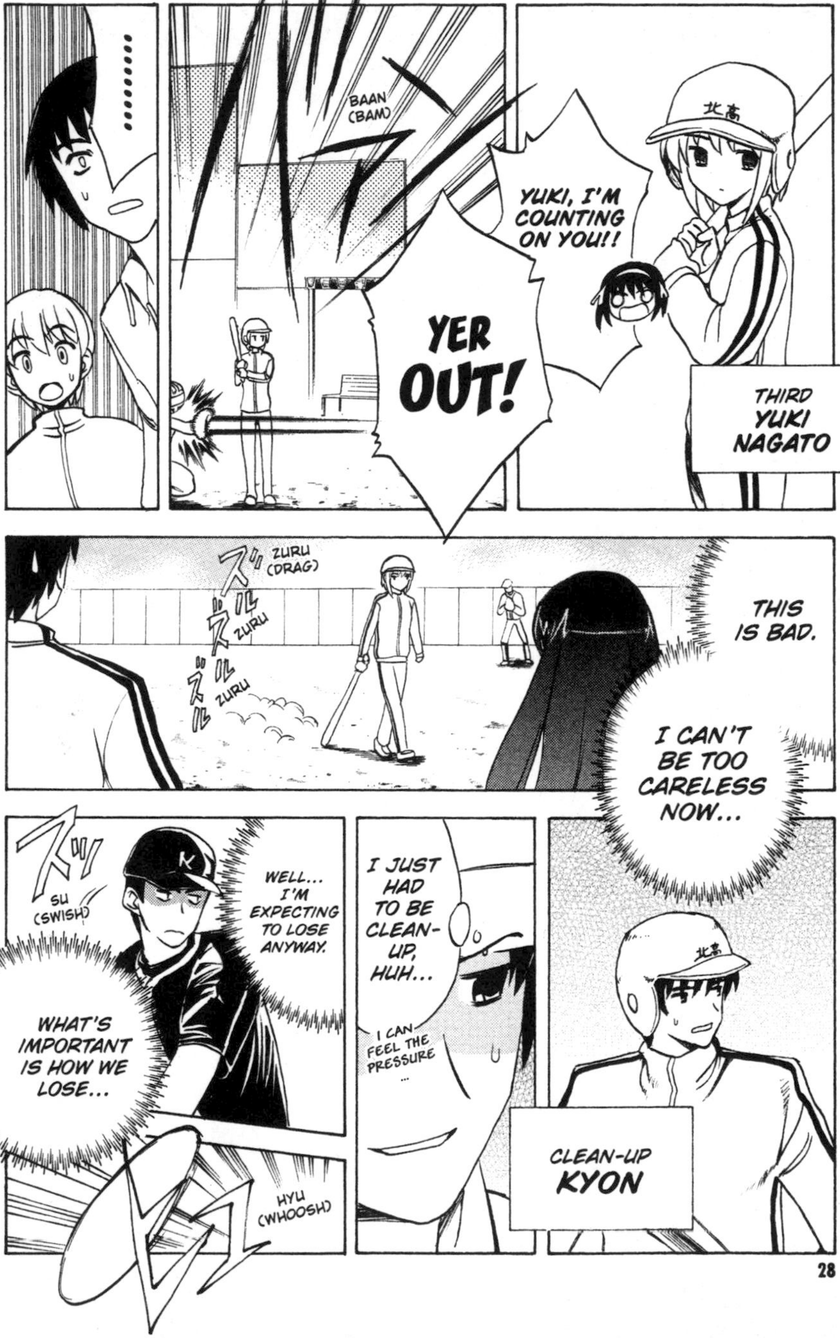
YUKI, I'M COUNTING ON YOU!!
THIRD YUKI NAGATO
BAAN (BAM)
YER OUT!
……
THIS IS BAD.
I CAN'T BE TOO CARELESS NOW...
ZURU (DRAG)
ZURU
ZURU
CLEAN-UP KYON
I JUST HAD TO BE CLEAN-UP, HUH...
I CAN FEEL THE PRESSURE ...
WELL... I'M EXPECTING TO LOSE ANYWAY.
SU (SWISH)
WHAT'S IMPORTANT IS HOW WE LOSE...
HYU (WHOOSH)

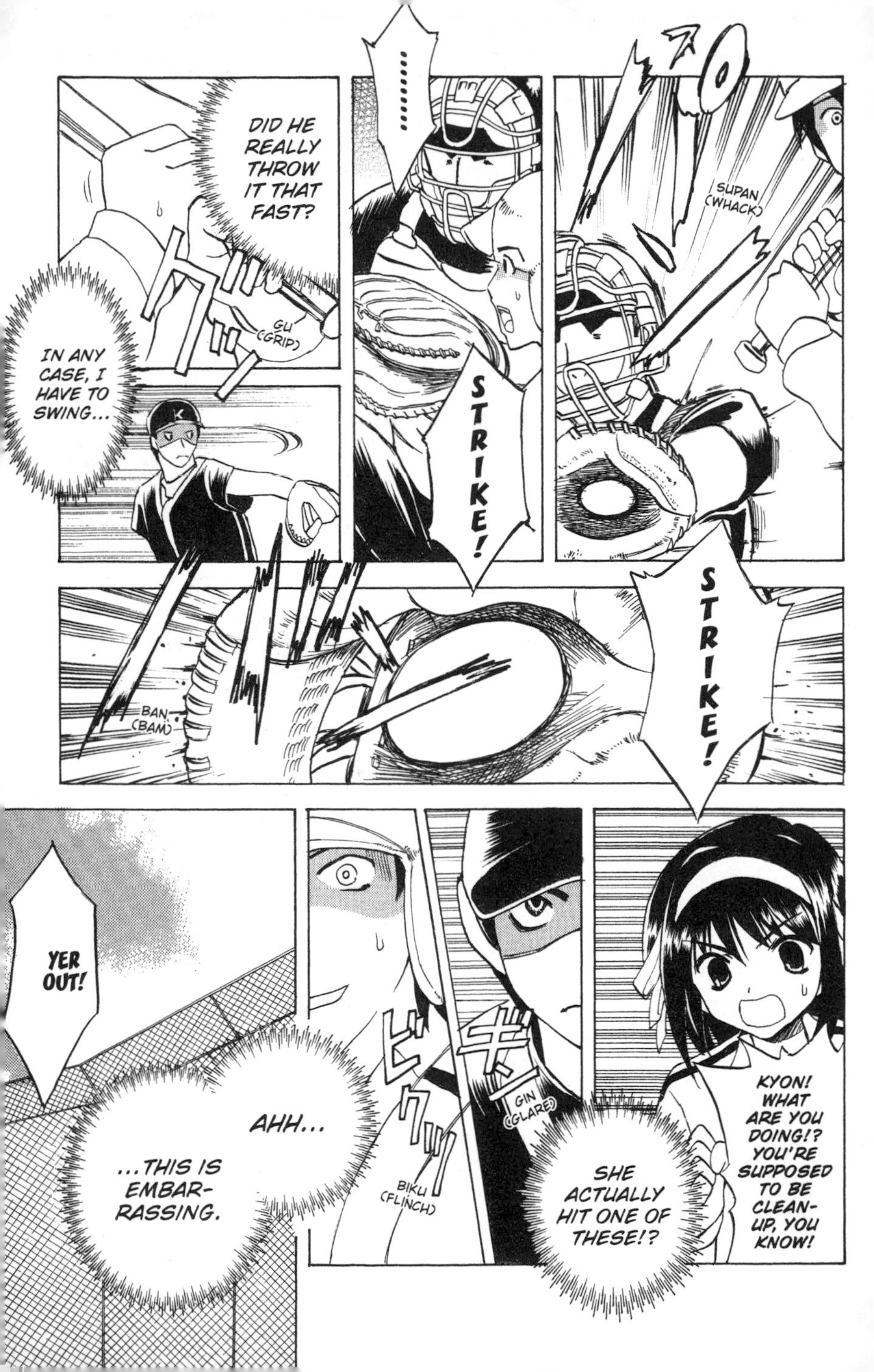
SUPAN (WHACK)
......
STRIKE!
DID HE REALLY THROW IT THAT FAST?
GU (GRIP)
IN ANY CASE, I HAVE TO SWING...
STRIKE!
BAN (BAM)
KYON! WHAT ARE YOU DOING!? YOU'RE SUPPOSED TO BE CLEAN-UP, YOU KNOW!
SHE ACTUALLY HIT ONE OF THESE!?
GIN (GLARE)
BIKU (FLINCH)
YER OUT!
AHH...
...THIS IS EMBAR-RASSING.

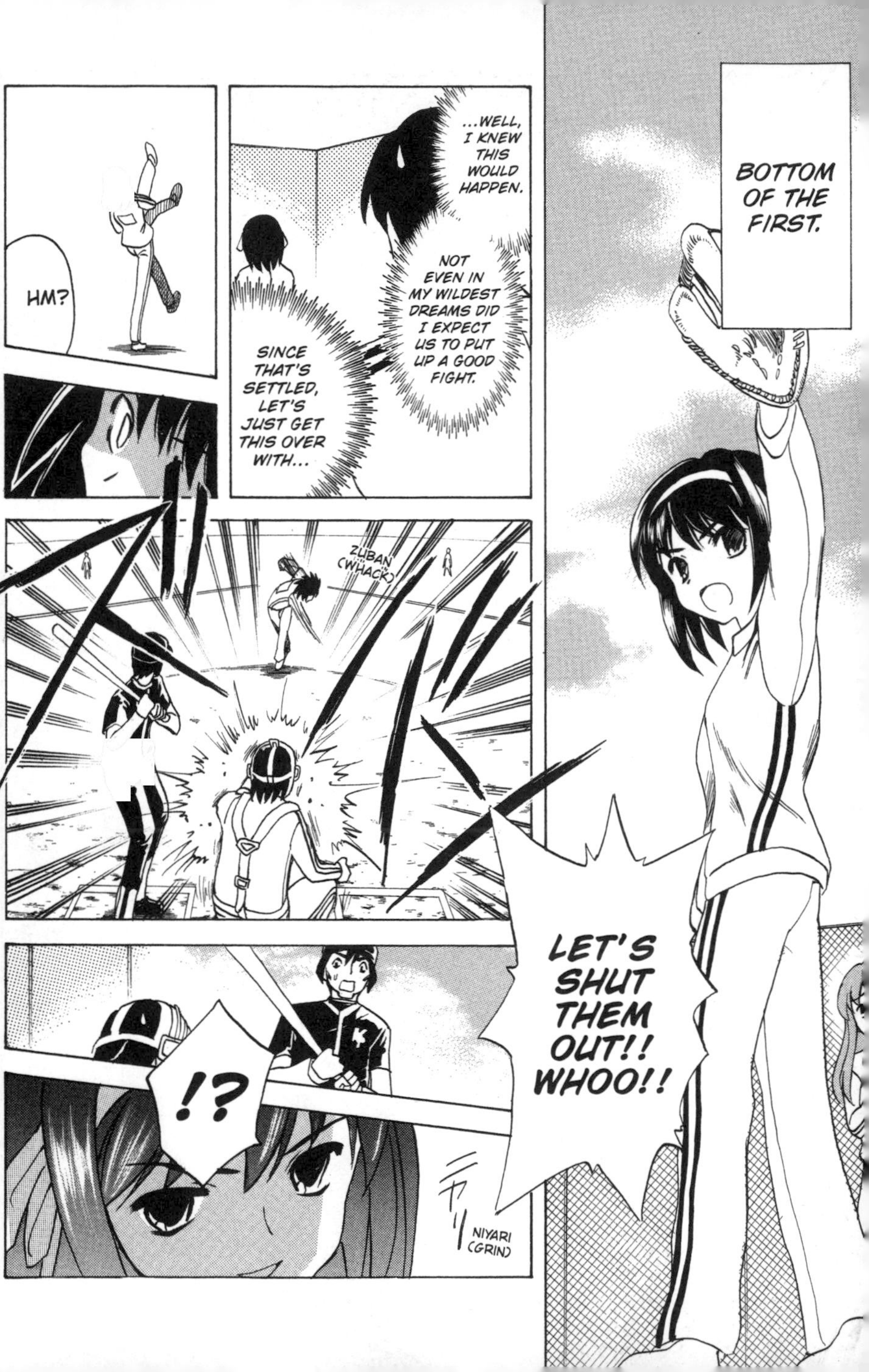
BOTTOM OF THE FIRST.
LET'S SHUT THEM OUT!! WHOO!!
...WELL, I KNEW THIS WOULD HAPPEN.
NOT EVEN IN MY WILDEST DREAMS DID I EXPECT US TO PUT UP A GOOD FIGHT.
SINCE THAT'S SETTLED, LET'S JUST GET THIS OVER WITH...
HM?
ZUBAN (WHACK)
!?
NIYARI (GRIN)

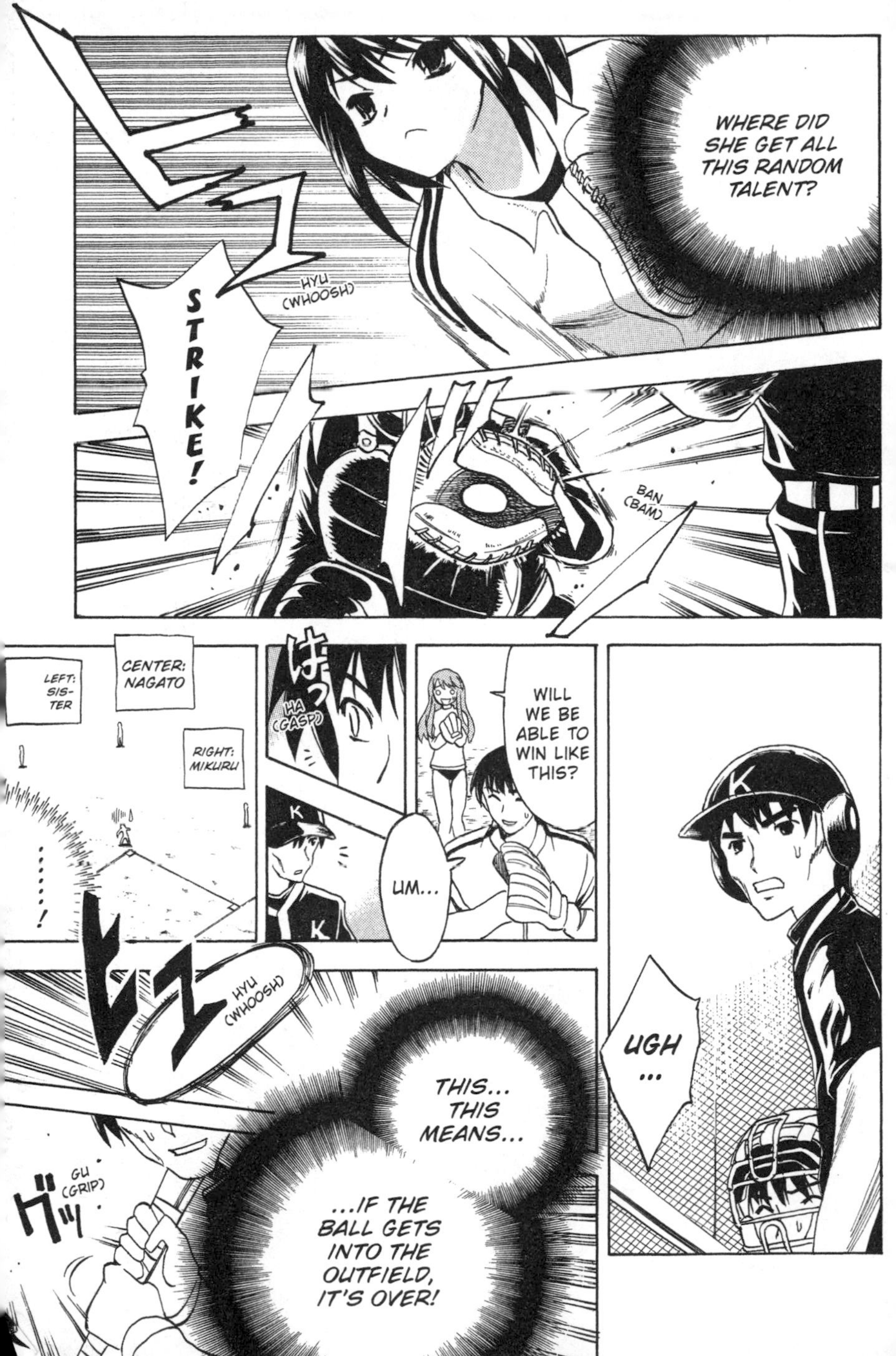
WHERE DID SHE GET ALL THIS RANDOM TALENT?
HYU (WHOOSH)
STRIKE!
BAN (BAM)
UGH...
WILL WE BE ABLE TO WIN LIKE THIS?
UM...
はっ
HA (GASP)
CENTER: NAGATO
LEFT: SISTER
RIGHT: MIKURU
......!
HYU (WHOOSH)
THIS... THIS MEANS...
...IF THE BALL GETS INTO THE OUTFIELD, IT'S OVER!
GU (GRIP)

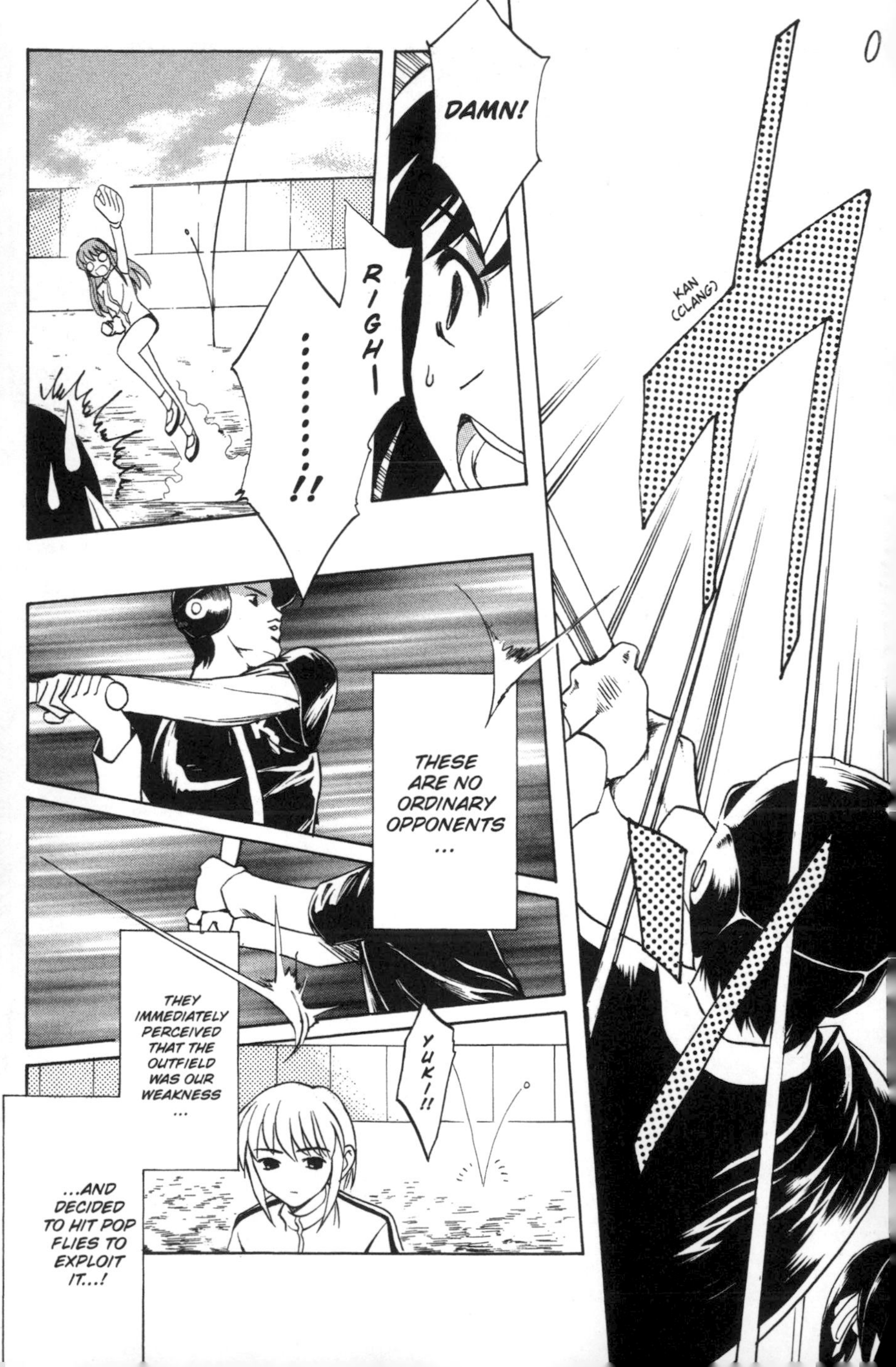
KAN (CLANG)
DAMN!
RIGHI
..........!!
THESE ARE NO ORDINARY OPPONENTS ...
YUKI!!
THEY IMMEDIATELY PERCEIVED THAT THE OUTFIELD WAS OUR WEAKNESS ...
...AND DECIDED TO HIT POP FLIES TO EXPLOIT IT...!

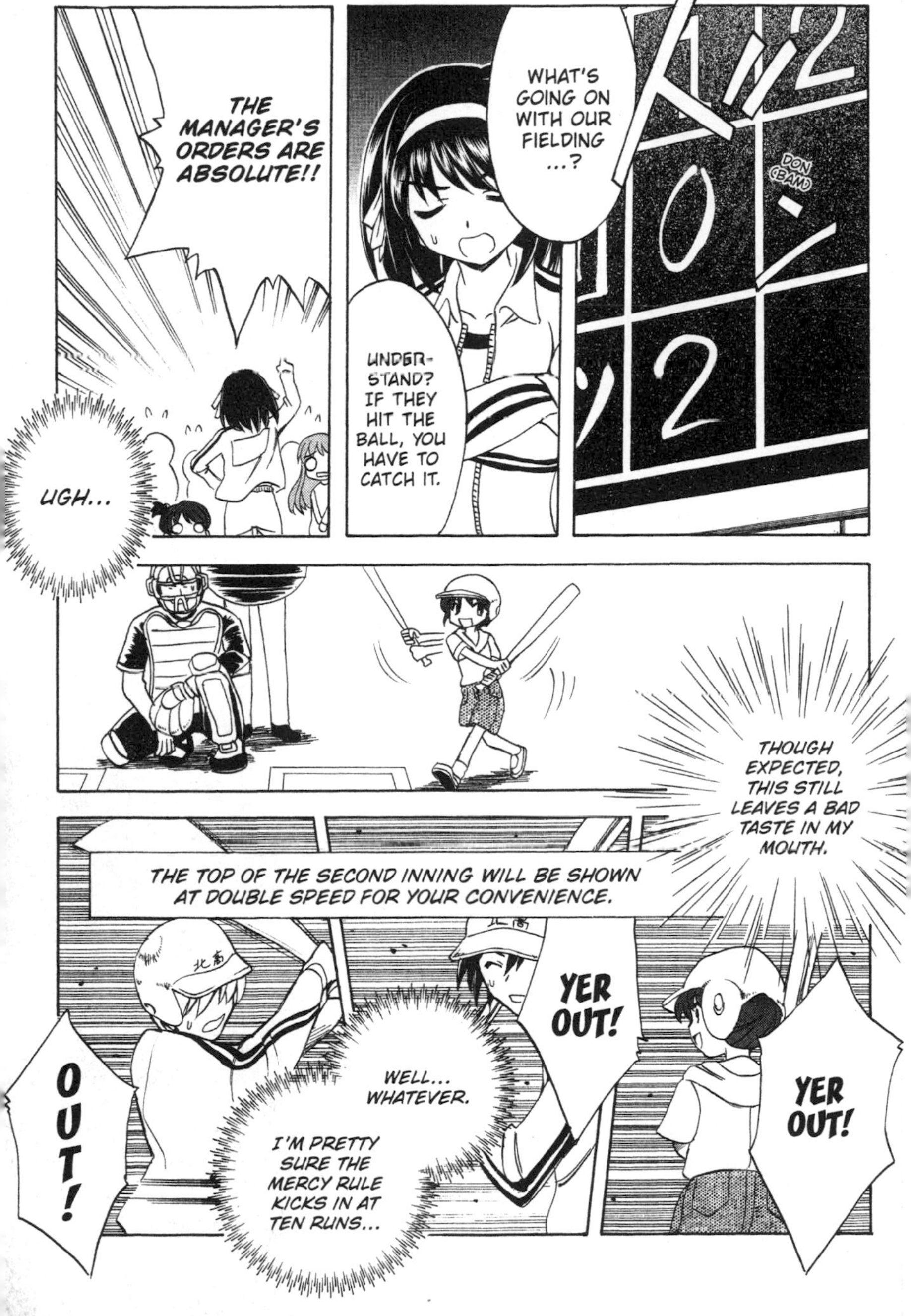
DON (BAM)
WHAT'S GOING ON WITH OUR FIELDING ...?
UNDER-STAND? IF THEY HIT THE BALL, YOU HAVE TO CATCH IT.
THE MANAGER'S ORDERS ARE ABSOLUTE!!
UGH...
THOUGH EXPECTED, THIS STILL LEAVES A BAD TASTE IN MY MOUTH.
THE TOP OF THE SECOND INNING WILL BE SHOWN AT DOUBLE SPEED FOR YOUR CONVENIENCE.
YER OUT!
YER OUT!
WELL... WHATEVER.
I'M PRETTY SURE THE MERCY RULE KICKS IN AT TEN RUNS...
OUT!

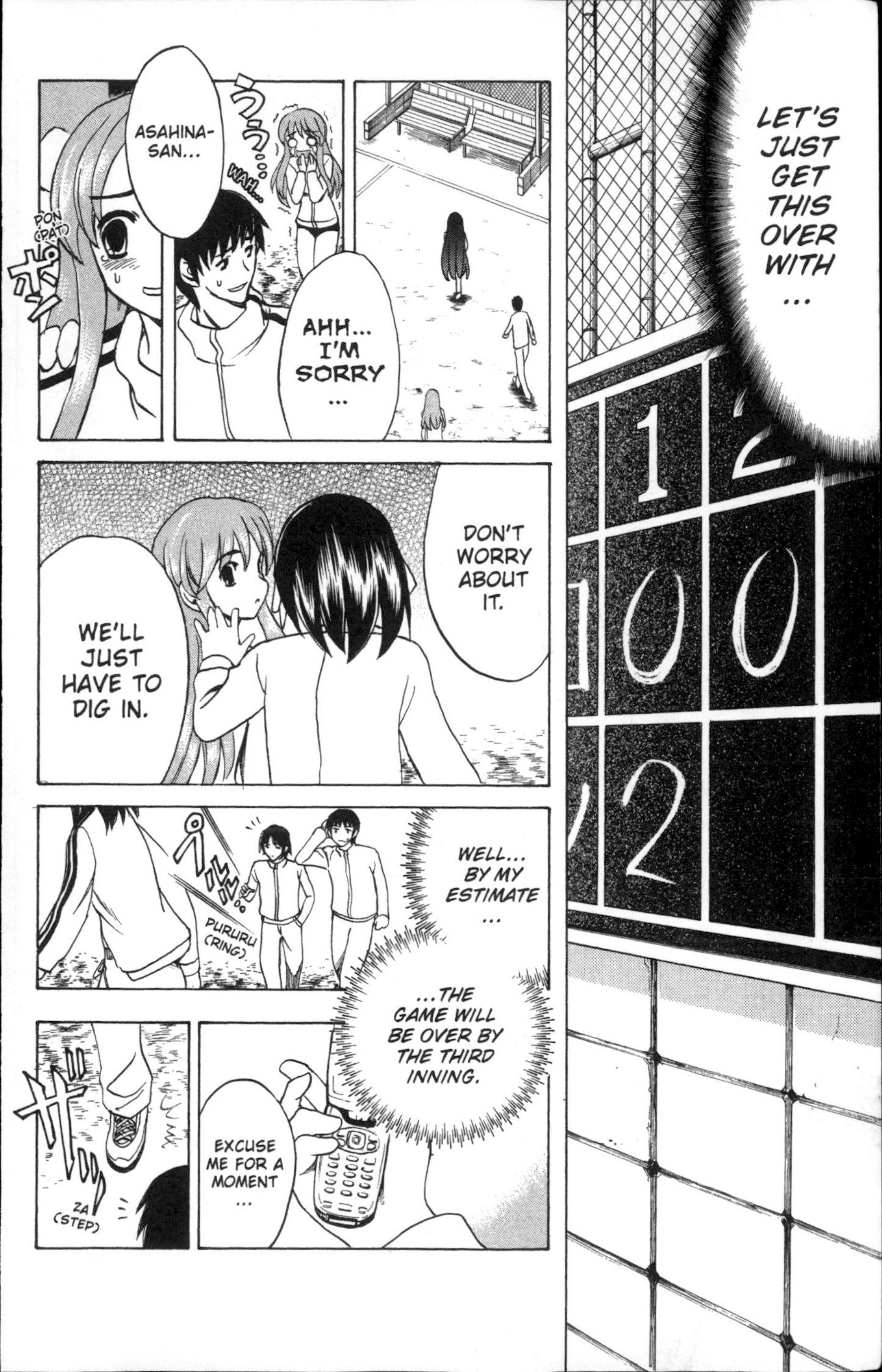
LET'S JUST GET THIS OVER WITH...
WAH...
ASAHINA-SAN...
AHH... I'M SORRY...
PON (PAT)
DON'T WORRY ABOUT IT.
WE'LL JUST HAVE TO DIG IN.
WELL... BY MY ESTIMATE...
PURURU (RING)
...THE GAME WILL BE OVER BY THE THIRD INNING.
EXCUSE ME FOR A MOMENT...
ZA (STEP)

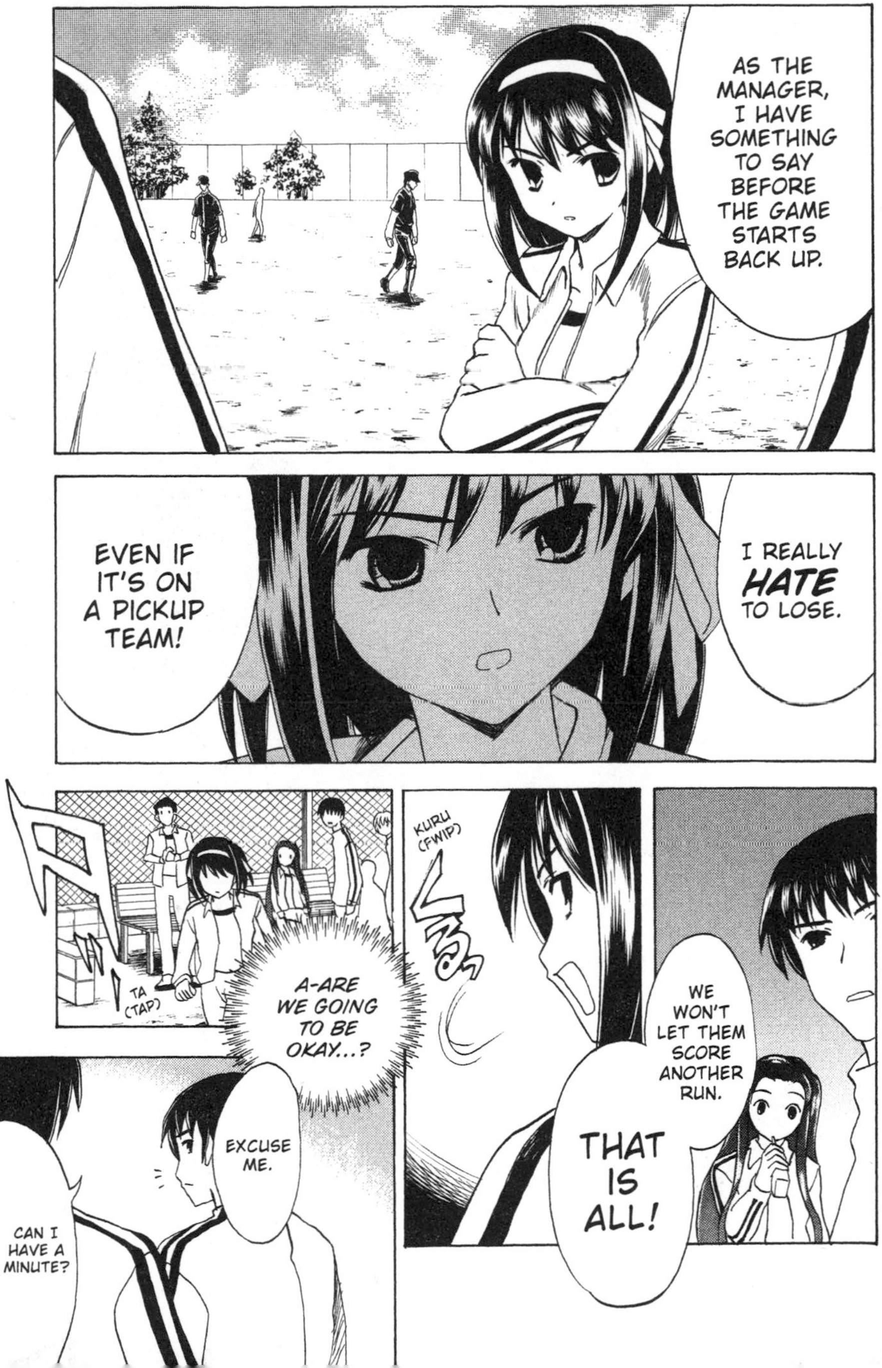
AS THE MANAGER, I HAVE SOMETHING TO SAY BEFORE THE GAME STARTS BACK UP.
I REALLY *HATE* TO LOSE.
EVEN IF IT'S ON A PICKUP TEAM!
WE WON'T LET THEM SCORE ANOTHER RUN.
THAT IS ALL!
KURU (FWIP)
TA (TAP)
A-ARE WE GOING TO BE OKAY...?
EXCUSE ME.
CAN I HAVE A MINUTE?

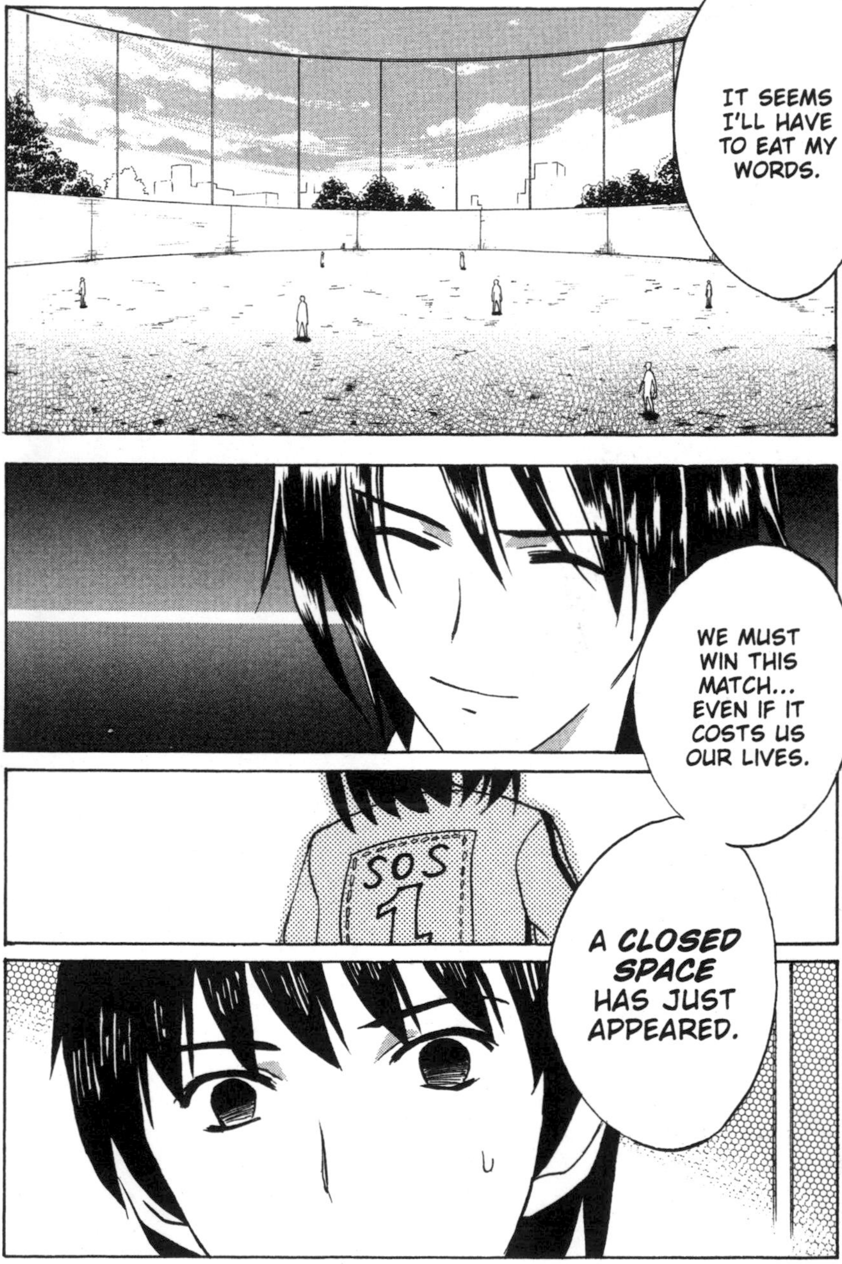
IT SEEMS I'LL HAVE TO EAT MY WORDS.
WE MUST WIN THIS MATCH... EVEN IF IT COSTS US OUR LIVES.
SOS 1
A *CLOSED SPACE* HAS JUST APPEARED.

The Boredom of Haruhi Suzumiya I : END

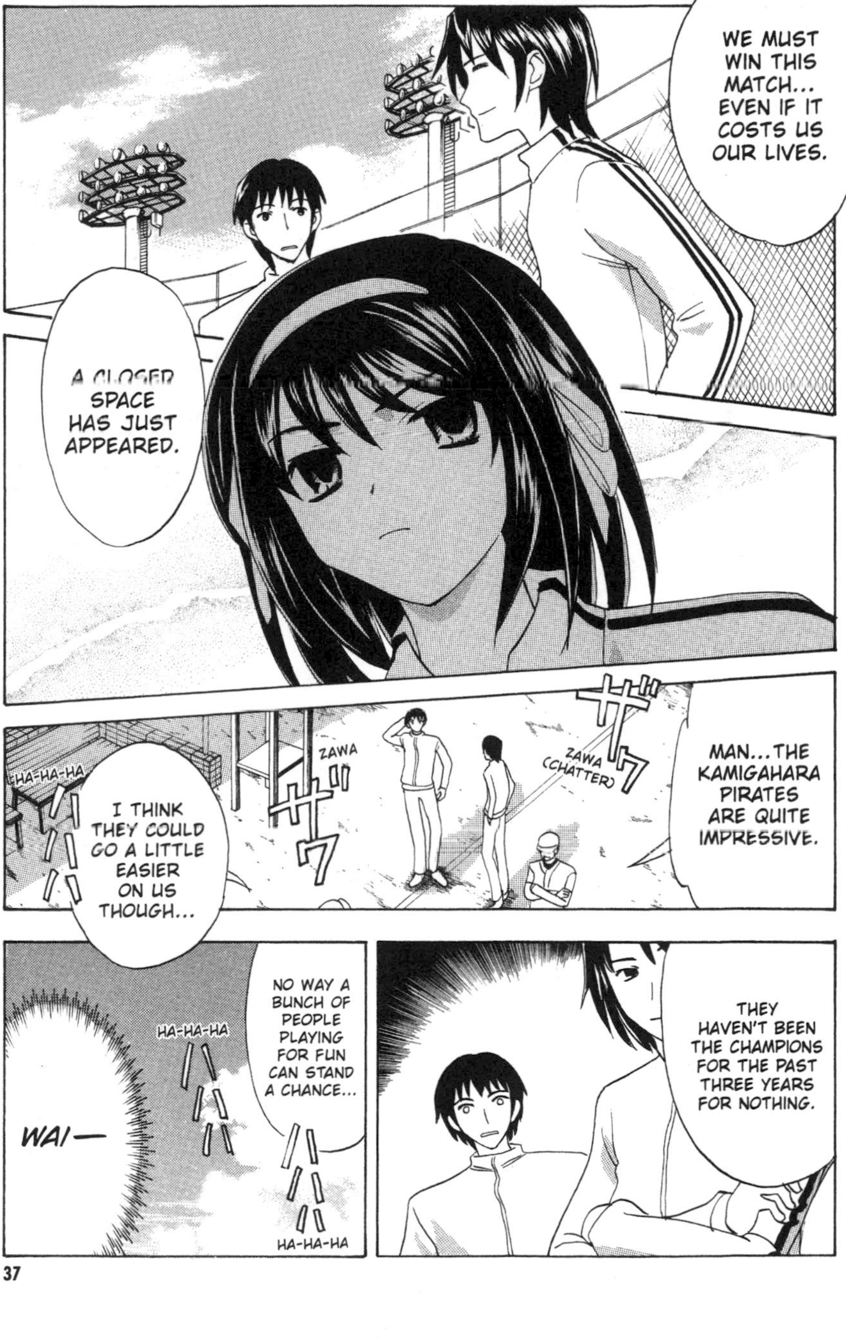
WE MUST WIN THIS MATCH... EVEN IF IT COSTS US OUR LIVES.
A CLOSED SPACE HAS JUST APPEARED.
MAN...THE KAMIGAHARA PIRATES ARE QUITE IMPRESSIVE.
ZAWA (CHATTER)
ZAWA
I THINK THEY COULD GO A LITTLE EASIER ON US THOUGH...
HA-HA-HA
THEY HAVEN'T BEEN THE CHAMPIONS FOR THE PAST THREE YEARS FOR NOTHING.
NO WAY A BUNCH OF PEOPLE PLAYING FOR FUN CAN STAND A CHANCE...
HA-HA-HA
HA-HA-HA
WAI—

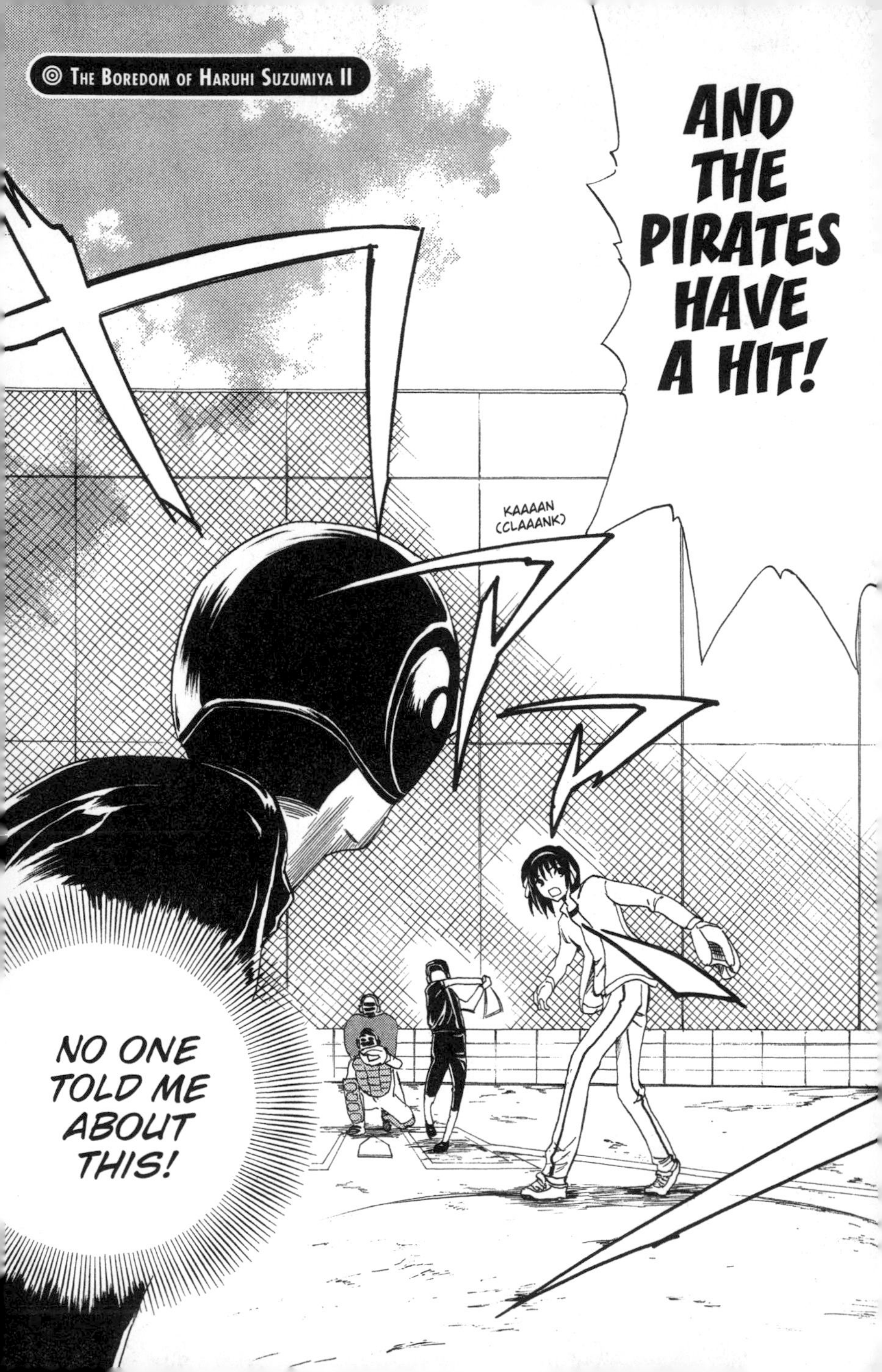
AND THE PIRATES HAVE A HIT!
KAAAAN (CLAAANK)
NO ONE TOLD ME ABOUT THIS!

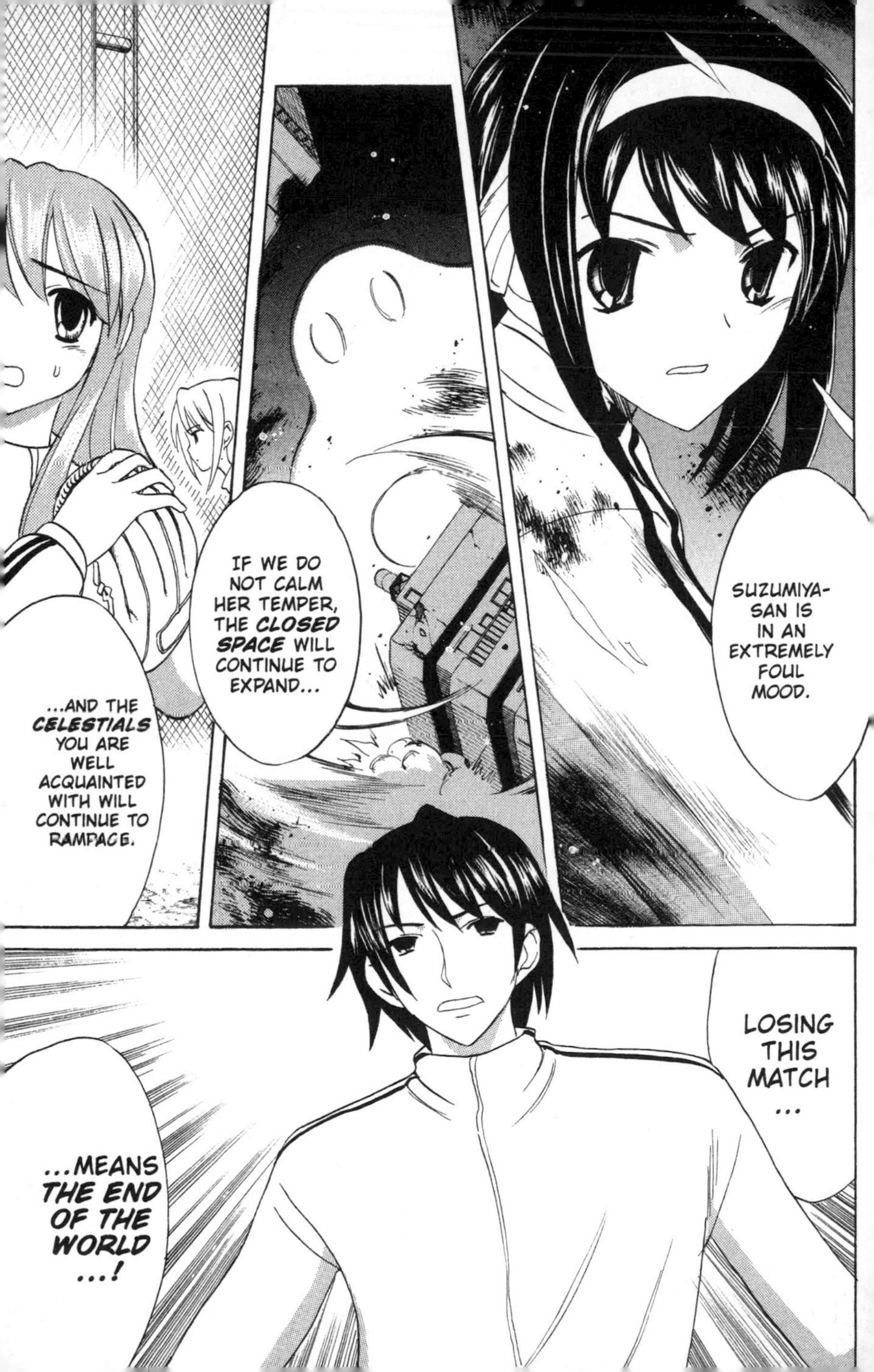
SUZUMIYA-SAN IS IN AN EXTREMELY FOUL MOOD.
IF WE DO NOT CALM HER TEMPER, THE CLOSED SPACE WILL CONTINUE TO EXPAND...
...AND THE CELESTIALS YOU ARE WELL ACQUAINTED WITH WILL CONTINUE TO RAMPAGE.
LOSING THIS MATCH ...
...MEANS THE END OF THE WORLD ...!

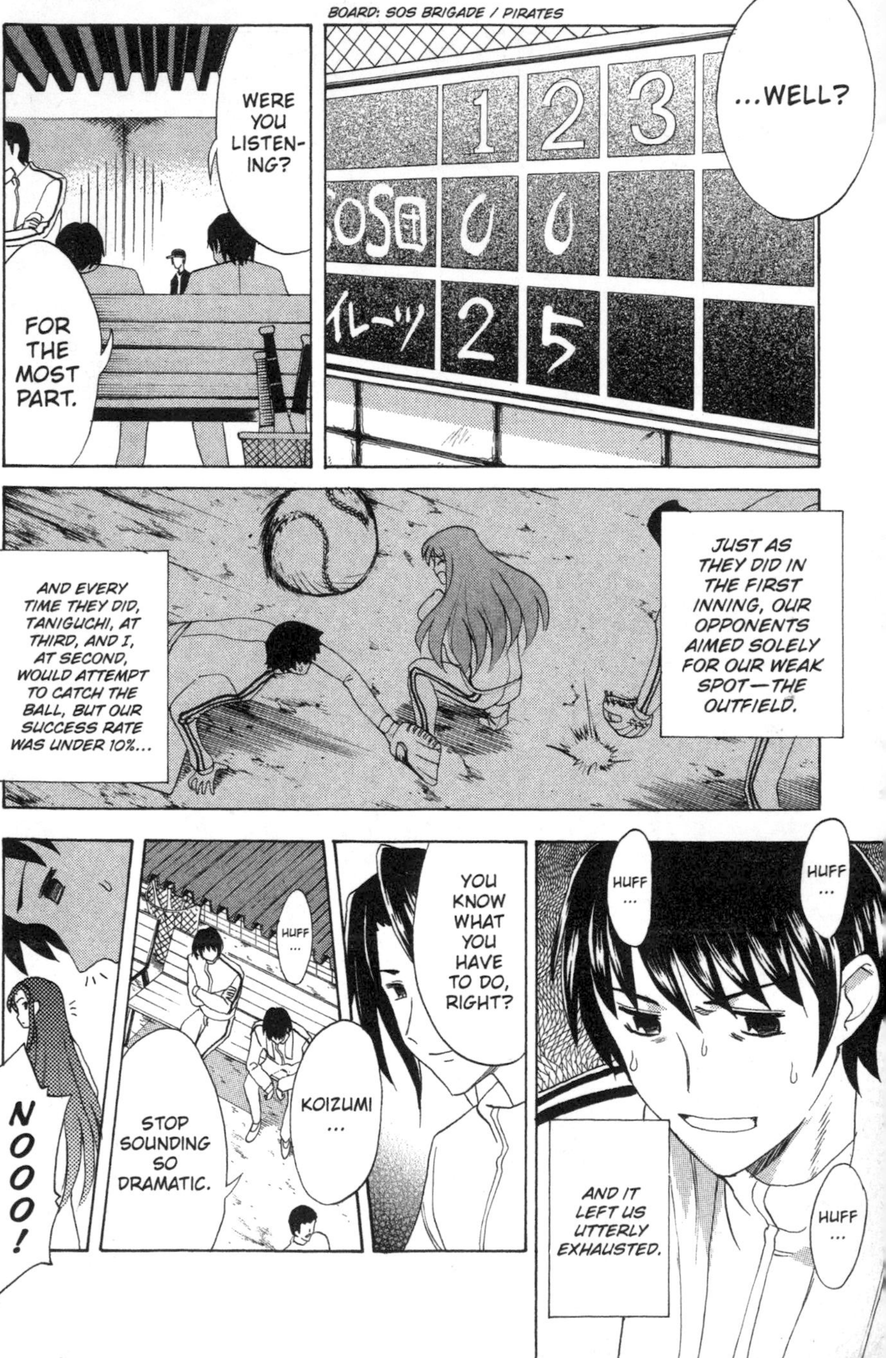
BOARD: SOS BRIGADE / PIRATES
...WELL?
WERE YOU LISTENING?
FOR THE MOST PART.
JUST AS THEY DID IN THE FIRST INNING, OUR OPPONENTS AIMED SOLELY FOR OUR WEAK SPOT—THE OUTFIELD.
AND EVERY TIME THEY DID, TANIGUCHI, AT THIRD, AND I, AT SECOND, WOULD ATTEMPT TO CATCH THE BALL, BUT OUR SUCCESS RATE WAS UNDER 10%...
HUFF...
HUFF...
AND IT LEFT US UTTERLY EXHAUSTED.
HUFF...
YOU KNOW WHAT YOU HAVE TO DO, RIGHT?
KOIZUMI...
HUFF...
STOP SOUNDING SO DRAMATIC.
NOOOO!

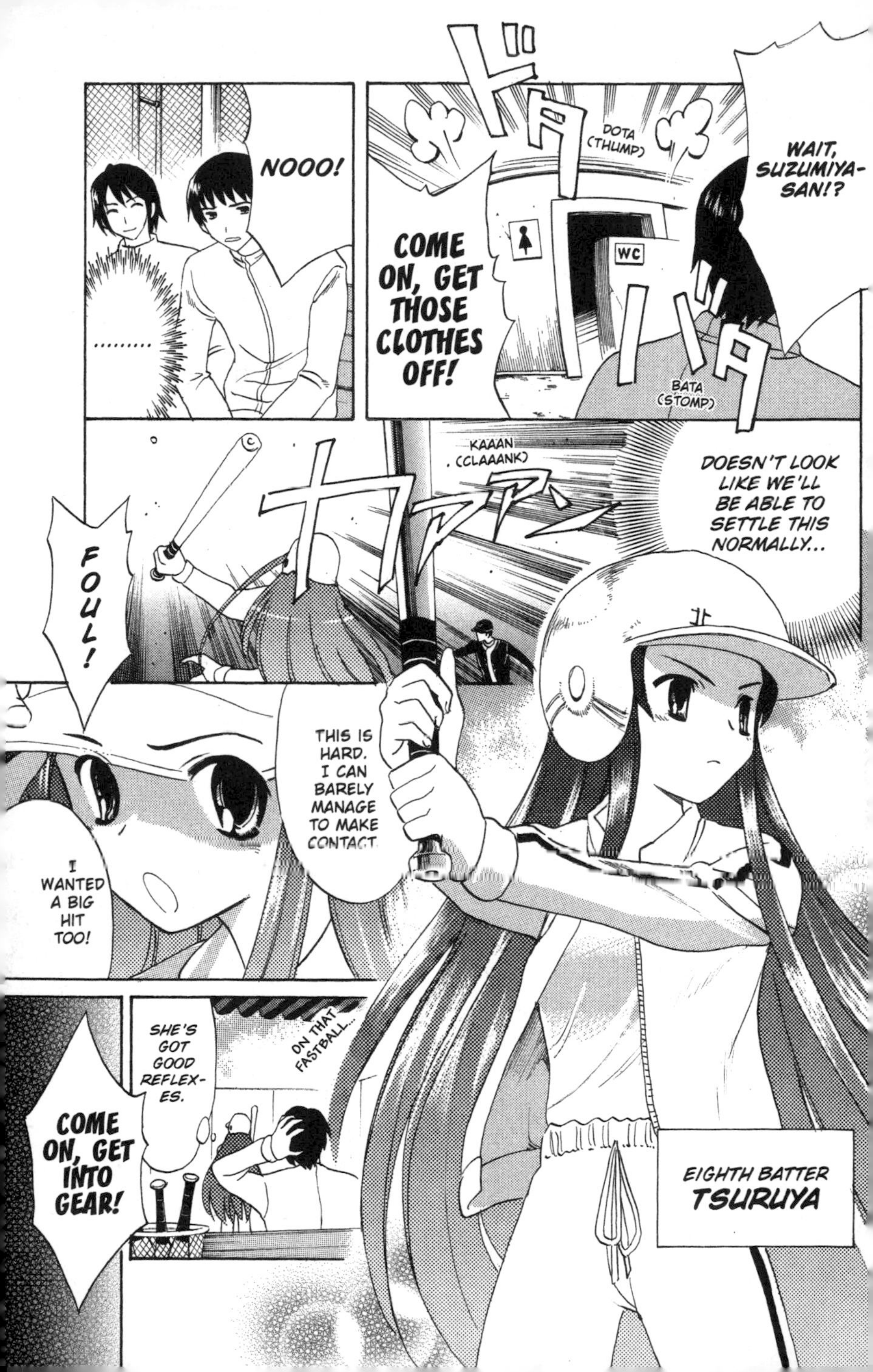
WAIT, SUZUMIYA-SAN!?
DOTA (THUMP)
COME ON, GET THOSE CLOTHES OFF!
BATA (STOMP)
NOOO!
....
DOESN'T LOOK LIKE WE'LL BE ABLE TO SETTLE THIS NORMALLY...
KAAAN (CLAAANK)
FOUL!
THIS IS HARD. I CAN BARELY MANAGE TO MAKE CONTACT.
I WANTED A BIG HIT TOO!
EIGHTH BATTER TSURUYA
ON THAT FASTBALL...
SHE'S GOT GOOD REFLEXES.
COME ON, GET INTO GEAR!

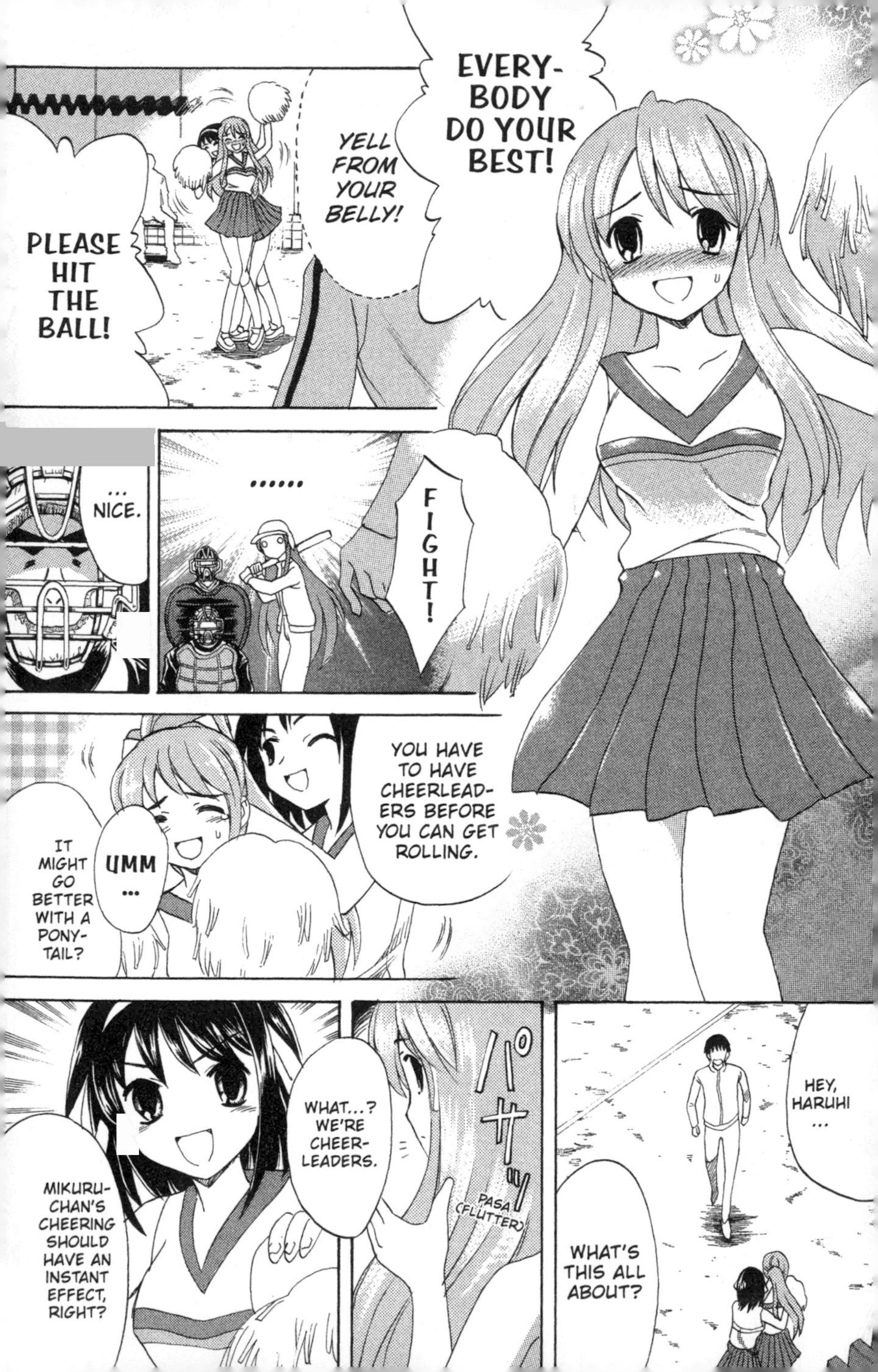
EVERY-BODY DO YOUR BEST!
FIGHT!
YELL FROM YOUR BELLY!
PLEASE HIT THE BALL!
......
... NICE.
YOU HAVE TO HAVE CHEERLEAD-ERS BEFORE YOU CAN GET ROLLING.
UMM ...
IT MIGHT GO BETTER WITH A PONY-TAIL?
HEY, HARUHI ...
WHAT'S THIS ALL ABOUT?
WHAT...? WE'RE CHEER-LEADERS.
PASA (FLUTTER)
MIKURU-CHAN'S CHEERING SHOULD HAVE AN INSTANT EFFECT, RIGHT?

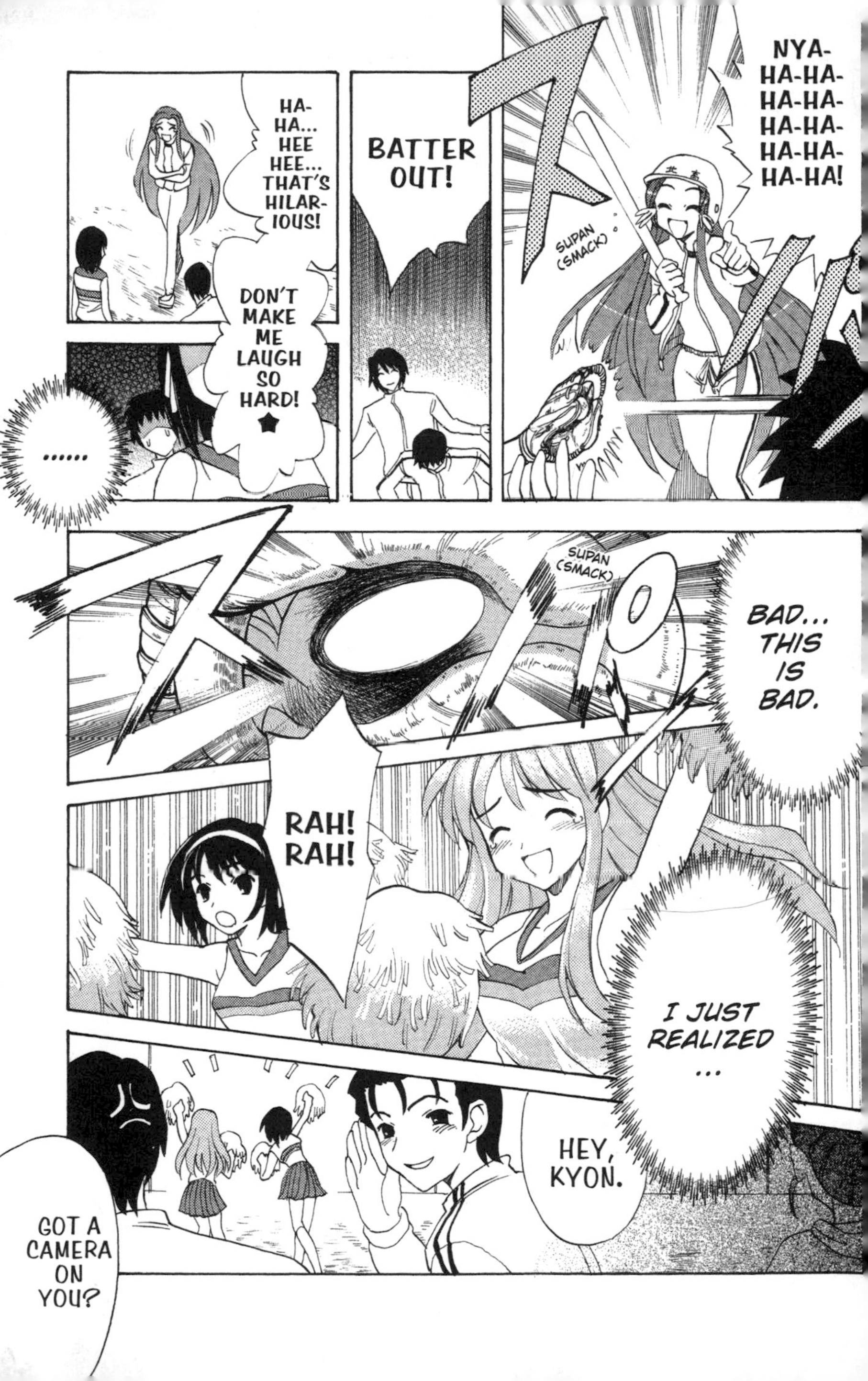
NYA-HA-HA-HA-HA-HA-HA-HA-HA-HA-HA!
SUPAN (SMACK)
BATTER OUT!
HA-HA... HEE HEE... THAT'S HILARIOUS!
DON'T MAKE ME LAUGH SO HARD! ★
......
SUPAN (SMACK)
BAD... THIS IS BAD.
I JUST REALIZED...
RAH! RAH!
HEY, KYON.
GOT A CAMERA ON YOU?

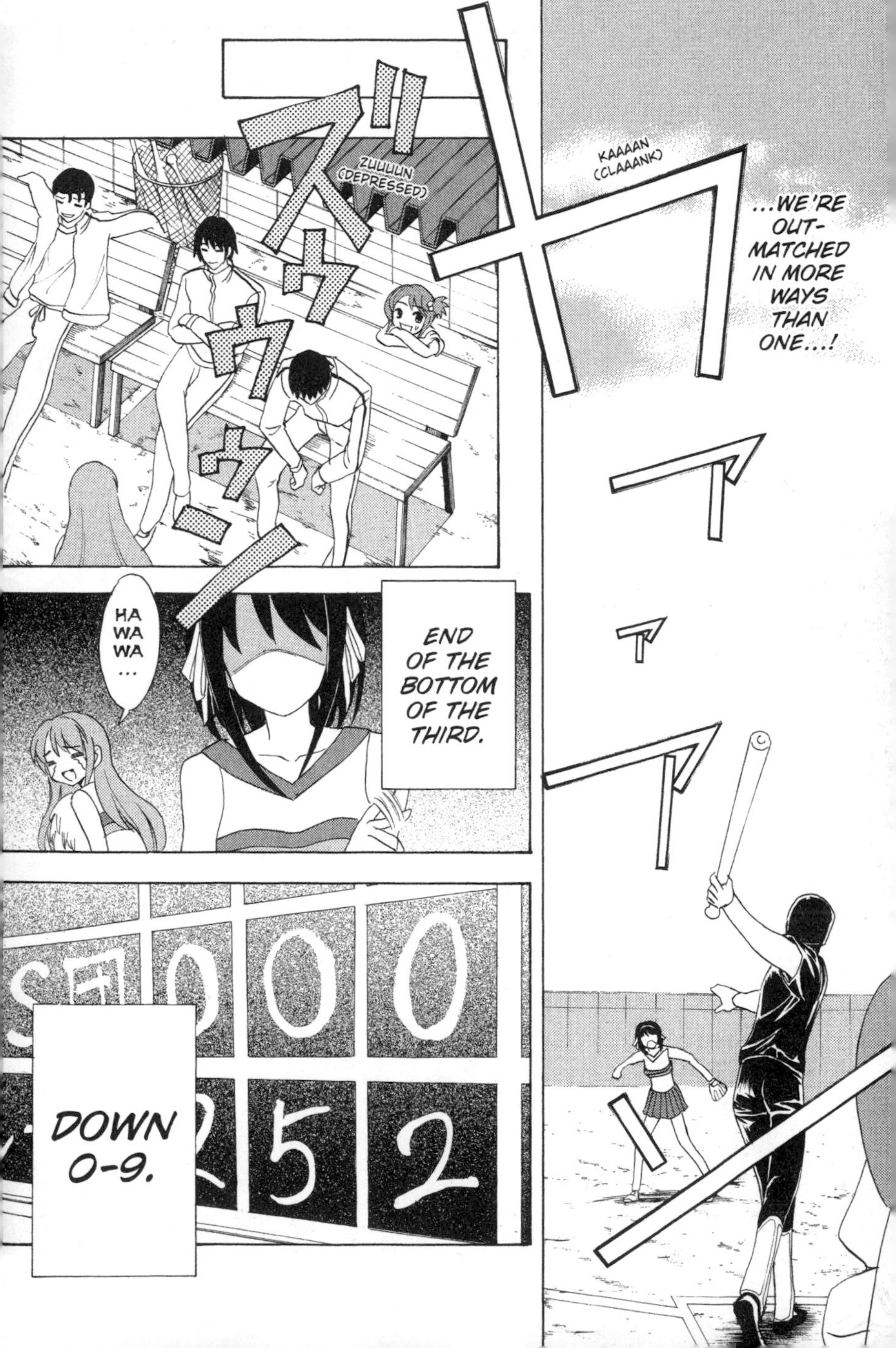
KAAAAN (CLAAANK)
...WE'RE OUT-MATCHED IN MORE WAYS THAN ONE...!
ZUUUUN (DEPRESSED)
END OF THE BOTTOM OF THE THIRD.
HA WA WA ...
DOWN 0-9.

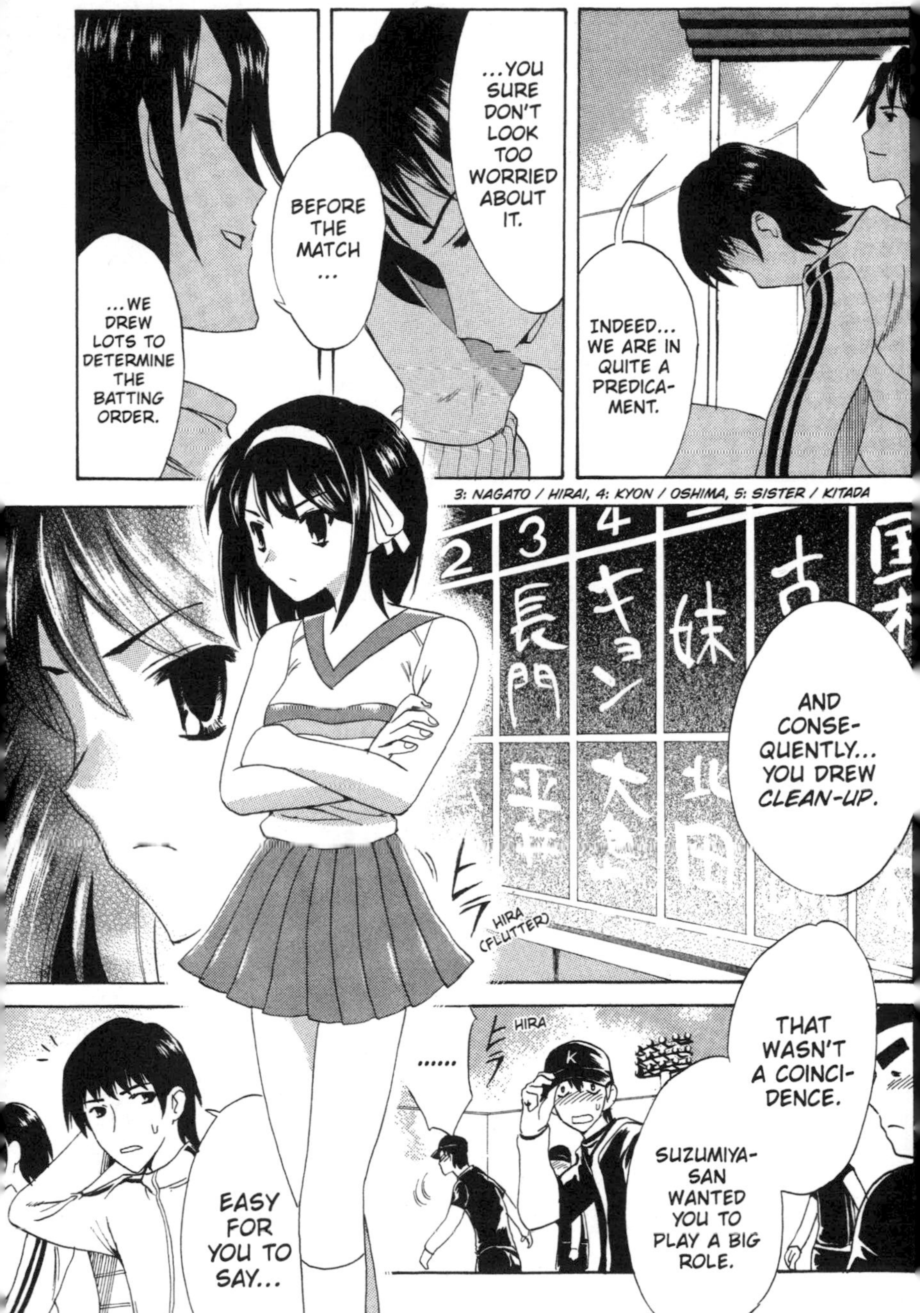
INDEED... WE ARE IN QUITE A PREDICAMENT.
...YOU SURE DON'T LOOK TOO WORRIED ABOUT IT.
BEFORE THE MATCH...
...WE DREW LOTS TO DETERMINE THE BATTING ORDER.
3: NAGATO / HIRAI, 4: KYON / OSHIMA, 5: SISTER / KITADA
2
3
4
長門
キョン
妹
AND CONSEQUENTLY... YOU DREW CLEAN-UP.
HIRA (FLUTTER)
THAT WASN'T A COINCIDENCE.
SUZUMIYA-SAN WANTED YOU TO PLAY A BIG ROLE.
HIRA
......
EASY FOR YOU TO SAY...

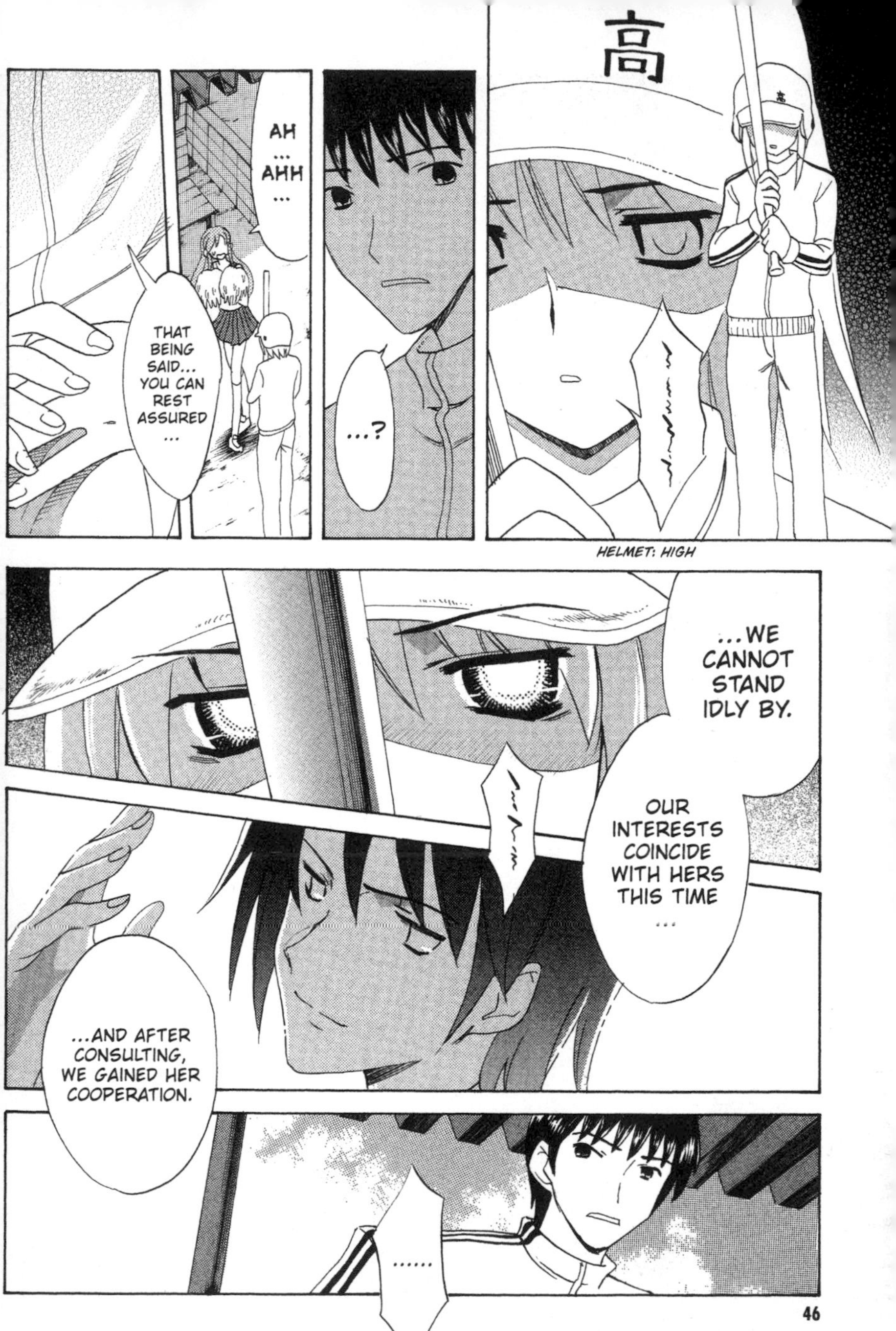
...?
AH ... AHH ...
THAT BEING SAID... YOU CAN REST ASSURED ...
...WE CANNOT STAND IDLY BY.
OUR INTERESTS COINCIDE WITH HERS THIS TIME ...
...AND AFTER CONSULTING, WE GAINED HER COOPERATION.
......
HELMET: HIGH

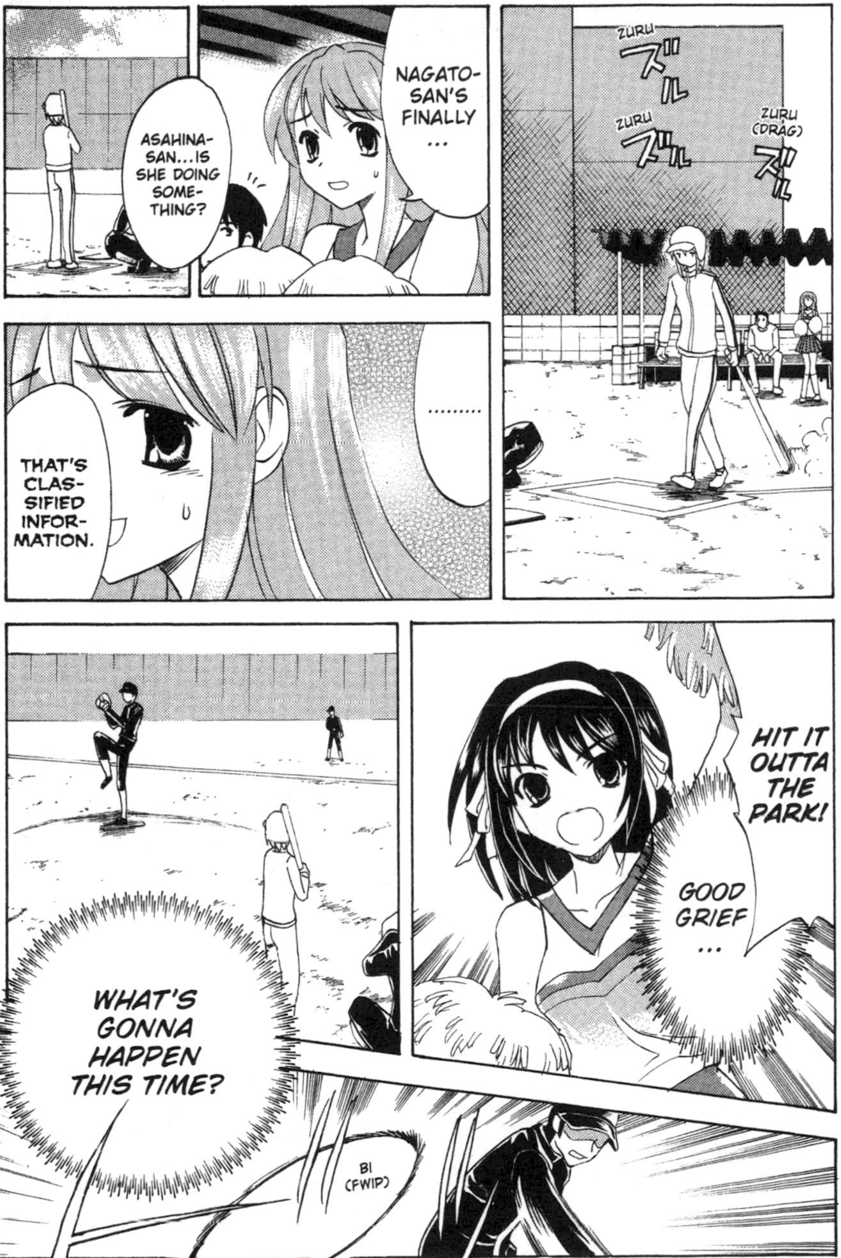
ZURU
ZURU
ZURU (DRAG)
NAGATO-SAN'S FINALLY...
ASAHINA-SAN...IS SHE DOING SOMETHING?
....
THAT'S CLASSIFIED INFORMATION.
HIT IT OUTTA THE PARK!
GOOD GRIEF...
WHAT'S GONNA HAPPEN THIS TIME?
BI (FWIP)

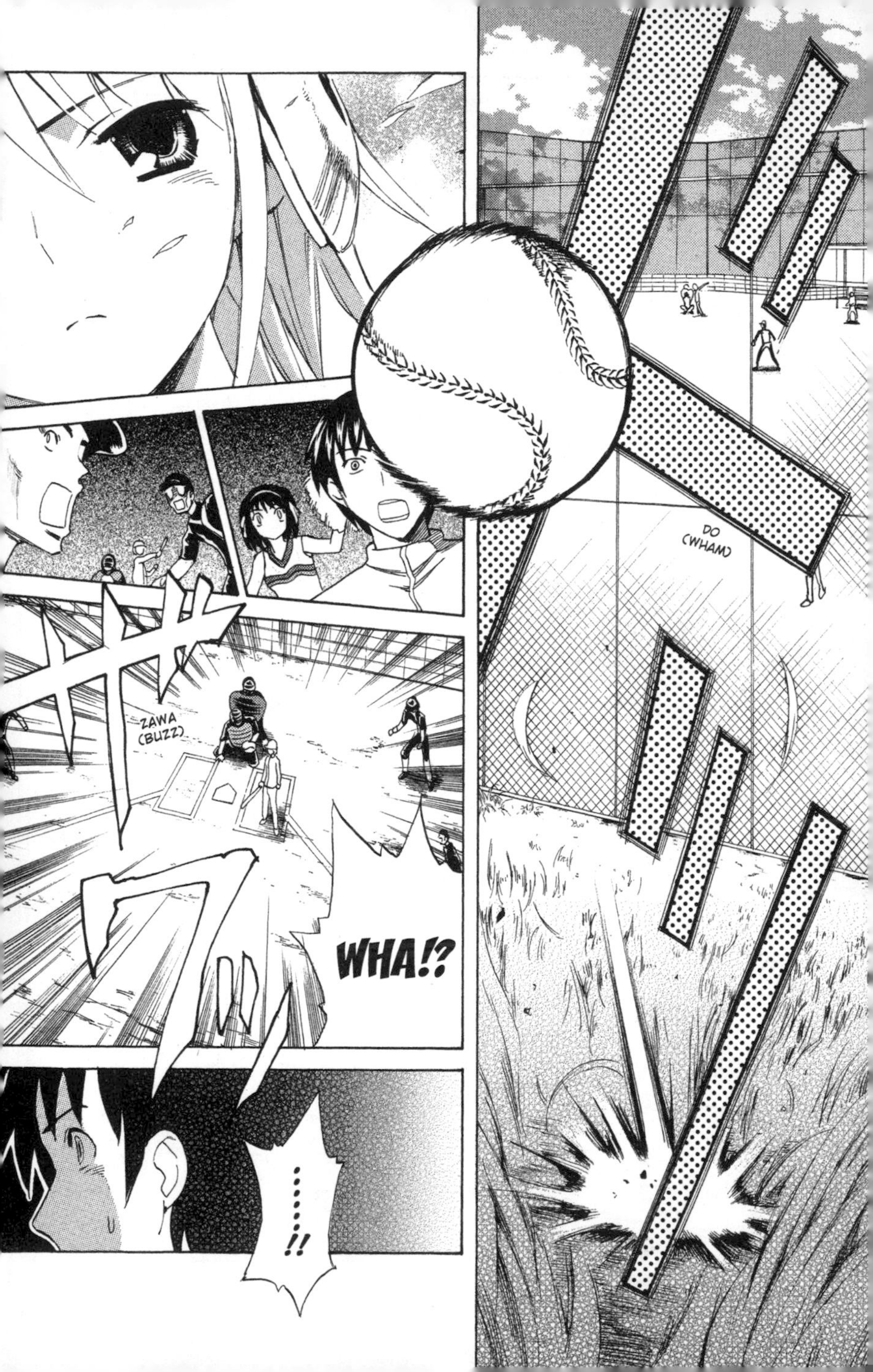
DO
(WHAM)
ZAWA
(BUZZ)
WHA!?
......!!

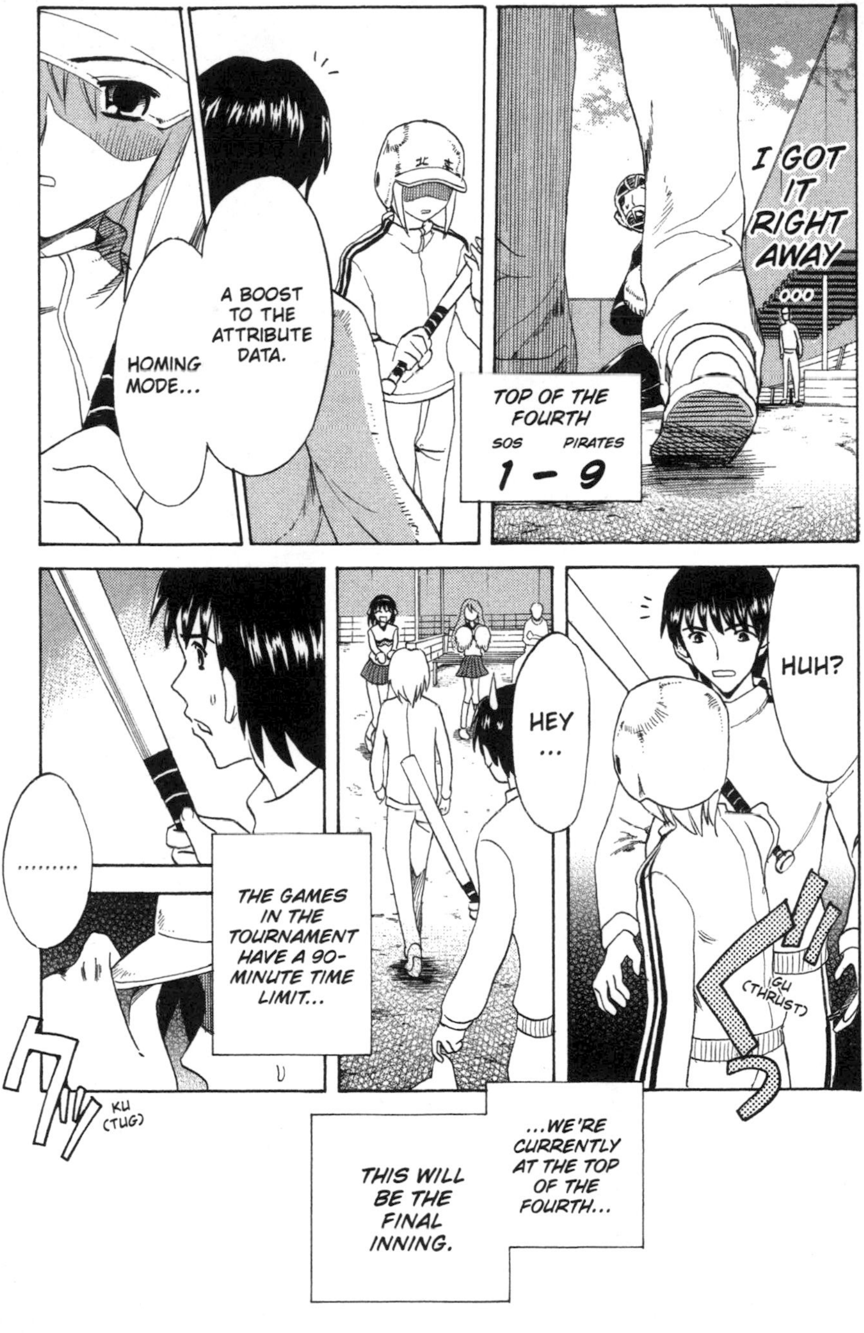
I GOT IT RIGHT AWAY
OOO
TOP OF THE FOURTH
SOS PIRATES
1 – 9
A BOOST TO THE ATTRIBUTE DATA.
HOMING MODE...
HUH?
HEY ...
GU (THRUST)
THE GAMES IN THE TOURNAMENT HAVE A 90-MINUTE TIME LIMIT...
....
KU (TUG)
...WE'RE CURRENTLY AT THE TOP OF THE FOURTH...
THIS WILL BE THE FINAL INNING.

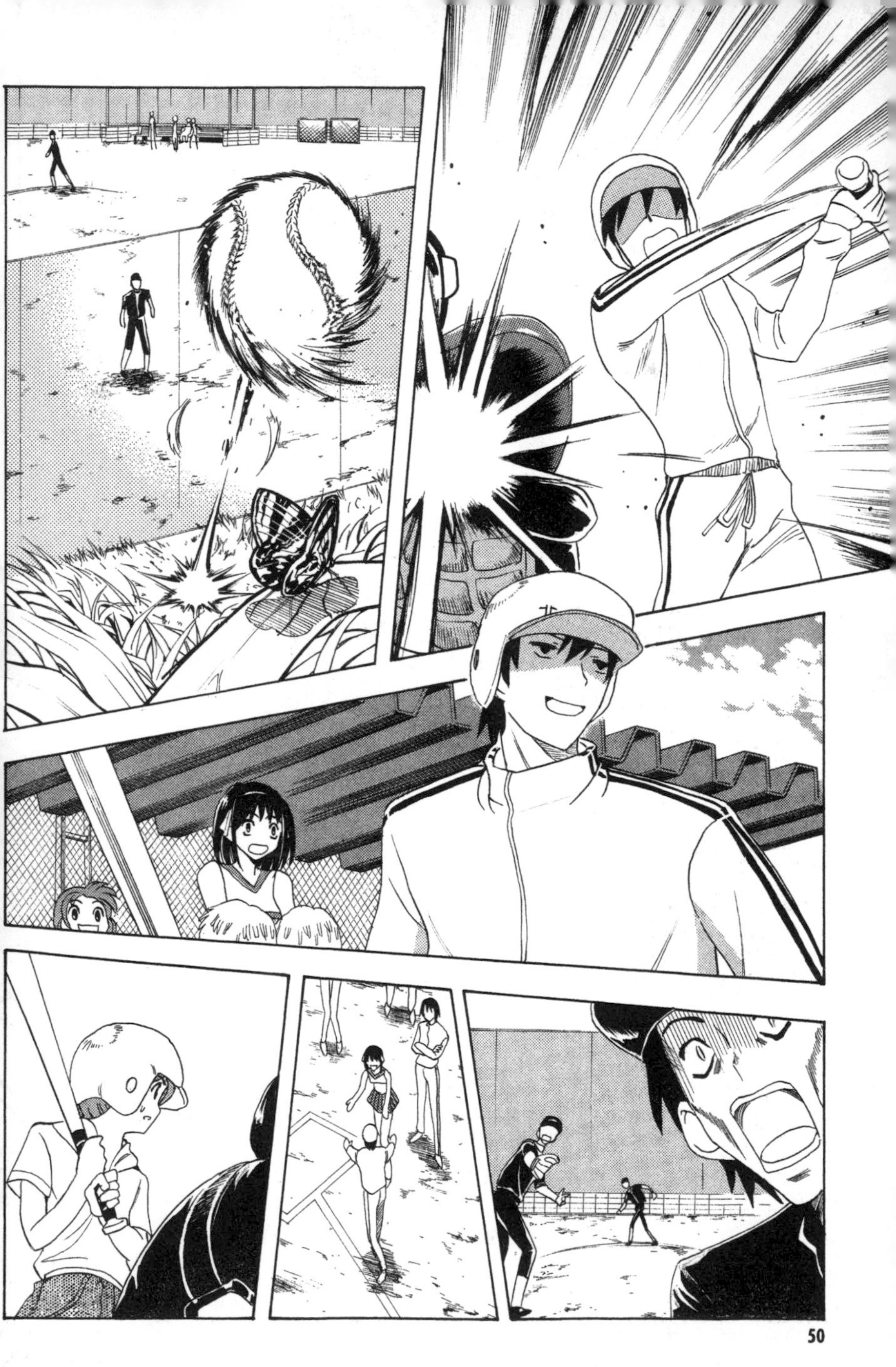

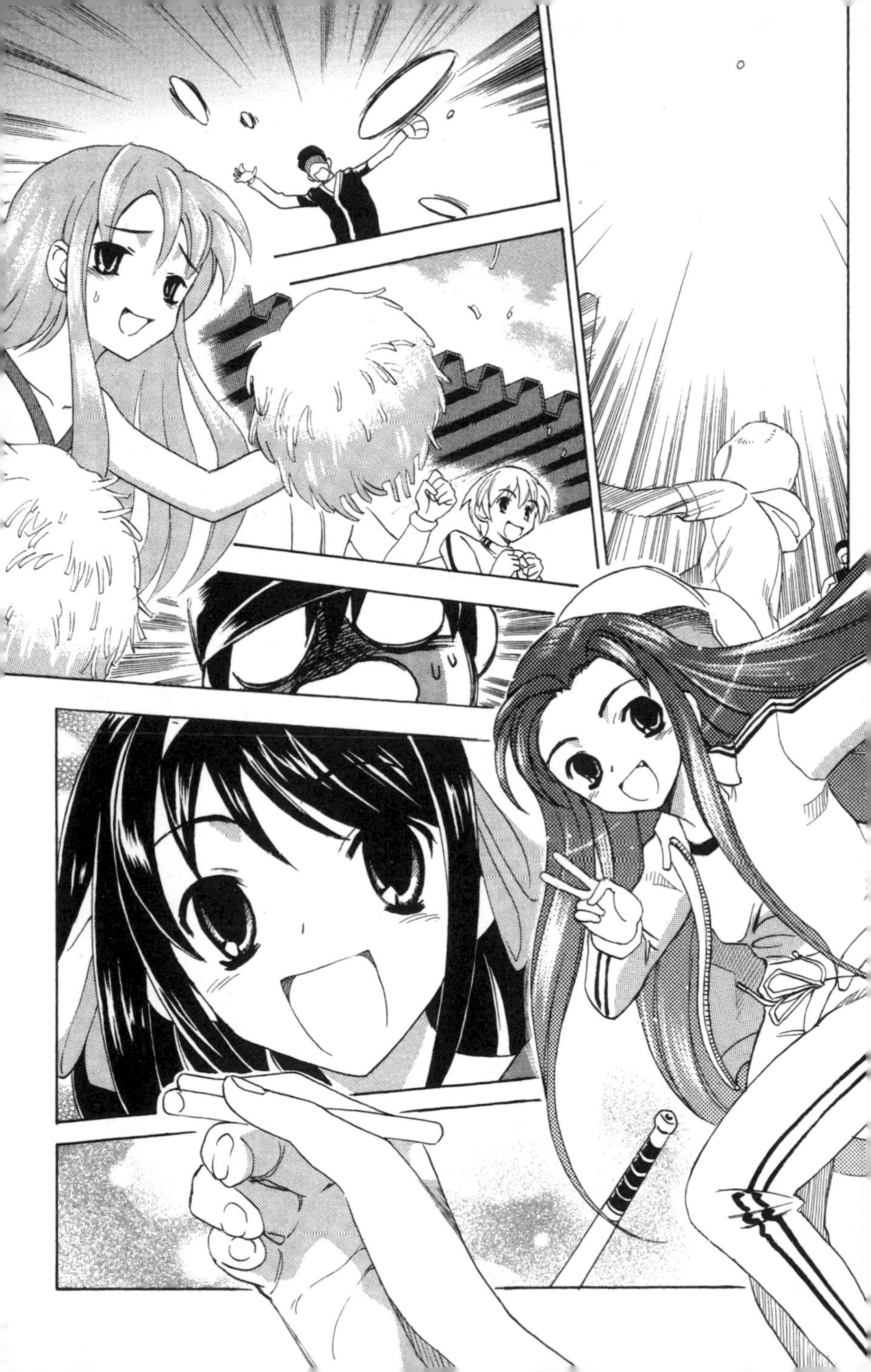

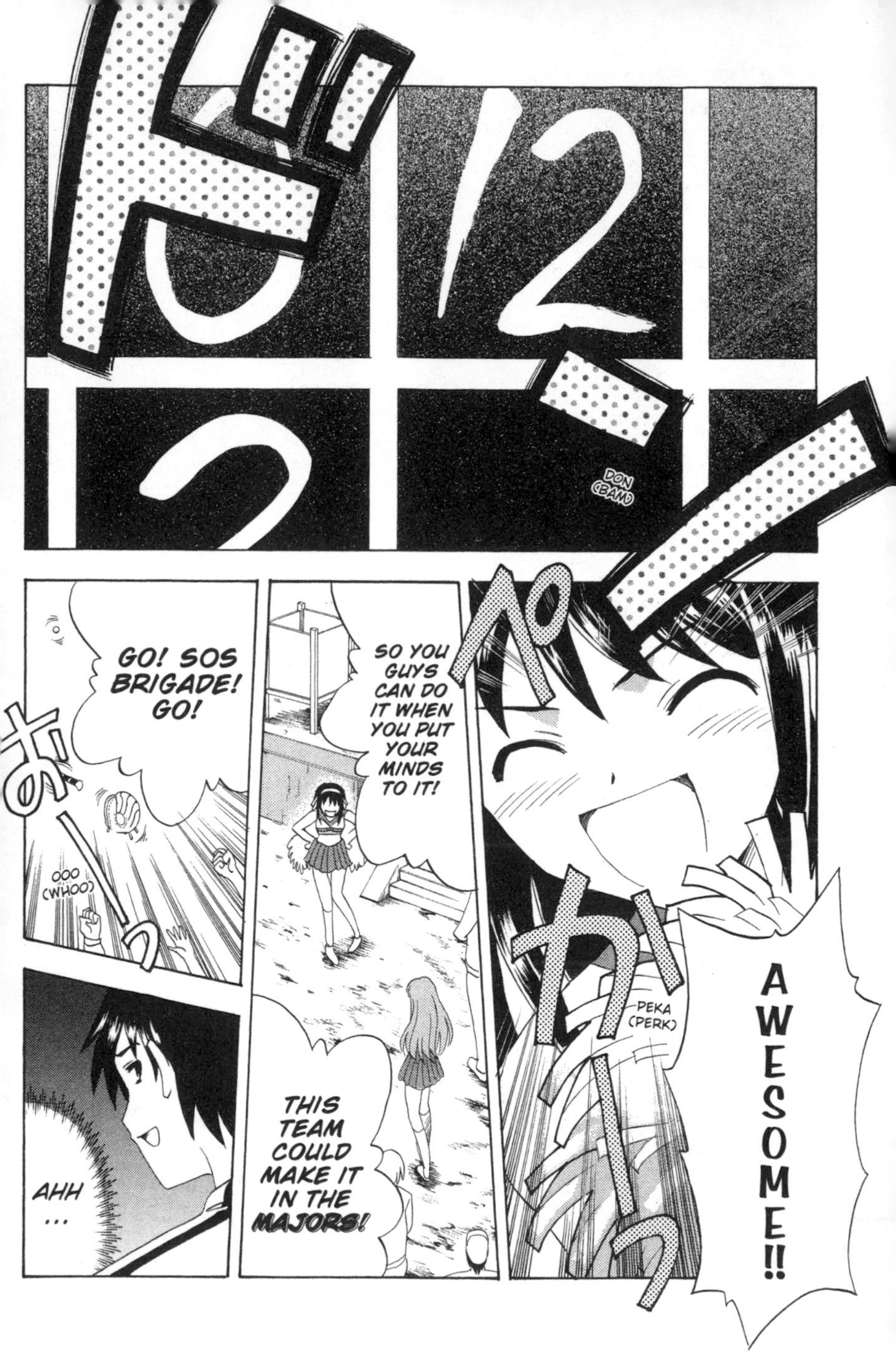
DON (BAM)
PEKA (PERK)
AWESOME!!
SO YOU GUYS CAN DO IT WHEN YOU PUT YOUR MINDS TO IT!
THIS TEAM COULD MAKE IT IN THE MAJORS!
GO! SOS BRIGADE! GO!
OOO (WHOO)
AHH ...

SFX: BUTSU (MUTTER) BUTSU BUTSU

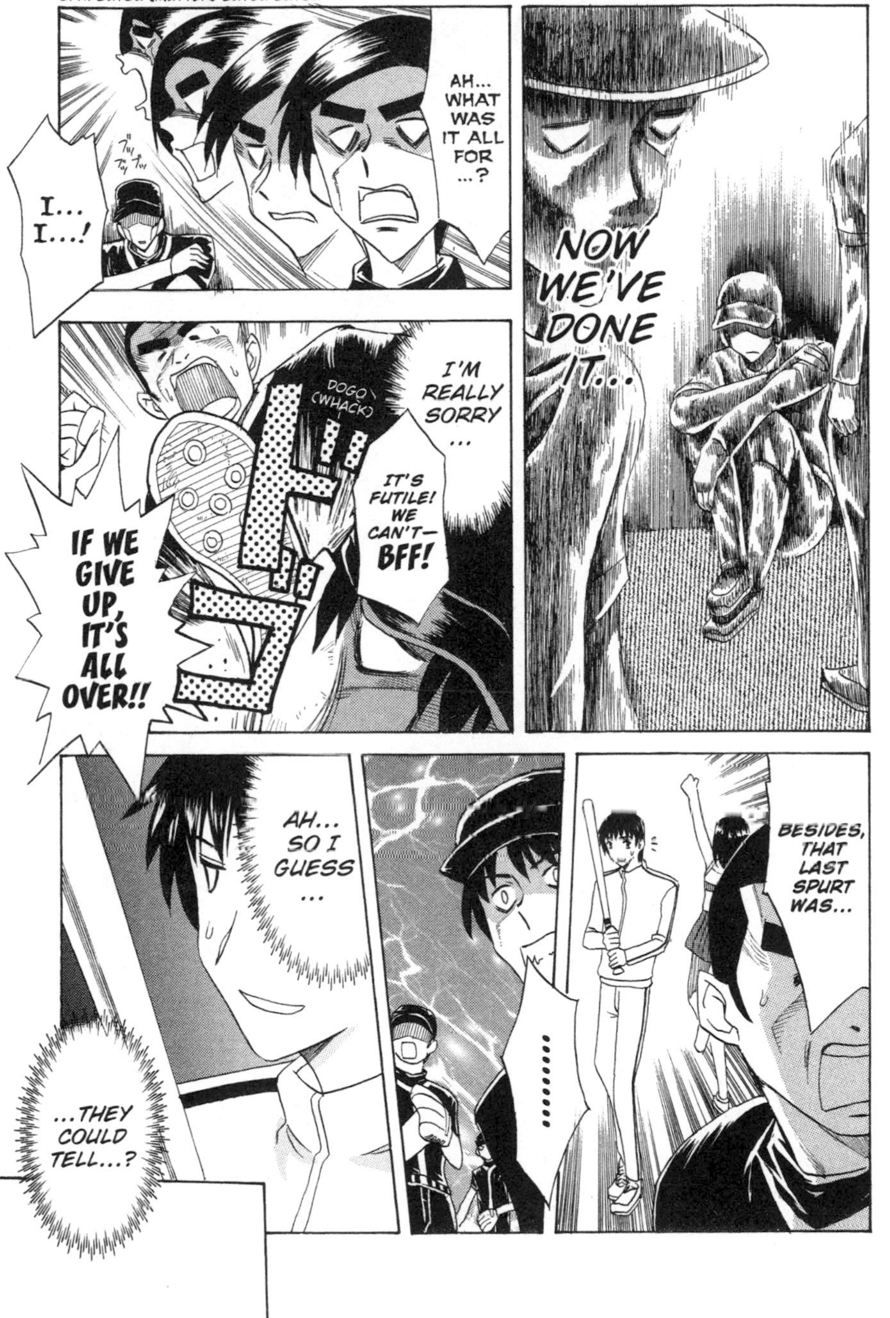
NOW WE'VE DONE IT...
AH... WHAT WAS IT ALL FOR ...?
I... I...!
I'M REALLY SORRY ...
IT'S FUTILE! WE CAN'T— BFF!
DOGO (WHACK)
IF WE GIVE UP, IT'S ALL OVER!!
BESIDES, THAT LAST SPURT WAS...
AH... SO I GUESS ...
....
...THEY COULD TELL...?

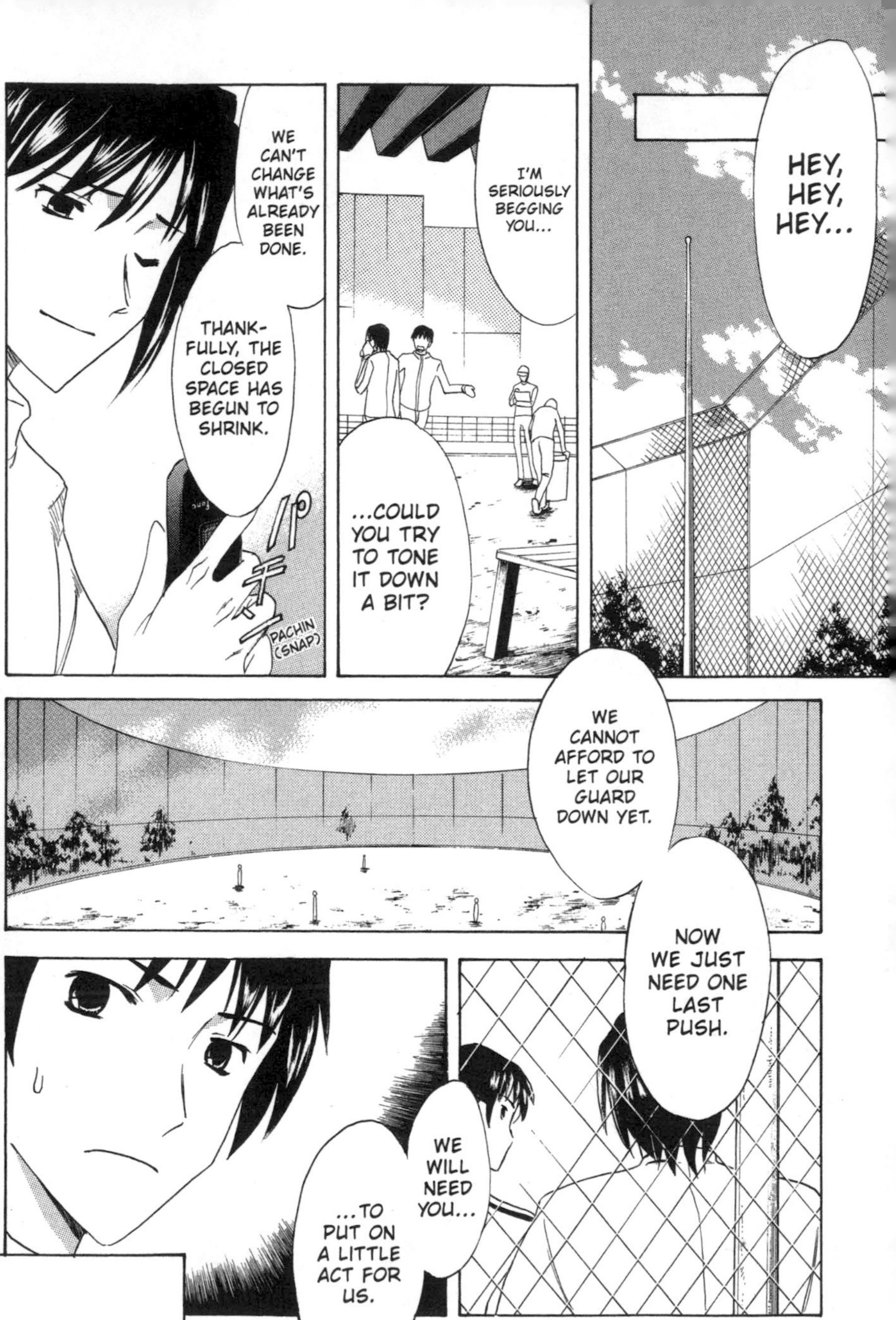
HEY, HEY, HEY...
I'M SERIOUSLY BEGGING YOU...
...COULD YOU TRY TO TONE IT DOWN A BIT?
WE CAN'T CHANGE WHAT'S ALREADY BEEN DONE.
THANK-FULLY, THE CLOSED SPACE HAS BEGUN TO SHRINK.
パチン
PACHIN (SNAP)
WE CANNOT AFFORD TO LET OUR GUARD DOWN YET.
NOW WE JUST NEED ONE LAST PUSH.
WE WILL NEED YOU...
...TO PUT ON A LITTLE ACT FOR US.

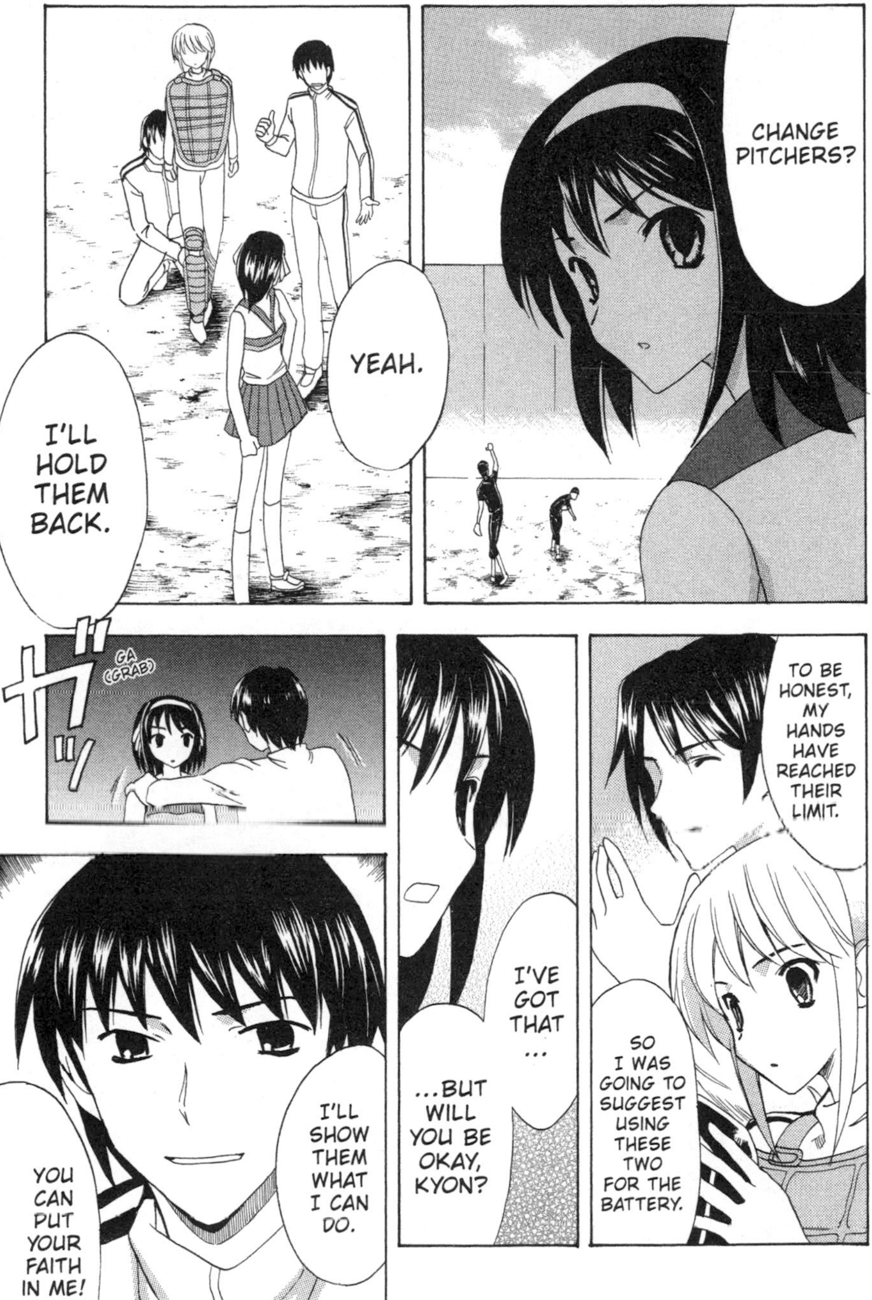
CHANGE PITCHERS?
YEAH.
I'LL HOLD THEM BACK.
TO BE HONEST, MY HANDS HAVE REACHED THEIR LIMIT.
SO I WAS GOING TO SUGGEST USING THESE TWO FOR THE BATTERY.
I'VE GOT THAT...
...BUT WILL YOU BE OKAY, KYON?
GA (GRAB)
I'LL SHOW THEM WHAT I CAN DO.
YOU CAN PUT YOUR FAITH IN ME!

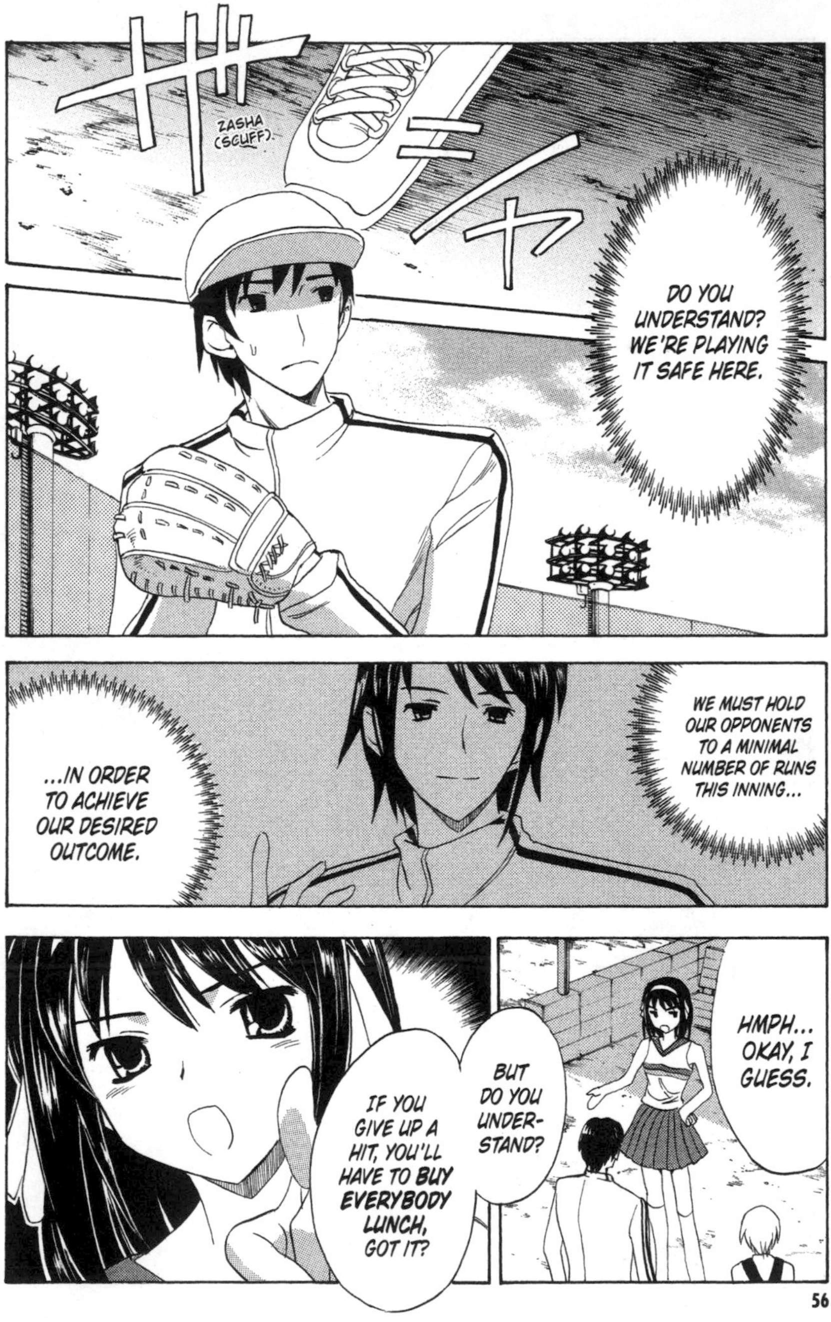
ZASHA (SCUFF).
DO YOU UNDERSTAND? WE'RE PLAYING IT SAFE HERE.
WE MUST HOLD OUR OPPONENTS TO A MINIMAL NUMBER OF RUNS THIS INNING...
...IN ORDER TO ACHIEVE OUR DESIRED OUTCOME.
HMPH... OKAY, I GUESS.
BUT DO YOU UNDER-STAND?
IF YOU GIVE UP A HIT, YOU'LL HAVE TO BUY EVERYBODY LUNCH, GOT IT?

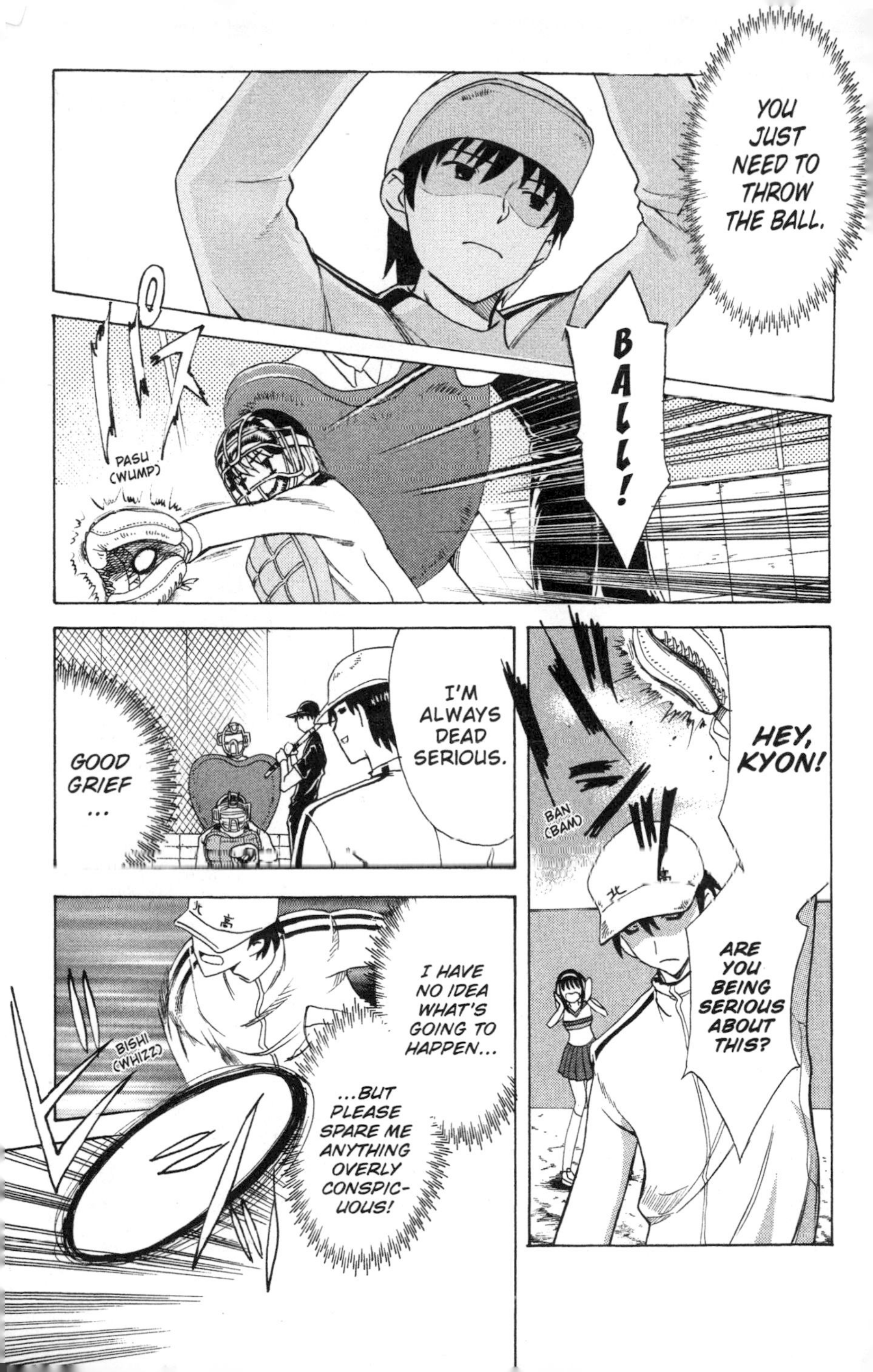
YOU JUST NEED TO THROW THE BALL.
BALL!
PASU (WUMP)
HEY, KYON!
BAN (BAM)
ARE YOU BEING SERIOUS ABOUT THIS?
I'M ALWAYS DEAD SERIOUS.
GOOD GRIEF...
I HAVE NO IDEA WHAT'S GOING TO HAPPEN...
...BUT PLEASE SPARE ME ANYTHING OVERLY CONSPICUOUS!
BISHI (WHIZZ)

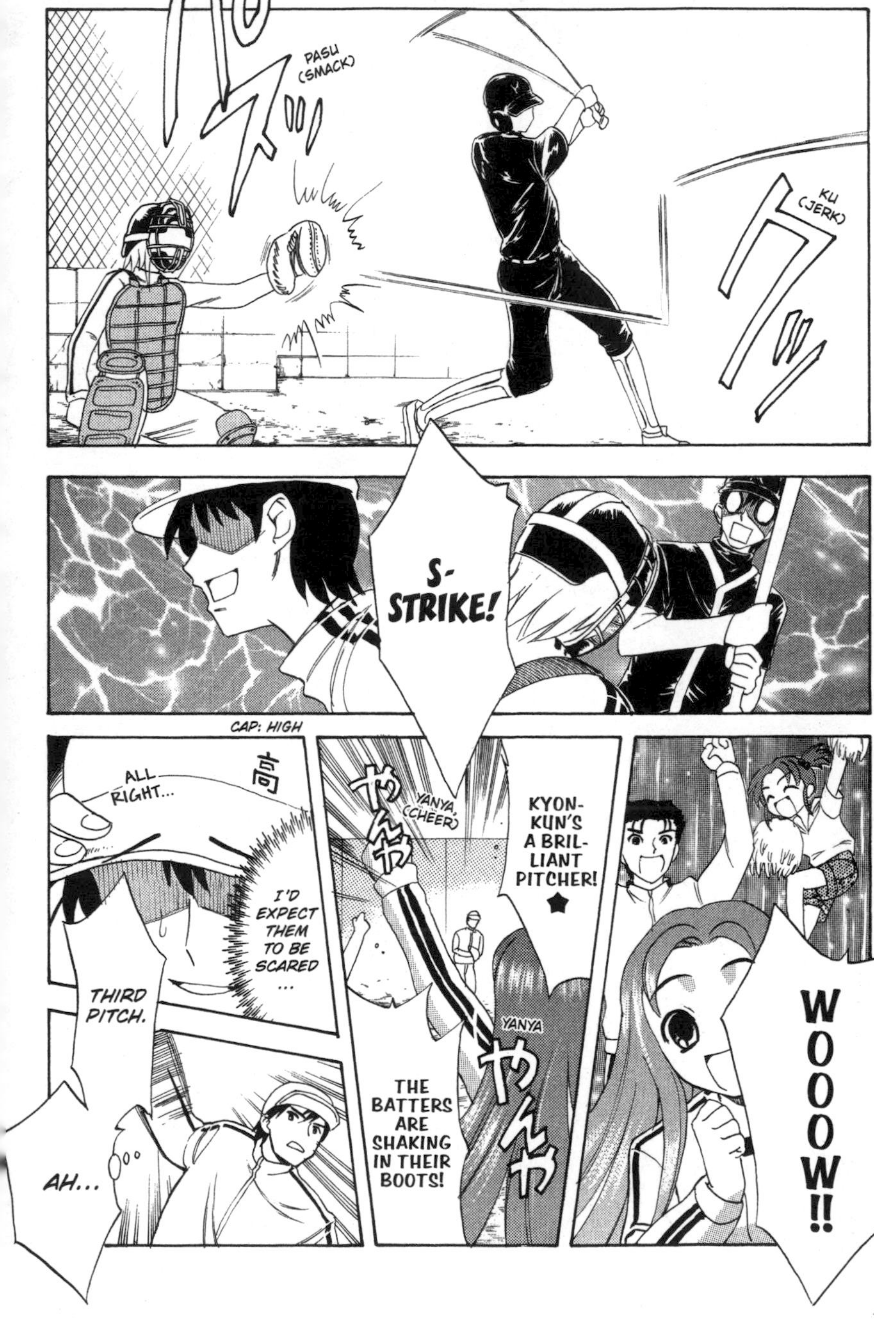
KU (JERK)
PASU (SMACK)
S-STRIKE!
CAP: HIGH
WOOOW!!
YANYA (CHEER)
KYON-KUN'S A BRILLIANT PITCHER! ★
YANYA
THE BATTERS ARE SHAKING IN THEIR BOOTS!
高
ALL RIGHT...
I'D EXPECT THEM TO BE SCARED...
THIRD PITCH.
AH...

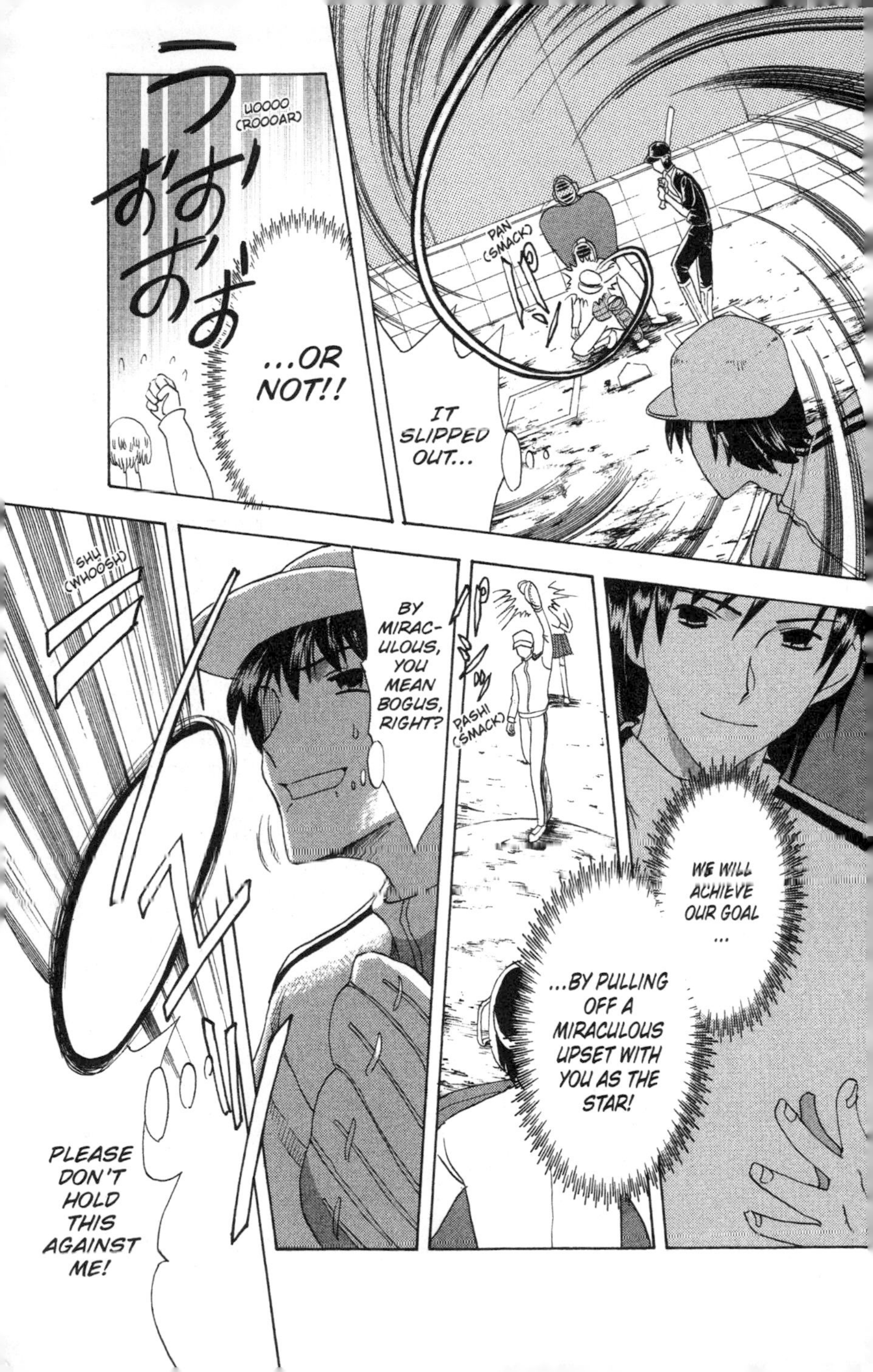
PAN (SMACK)
IT SLIPPED OUT...
うおおお
UOOOO (ROOOAR)
...OR NOT!!
WE WILL ACHIEVE OUR GOAL ...
...BY PULLING OFF A MIRACULOUS UPSET WITH YOU AS THE STAR!
PASHI (SMACK)
BY MIRACULOUS, YOU MEAN BOGUS, RIGHT?
SHU (WHOOSH)
PLEASE DON'T HOLD THIS AGAINST ME!

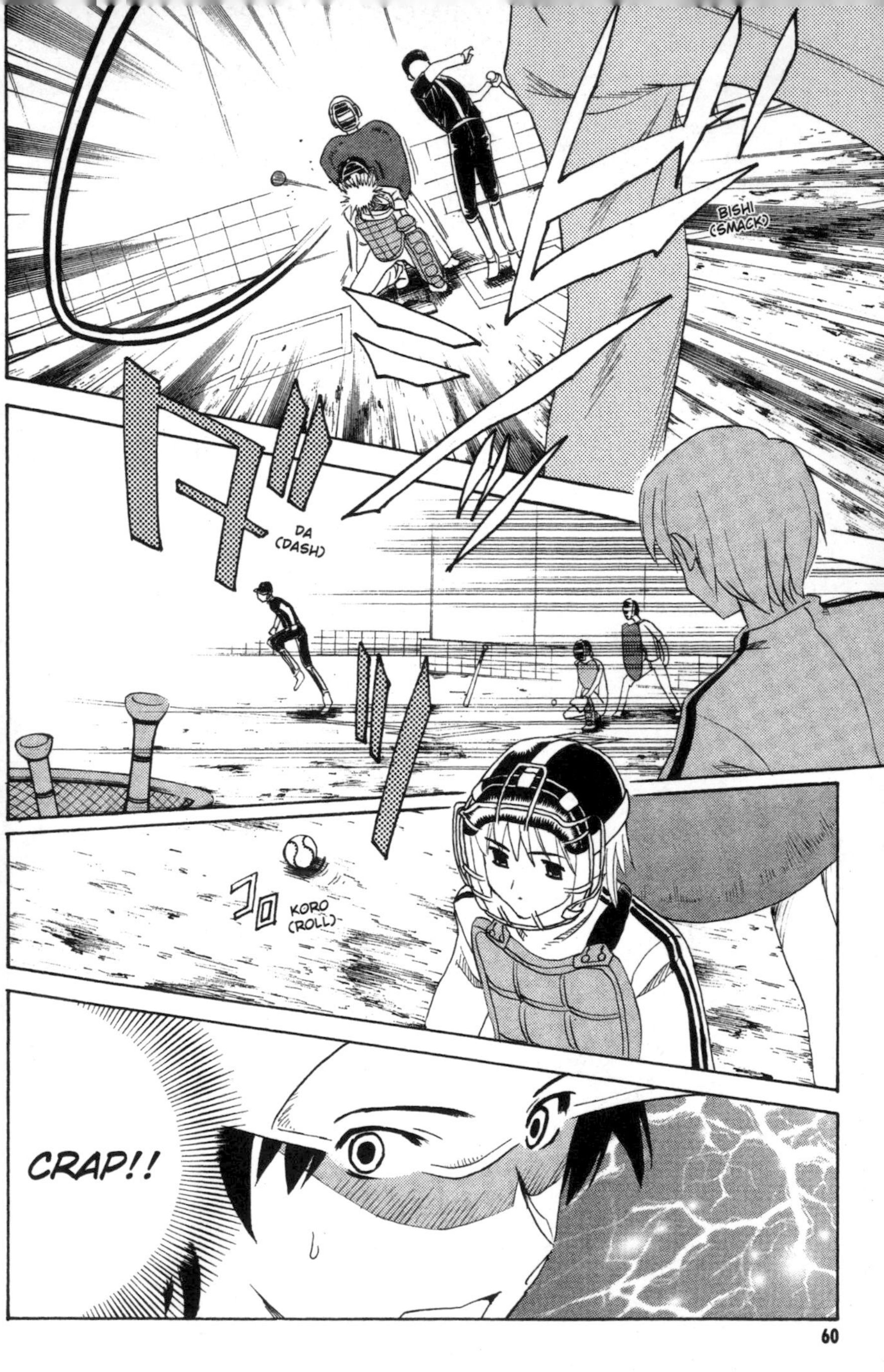
BISHI
(SMACK)
DA
(DASH)
KORO
(ROLL)
CRAP!!

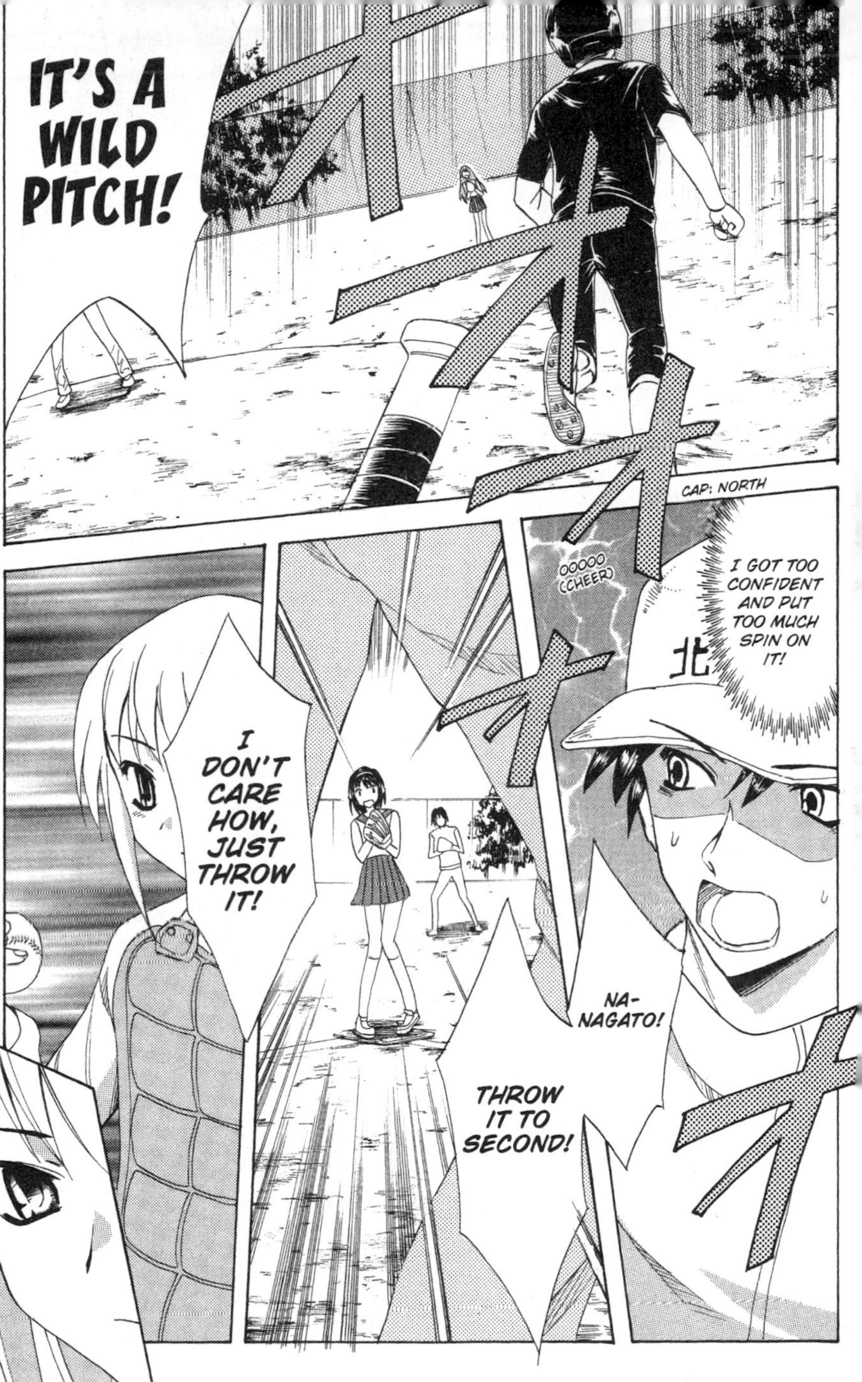
IT'S A WILD PITCH!
CAP: NORTH
OOOOO (CHEER)
I GOT TOO CONFIDENT AND PUT TOO MUCH SPIN ON IT!
NA-NAGATO!
THROW IT TO SECOND!
I DON'T CARE HOW, JUST THROW IT!

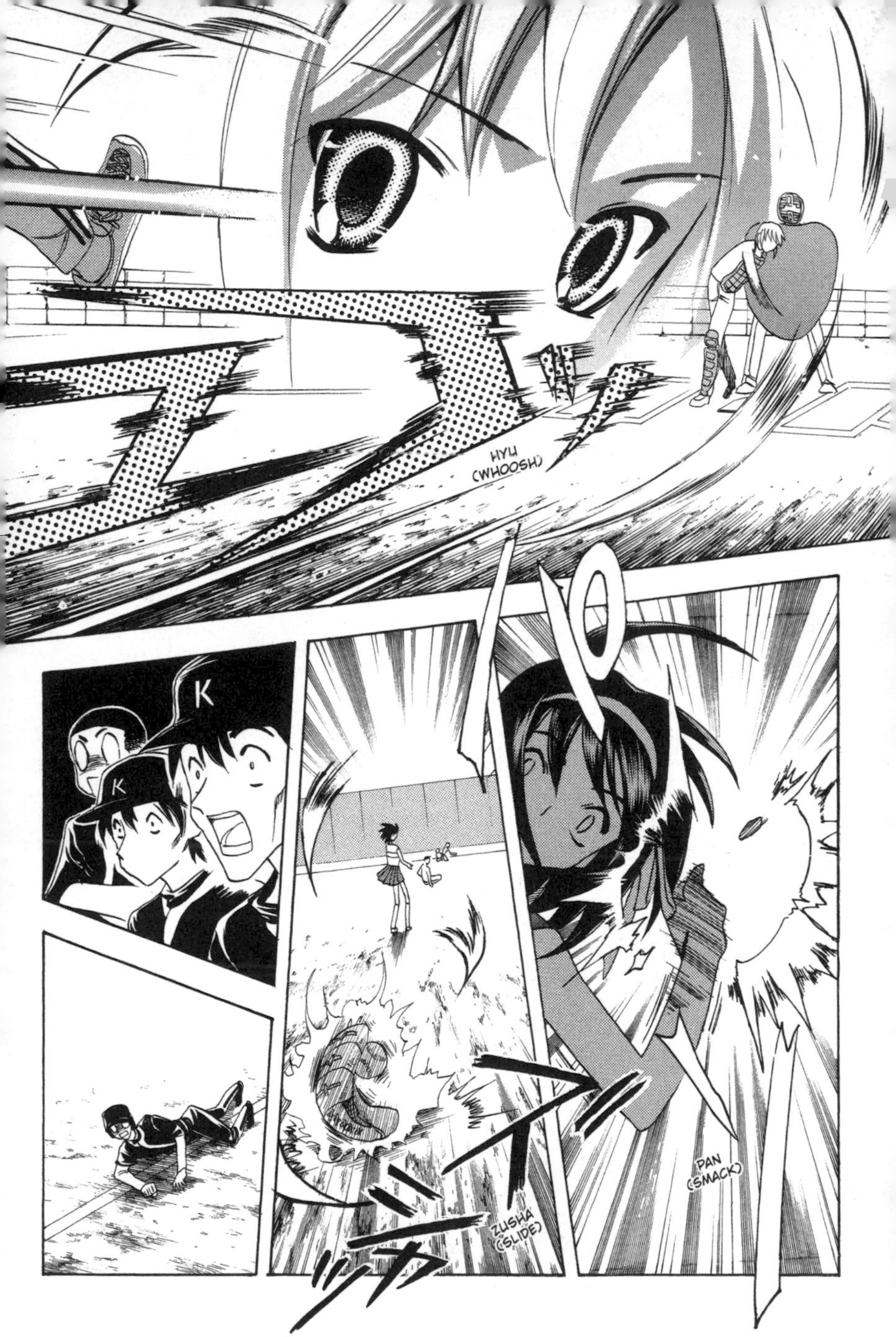
HYU (WHOOSH)
PAN (SMACK)
ZUSHA (SLIDE)

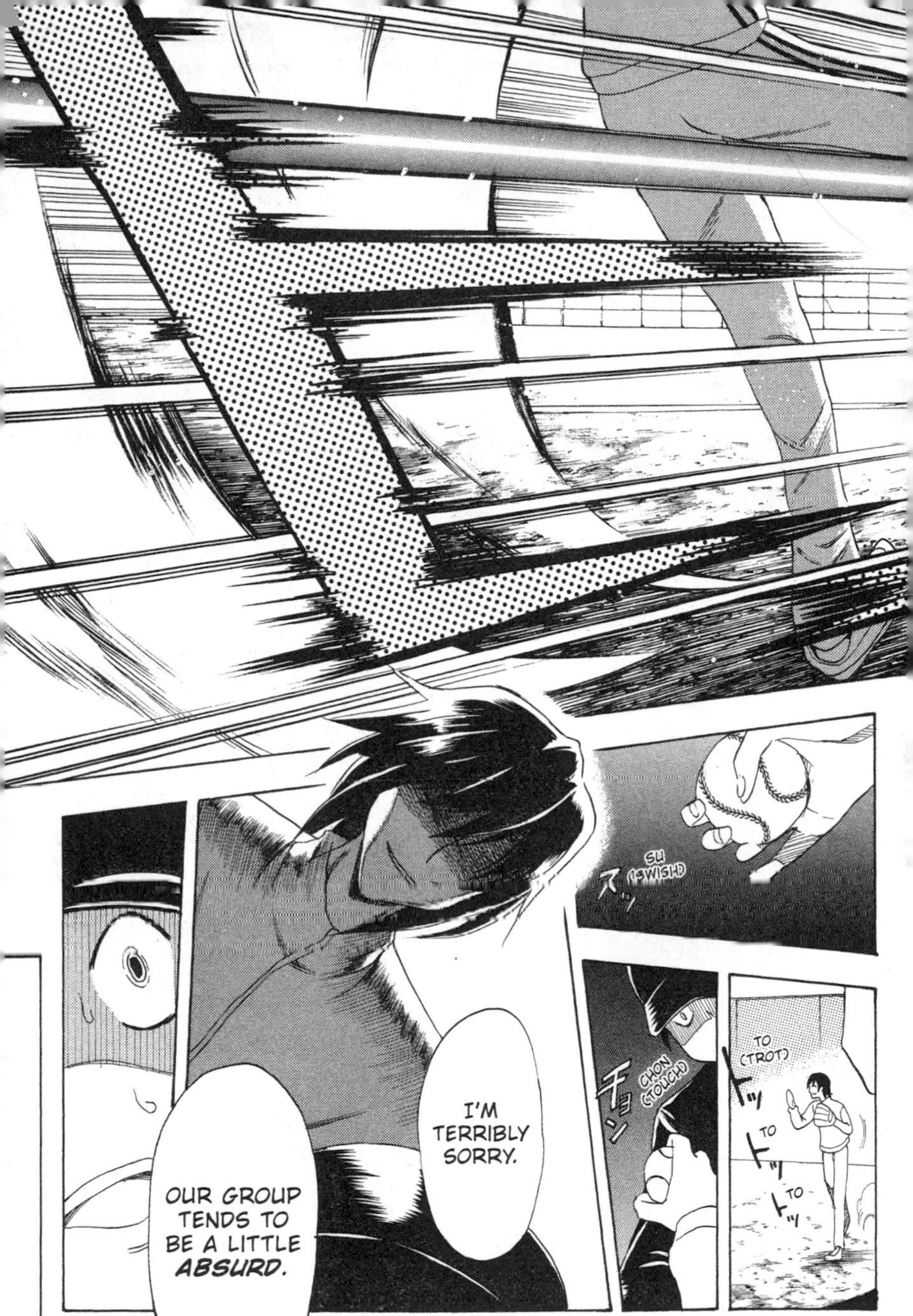
SU (SWISH)
TO (TROT)
TO
TO
CHON (TOUCH)
I'M TERRIBLY SORRY.
OUR GROUP TENDS TO BE A LITTLE ***ABSURD***.

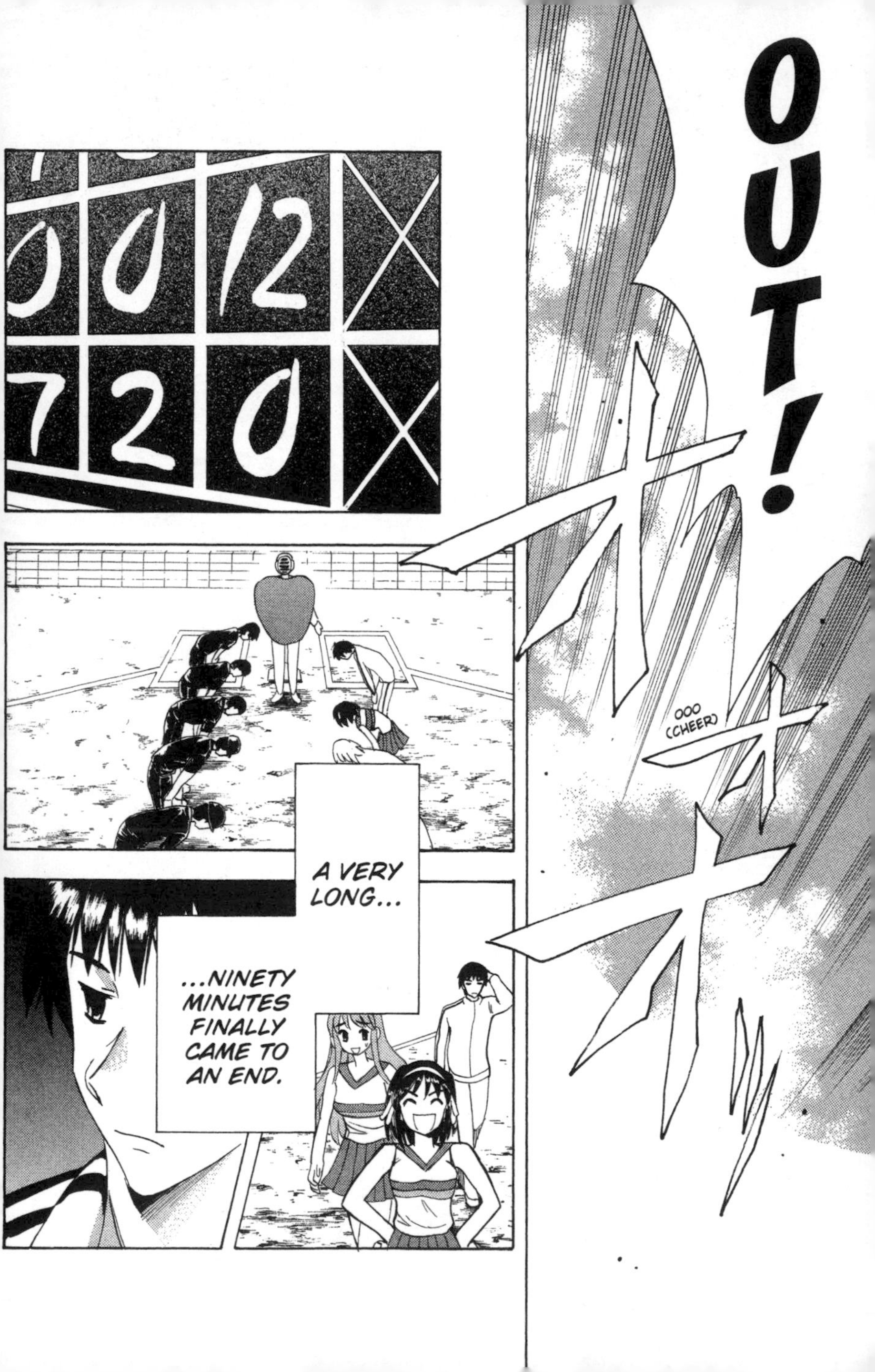
OUT!
OOO (CHEER)
A VERY LONG...
...NINETY MINUTES FINALLY CAME TO AN END.

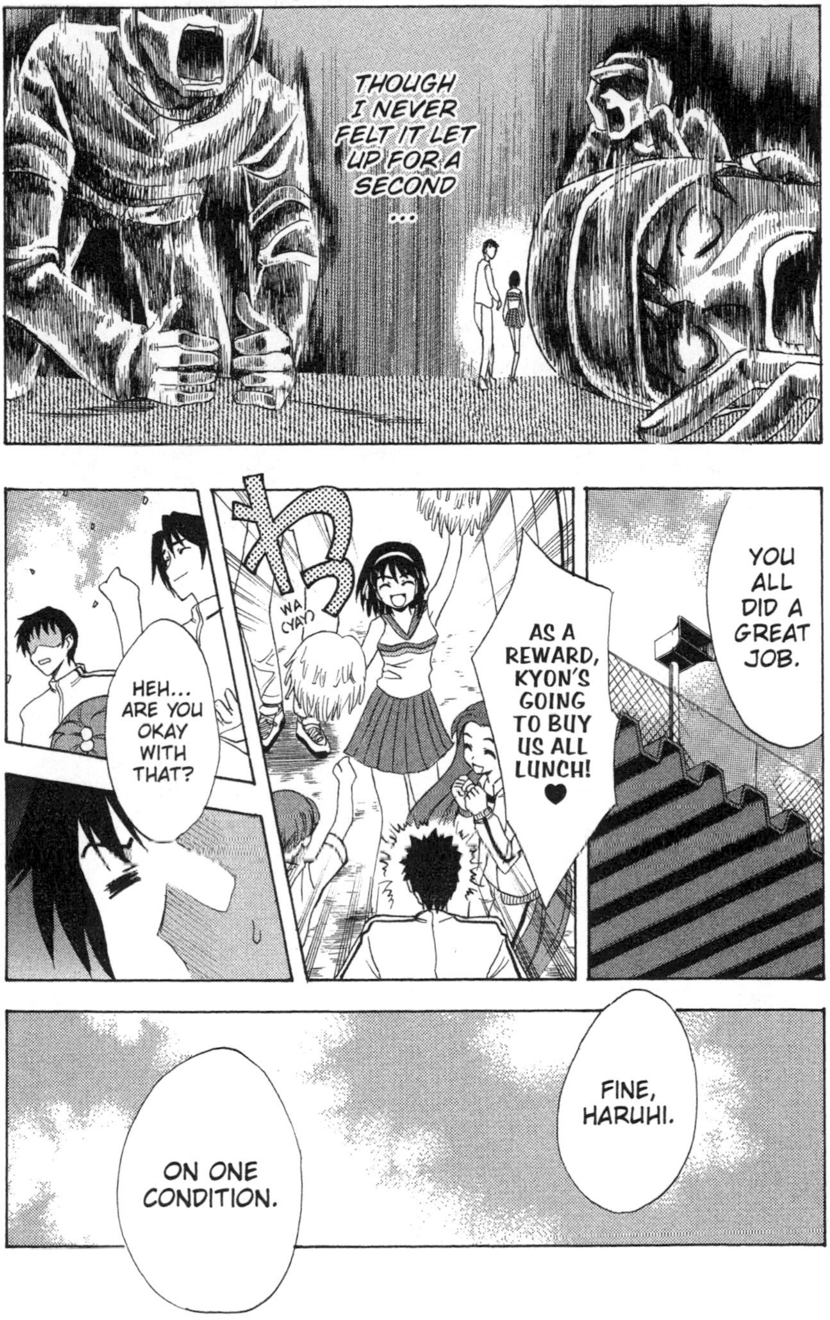
THOUGH I NEVER FELT IT LET UP FOR A SECOND ...
YOU ALL DID A GREAT JOB.
AS A REWARD, KYON'S GOING TO BUY US ALL LUNCH! ♥
わ
WA (YAY)
HEH... ARE YOU OKAY WITH THAT?
FINE, HARUHI.
ON ONE CONDITION.

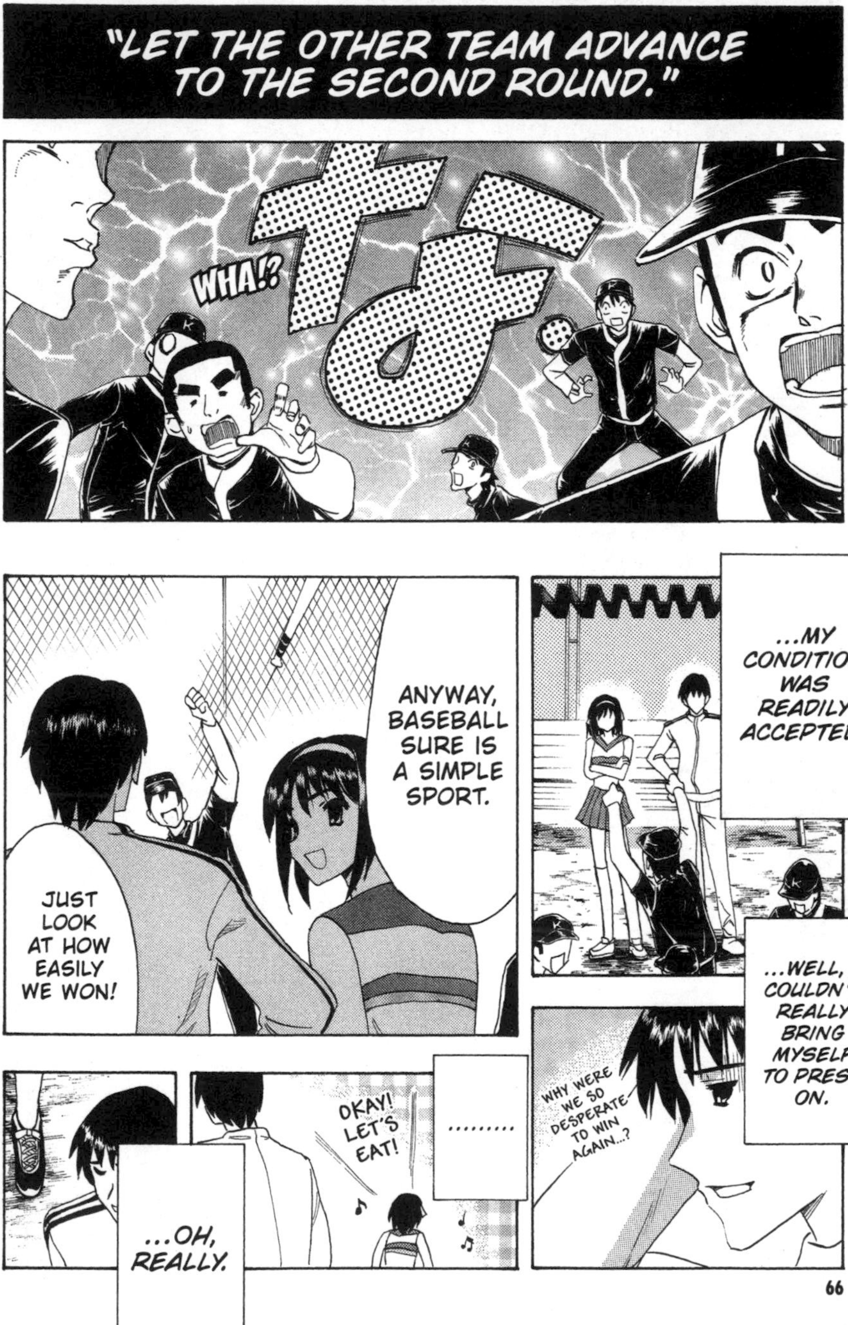
"LET THE OTHER TEAM ADVANCE TO THE SECOND ROUND."
WHA!?
...MY CONDITION WAS READILY ACCEPTED.
ANYWAY, BASEBALL SURE IS A SIMPLE SPORT.
JUST LOOK AT HOW EASILY WE WON!
...WELL, I COULDN'T REALLY BRING MYSELF TO PRESS ON.
WHY WERE WE SO DESPERATE TO WIN AGAIN...?
....
OKAY! LET'S EAT!
...OH, REALLY.

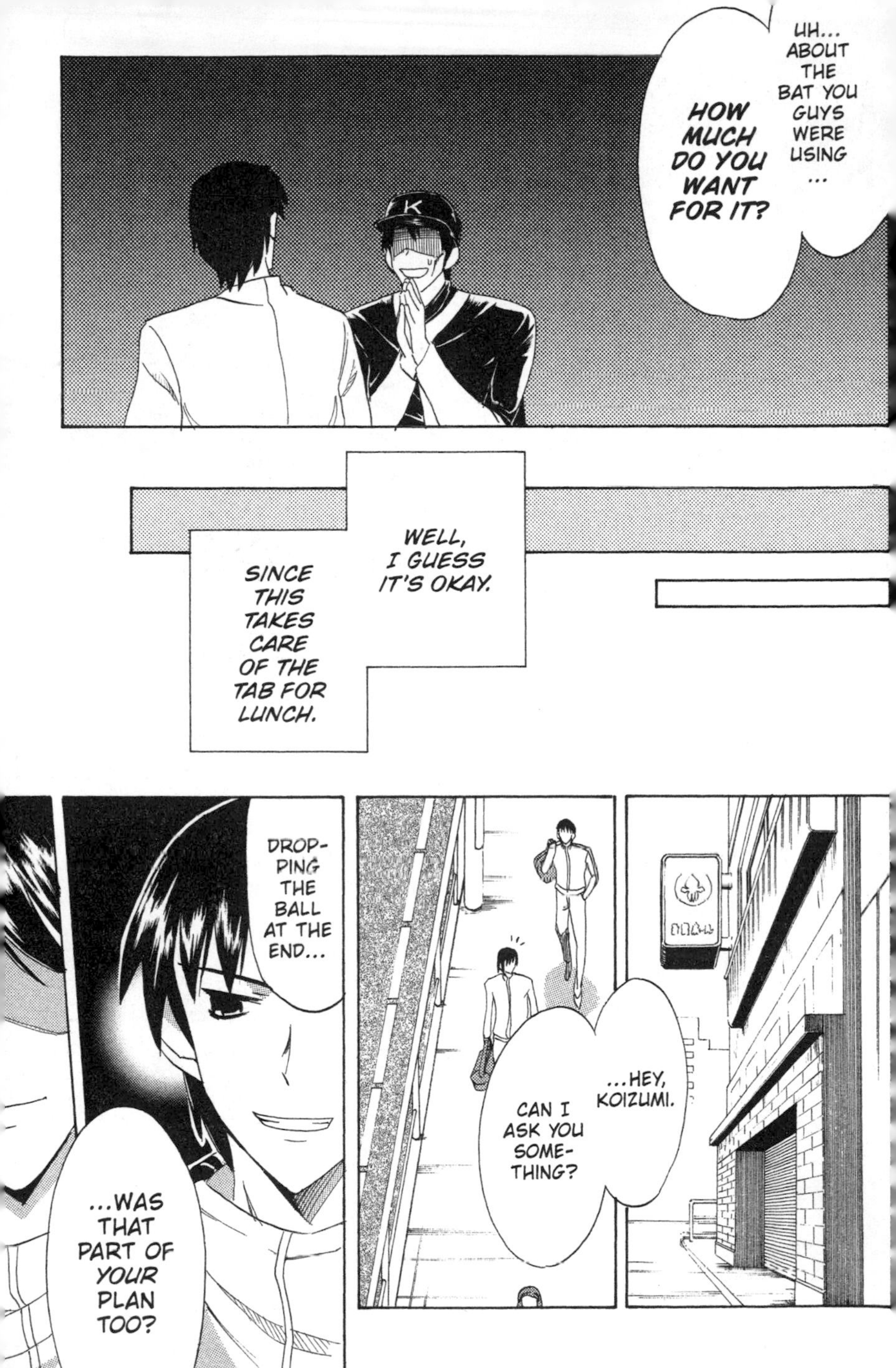
UH... ABOUT THE BAT YOU GUYS WERE USING...
HOW MUCH DO YOU WANT FOR IT?
WELL, I GUESS IT'S OKAY.
SINCE THIS TAKES CARE OF THE TAB FOR LUNCH.
...HEY, KOIZUMI.
CAN I ASK YOU SOMETHING?
DROPPING THE BALL AT THE END...
...WAS THAT PART OF YOUR PLAN TOO?

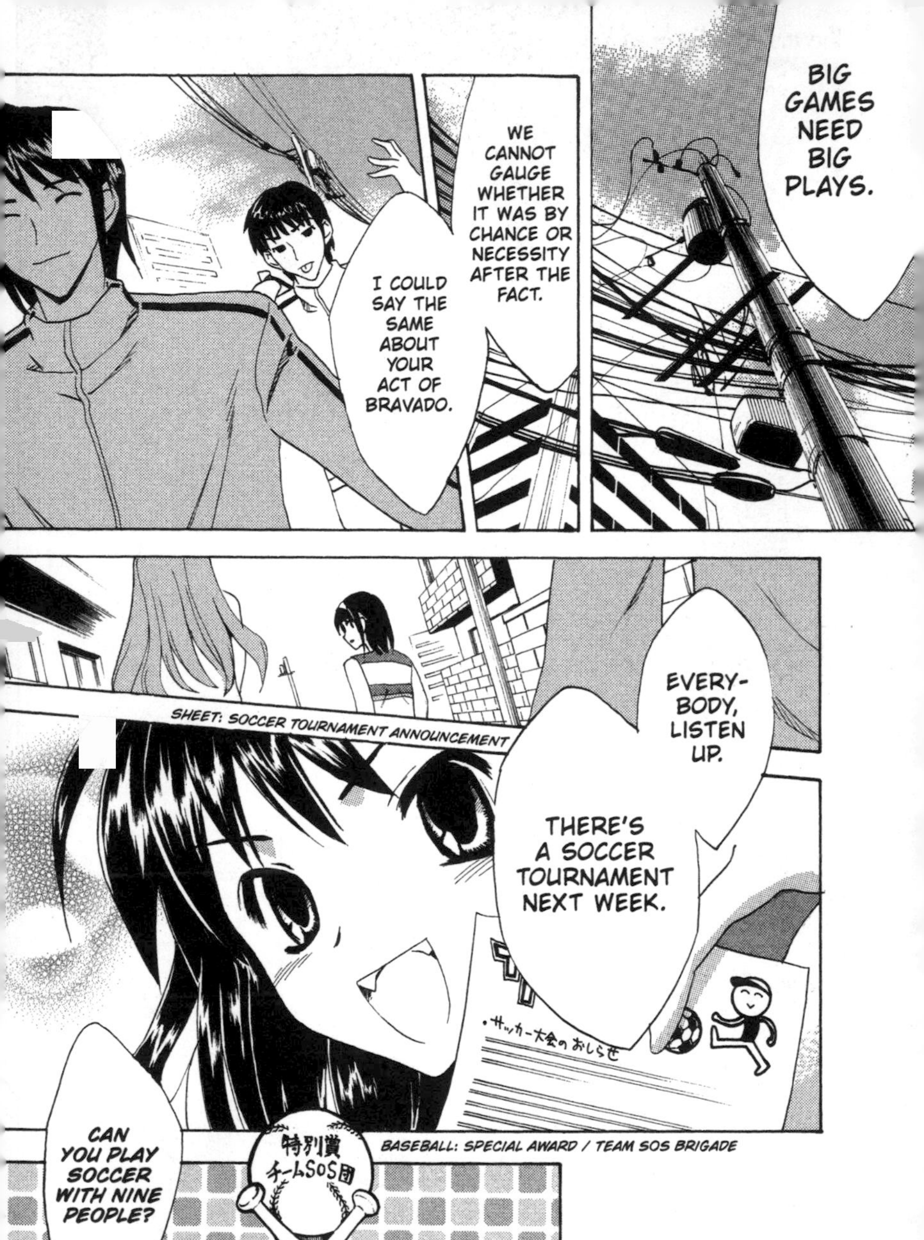
BIG GAMES NEED BIG PLAYS.
WE CANNOT GAUGE WHETHER IT WAS BY CHANCE OR NECESSITY AFTER THE FACT.
I COULD SAY THE SAME ABOUT YOUR ACT OF BRAVADO.
EVERY-BODY, LISTEN UP.
THERE'S A SOCCER TOURNAMENT NEXT WEEK.
SHEET: SOCCER TOURNAMENT ANNOUNCEMENT
・サッカー大会のおしらせ
CAN YOU PLAY SOCCER WITH NINE PEOPLE?
特別賞
チームSOS団
BASEBALL: SPECIAL AWARD / TEAM SOS BRIGADE

The Boredom of Haruhi Suzumiya II : END

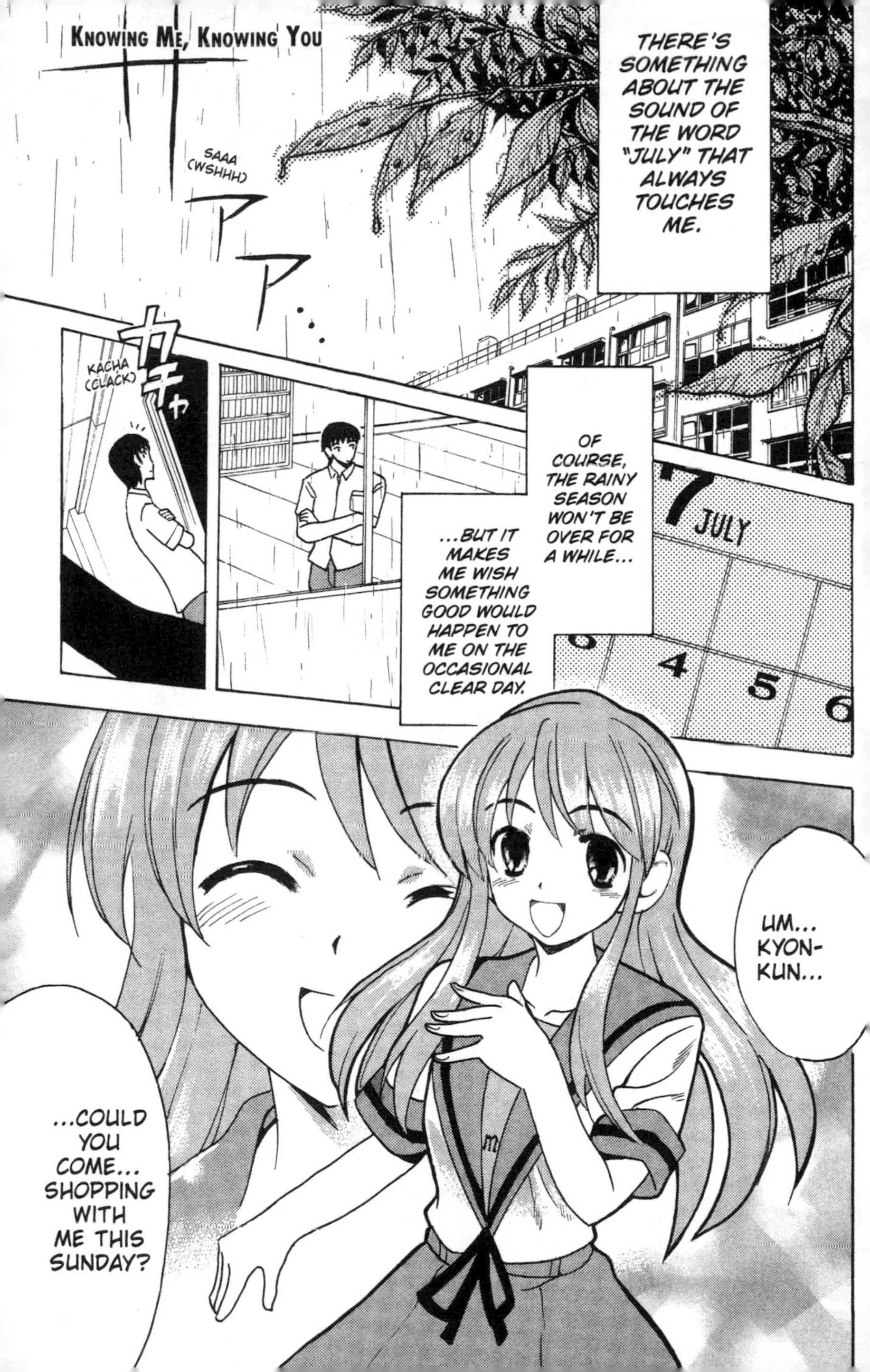
KNOWING ME, KNOWING YOU
THERE'S SOMETHING ABOUT THE SOUND OF THE WORD "JULY" THAT ALWAYS TOUCHES ME.
SAAA (WSHHH)
OF COURSE, THE RAINY SEASON WON'T BE OVER FOR A WHILE...
...BUT IT MAKES ME WISH SOMETHING GOOD WOULD HAPPEN TO ME ON THE OCCASIONAL CLEAR DAY.
7 JULY
4 5 6
KACHA (CLACK)
UM... KYON-KUN...
...COULD YOU COME... SHOPPING WITH ME THIS SUNDAY?

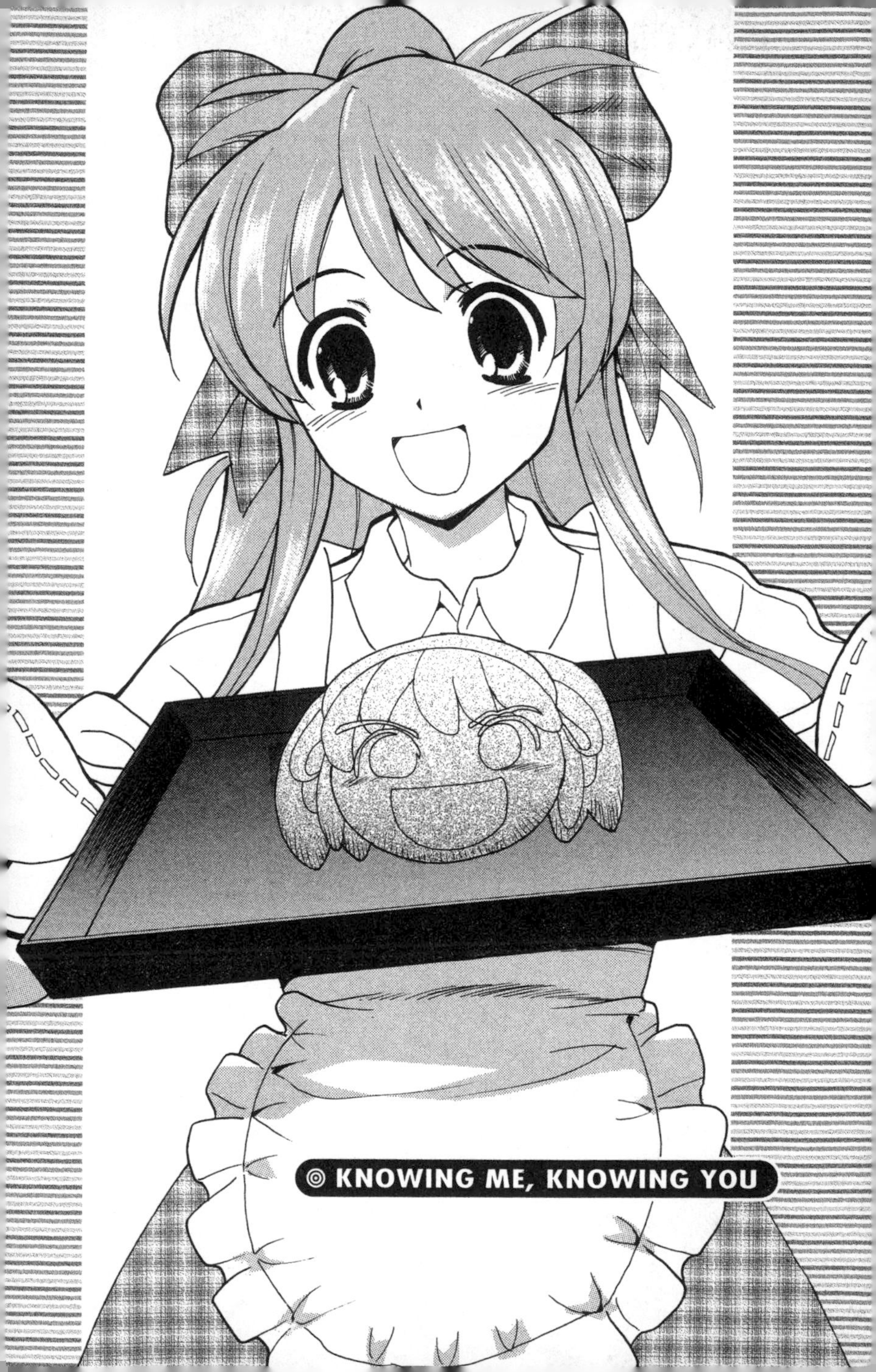
◎ KNOWING ME, KNOWING YOU

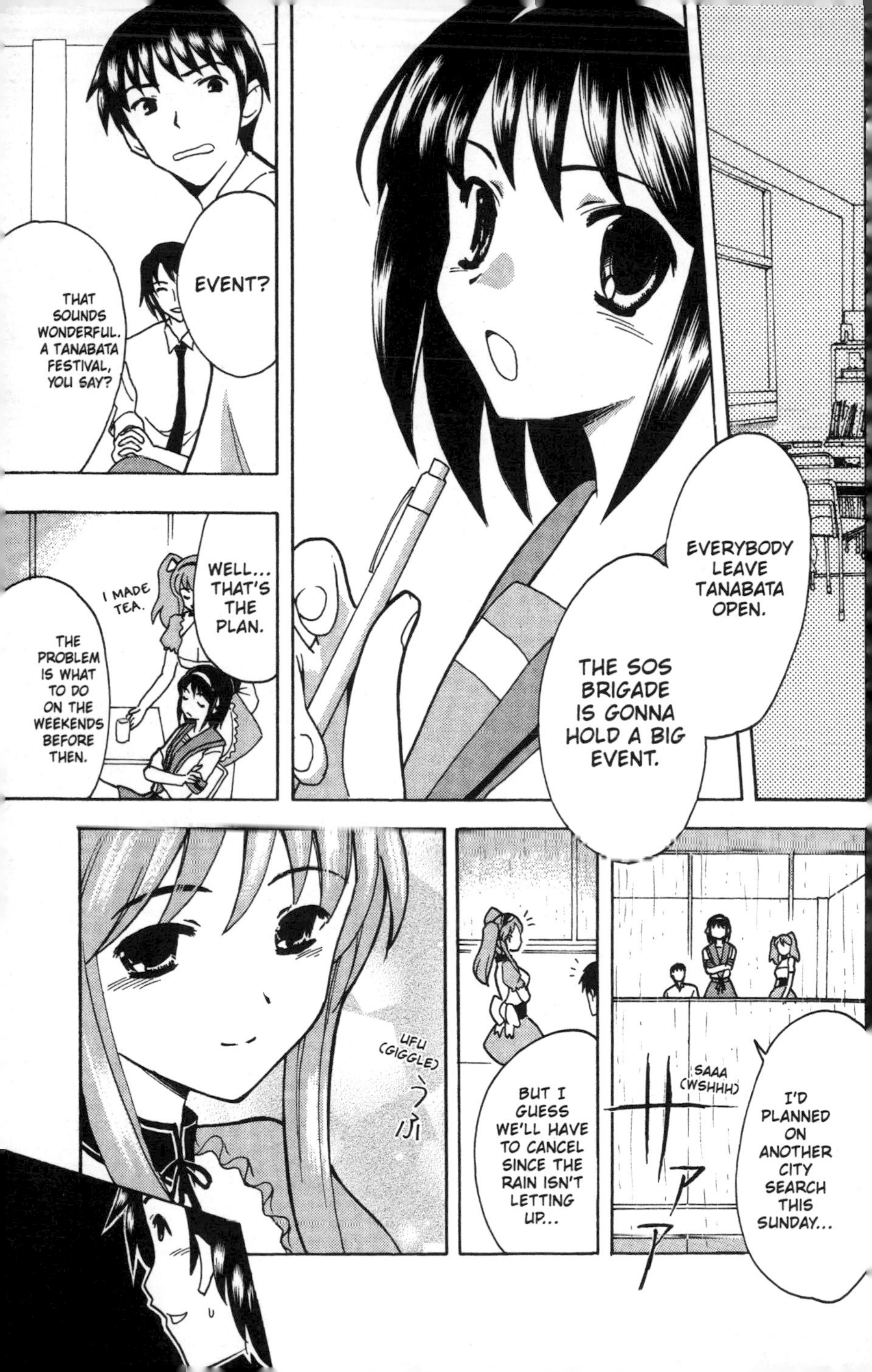
EVERYBODY LEAVE TANABATA OPEN.
THE SOS BRIGADE IS GONNA HOLD A BIG EVENT.
EVENT?
THAT SOUNDS WONDERFUL. A TANABATA FESTIVAL, YOU SAY?
WELL... THAT'S THE PLAN.
I MADE TEA.
THE PROBLEM IS WHAT TO DO ON THE WEEKENDS BEFORE THEN.
サァァ
SAAA (WSHHH)
I'D PLANNED ON ANOTHER CITY SEARCH THIS SUNDAY...
BUT I GUESS WE'LL HAVE TO CANCEL SINCE THE RAIN ISN'T LETTING UP...
うふ
UFU (GIGGLE)

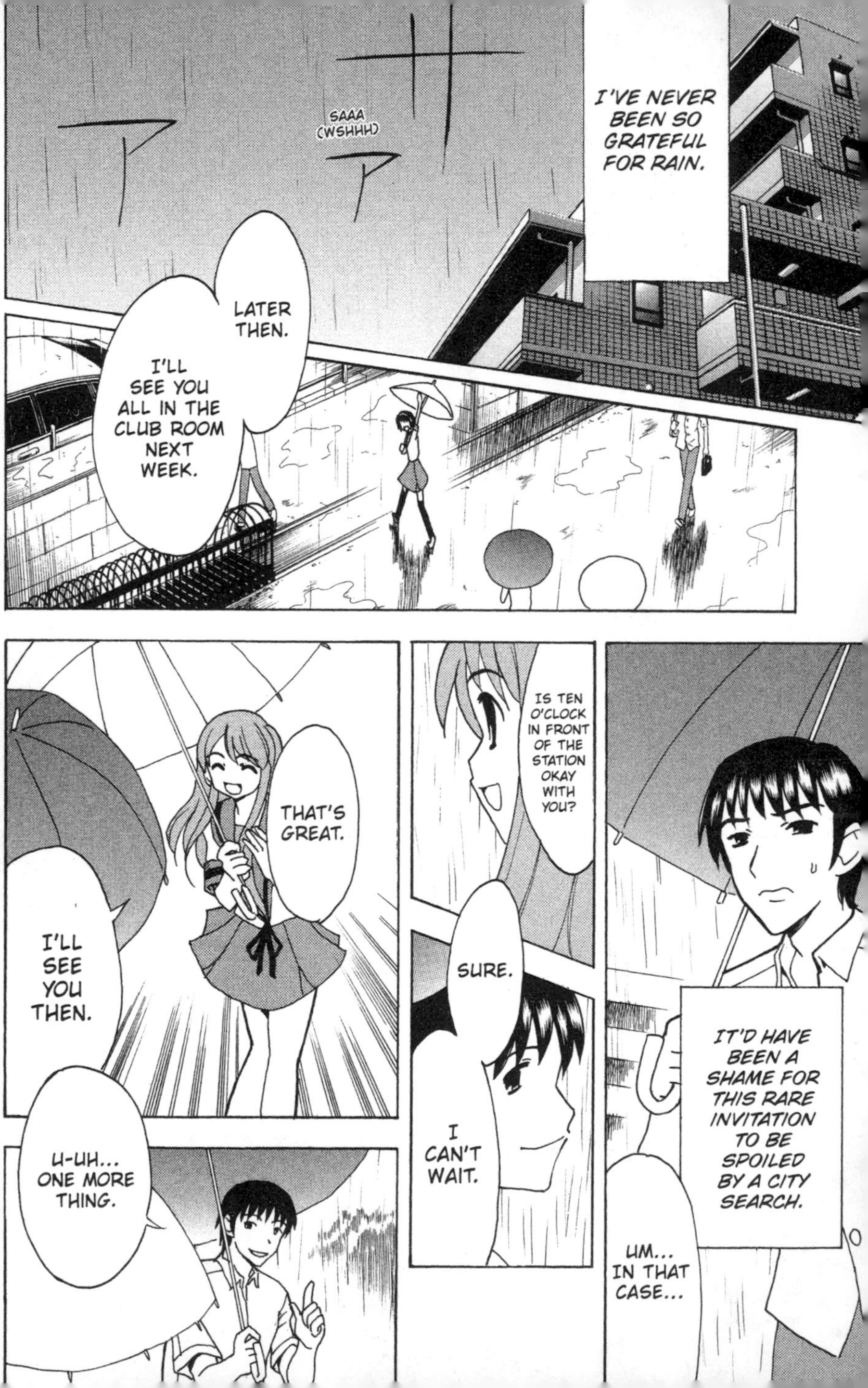
I'VE NEVER BEEN SO GRATEFUL FOR RAIN.
SAAA (WSHHH)
LATER THEN. I'LL SEE YOU ALL IN THE CLUB ROOM NEXT WEEK.
IT'D HAVE BEEN A SHAME FOR THIS RARE INVITATION TO BE SPOILED BY A CITY SEARCH.
UM... IN THAT CASE...
IS TEN O'CLOCK IN FRONT OF THE STATION OKAY WITH YOU?
SURE.
I CAN'T WAIT.
THAT'S GREAT.
I'LL SEE YOU THEN.
U-UH... ONE MORE THING.

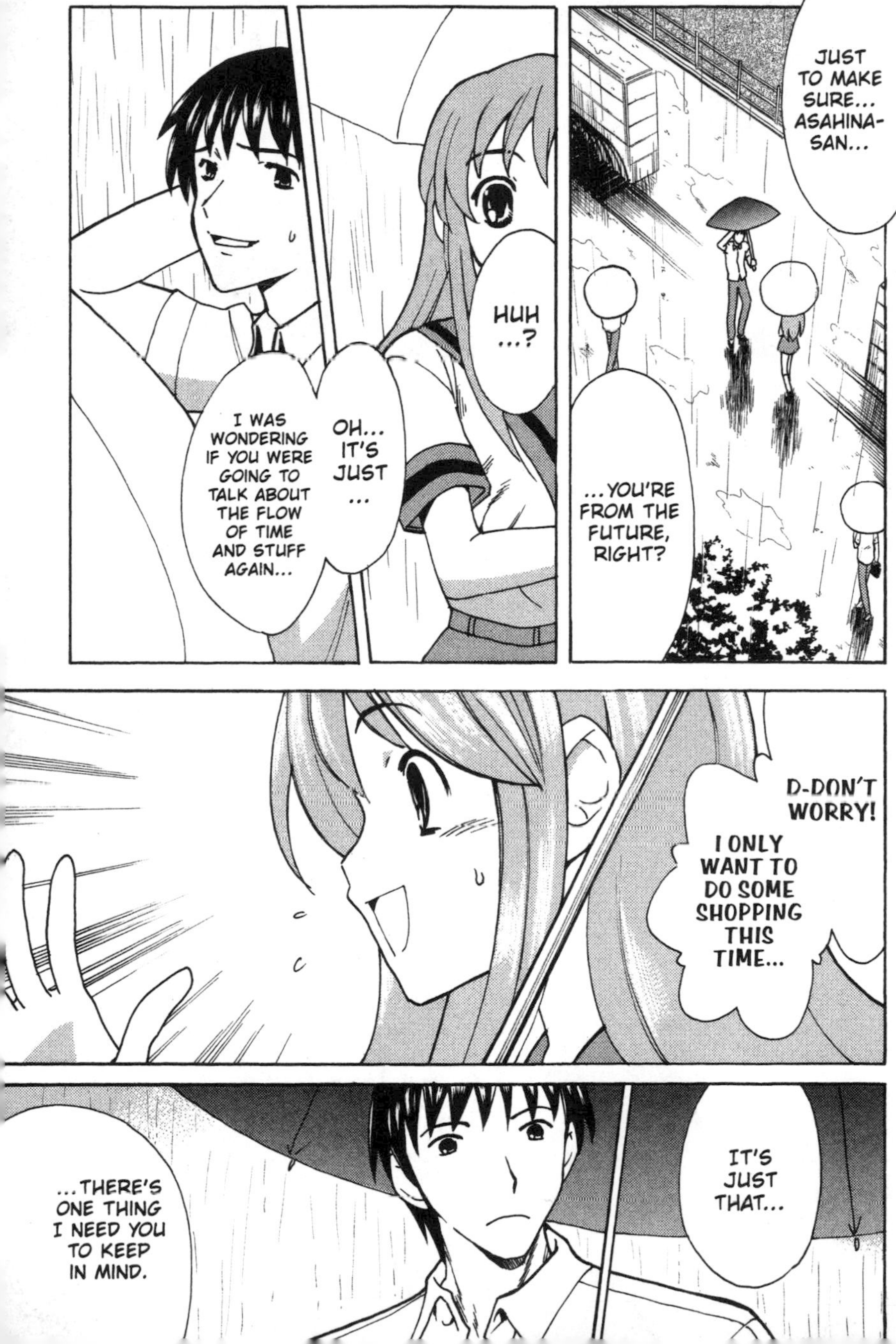
JUST TO MAKE SURE... ASAHINA-SAN...
...YOU'RE FROM THE FUTURE, RIGHT?
HUH ...?
OH... IT'S JUST ...
I WAS WONDERING IF YOU WERE GOING TO TALK ABOUT THE FLOW OF TIME AND STUFF AGAIN...
D-DON'T WORRY!
I ONLY WANT TO DO SOME SHOPPING THIS TIME...
IT'S JUST THAT...
...THERE'S ONE THING I NEED YOU TO KEEP IN MIND.

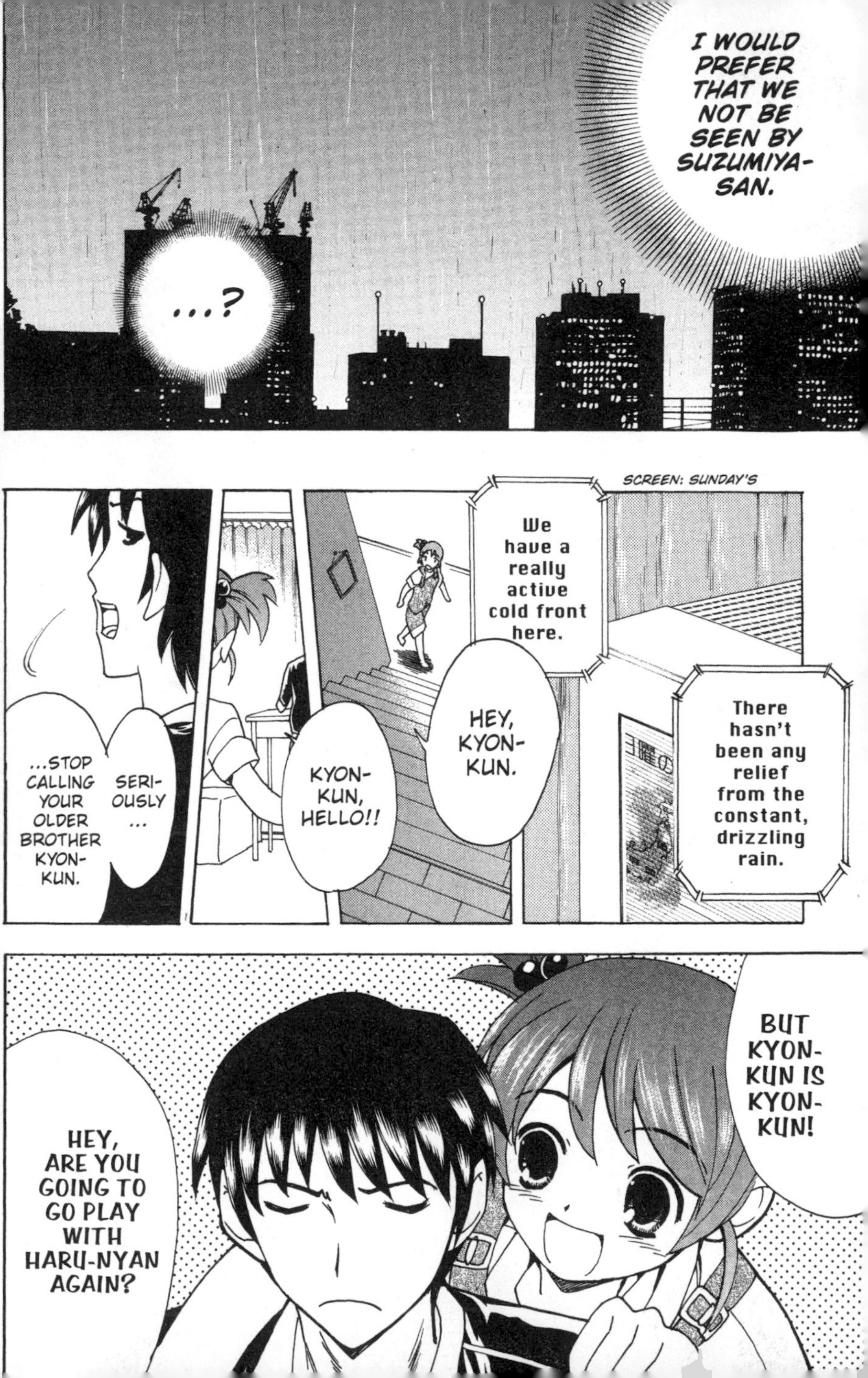
I WOULD PREFER THAT WE NOT BE SEEN BY SUZUMIYA-SAN.
...?
SCREEN: SUNDAY'S
We have a really active cold front here.
There hasn't been any relief from the constant, drizzling rain.
HEY, KYON-KUN.
KYON-KUN, HELLO!!
SERI-OUSLY ...
...STOP CALLING YOUR OLDER BROTHER KYON-KUN.
BUT KYON-KUN IS KYON-KUN!
HEY, ARE YOU GOING TO GO PLAY WITH HARU-NYAN AGAIN?

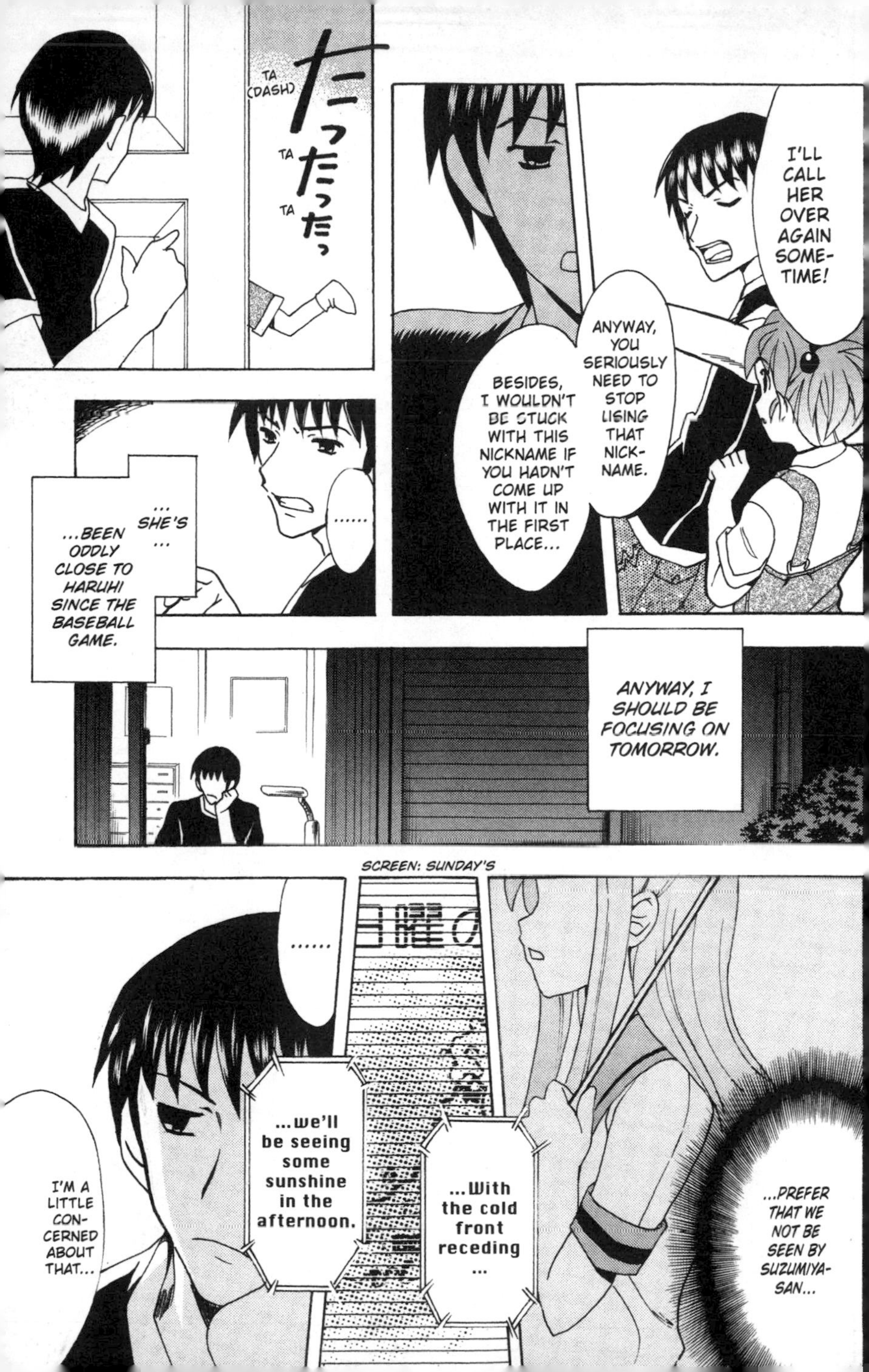
I'LL CALL HER OVER AGAIN SOME-TIME!
ANYWAY, YOU SERIOUSLY NEED TO STOP USING THAT NICK-NAME.
BESIDES, I WOULDN'T BE STUCK WITH THIS NICKNAME IF YOU HADN'T COME UP WITH IT IN THE FIRST PLACE...
たったったっ
TA (DASH)
TA
TA
......
...SHE'S...
...BEEN ODDLY CLOSE TO HARUHI SINCE THE BASEBALL GAME.
ANYWAY, I SHOULD BE FOCUSING ON TOMORROW.
SCREEN: SUNDAY'S
...PREFER THAT WE NOT BE SEEN BY SUZUMIYA-SAN...
...With the cold front receding...
...we'll be seeing some sunshine in the afternoon.
......
I'M A LITTLE CON-CERNED ABOUT THAT...

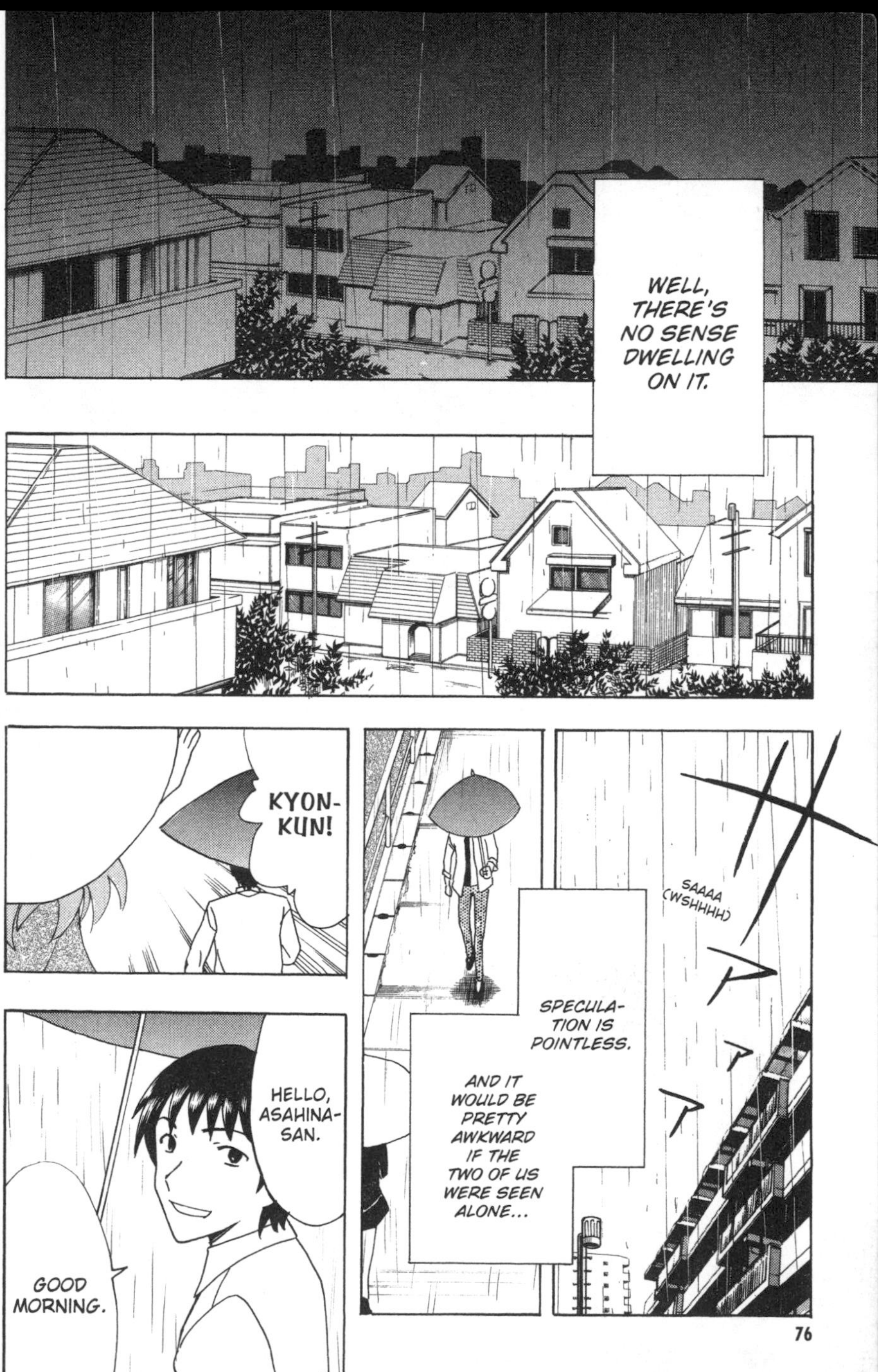
WELL, THERE'S NO SENSE DWELLING ON IT.
SAAAA (WSHHHH)
SPECULATION IS POINTLESS.
AND IT WOULD BE PRETTY AWKWARD IF THE TWO OF US WERE SEEN ALONE...
KYON-KUN!
HELLO, ASAHINA-SAN.
GOOD MORNING.

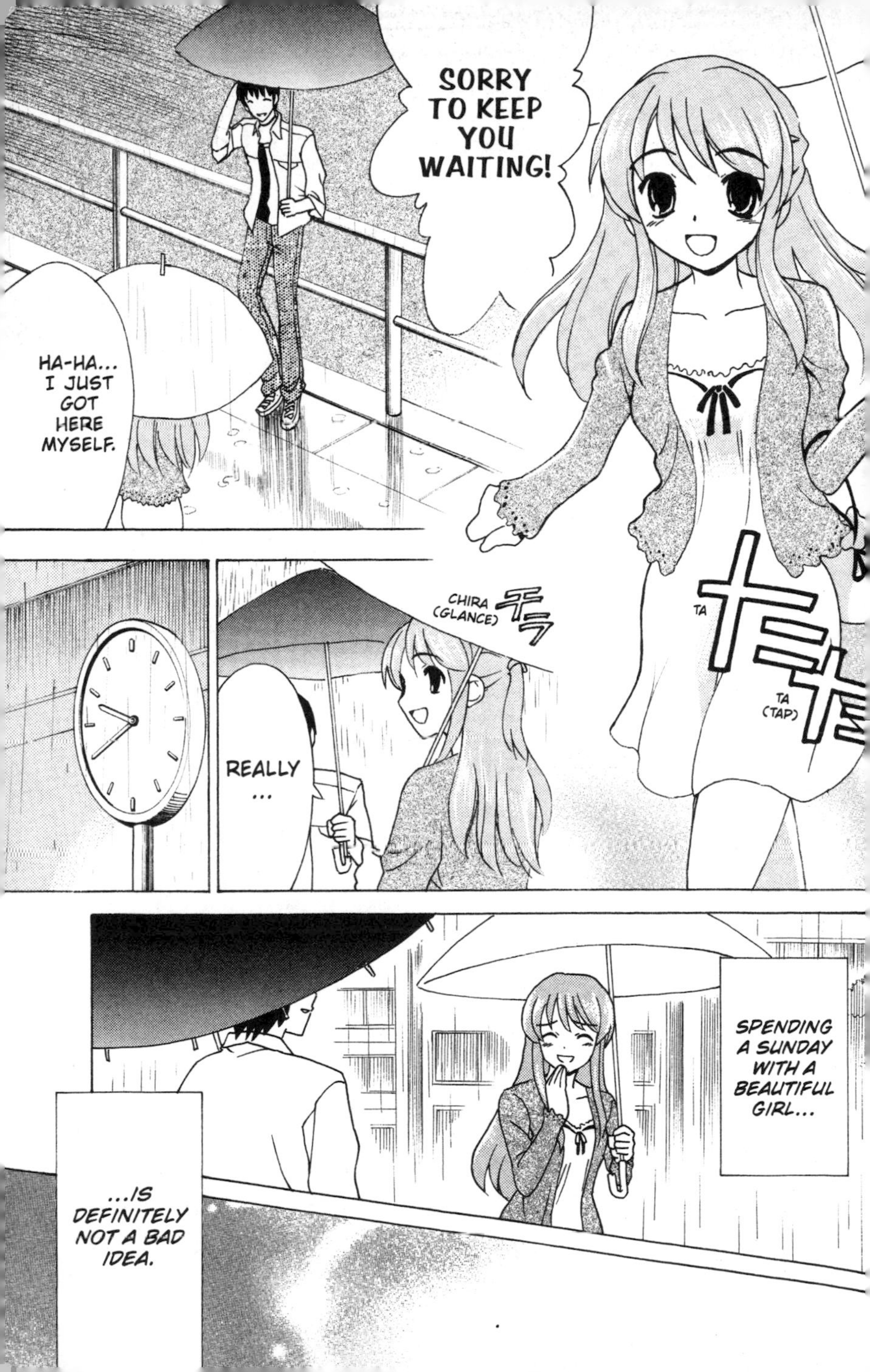
SORRY TO KEEP YOU WAITING!
TA
TA (TAP)
HA-HA... I JUST GOT HERE MYSELF.
CHIRA (GLANCE)
REALLY ...
SPENDING A SUNDAY WITH A BEAUTIFUL GIRL...
...IS DEFINITELY NOT A BAD IDEA.

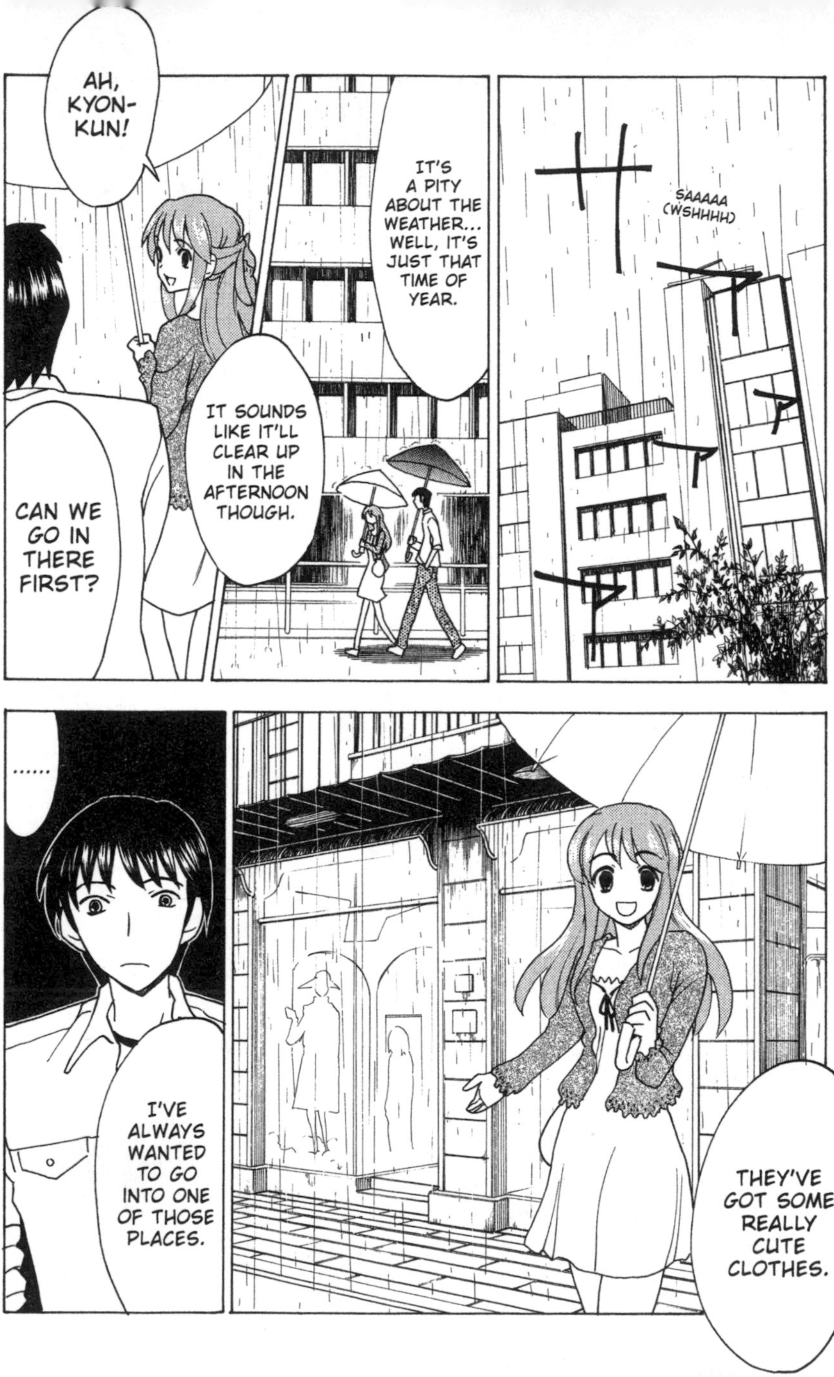
SAAAAA (WSHHHH)
IT'S A PITY ABOUT THE WEATHER... WELL, IT'S JUST THAT TIME OF YEAR.
IT SOUNDS LIKE IT'LL CLEAR UP IN THE AFTERNOON THOUGH.
AH, KYON-KUN!
CAN WE GO IN THERE FIRST?
THEY'VE GOT SOME REALLY CUTE CLOTHES.
I'VE ALWAYS WANTED TO GO INTO ONE OF THOSE PLACES.
......

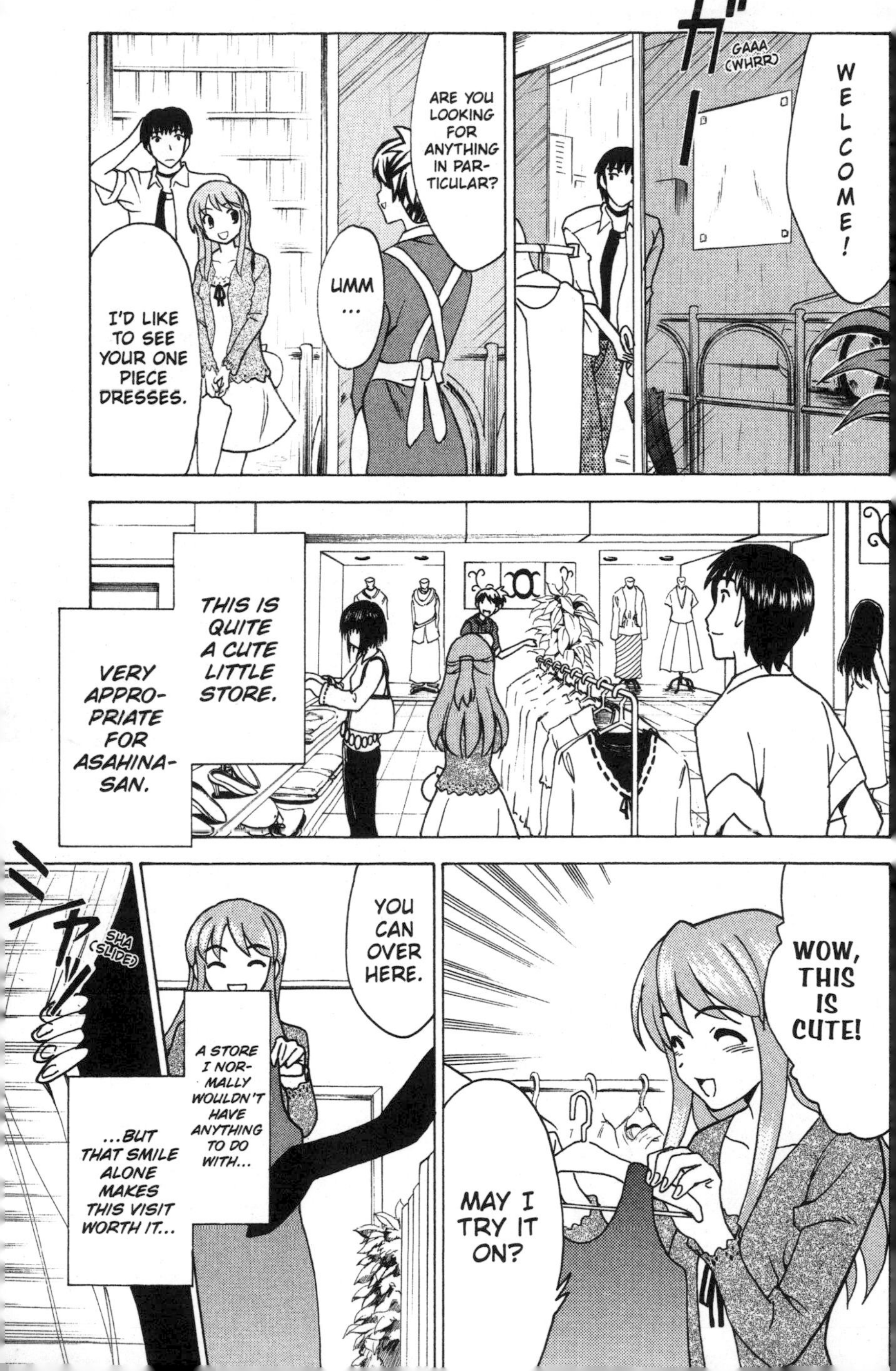
GAAA (WHRR)
WELCOME!
ARE YOU LOOKING FOR ANYTHING IN PARTICULAR?
UMM ...
I'D LIKE TO SEE YOUR ONE PIECE DRESSES.
THIS IS QUITE A CUTE LITTLE STORE.
VERY APPROPRIATE FOR ASAHINA-SAN.
WOW, THIS IS CUTE!
MAY I TRY IT ON?
YOU CAN OVER HERE.
SHA (SLIDE)
A STORE I NORMALLY WOULDN'T HAVE ANYTHING TO DO WITH...
...BUT THAT SMILE ALONE MAKES THIS VISIT WORTH IT...

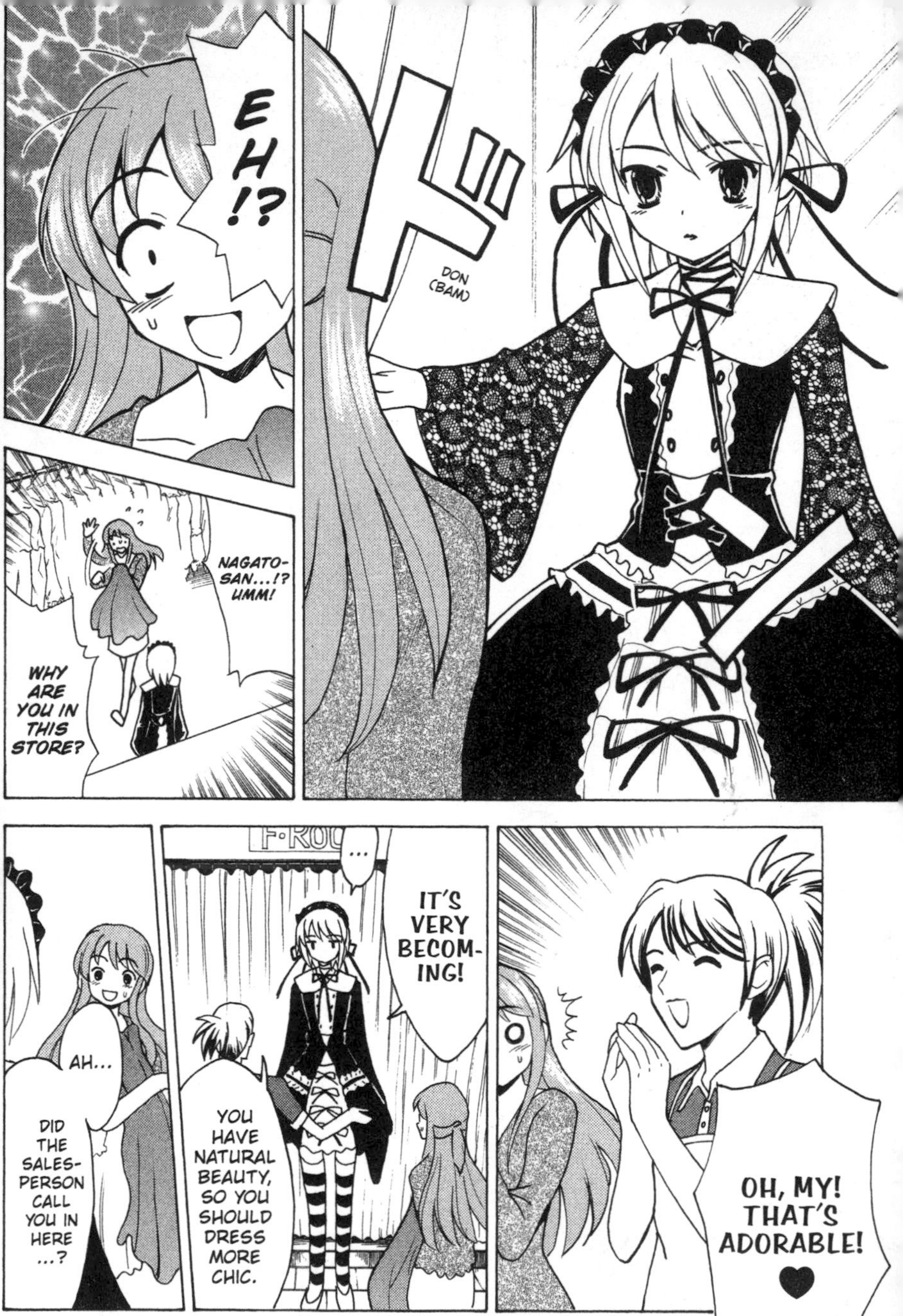
DON (BAM)
EH!?
NAGATO-SAN...!? UMM!
WHY ARE YOU IN THIS STORE?
OH, MY! THAT'S ADORABLE!
...
IT'S VERY BECOMING!
YOU HAVE NATURAL BEAUTY, SO YOU SHOULD DRESS MORE CHIC.
AH...
DID THE SALES-PERSON CALL YOU IN HERE ...?

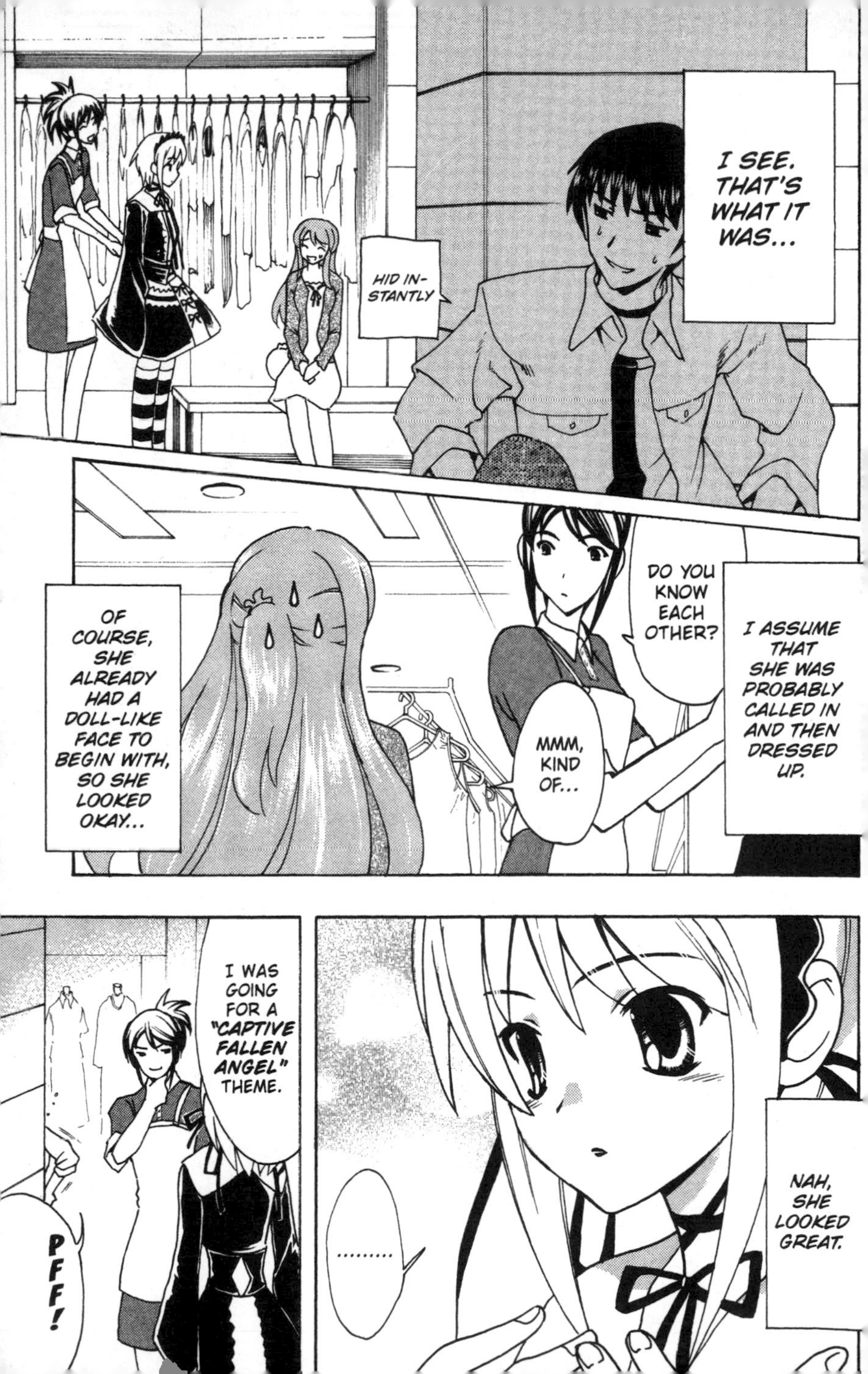
I SEE. THAT'S WHAT IT WAS...
HID IN-STANTLY
I ASSUME THAT SHE WAS PROBABLY CALLED IN AND THEN DRESSED UP.
DO YOU KNOW EACH OTHER?
MMM, KIND OF...
OF COURSE, SHE ALREADY HAD A DOLL-LIKE FACE TO BEGIN WITH, SO SHE LOOKED OKAY...
NAH, SHE LOOKED GREAT.
....
I WAS GOING FOR A "CAPTIVE FALLEN ANGEL" THEME.
PFF!

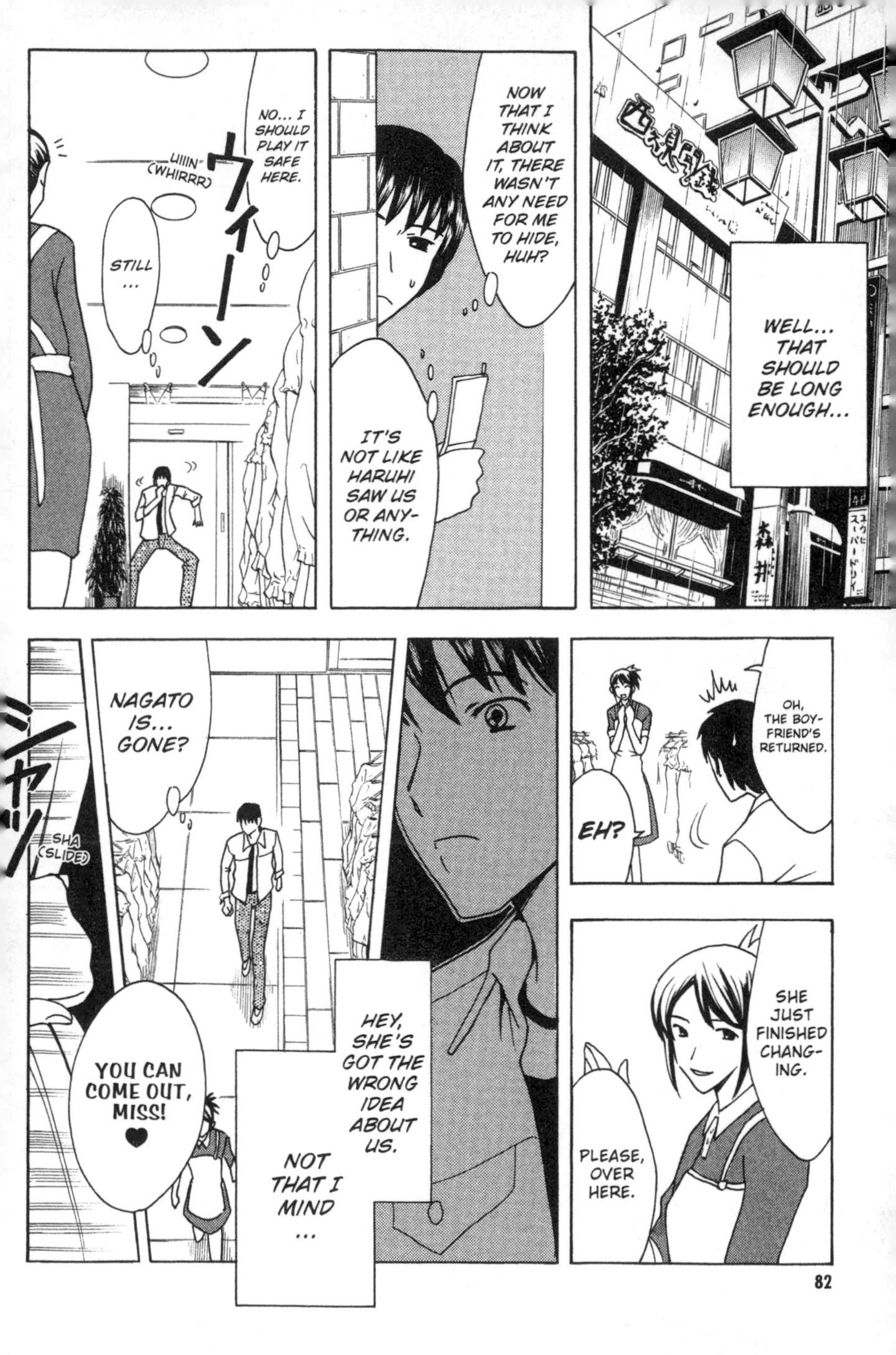
WELL... THAT SHOULD BE LONG ENOUGH...
NOW THAT I THINK ABOUT IT, THERE WASN'T ANY NEED FOR ME TO HIDE, HUH?
IT'S NOT LIKE HARUHI SAW US OR ANYTHING.
NO... I SHOULD PLAY IT SAFE HERE.
UIIIN (WHIRRR)
STILL...
OH, THE BOYFRIEND'S RETURNED.
EH?
SHE JUST FINISHED CHANGING.
PLEASE, OVER HERE.
HEY, SHE'S GOT THE WRONG IDEA ABOUT US.
NOT THAT I MIND...
NAGATO IS... GONE?
SHA (SLIDE)
YOU CAN COME OUT, MISS! ♥

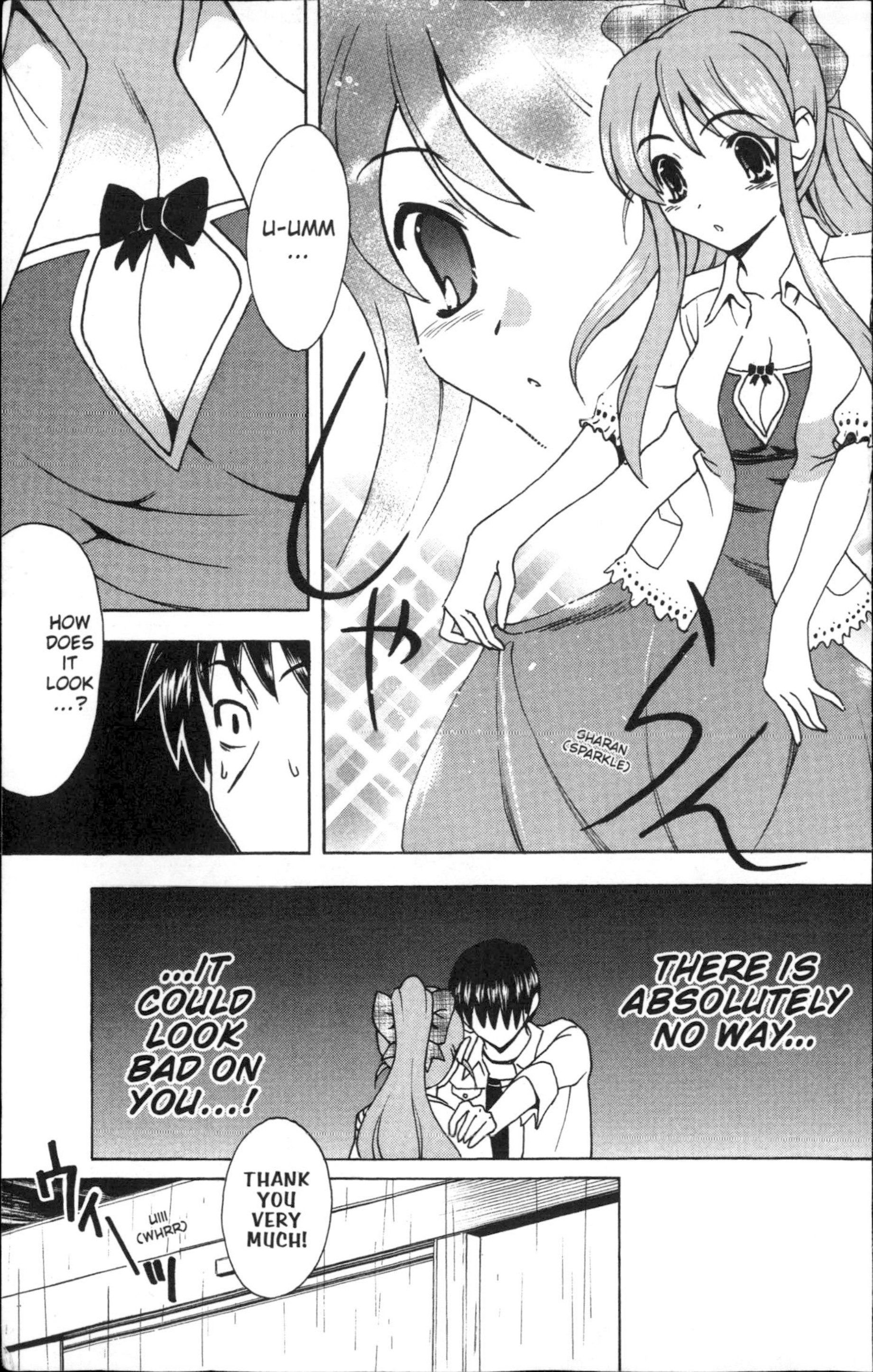
U-UMM ...
SHARAN (SPARKLE)
HOW DOES IT LOOK ...?
THERE IS ABSOLUTELY NO WAY...
...IT COULD LOOK BAD ON YOU...!
THANK YOU VERY MUCH!
UIII (WHRR)

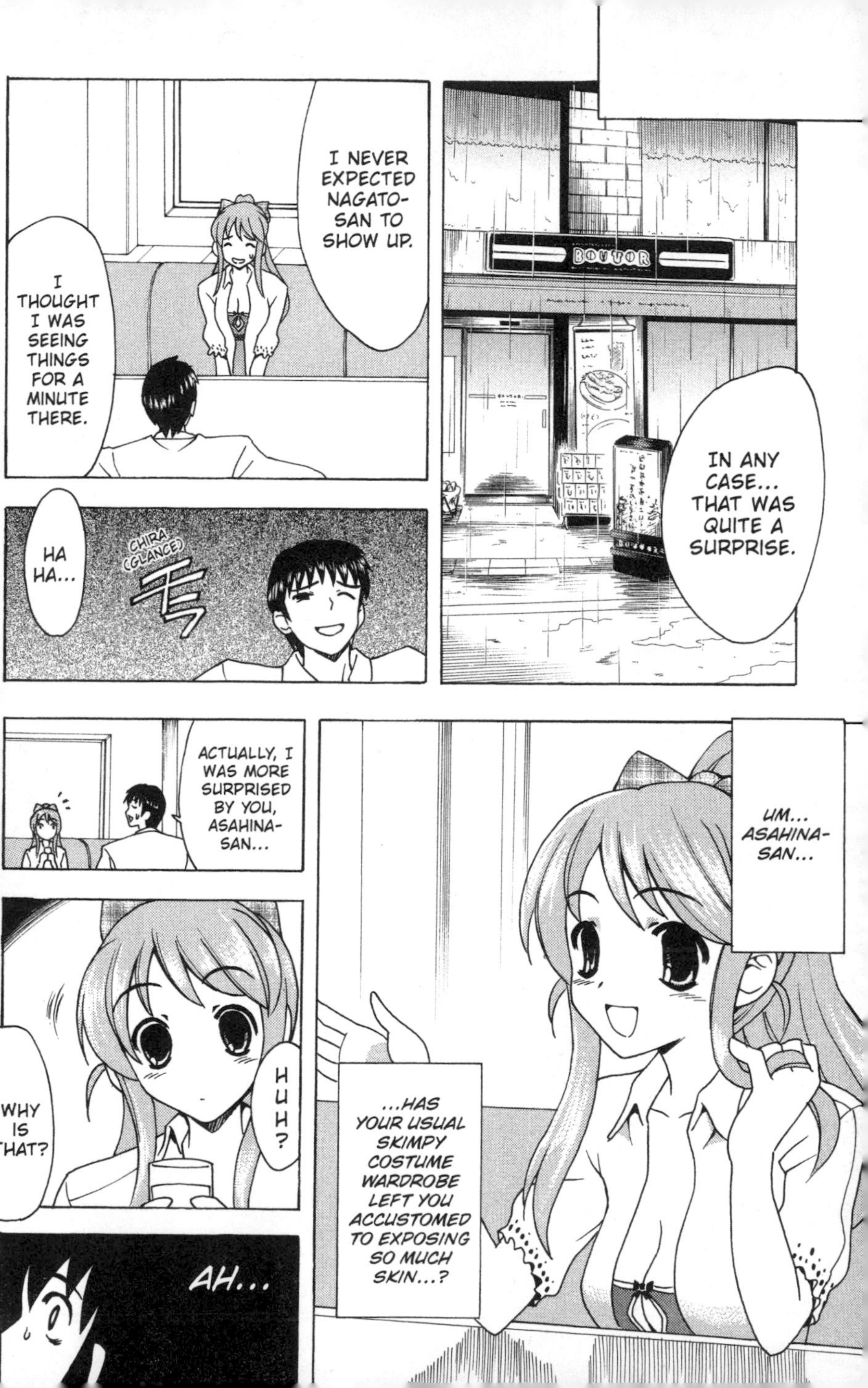
IN ANY CASE... THAT WAS QUITE A SURPRISE.
I NEVER EXPECTED NAGATO-SAN TO SHOW UP.
I THOUGHT I WAS SEEING THINGS FOR A MINUTE THERE.
CHIRA (GLANCE)
HA HA...
UM... ASAHINA-SAN...
...HAS YOUR USUAL SKIMPY COSTUME WARDROBE LEFT YOU ACCUSTOMED TO EXPOSING SO MUCH SKIN...?
ACTUALLY, I WAS MORE SURPRISED BY YOU, ASAHINA-SAN...
HUH?
WHY IS THAT?
AH...

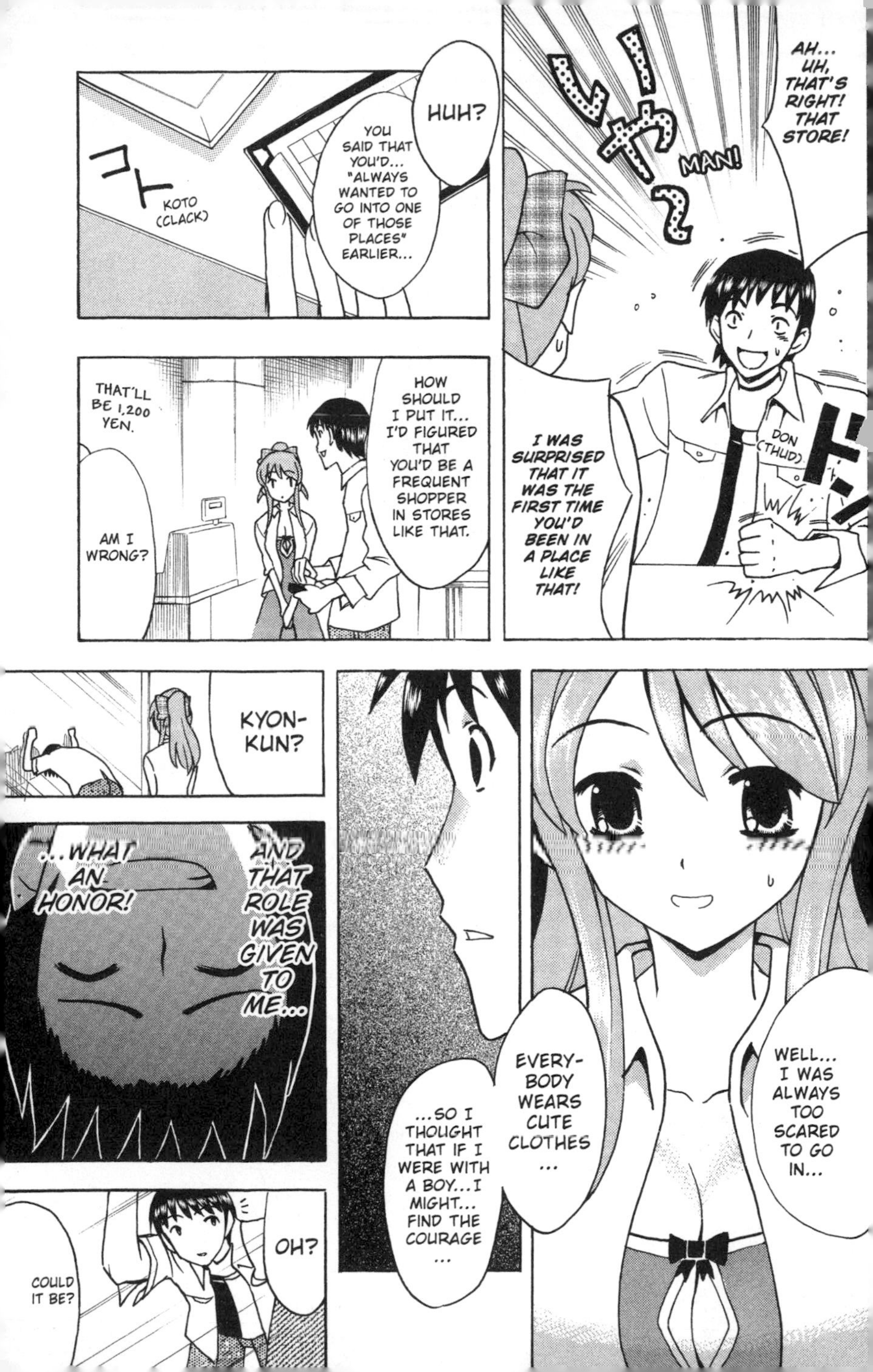
AH... UH, THAT'S RIGHT! THAT STORE!
いやぁ~
MAN!
DON (THUD)
ドン
I WAS SURPRISED THAT IT WAS THE FIRST TIME YOU'D BEEN IN A PLACE LIKE THAT!
HUH?
YOU SAID THAT YOU'D... "ALWAYS WANTED TO GO INTO ONE OF THOSE PLACES" EARLIER...
コト
KOTO (CLACK)
HOW SHOULD I PUT IT... I'D FIGURED THAT YOU'D BE A FREQUENT SHOPPER IN STORES LIKE THAT.
THAT'LL BE 1,200 YEN.
AM I WRONG?
WELL... I WAS ALWAYS TOO SCARED TO GO IN...
EVERY-BODY WEARS CUTE CLOTHES...
...SO I THOUGHT THAT IF I WERE WITH A BOY... I MIGHT... FIND THE COURAGE...
KYON-KUN?
AND THAT ROLE WAS GIVEN TO ME...
...WHAT AN HONOR!
OH?
COULD IT BE?

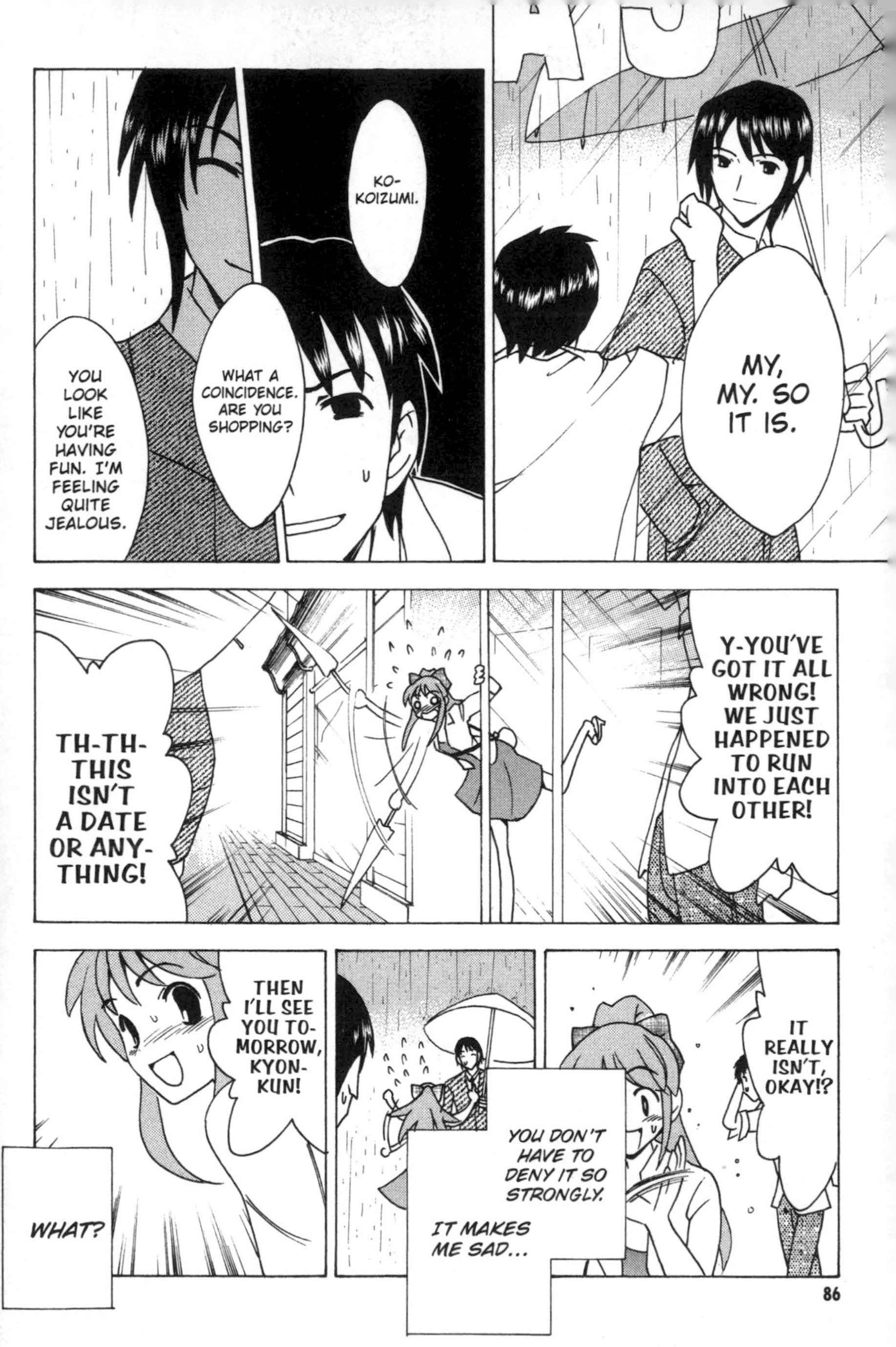

MY, MY. SO IT IS.
KO-KOIZUMI.
WHAT A COINCIDENCE. ARE YOU SHOPPING?
YOU LOOK LIKE YOU'RE HAVING FUN. I'M FEELING QUITE JEALOUS.
Y-YOU'VE GOT IT ALL WRONG! WE JUST HAPPENED TO RUN INTO EACH OTHER!
TH-TH-THIS ISN'T A DATE OR ANY-THING!
IT REALLY ISN'T, OKAY!?
YOU DON'T HAVE TO DENY IT SO STRONGLY.
IT MAKES ME SAD...
THEN I'LL SEE YOU TO-MORROW, KYON-KUN!
WHAT?

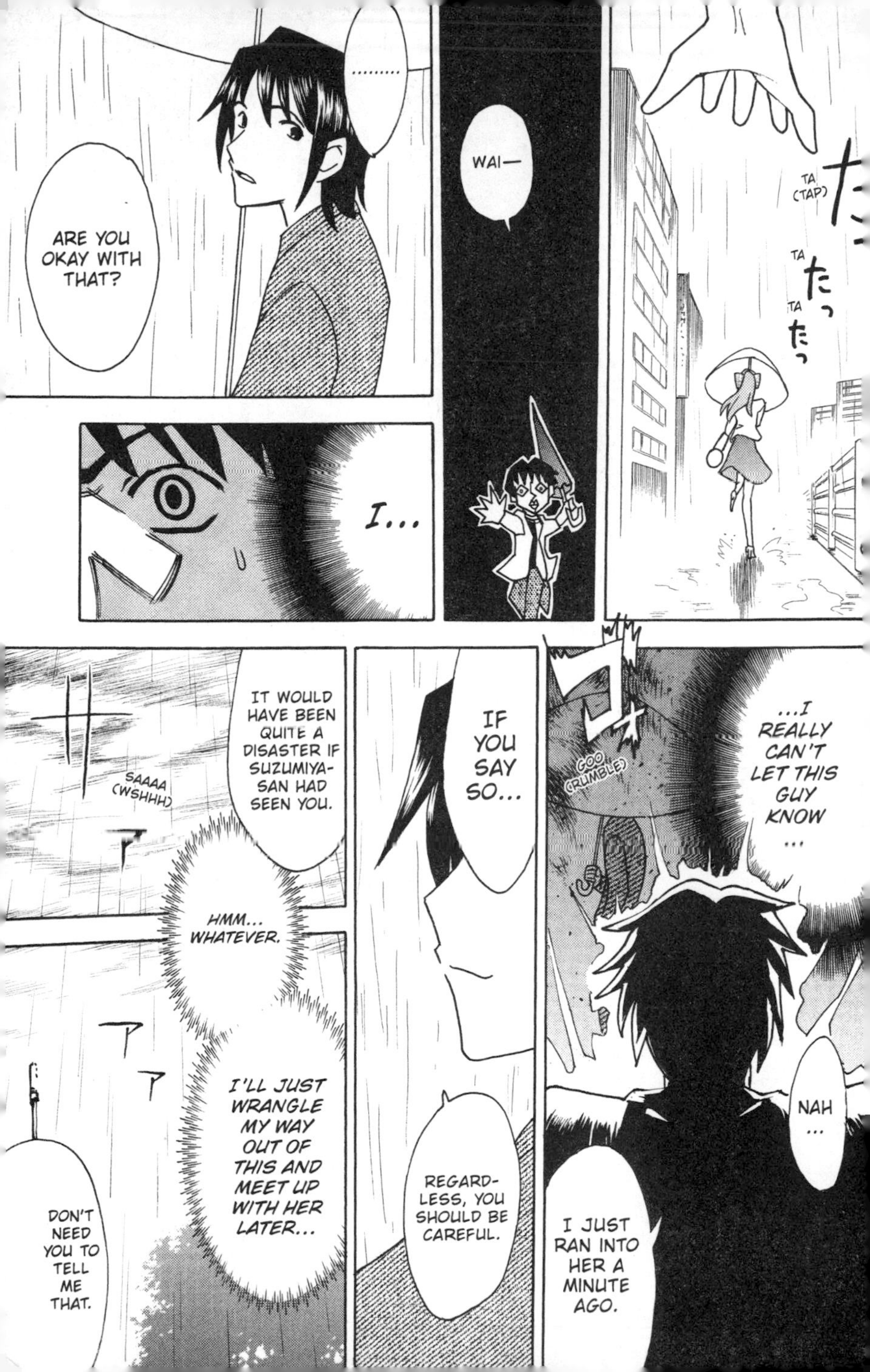
TA (TAP)
TA
TA
WAI—
......
ARE YOU OKAY WITH THAT?
I...
GOO (RUMBLE)
...I REALLY CAN'T LET THIS GUY KNOW...
NAH...
I JUST RAN INTO HER A MINUTE AGO.
IF YOU SAY SO...
REGARDLESS, YOU SHOULD BE CAREFUL.
IT WOULD HAVE BEEN QUITE A DISASTER IF SUZUMIYA-SAN HAD SEEN YOU.
SAAAA (WSHHH)
HMM... WHATEVER.
I'LL JUST WRANGLE MY WAY OUT OF THIS AND MEET UP WITH HER LATER...
DON'T NEED YOU TO TELL ME THAT.

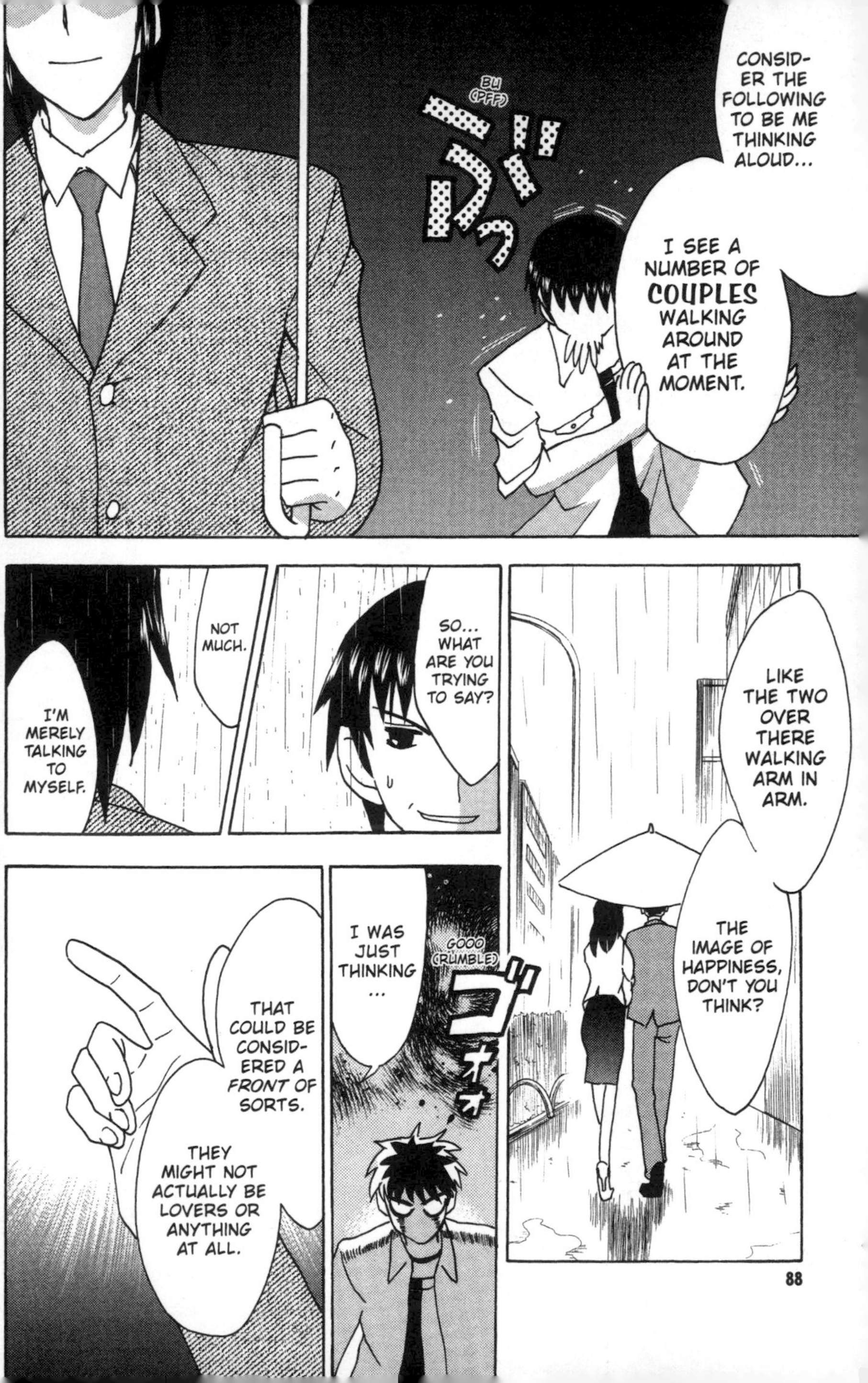
CONSID-ER THE FOLLOWING TO BE ME THINKING ALOUD...
I SEE A NUMBER OF **COUPLES** WALKING AROUND AT THE MOMENT.
BU (PFF)
LIKE THE TWO OVER THERE WALKING ARM IN ARM.
THE IMAGE OF HAPPINESS, DON'T YOU THINK?
SO... WHAT ARE YOU TRYING TO SAY?
NOT MUCH.
I'M MERELY TALKING TO MYSELF.
I WAS JUST THINKING ...
GOOO (RUMBLE)
THAT COULD BE CONSID-ERED A *FRONT* OF SORTS.
THEY MIGHT NOT ACTUALLY BE LOVERS OR ANYTHING AT ALL.

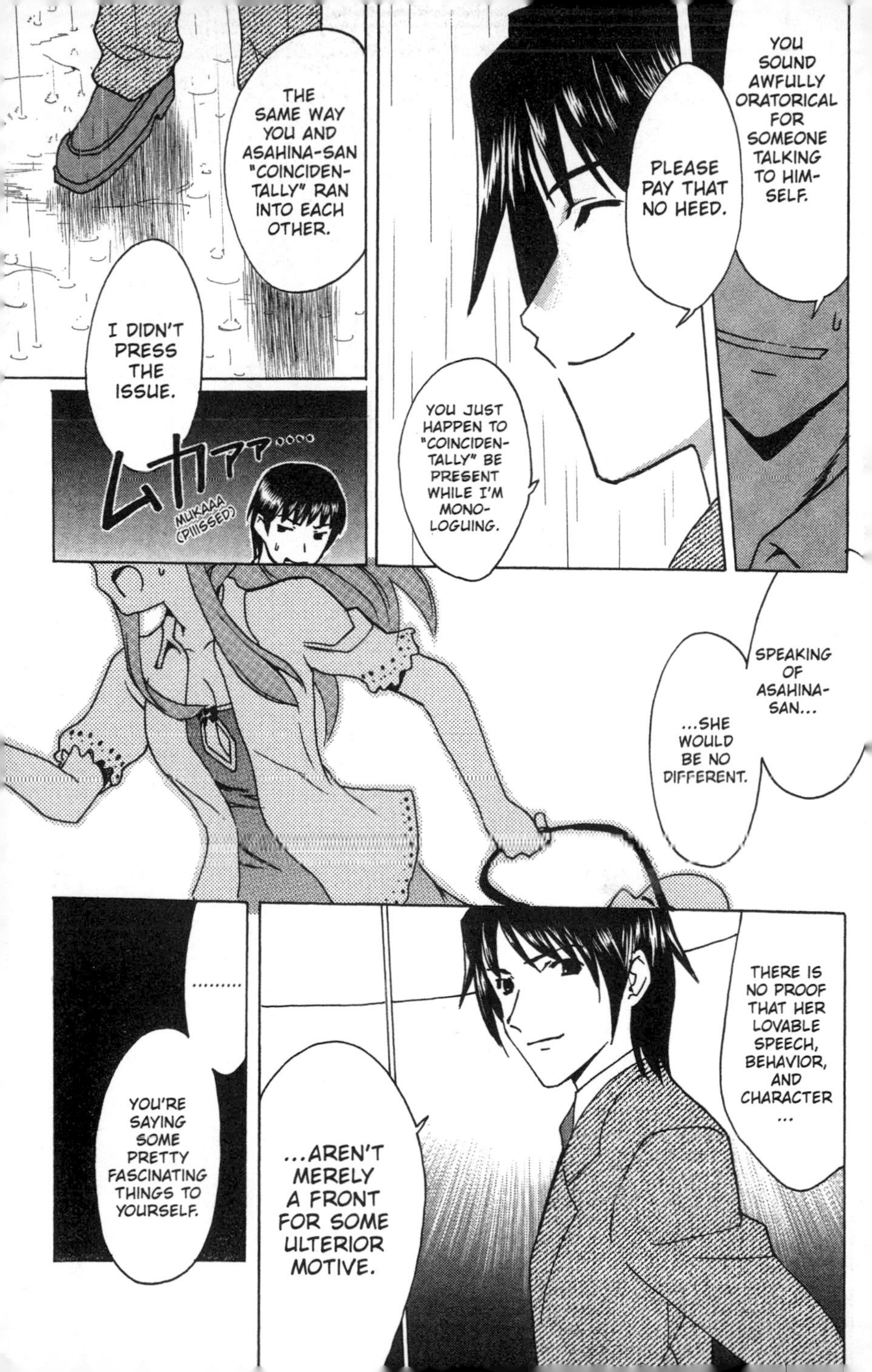

YOU SOUND AWFULLY ORATORICAL FOR SOMEONE TALKING TO HIM-SELF.
PLEASE PAY THAT NO HEED.
YOU JUST HAPPEN TO "COINCIDEN-TALLY" BE PRESENT WHILE I'M MONO-LOGUING.
THE SAME WAY YOU AND ASAHINA-SAN "COINCIDEN-TALLY" RAN INTO EACH OTHER.
I DIDN'T PRESS THE ISSUE.
ムカァァ
MUKAAA (PIIISSED)
SPEAKING OF ASAHINA-SAN...
...SHE WOULD BE NO DIFFERENT.
THERE IS NO PROOF THAT HER LOVABLE SPEECH, BEHAVIOR, AND CHARACTER...
...AREN'T MERELY A FRONT FOR SOME ULTERIOR MOTIVE.
....
YOU'RE SAYING SOME PRETTY FASCINATING THINGS TO YOURSELF.

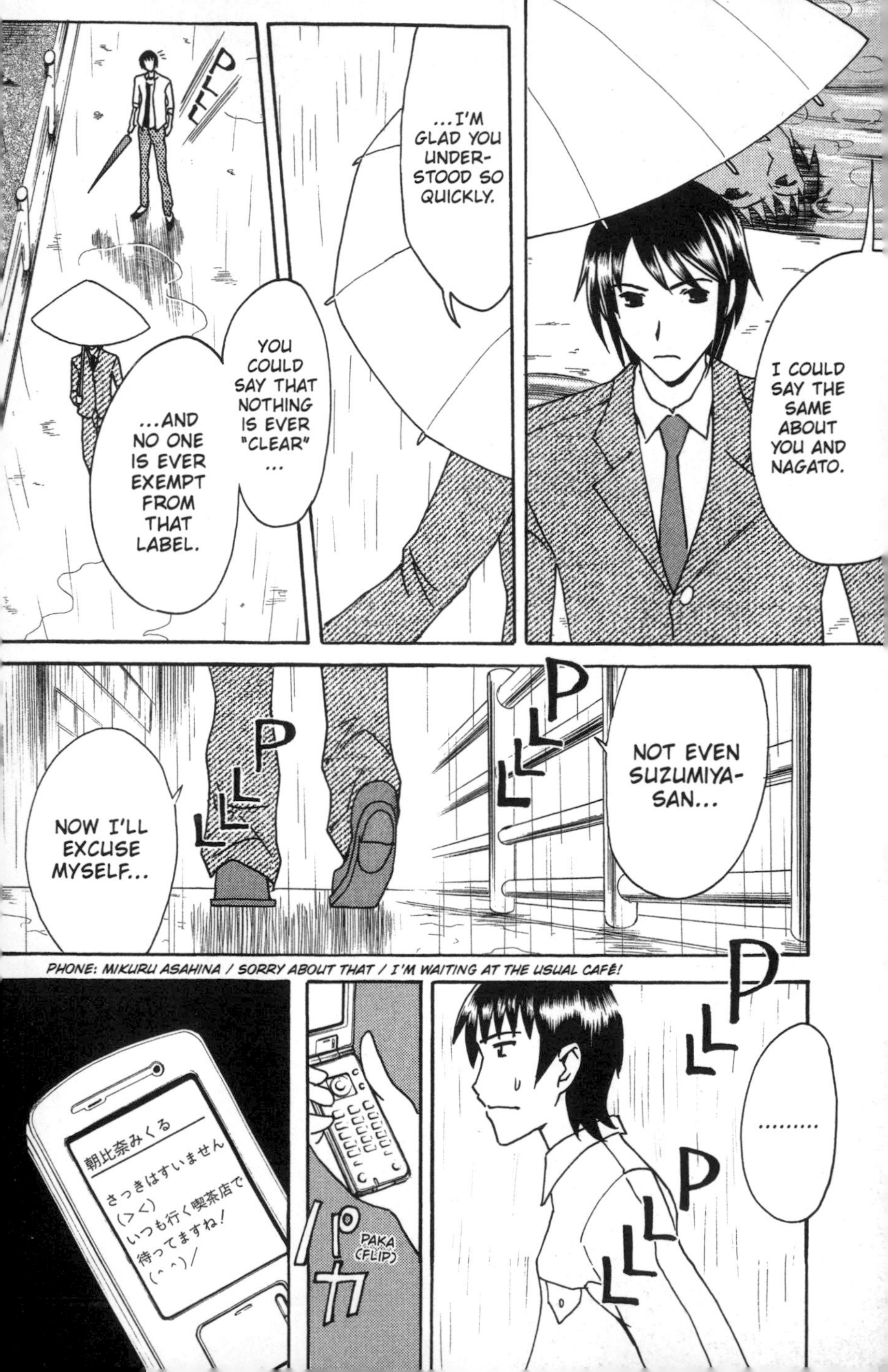
I COULD SAY THE SAME ABOUT YOU AND NAGATO.
...I'M GLAD YOU UNDERSTOOD SO QUICKLY.
PLLL
YOU COULD SAY THAT NOTHING IS EVER "CLEAR" ...
...AND NO ONE IS EVER EXEMPT FROM THAT LABEL.
PLLL
NOT EVEN SUZUMIYA-SAN...
PLLL
NOW I'LL EXCUSE MYSELF...
PHONE: MIKURU ASAHINA / SORRY ABOUT THAT / I'M WAITING AT THE USUAL CAFÉ!
PLLL
....
PLLL
パカ
PAKA (FLIP)
朝比奈みくる
さっきはすいません
(><)
いつも行く喫茶店で
待ってますね!
(^^)/

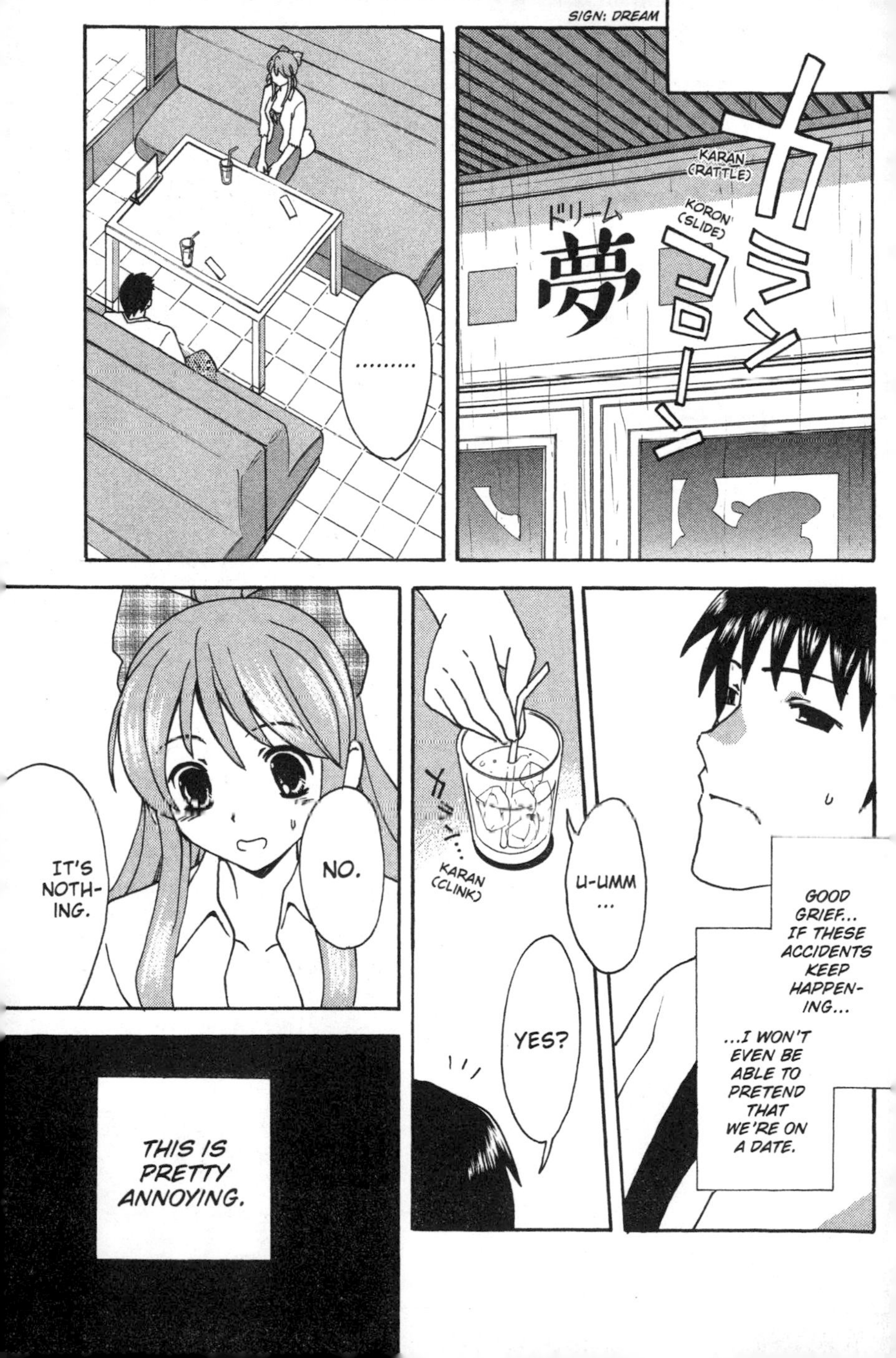
SIGN: DREAM
KARAN (RATTLE)
KORON (SLIDE)
ドリーム
夢
....
GOOD GRIEF... IF THESE ACCIDENTS KEEP HAPPEN-ING...
...I WON'T EVEN BE ABLE TO PRETEND THAT WE'RE ON A DATE.
KARAN (CLINK)
U-UMM...
YES?
NO.
IT'S NOTH-ING.
THIS IS PRETTY ANNOYING.

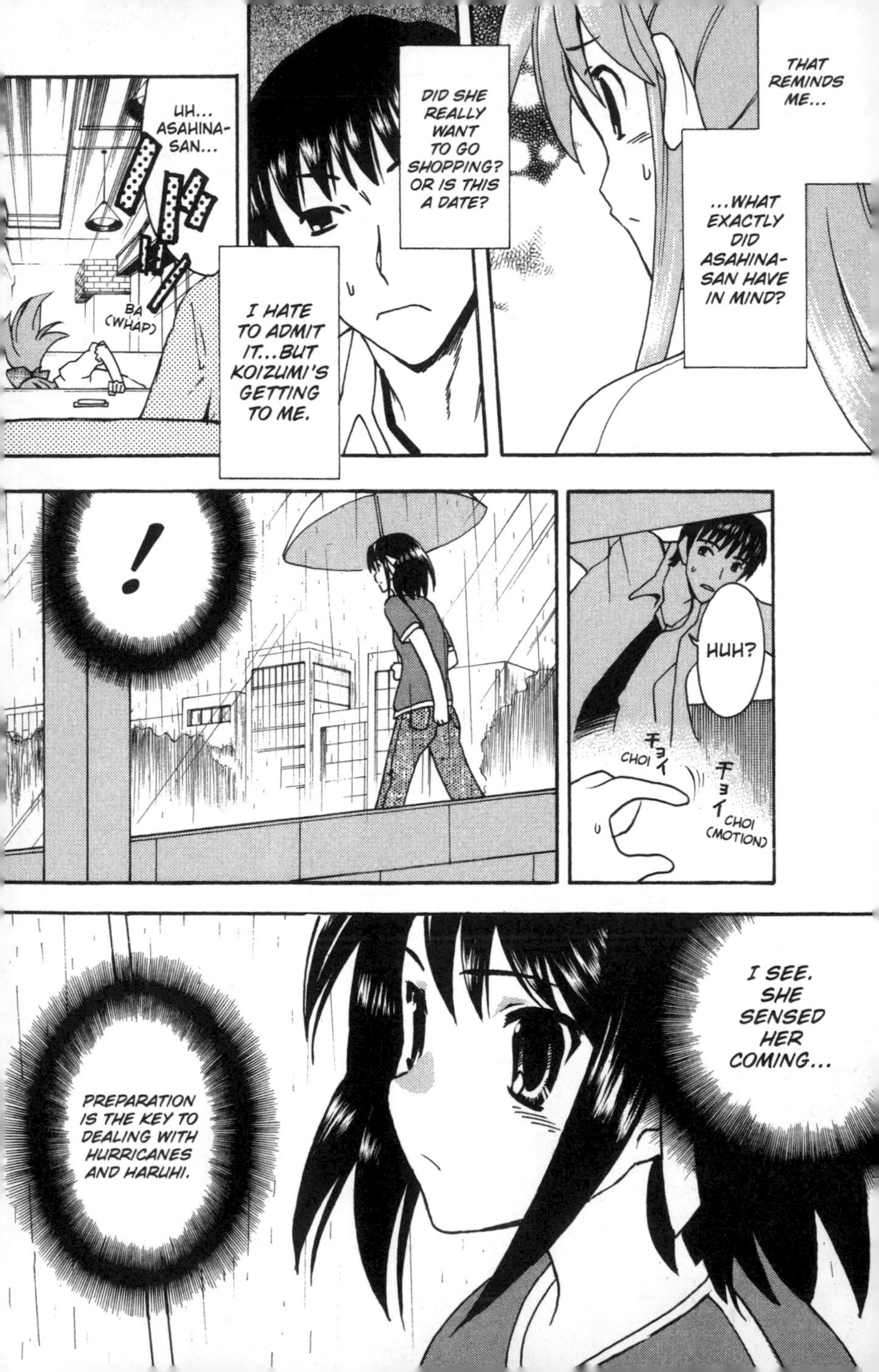
THAT REMINDS ME...
...WHAT EXACTLY DID ASAHINA-SAN HAVE IN MIND?
DID SHE REALLY WANT TO GO SHOPPING? OR IS THIS A DATE?
I HATE TO ADMIT IT...BUT KOIZUMI'S GETTING TO ME.
UH... ASAHINA-SAN...
BA (WHAP)
HUH?
チョイ CHOI
チョイ CHOI (MOTION)
!
I SEE. SHE SENSED HER COMING...
PREPARATION IS THE KEY TO DEALING WITH HURRICANES AND HARUHI.

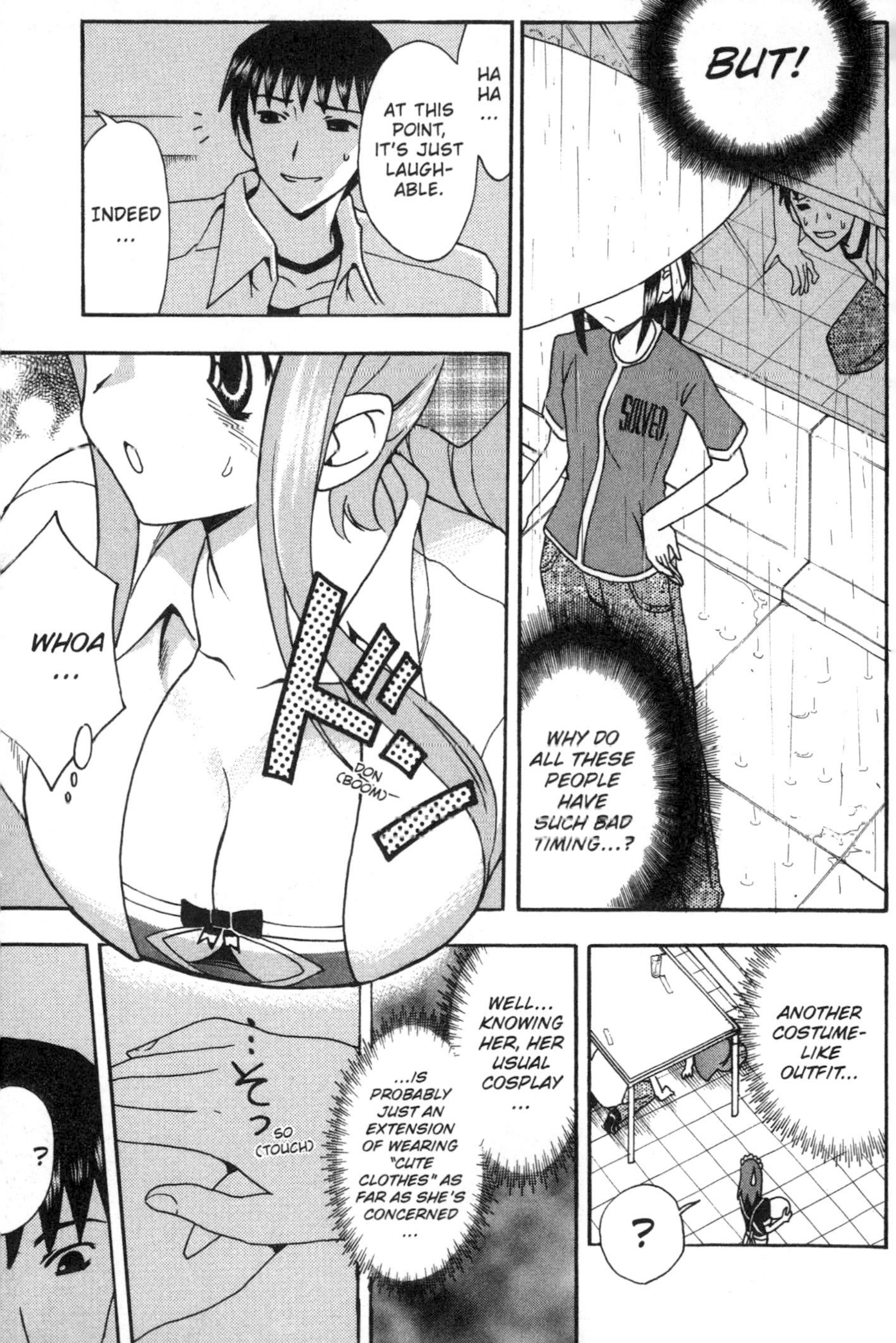
BUT!
WHY DO ALL THESE PEOPLE HAVE SUCH BAD TIMING...?
HA HA ...
AT THIS POINT, IT'S JUST LAUGHABLE.
INDEED ...
DON (BOOM)
WHOA ...
ANOTHER COSTUME-LIKE OUTFIT...
?
WELL... KNOWING HER, HER USUAL COSPLAY ...
...IS PROBABLY JUST AN EXTENSION OF WEARING "CUTE CLOTHES" AS FAR AS SHE'S CONCERNED ...
…そっ
SO (TOUCH)
?

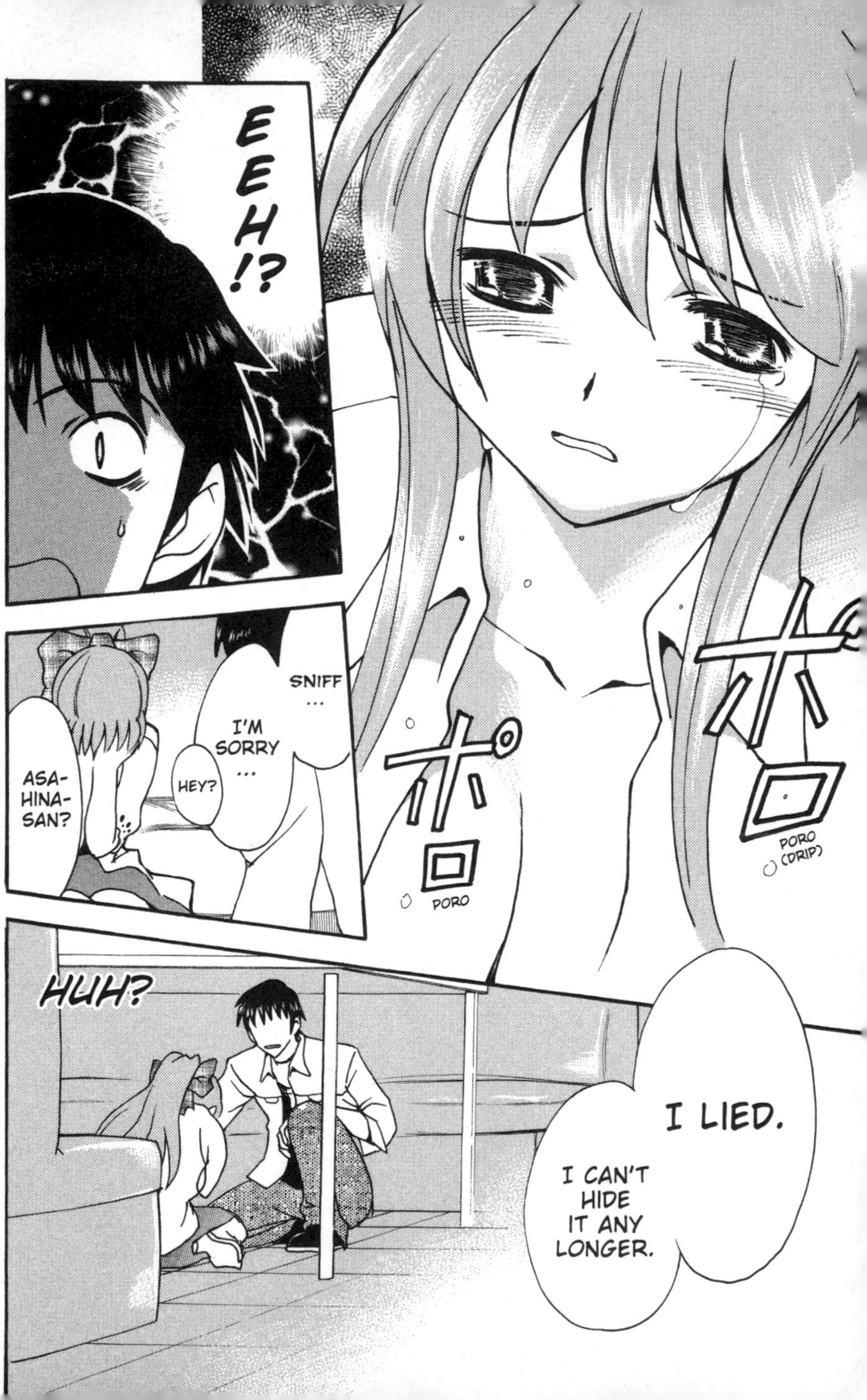
ポロ
PORO (DRIP)
ポロ
PORO
EEEH!?
SNIFF ...
I'M SORRY ...
HEY?
ASA-HINA-SAN?
I LIED.
I CAN'T HIDE IT ANY LONGER.
HUH?

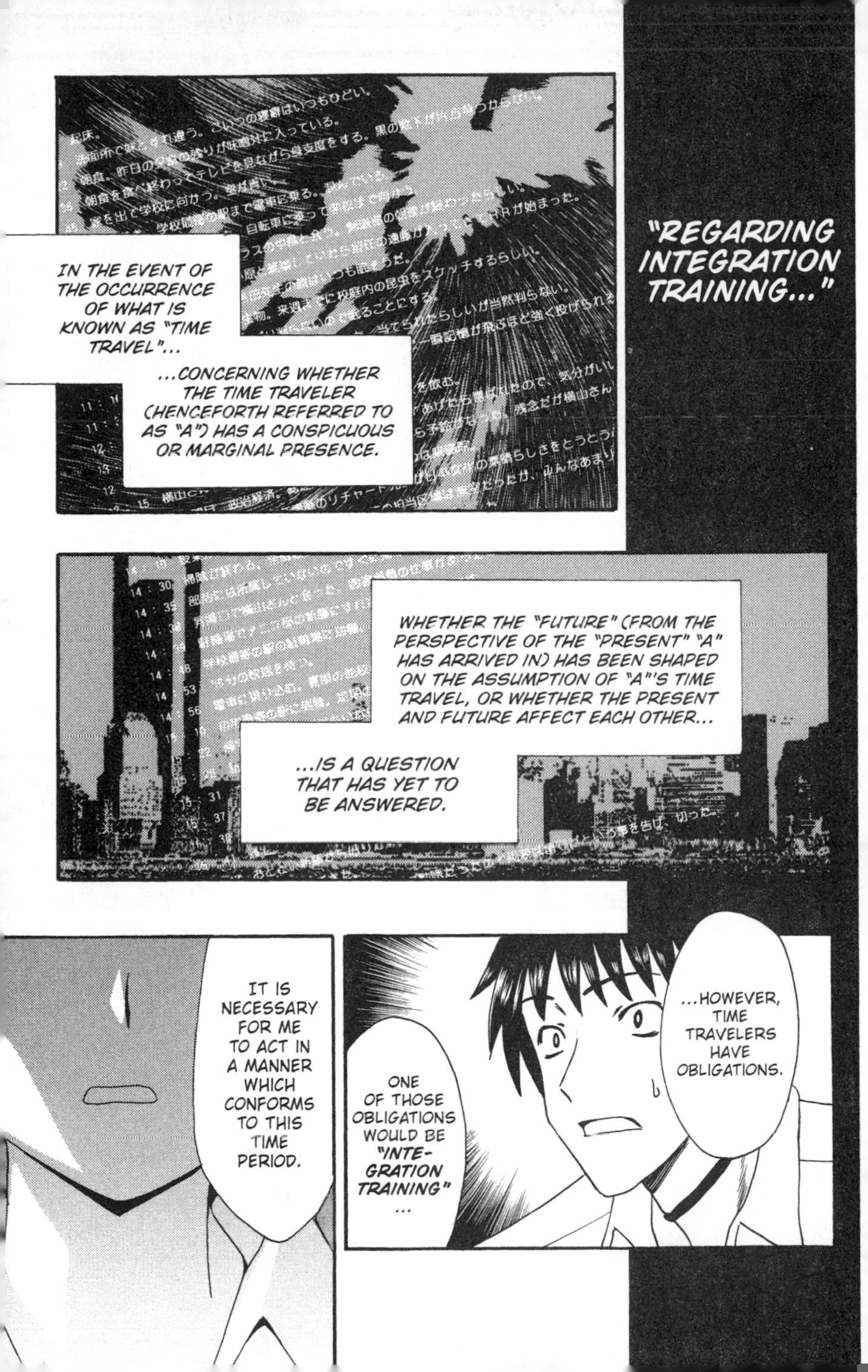
"REGARDING INTEGRATION TRAINING..."
IN THE EVENT OF THE OCCURRENCE OF WHAT IS KNOWN AS "TIME TRAVEL"...
...CONCERNING WHETHER THE TIME TRAVELER (HENCEFORTH REFERRED TO AS "A") HAS A CONSPICUOUS OR MARGINAL PRESENCE.
WHETHER THE "FUTURE" (FROM THE PERSPECTIVE OF THE "PRESENT" "A" HAS ARRIVED IN) HAS BEEN SHAPED ON THE ASSUMPTION OF "A"'S TIME TRAVEL, OR WHETHER THE PRESENT AND FUTURE AFFECT EACH OTHER...
...IS A QUESTION THAT HAS YET TO BE ANSWERED.
...HOWEVER, TIME TRAVELERS HAVE OBLIGATIONS.
ONE OF THOSE OBLIGATIONS WOULD BE "INTEGRATION TRAINING"...
IT IS NECESSARY FOR ME TO ACT IN A MANNER WHICH CONFORMS TO THIS TIME PERIOD.

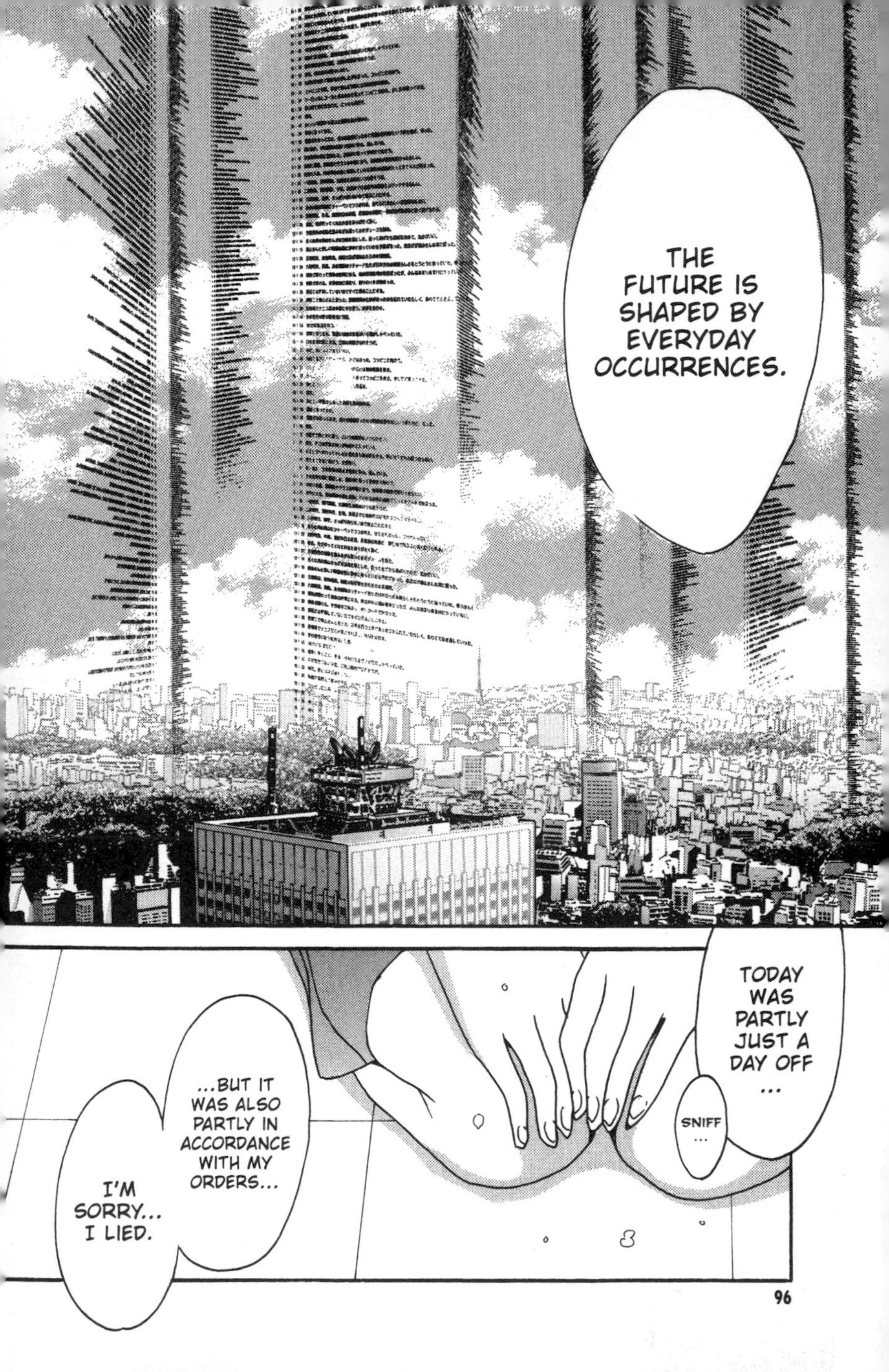
THE FUTURE IS SHAPED BY EVERYDAY OCCURRENCES.
TODAY WAS PARTLY JUST A DAY OFF ...
SNIFF ...
...BUT IT WAS ALSO PARTLY IN ACCORDANCE WITH MY ORDERS...
I'M SORRY... I LIED.

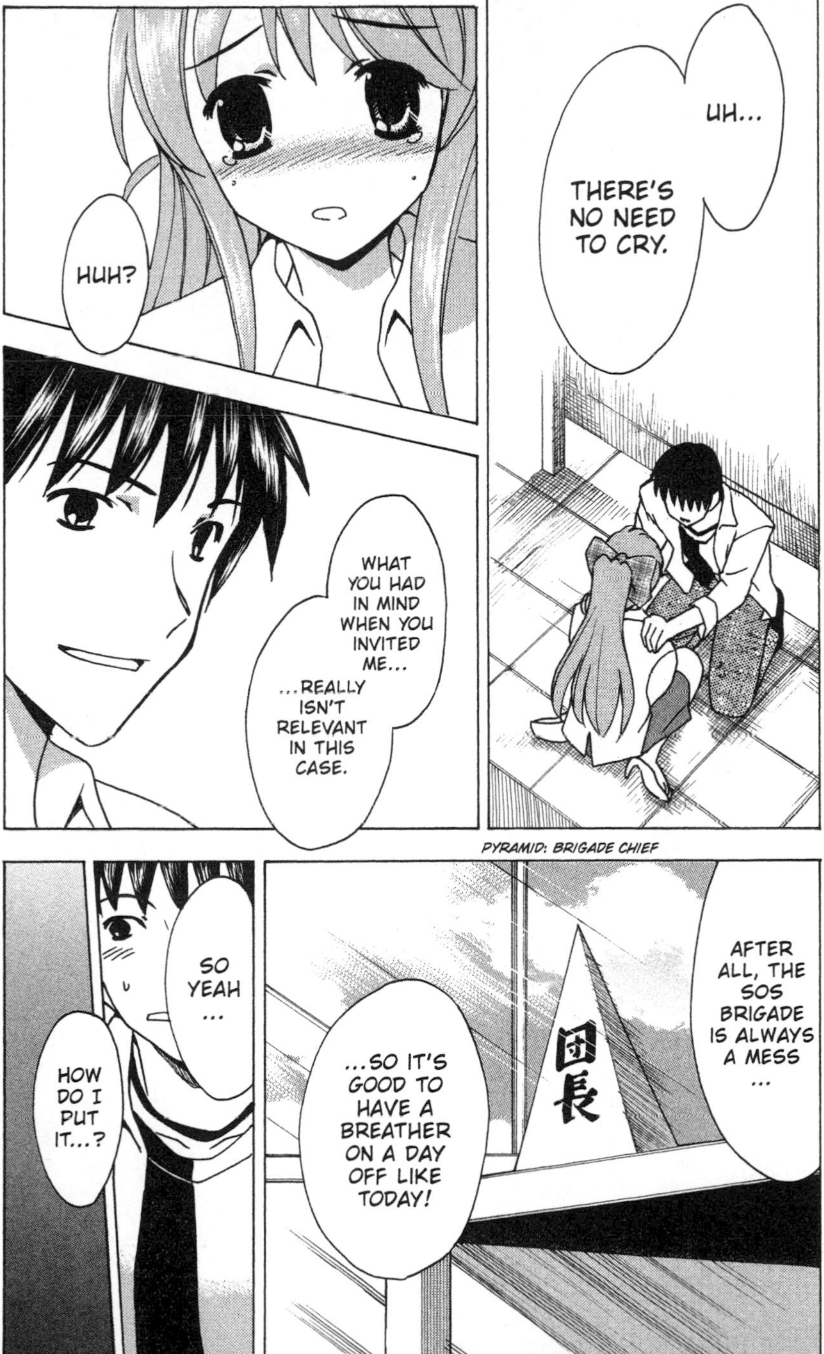
UH...
THERE'S NO NEED TO CRY.
HUH?
WHAT YOU HAD IN MIND WHEN YOU INVITED ME...
...REALLY ISN'T RELEVANT IN THIS CASE.
PYRAMID: BRIGADE CHIEF
AFTER ALL, THE SOS BRIGADE IS ALWAYS A MESS ...
団長
...SO IT'S GOOD TO HAVE A BREATHER ON A DAY OFF LIKE TODAY!
SO YEAH ...
HOW DO I PUT IT...?

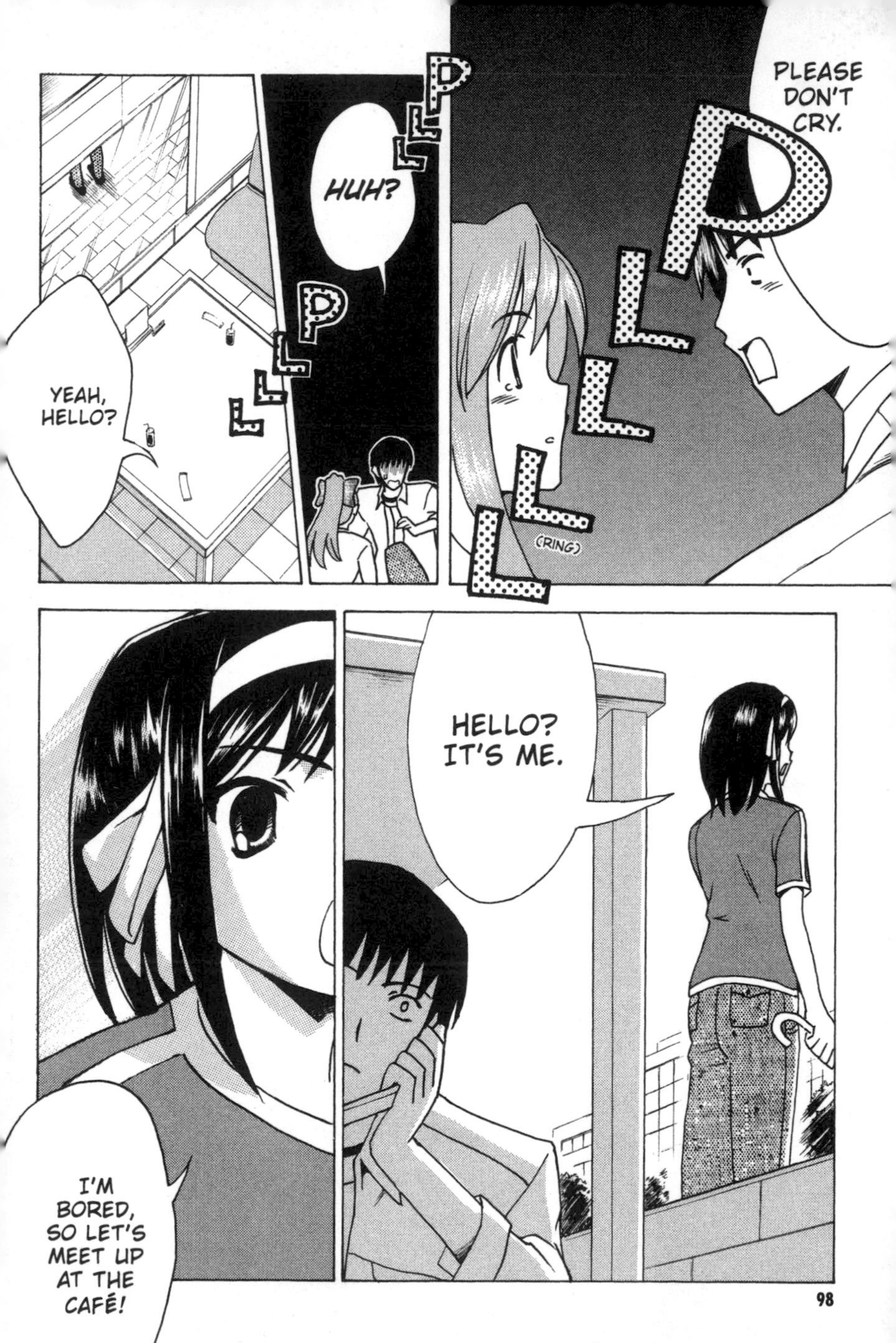
PLEASE DON'T CRY.
PLLLL
(RING)
PLLL
HUH?
PLLL
YEAH, HELLO?
HELLO? IT'S ME.
I'M BORED, SO LET'S MEET UP AT THE CAFÉ!

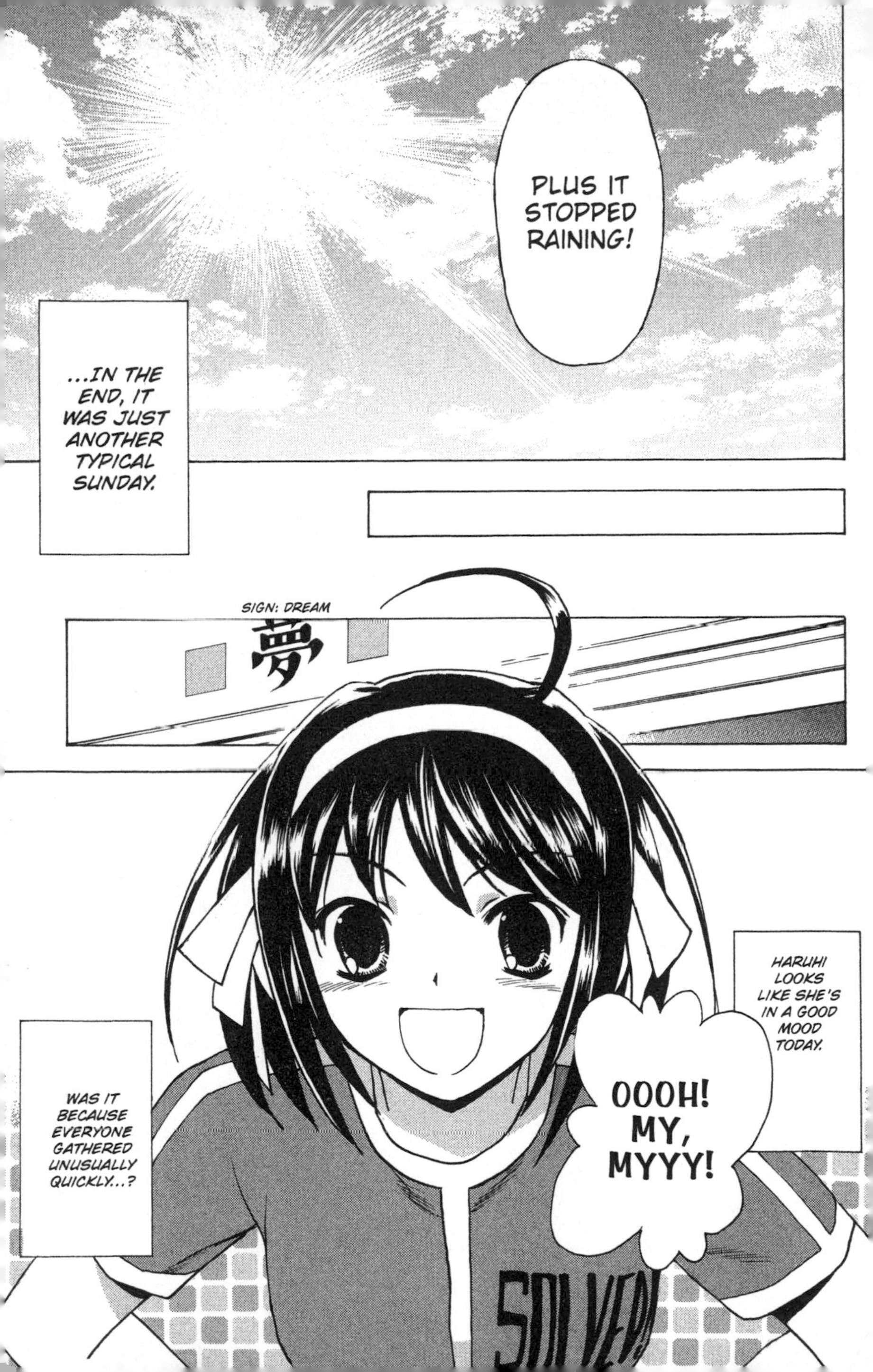
PLUS IT STOPPED RAINING!
...IN THE END, IT WAS JUST ANOTHER TYPICAL SUNDAY.
SIGN: DREAM
夢
HARUHI LOOKS LIKE SHE'S IN A GOOD MOOD TODAY.
OOOH! MY, MYYY!
WAS IT BECAUSE EVERYONE GATHERED UNUSUALLY QUICKLY...?

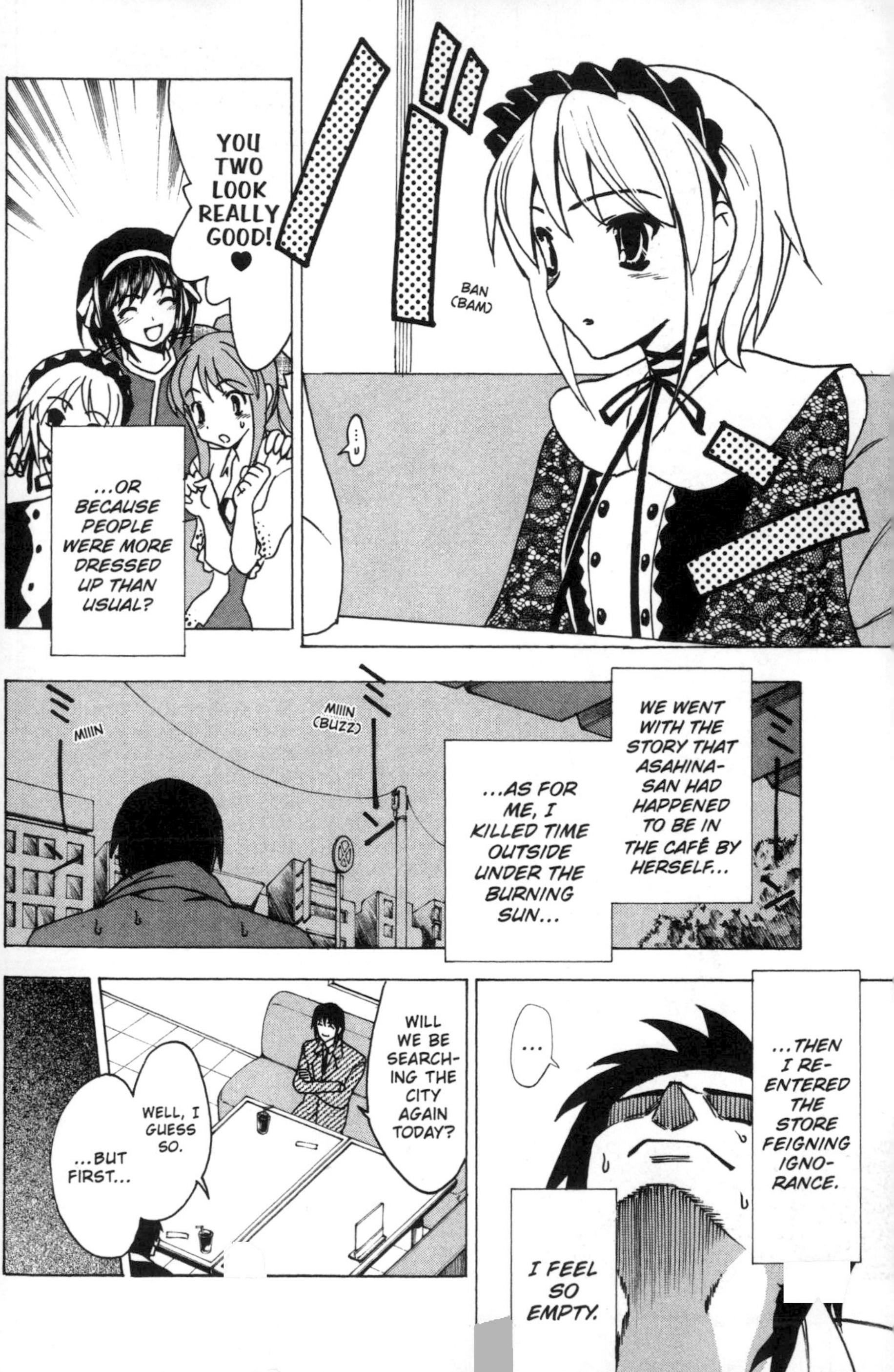
BAN (BAM)
...
YOU TWO LOOK REALLY GOOD! ♥
...OR BECAUSE PEOPLE WERE MORE DRESSED UP THAN USUAL?
WE WENT WITH THE STORY THAT ASAHINA-SAN HAD HAPPENED TO BE IN THE CAFÉ BY HERSELF...
...AS FOR ME, I KILLED TIME OUTSIDE UNDER THE BURNING SUN...
MIIIN (BUZZ)
MIIIN
...THEN I RE-ENTERED THE STORE FEIGNING IGNORANCE.
...
I FEEL SO EMPTY.
WILL WE BE SEARCHING THE CITY AGAIN TODAY?
WELL, I GUESS SO.
...BUT FIRST...

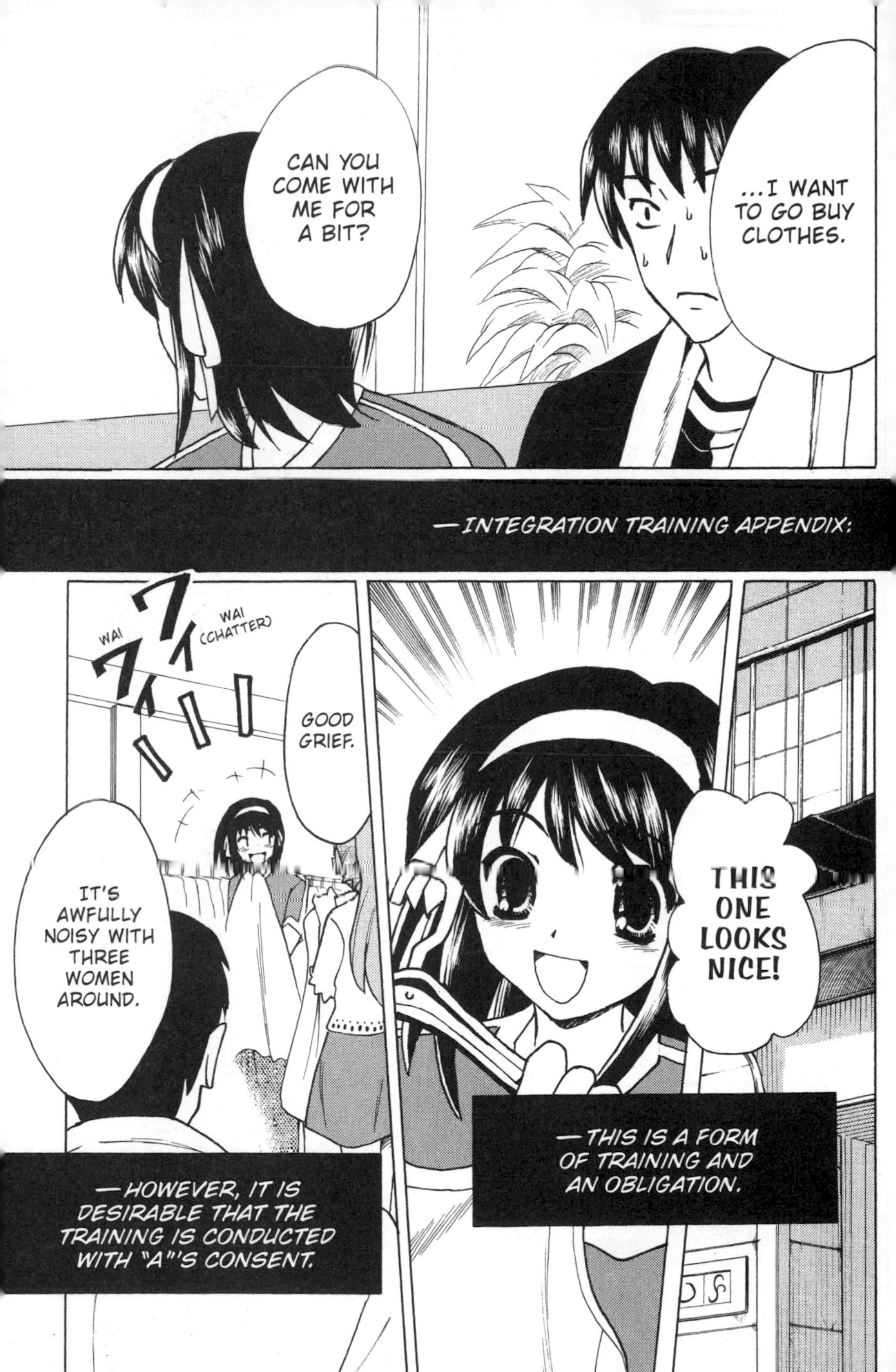
...I WANT TO GO BUY CLOTHES.
CAN YOU COME WITH ME FOR A BIT?
—INTEGRATION TRAINING APPENDIX:
THIS ONE LOOKS NICE!
—THIS IS A FORM OF TRAINING AND AN OBLIGATION.
ワイワイ
WAI
WAI (CHATTER)
GOOD GRIEF.
IT'S AWFULLY NOISY WITH THREE WOMEN AROUND.
—HOWEVER, IT IS DESIRABLE THAT THE TRAINING IS CONDUCTED WITH "A"'S CONSENT.

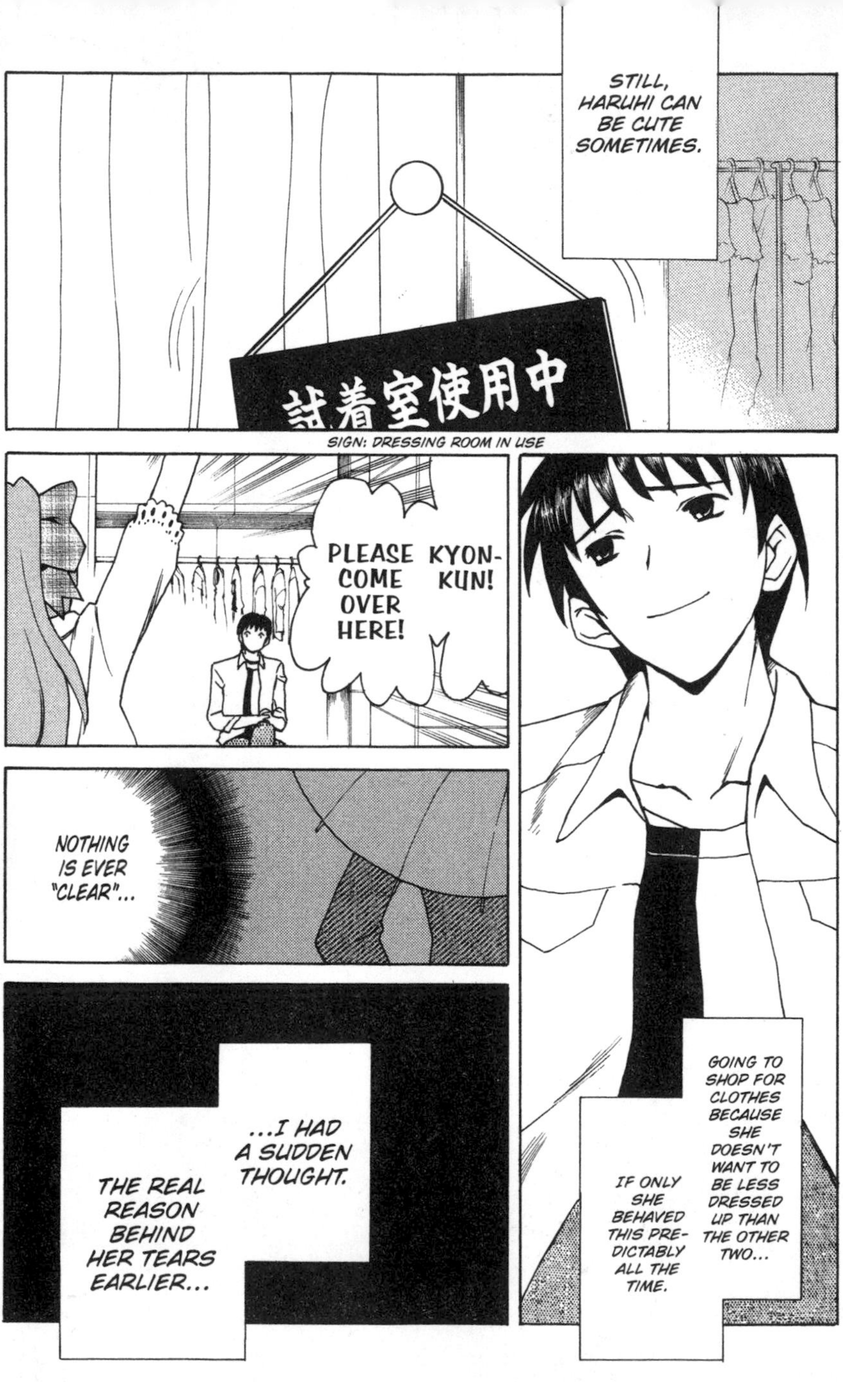
STILL, HARUHI CAN BE CUTE SOMETIMES.
試着室使用中
SIGN: DRESSING ROOM IN USE
GOING TO SHOP FOR CLOTHES BECAUSE SHE DOESN'T WANT TO BE LESS DRESSED UP THAN THE OTHER TWO...
IF ONLY SHE BEHAVED THIS PRE-DICTABLY ALL THE TIME.
KYON-KUN! PLEASE COME OVER HERE!
NOTHING IS EVER "CLEAR"...
...I HAD A SUDDEN THOUGHT.
THE REAL REASON BEHIND HER TEARS EARLIER...

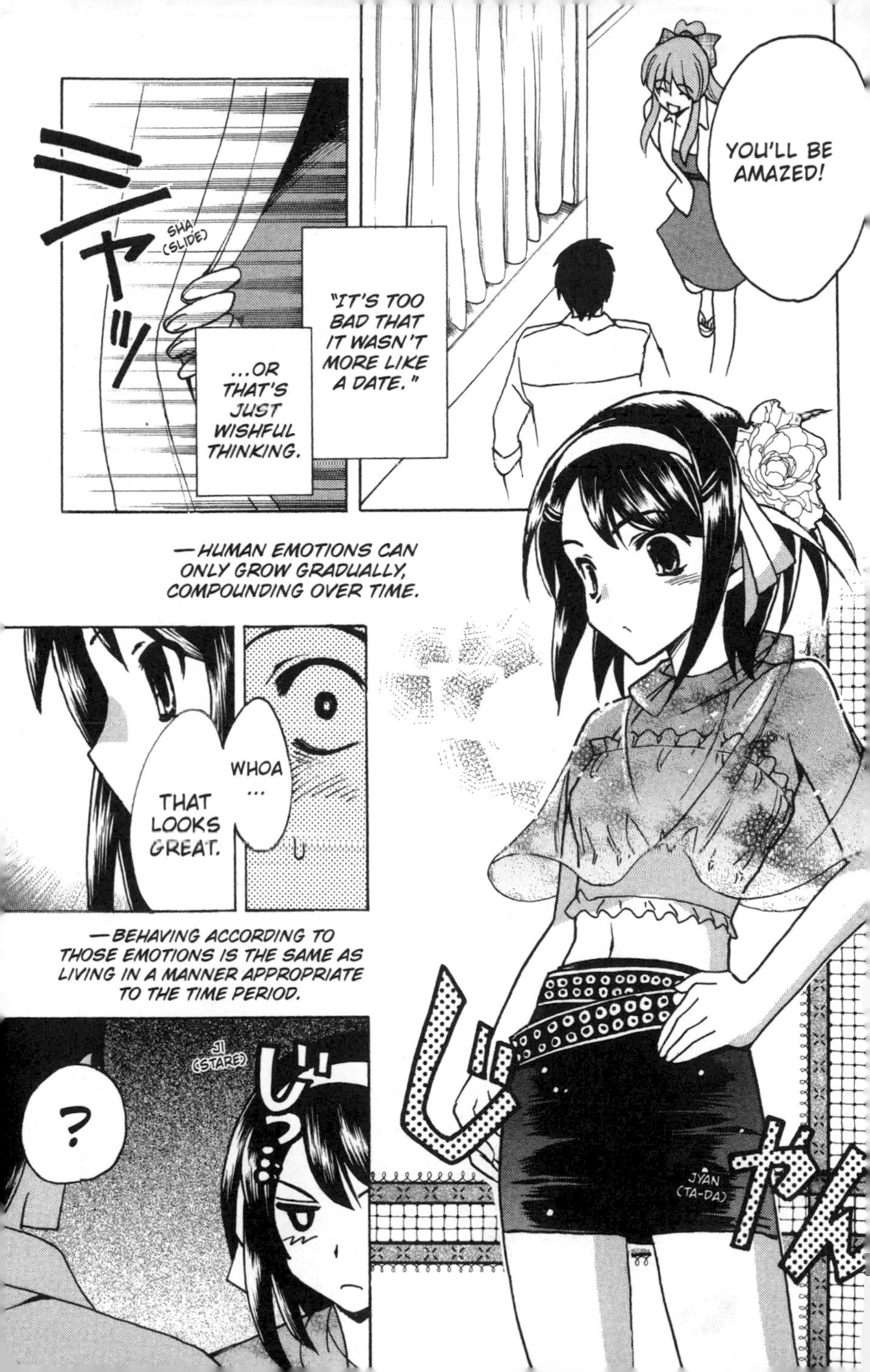

YOU'LL BE AMAZED!
"IT'S TOO BAD THAT IT WASN'T MORE LIKE A DATE."
...OR THAT'S JUST WISHFUL THINKING.
SHA (SLIDE)
JYAN (TA-DA)
—HUMAN EMOTIONS CAN ONLY GROW GRADUALLY, COMPOUNDING OVER TIME.
WHOA ...
THAT LOOKS GREAT.
—BEHAVING ACCORDING TO THOSE EMOTIONS IS THE SAME AS LIVING IN A MANNER APPROPRIATE TO THE TIME PERIOD.
JI (STARE)
?

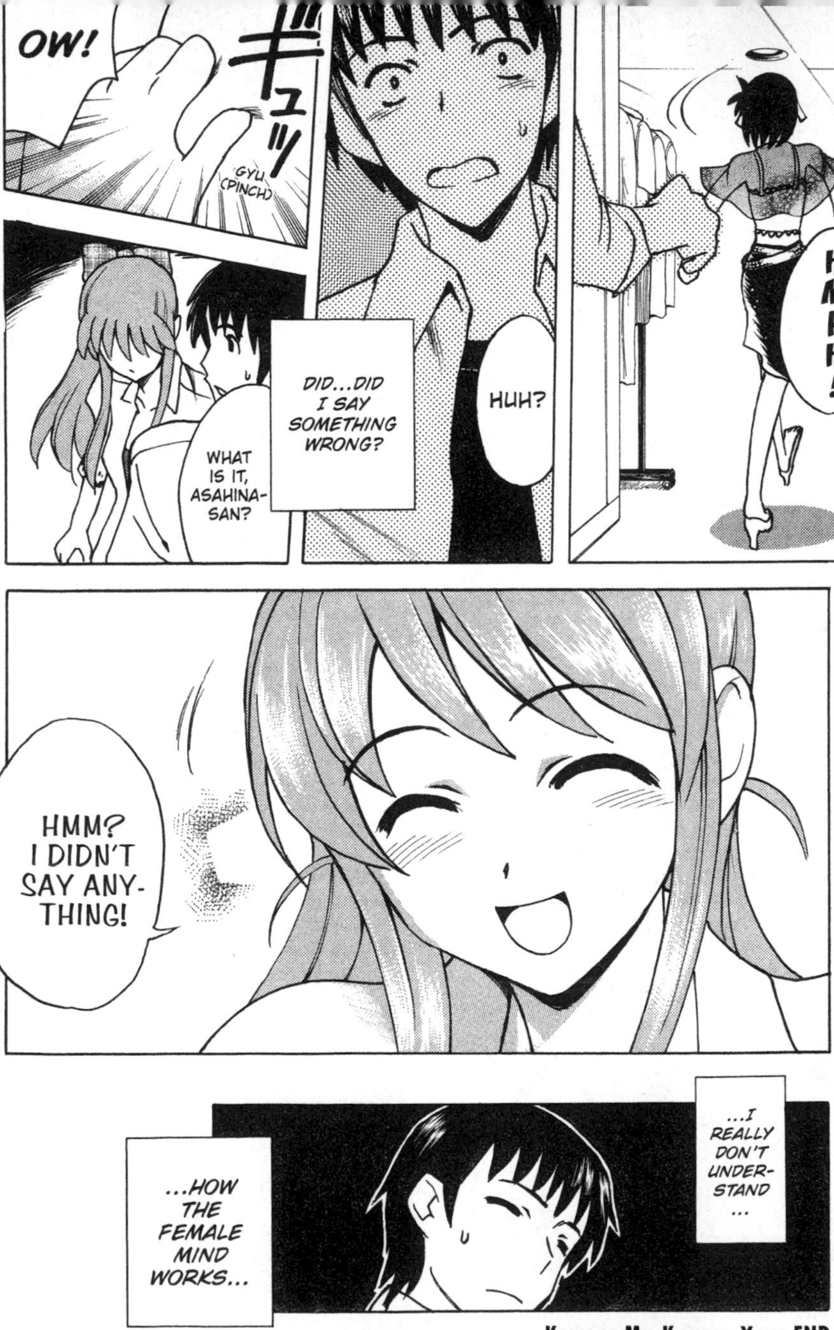
HMPH!
HUH?
DID...DID I SAY SOMETHING WRONG?
OW!
ギュッ
GYU (PINCH)
WHAT IS IT, ASAHINA-SAN?
HMM? I DIDN'T SAY ANY-THING!
...I REALLY DON'T UNDER-STAND...
...HOW THE FEMALE MIND WORKS...

Knowing Me, Knowing You : END

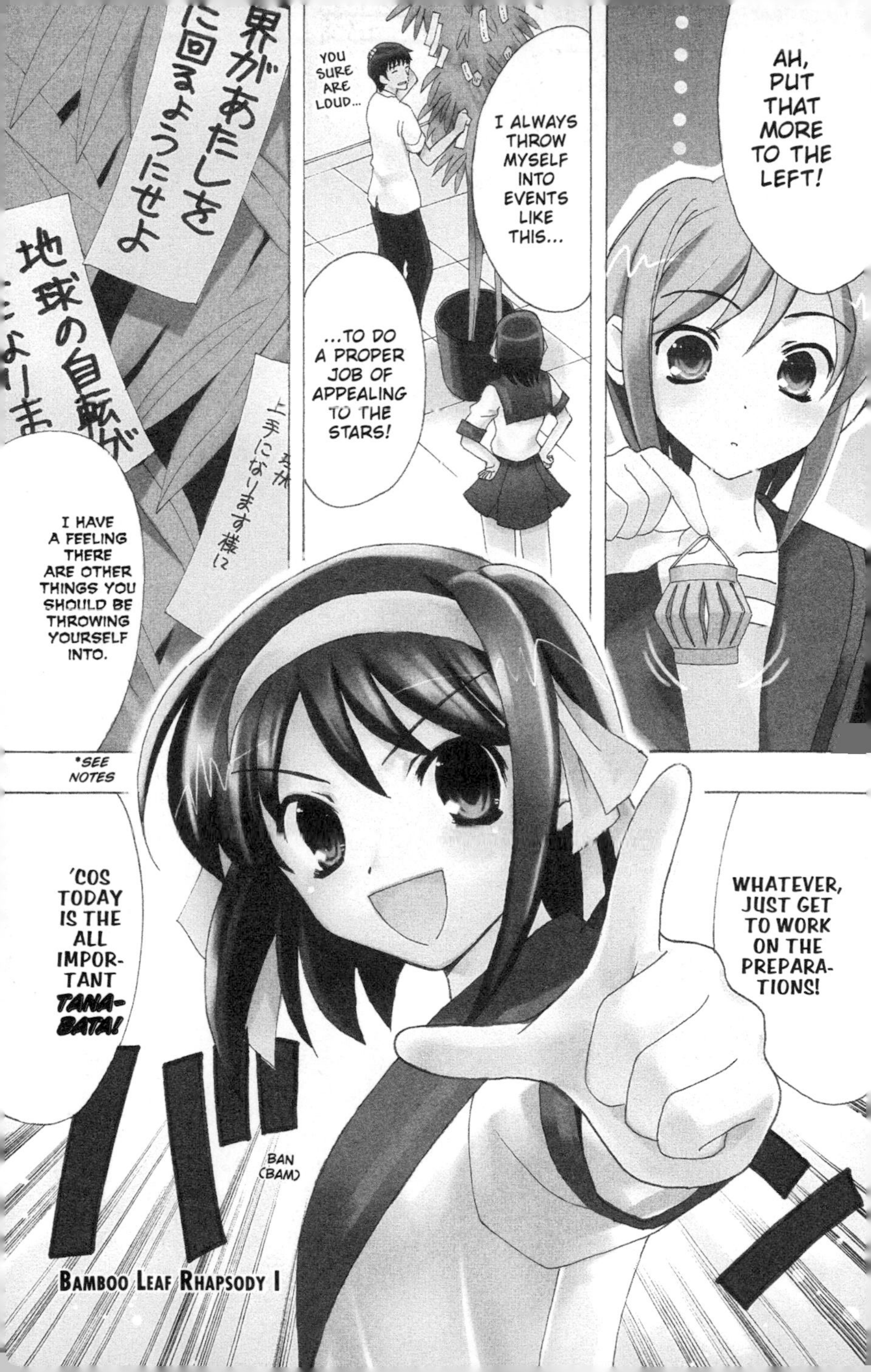
AH, PUT THAT MORE TO THE LEFT!
I ALWAYS THROW MYSELF INTO EVENTS LIKE THIS...
...TO DO A PROPER JOB OF APPEALING TO THE STARS!
YOU SURE ARE LOUD...
界があたしを
に回るようにせよ
地球の自転が
上手になります様に
I HAVE A FEELING THERE ARE OTHER THINGS YOU SHOULD BE THROWING YOURSELF INTO.
*SEE NOTES
WHATEVER, JUST GET TO WORK ON THE PREPARATIONS!
'COS TODAY IS THE ALL IMPORTANT TANABATA!
BAN (BAM)
BAMBOO LEAF RHAPSODY I

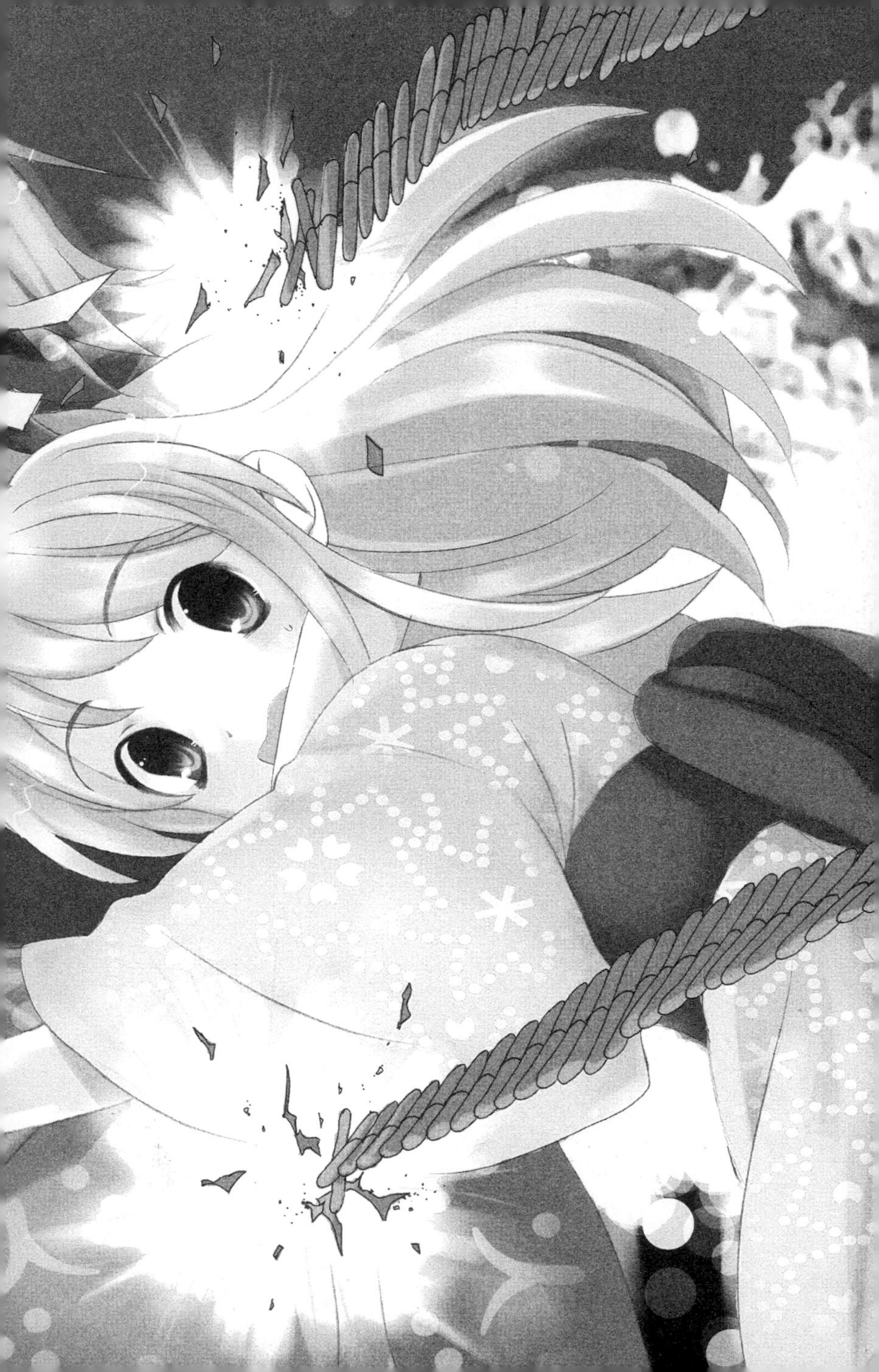

◎ Bamboo Leaf Rhapsody I

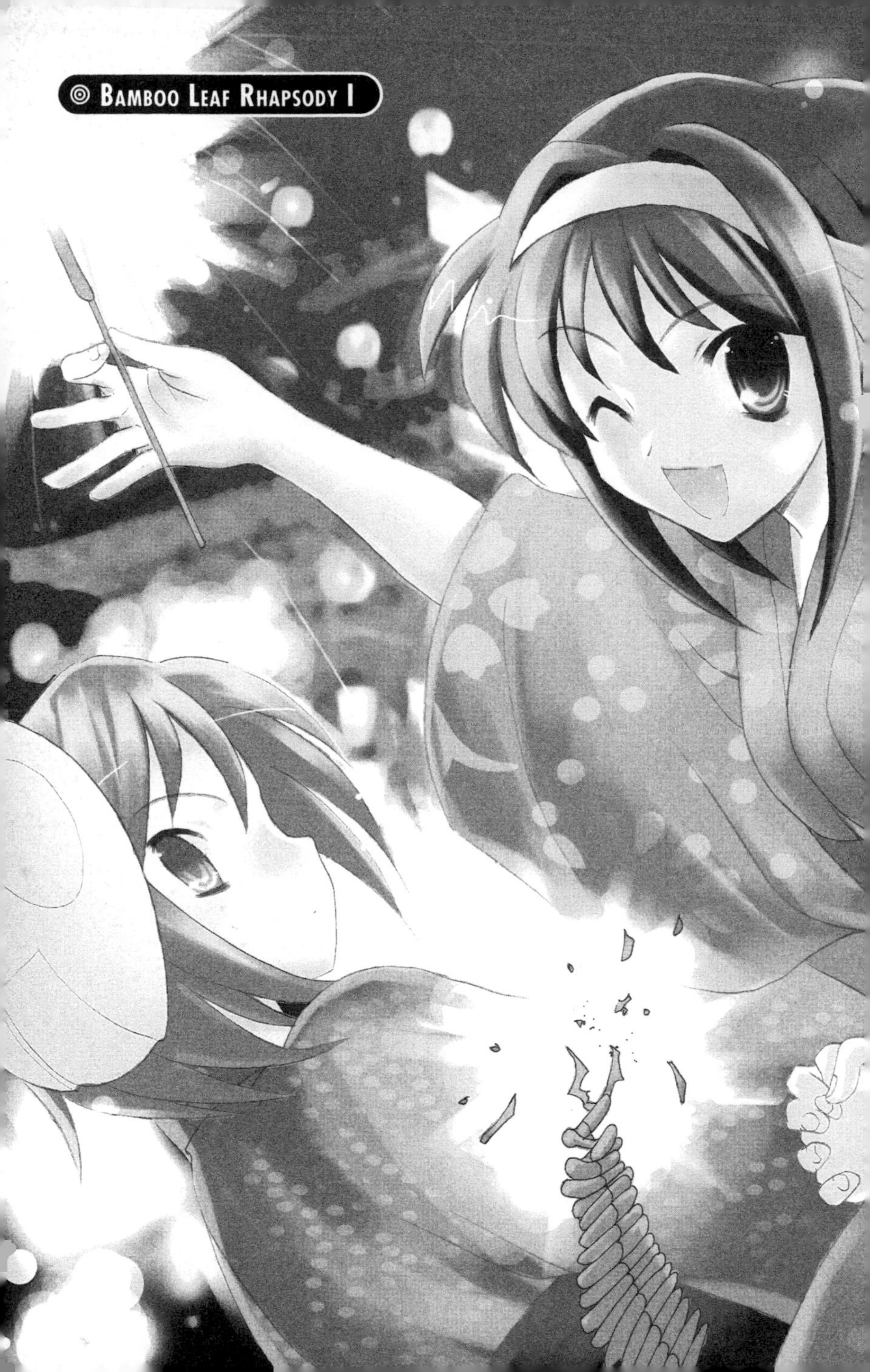

THE MELANCHOLY OF HARUHI SUZUMIYA

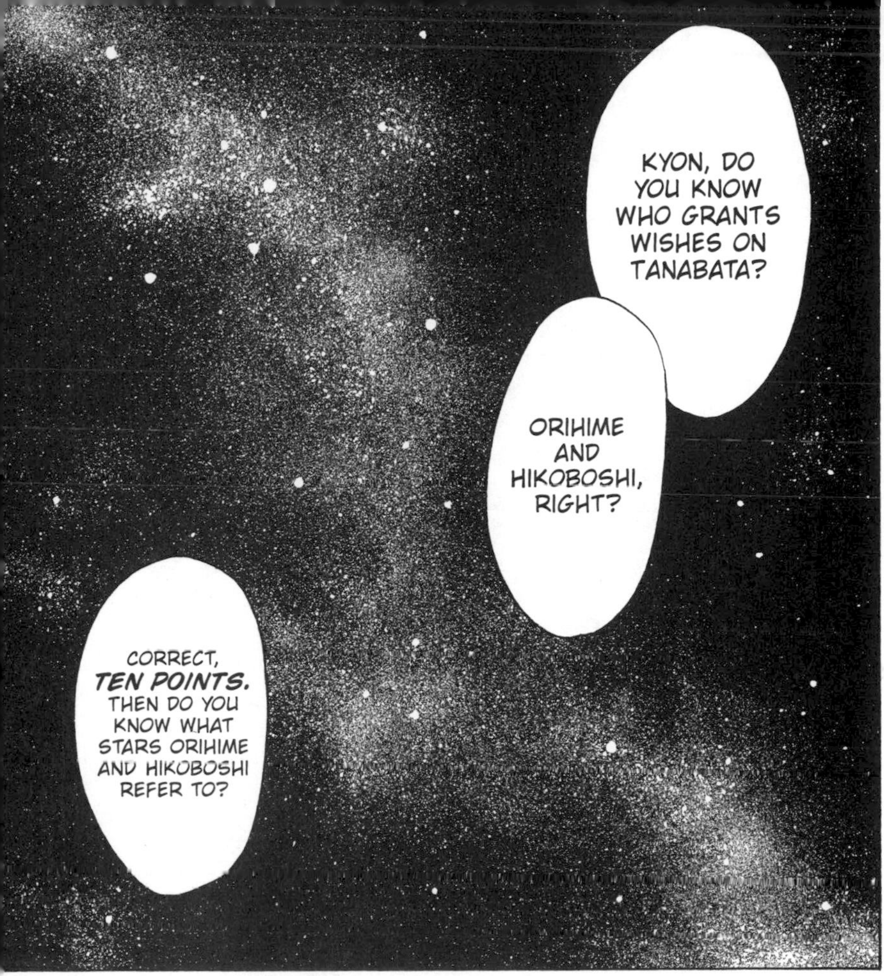
KYON, DO YOU KNOW WHO GRANTS WISHES ON TANABATA?
ORIHIME AND HIKOBOSHI, RIGHT?
CORRECT, **TEN POINTS.** THEN DO YOU KNOW WHAT STARS ORIHIME AND HIKOBOSHI REFER TO?
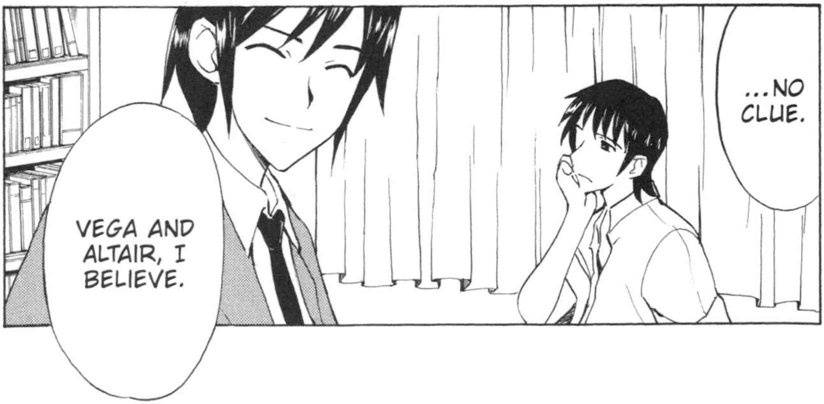
...NO CLUE.
VEGA AND ALTAIR, I BELIEVE.

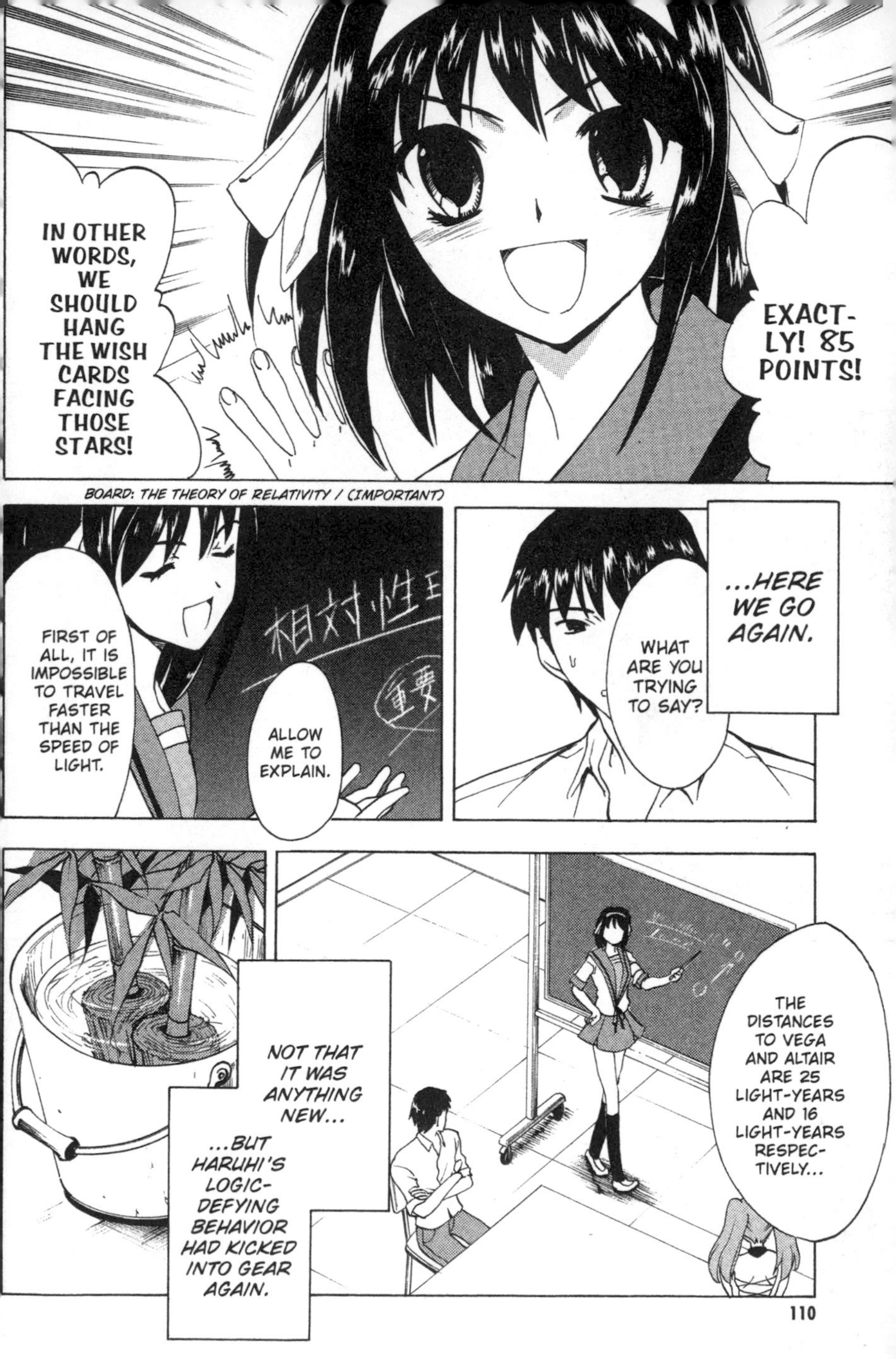

IN OTHER WORDS, WE SHOULD HANG THE WISH CARDS FACING THOSE STARS!
EXACT-LY! 85 POINTS!
...HERE WE GO AGAIN.
WHAT ARE YOU TRYING TO SAY?
BOARD: THE THEORY OF RELATIVITY / (IMPORTANT)
ALLOW ME TO EXPLAIN.
FIRST OF ALL, IT IS IMPOSSIBLE TO TRAVEL FASTER THAN THE SPEED OF LIGHT.
THE DISTANCES TO VEGA AND ALTAIR ARE 25 LIGHT-YEARS AND 16 LIGHT-YEARS RESPEC-TIVELY...
NOT THAT IT WAS ANYTHING NEW...
...BUT HARUHI'S LOGIC-DEFYING BEHAVIOR HAD KICKED INTO GEAR AGAIN.

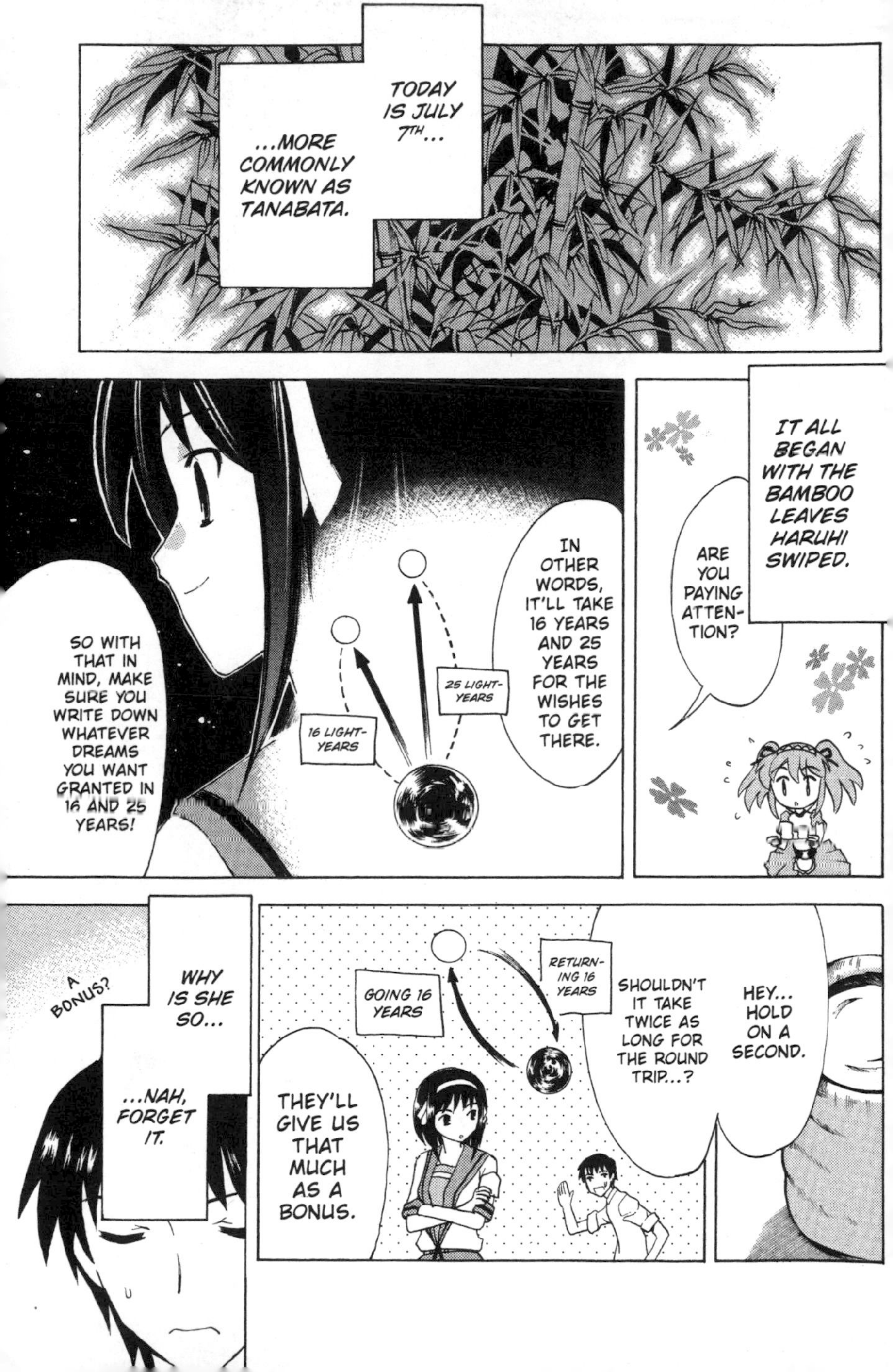
TODAY IS JULY 7TH...
...MORE COMMONLY KNOWN AS TANABATA.
IT ALL BEGAN WITH THE BAMBOO LEAVES HARUHI SWIPED.
ARE YOU PAYING ATTEN-TION?
IN OTHER WORDS, IT'LL TAKE 16 YEARS AND 25 YEARS FOR THE WISHES TO GET THERE.
25 LIGHT-YEARS
16 LIGHT-YEARS
SO WITH THAT IN MIND, MAKE SURE YOU WRITE DOWN WHATEVER DREAMS YOU WANT GRANTED IN 16 AND 25 YEARS!
HEY... HOLD ON A SECOND.
SHOULDN'T IT TAKE TWICE AS LONG FOR THE ROUND TRIP...?
RETURN-ING 16 YEARS
GOING 16 YEARS
THEY'LL GIVE US THAT MUCH AS A BONUS.
A BONUS?
WHY IS SHE SO...
...NAH, FORGET IT.

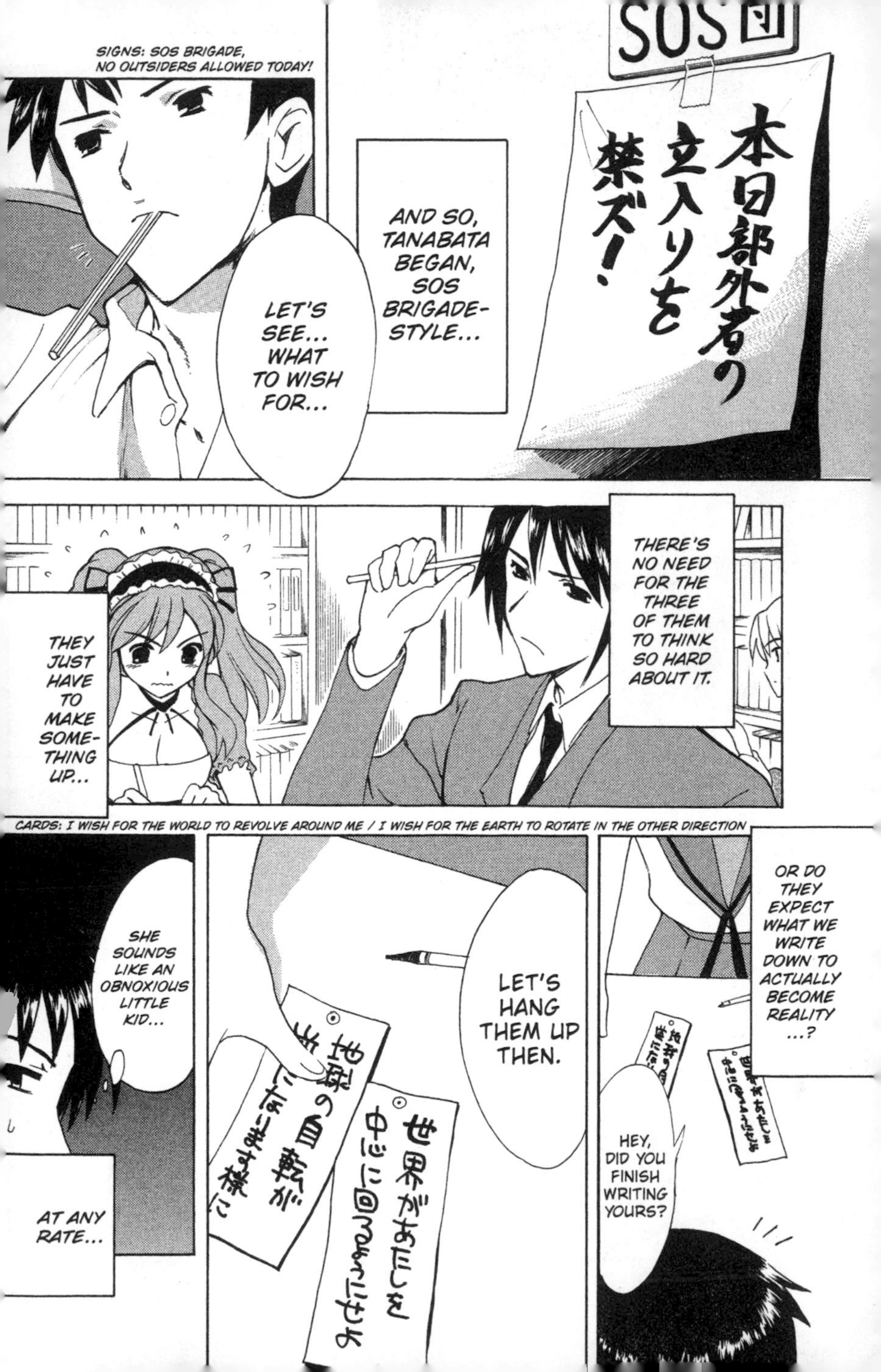
SOS団
本日部外者の立入りを禁ズ！
SIGNS: SOS BRIGADE, NO OUTSIDERS ALLOWED TODAY!
AND SO, TANABATA BEGAN, SOS BRIGADE-STYLE...
LET'S SEE... WHAT TO WISH FOR...
THERE'S NO NEED FOR THE THREE OF THEM TO THINK SO HARD ABOUT IT.
THEY JUST HAVE TO MAKE SOMETHING UP...
CARDS: I WISH FOR THE WORLD TO REVOLVE AROUND ME / I WISH FOR THE EARTH TO ROTATE IN THE OTHER DIRECTION
OR DO THEY EXPECT WHAT WE WRITE DOWN TO ACTUALLY BECOME REALITY ...?
HEY, DID YOU FINISH WRITING YOURS?
LET'S HANG THEM UP THEN.
世界があたしを中心に回るようにせよ
地球の自転が逆になります様に
SHE SOUNDS LIKE AN OBNOXIOUS LITTLE KID...
AT ANY RATE...

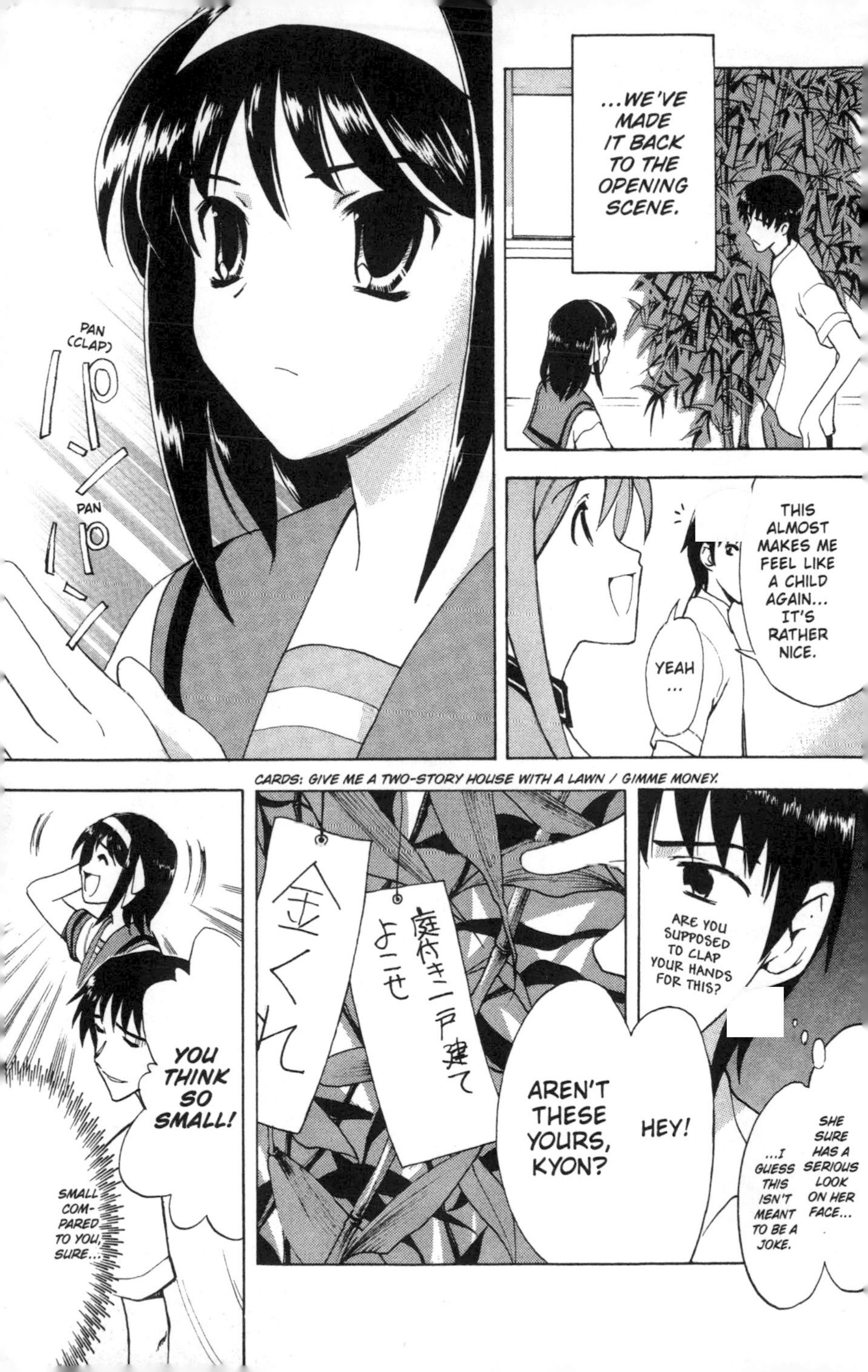
...WE'VE MADE IT BACK TO THE OPENING SCENE.
THIS ALMOST MAKES ME FEEL LIKE A CHILD AGAIN... IT'S RATHER NICE.
YEAH...
PAN (CLAP)
PAN
CARDS: GIVE ME A TWO-STORY HOUSE WITH A LAWN / GIMME MONEY.
ARE YOU SUPPOSED TO CLAP YOUR HANDS FOR THIS?
SHE SURE HAS A SERIOUS LOOK ON HER FACE...
...I GUESS THIS ISN'T MEANT TO BE A JOKE.
庭付き一戸建てよこせ
金くれ
HEY!
AREN'T THESE YOURS, KYON?
YOU THINK SO SMALL!
SMALL COMPARED TO YOU, SURE...

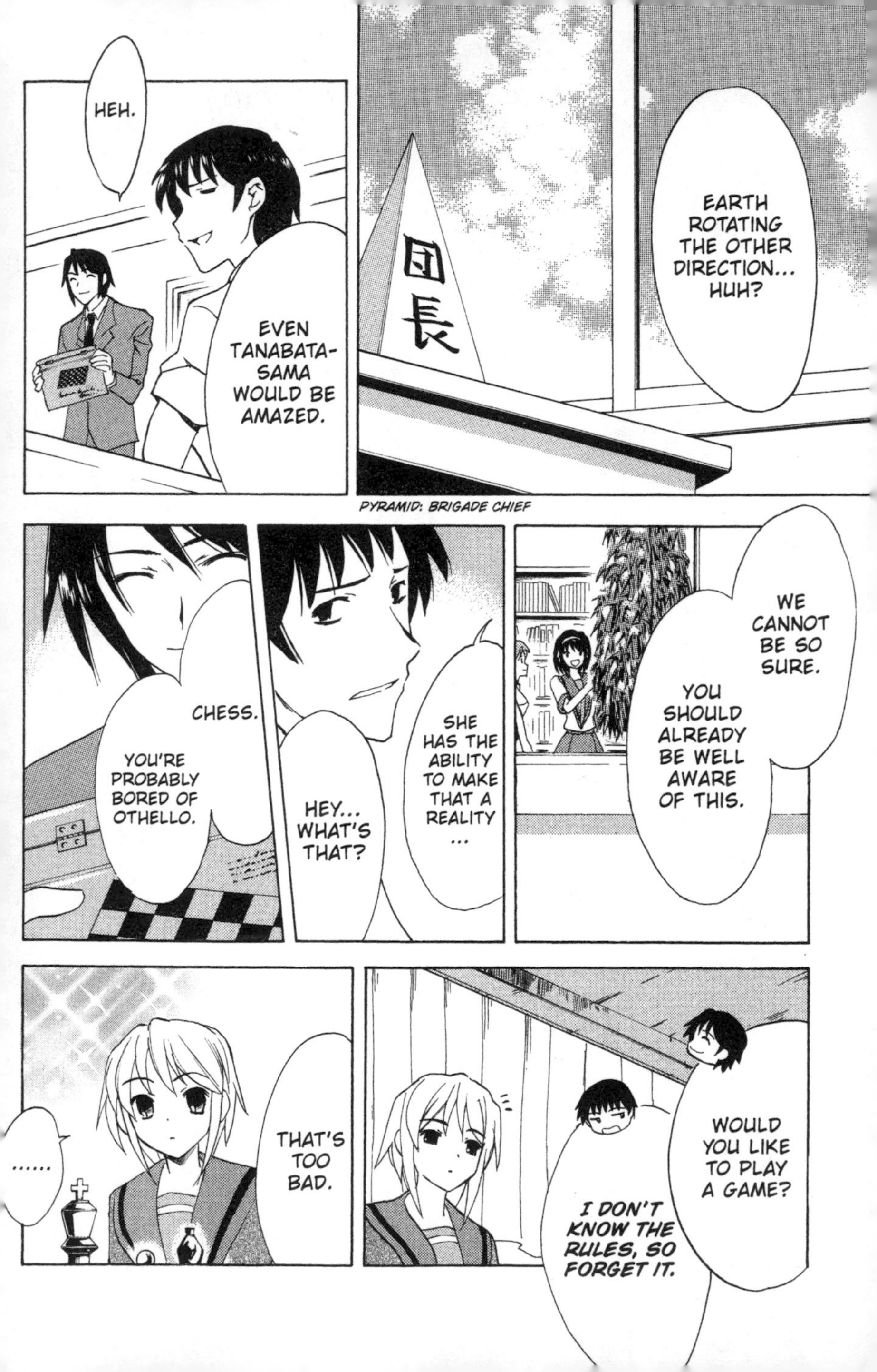
EARTH ROTATING THE OTHER DIRECTION... HUH?
團長
HEH.
EVEN TANABATA-SAMA WOULD BE AMAZED.
PYRAMID: BRIGADE CHIEF
WE CANNOT BE SO SURE.
YOU SHOULD ALREADY BE WELL AWARE OF THIS.
SHE HAS THE ABILITY TO MAKE THAT A REALITY...
HEY... WHAT'S THAT?
CHESS.
YOU'RE PROBABLY BORED OF OTHELLO.
WOULD YOU LIKE TO PLAY A GAME?
I DON'T KNOW THE RULES, SO FORGET IT.
THAT'S TOO BAD.
......

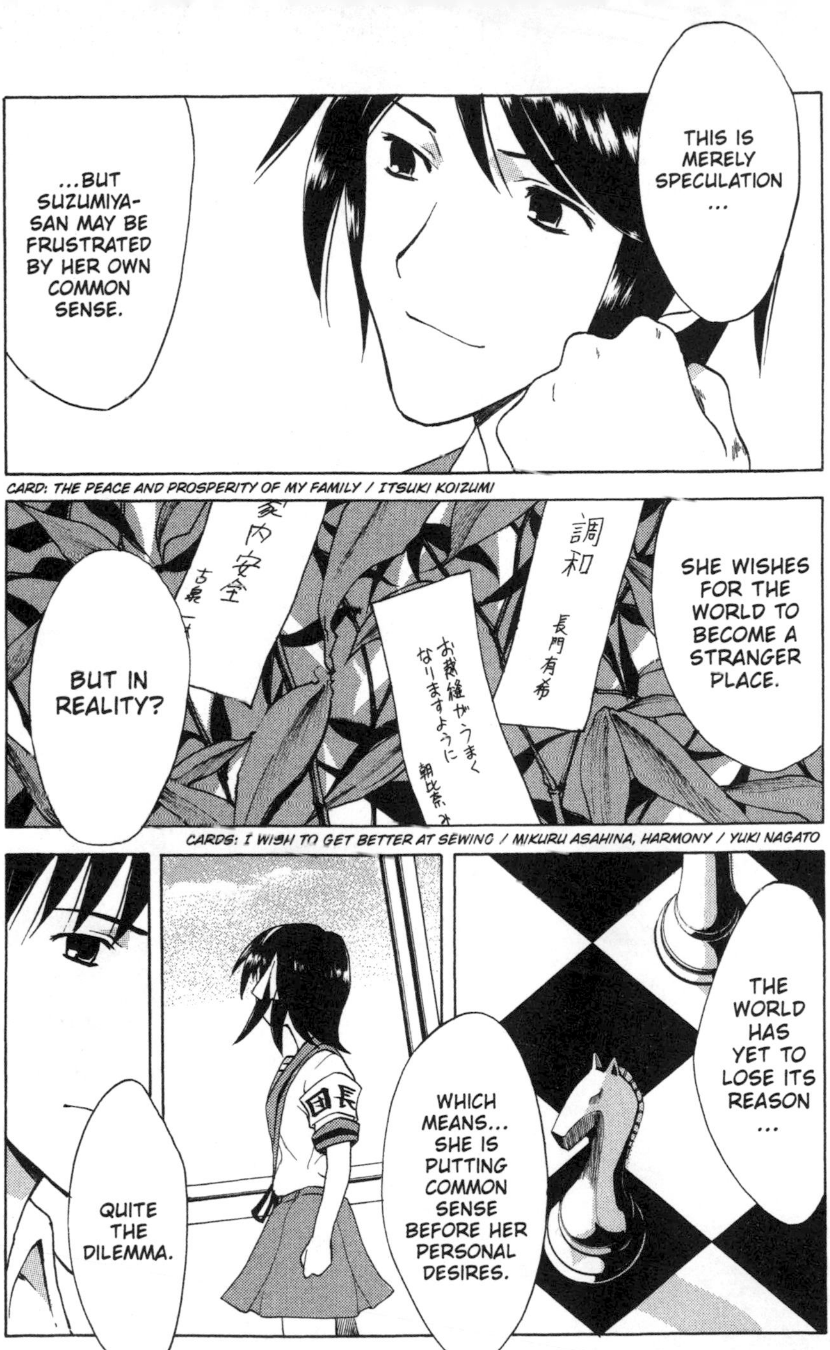
THIS IS MERELY SPECULATION ...
...BUT SUZUMIYA-SAN MAY BE FRUSTRATED BY HER OWN COMMON SENSE.
CARD: THE PEACE AND PROSPERITY OF MY FAMILY / ITSUKI KOIZUMI
SHE WISHES FOR THE WORLD TO BECOME A STRANGER PLACE.
調和 長門有希
お裁縫がうまくなりますように 朝比奈み
家内安全 古泉一
BUT IN REALITY?
CARDS: I WISH TO GET BETTER AT SEWING / MIKURU ASAHINA, HARMONY / YUKI NAGATO
THE WORLD HAS YET TO LOSE ITS REASON ...
WHICH MEANS... SHE IS PUTTING COMMON SENSE BEFORE HER PERSONAL DESIRES.
QUITE THE DILEMMA.

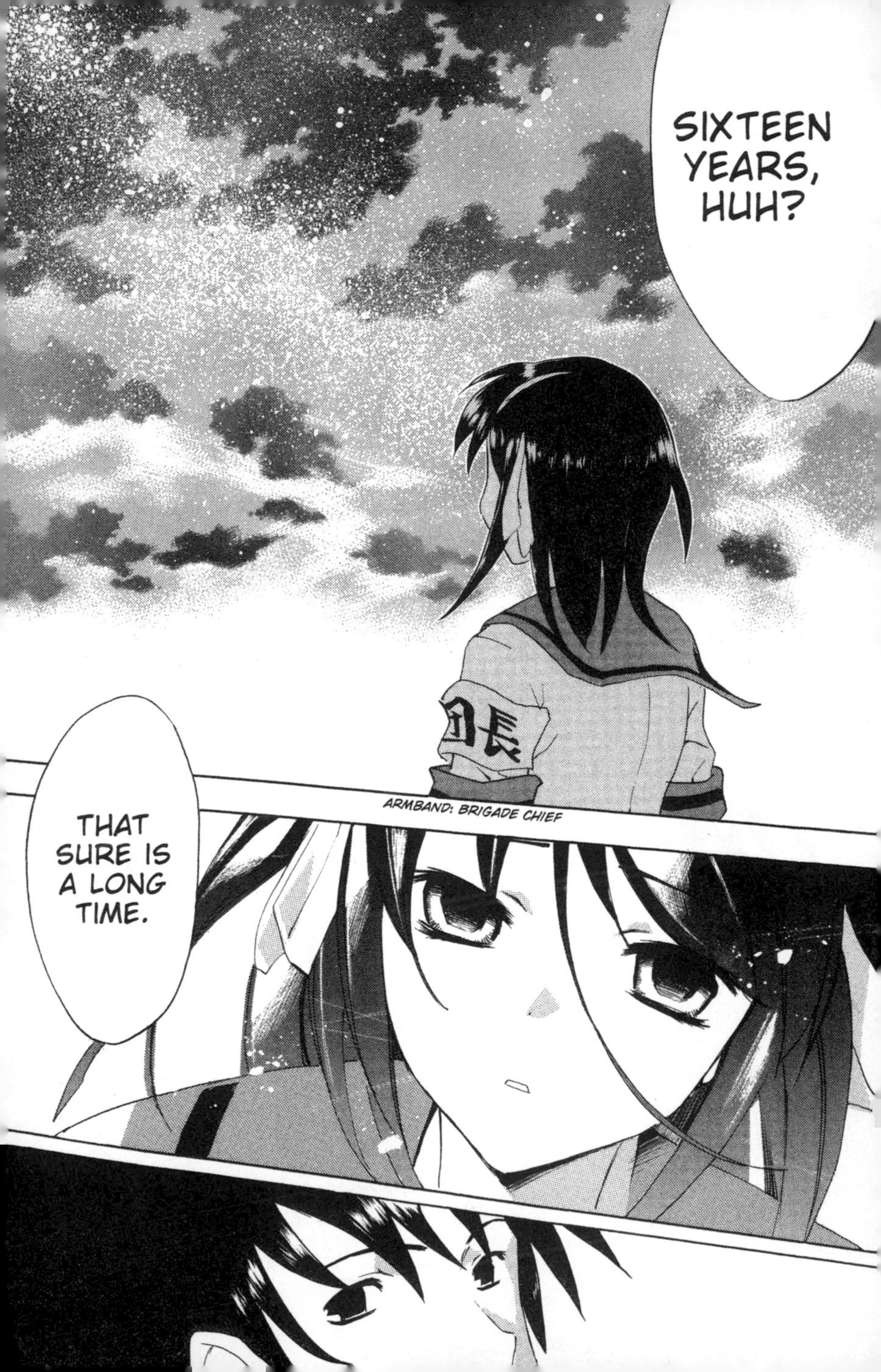
SIXTEEN YEARS, HUH?
ARMBAND: BRIGADE CHIEF
THAT SURE IS A LONG TIME.

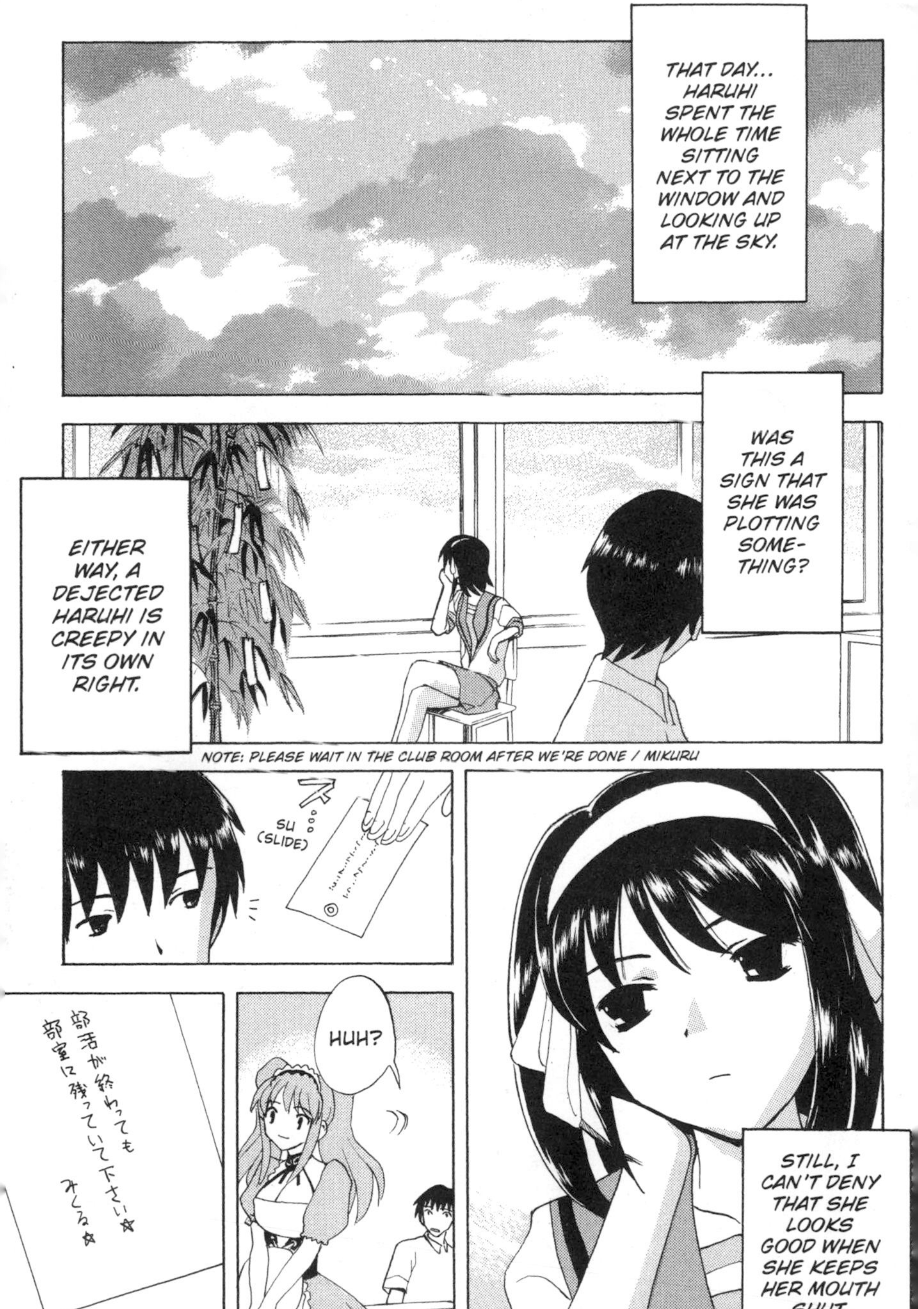
THAT DAY... HARUHI SPENT THE WHOLE TIME SITTING NEXT TO THE WINDOW AND LOOKING UP AT THE SKY.
WAS THIS A SIGN THAT SHE WAS PLOTTING SOME-THING?
EITHER WAY, A DEJECTED HARUHI IS CREEPY IN ITS OWN RIGHT.
NOTE: PLEASE WAIT IN THE CLUB ROOM AFTER WE'RE DONE / MIKURU
STILL, I CAN'T DENY THAT SHE LOOKS GOOD WHEN SHE KEEPS HER MOUTH SHUT.
SU (SLIDE)
HUH?
部活が終わっても部室に残っていて下さい☆
みくる☆

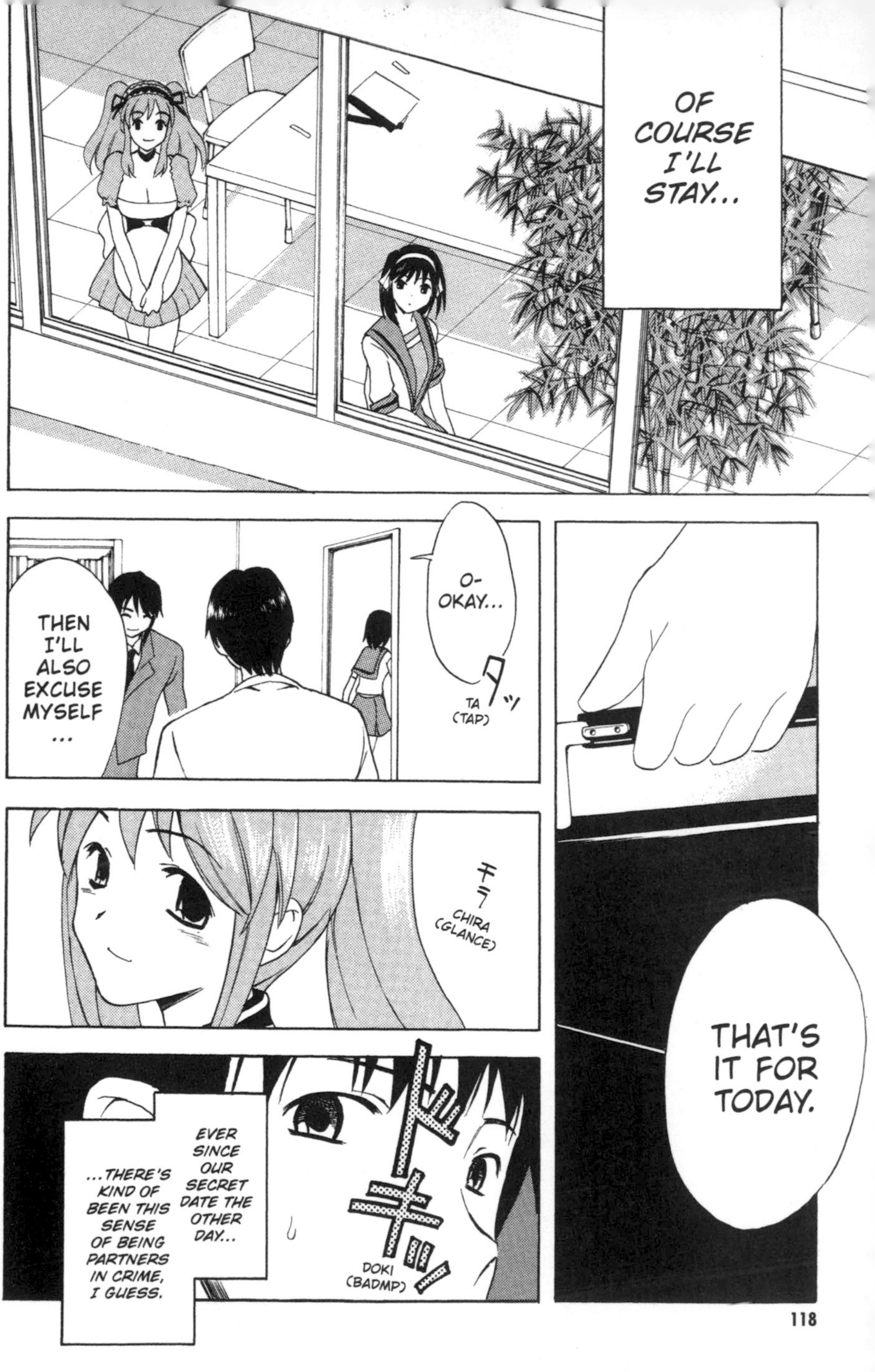
OF COURSE I'LL STAY...
THAT'S IT FOR TODAY.
O-OKAY...
タッ
TA (TAP)
THEN I'LL ALSO EXCUSE MYSELF...
チラ
CHIRA (GLANCE)
ドキッ
DOKI (BADMP)
EVER SINCE OUR SECRET DATE THE OTHER DAY...
...THERE'S KIND OF BEEN THIS SENSE OF BEING PARTNERS IN CRIME, I GUESS.

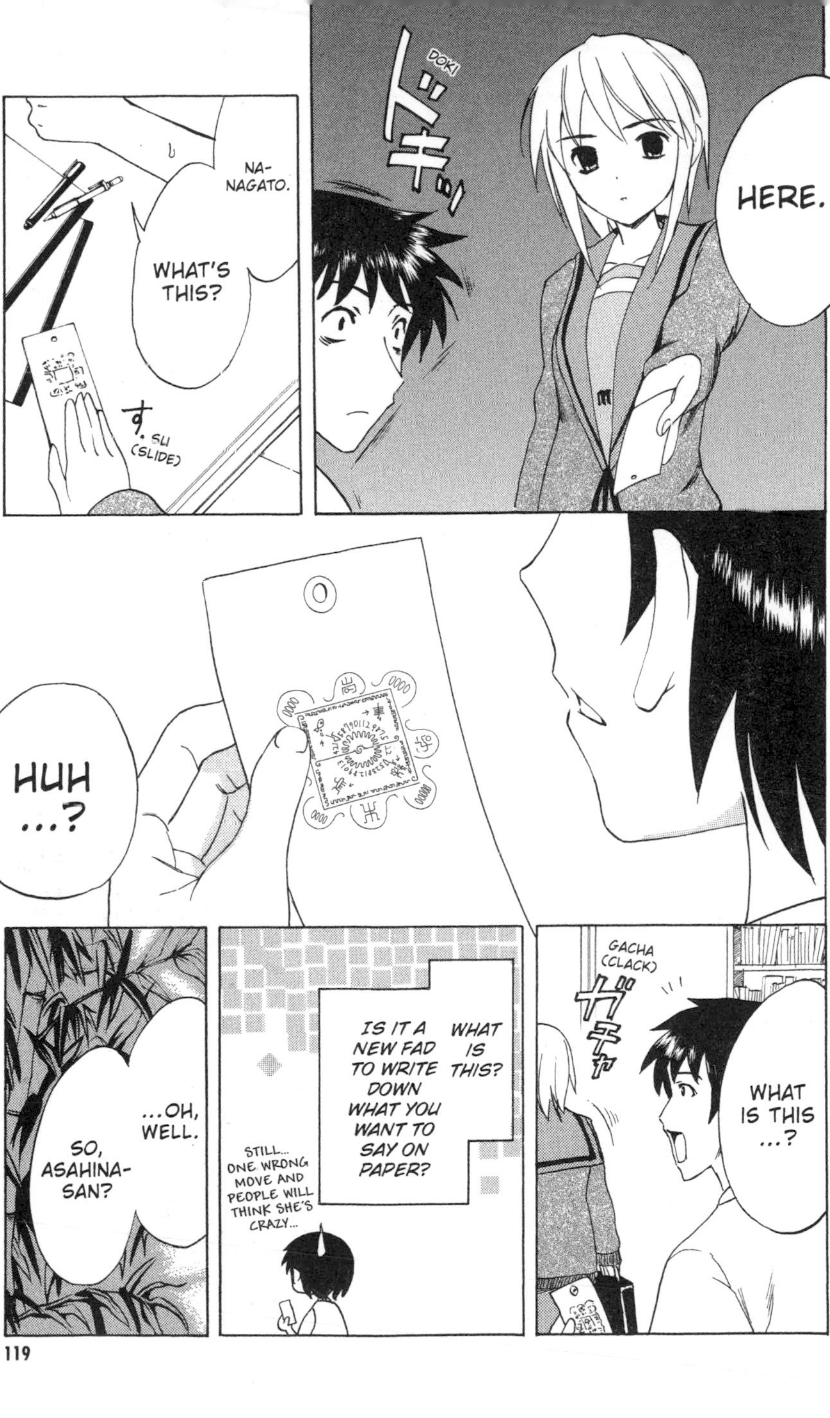
DOKI
ドキッ
HERE.
NA-NAGATO.
WHAT'S THIS?
す
SU (SLIDE)
HUH ...?
GACHA (CLACK)
ガチャ
WHAT IS THIS ...?
WHAT IS THIS?
IS IT A NEW FAD TO WRITE DOWN WHAT YOU WANT TO SAY ON PAPER?
STILL... ONE WRONG MOVE AND PEOPLE WILL THINK SHE'S CRAZY...
...OH, WELL.
SO, ASAHINA-SAN?

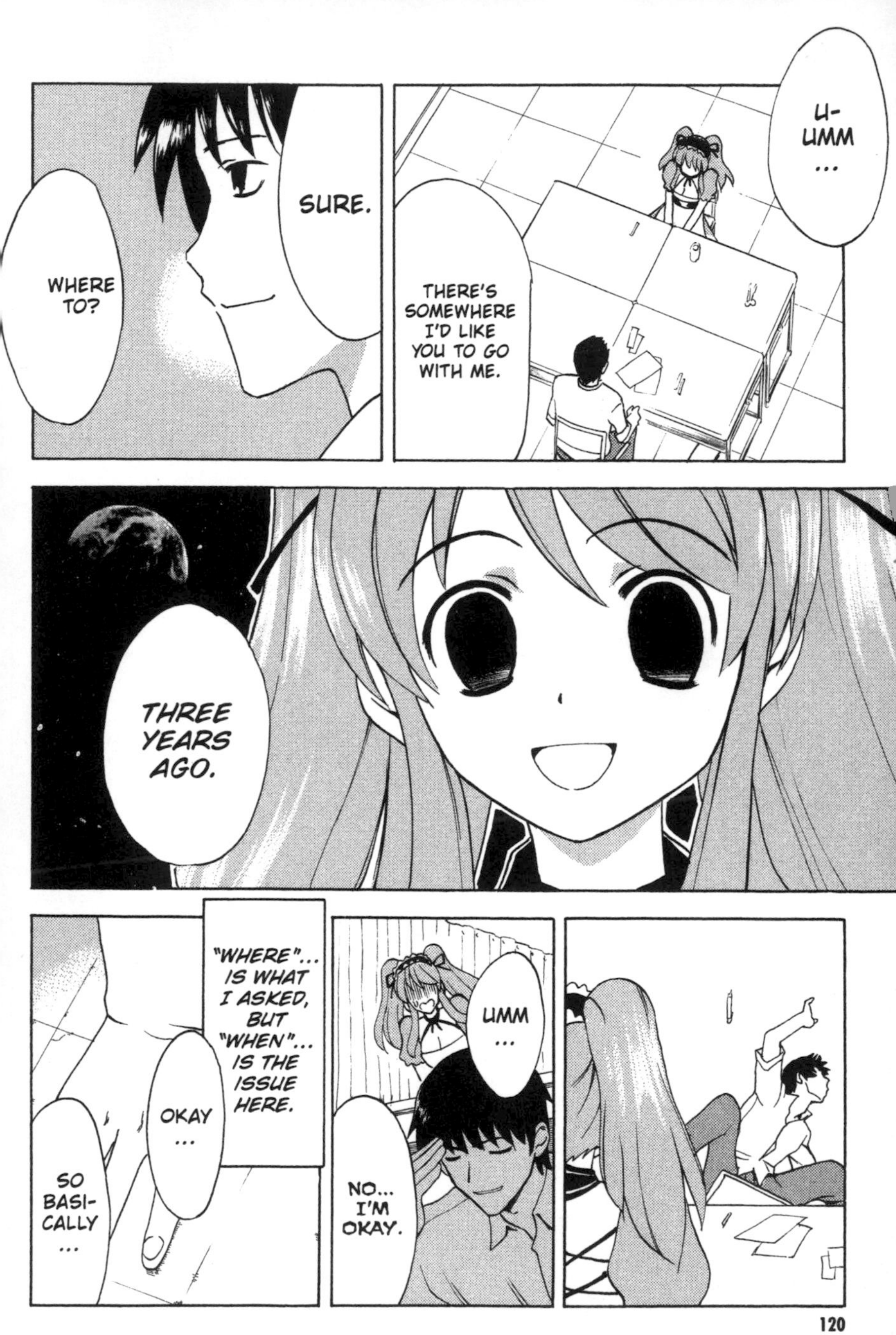
U-UMM...
THERE'S SOMEWHERE I'D LIKE YOU TO GO WITH ME.
SURE.
WHERE TO?
THREE YEARS AGO.
UMM...
NO... I'M OKAY.
"WHERE"... IS WHAT I ASKED, BUT "WHEN"... IS THE ISSUE HERE.
OKAY...
SO BASICALLY...

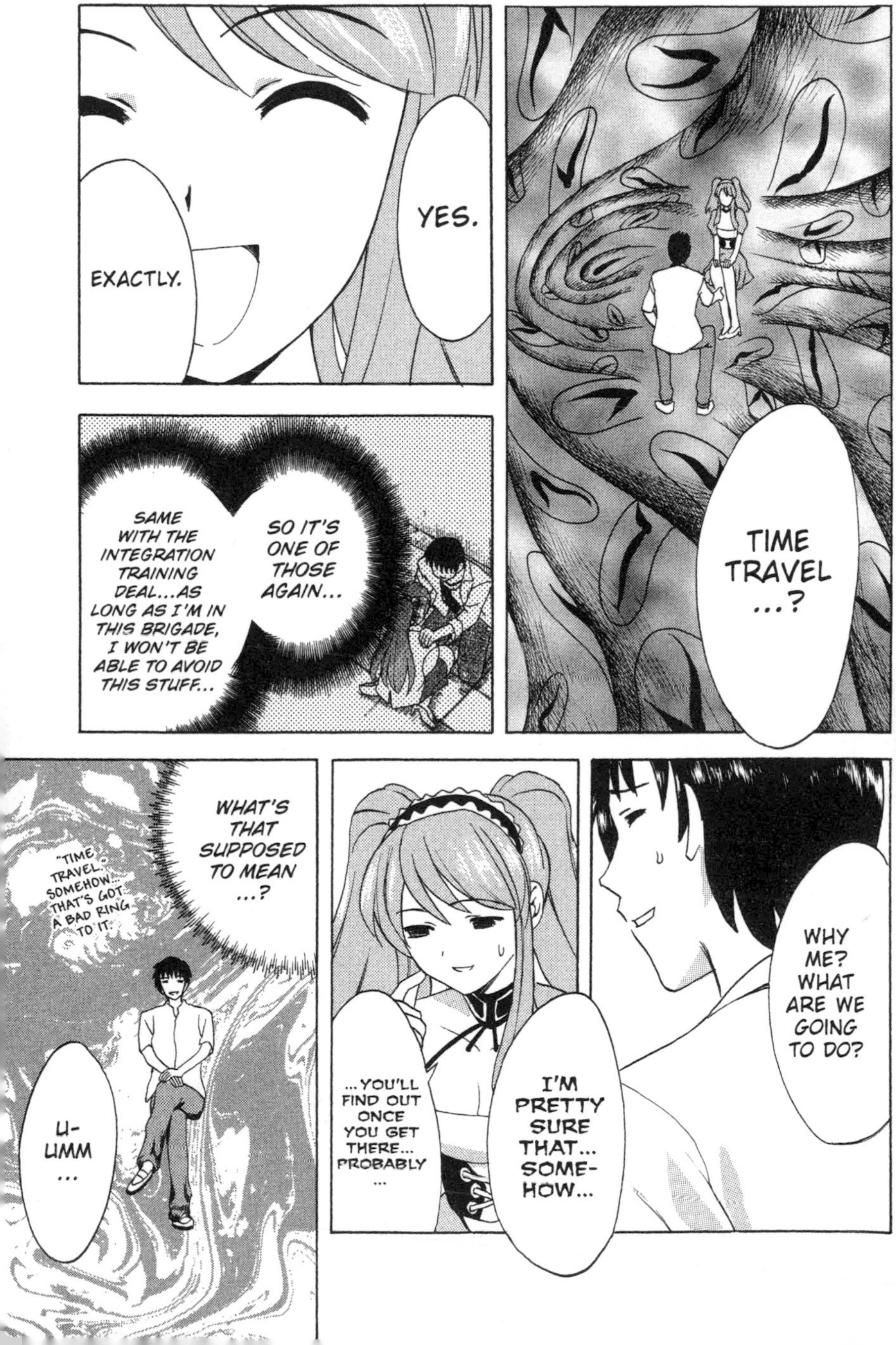
TIME TRAVEL ...?
YES.
EXACTLY.
SO IT'S ONE OF THOSE AGAIN...
SAME WITH THE INTEGRATION TRAINING DEAL...AS LONG AS I'M IN THIS BRIGADE, I WON'T BE ABLE TO AVOID THIS STUFF...
WHY ME? WHAT ARE WE GOING TO DO?
I'M PRETTY SURE THAT... SOME-HOW...
...YOU'LL FIND OUT ONCE YOU GET THERE... PROBABLY ...
WHAT'S THAT SUPPOSED TO MEAN ...?
"TIME TRAVEL." SOMEHOW... THAT'S GOT A BAD RING TO IT.
U-UMM ...

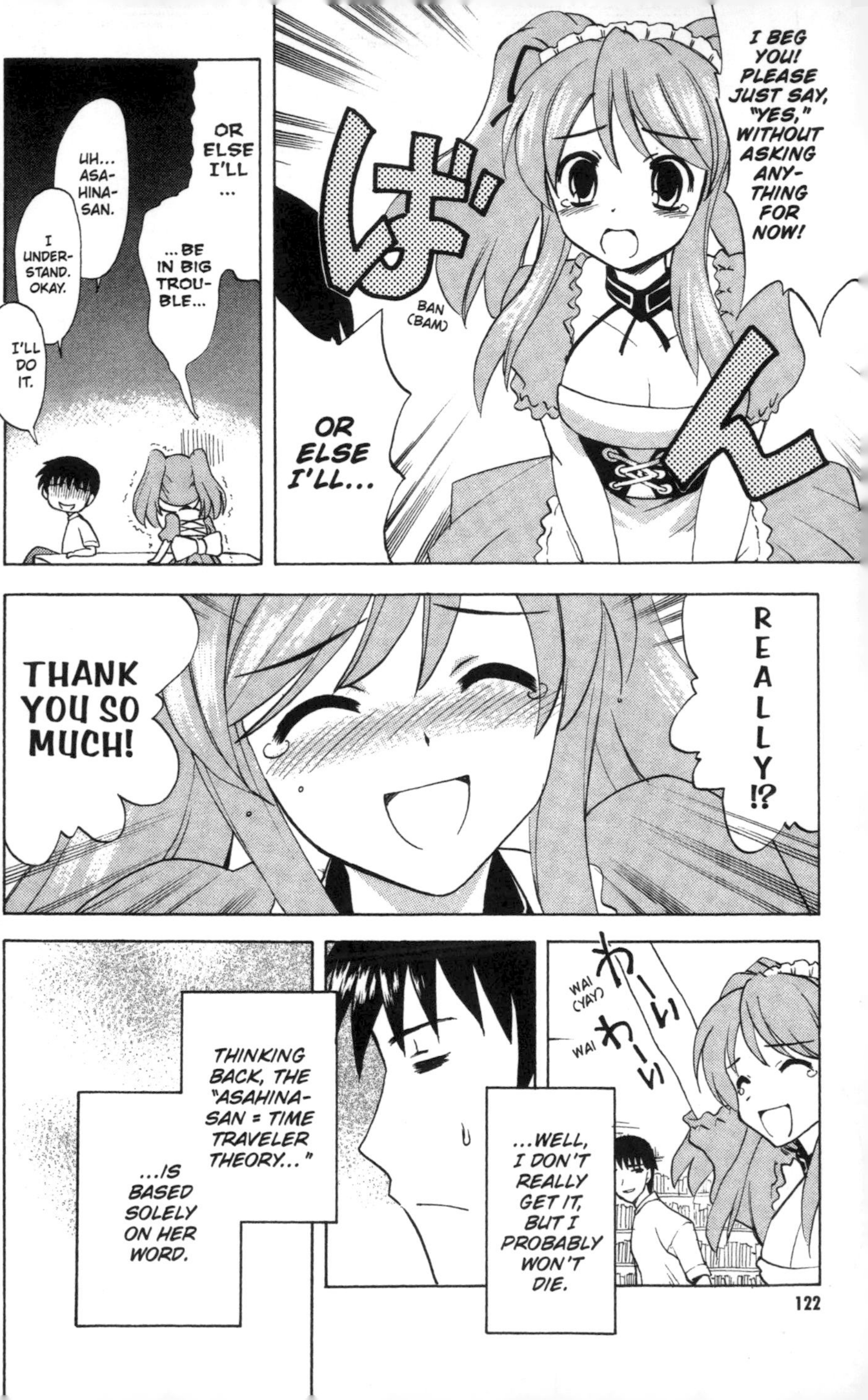
I BEG YOU! PLEASE JUST SAY, "YES," WITHOUT ASKING ANYTHING FOR NOW!
ばん
BAN (BAM)
OR ELSE I'LL...
OR ELSE I'LL ...
...BE IN BIG TROUBLE...
UH... ASAHINA-SAN.
I UNDERSTAND. OKAY.
I'LL DO IT.
REALLY!?
THANK YOU SO MUCH!
わーい
WAI (YAY)
わーい
WAI
...WELL, I DON'T REALLY GET IT, BUT I PROBABLY WON'T DIE.
THINKING BACK, THE "ASAHINA-SAN = TIME TRAVELER THEORY..."
...IS BASED SOLELY ON HER WORD.

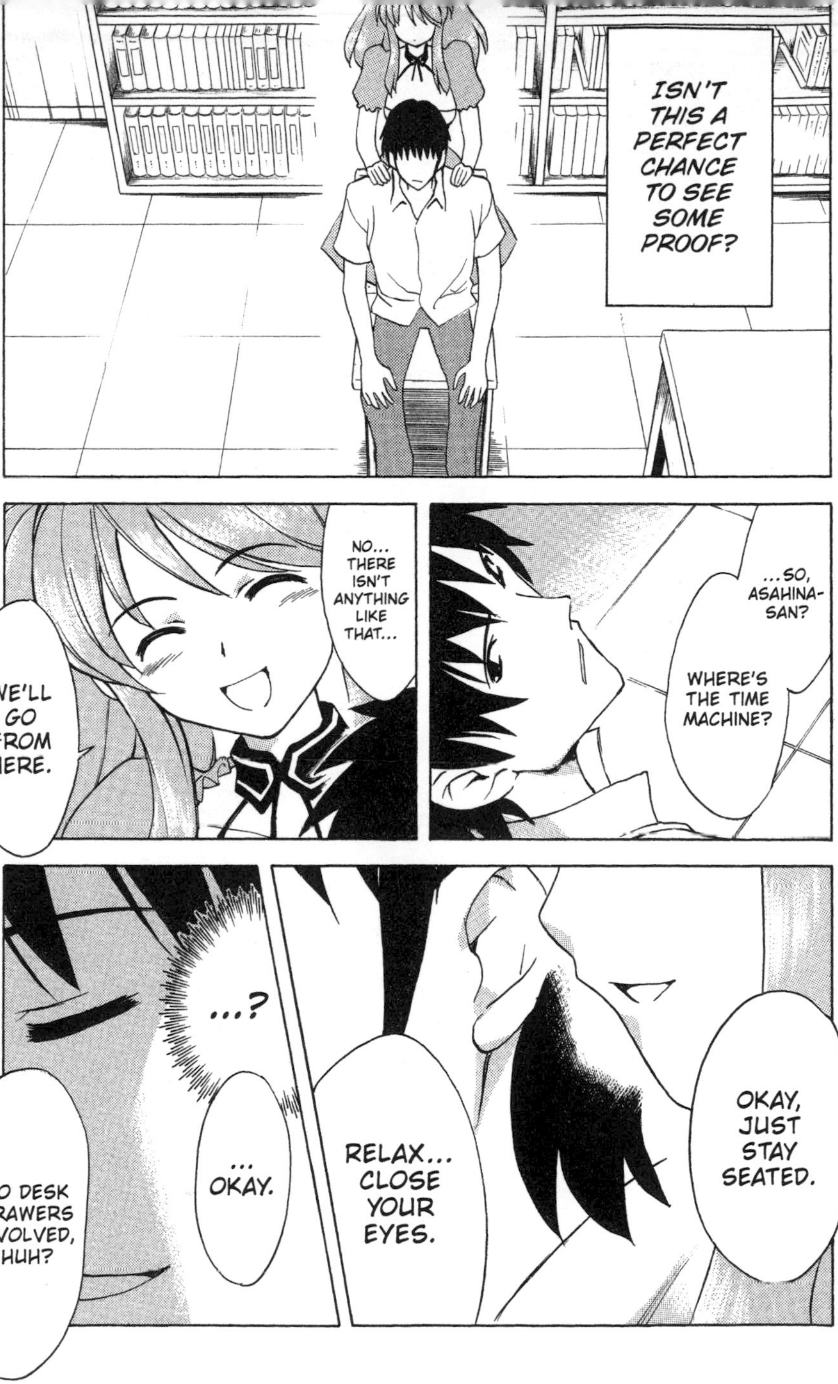
ISN'T THIS A PERFECT CHANCE TO SEE SOME PROOF?
...SO, ASAHINA-SAN?
WHERE'S THE TIME MACHINE?
NO... THERE ISN'T ANYTHING LIKE THAT...
WE'LL GO FROM HERE.
OKAY, JUST STAY SEATED.
RELAX... CLOSE YOUR EYES.
...?
...OKAY.
NO DESK DRAWERS INVOLVED, HUH?

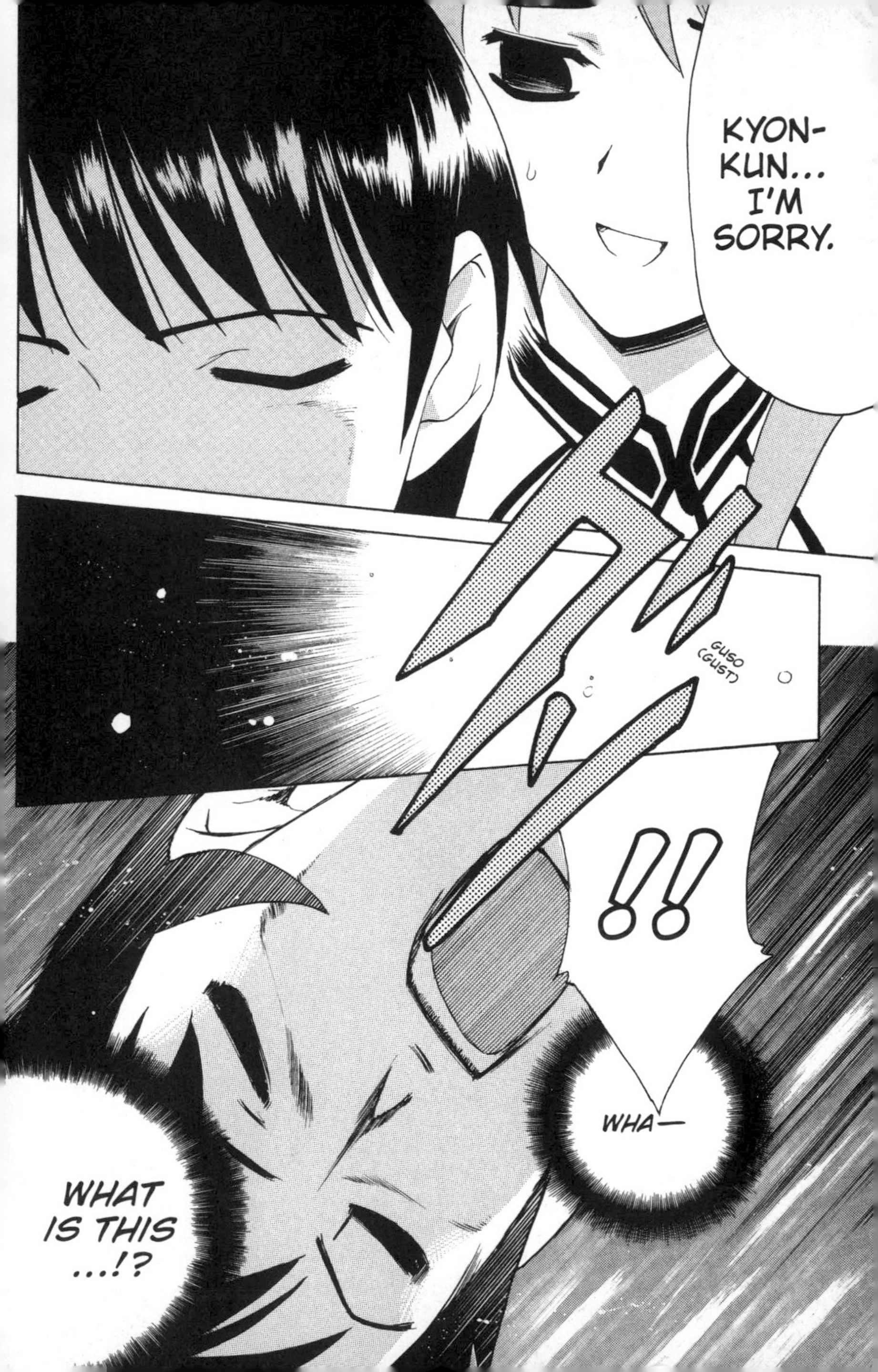
KYON-KUN... I'M SORRY.
GUSO (GUST)
!!
WHA—
WHAT IS THIS ...!?

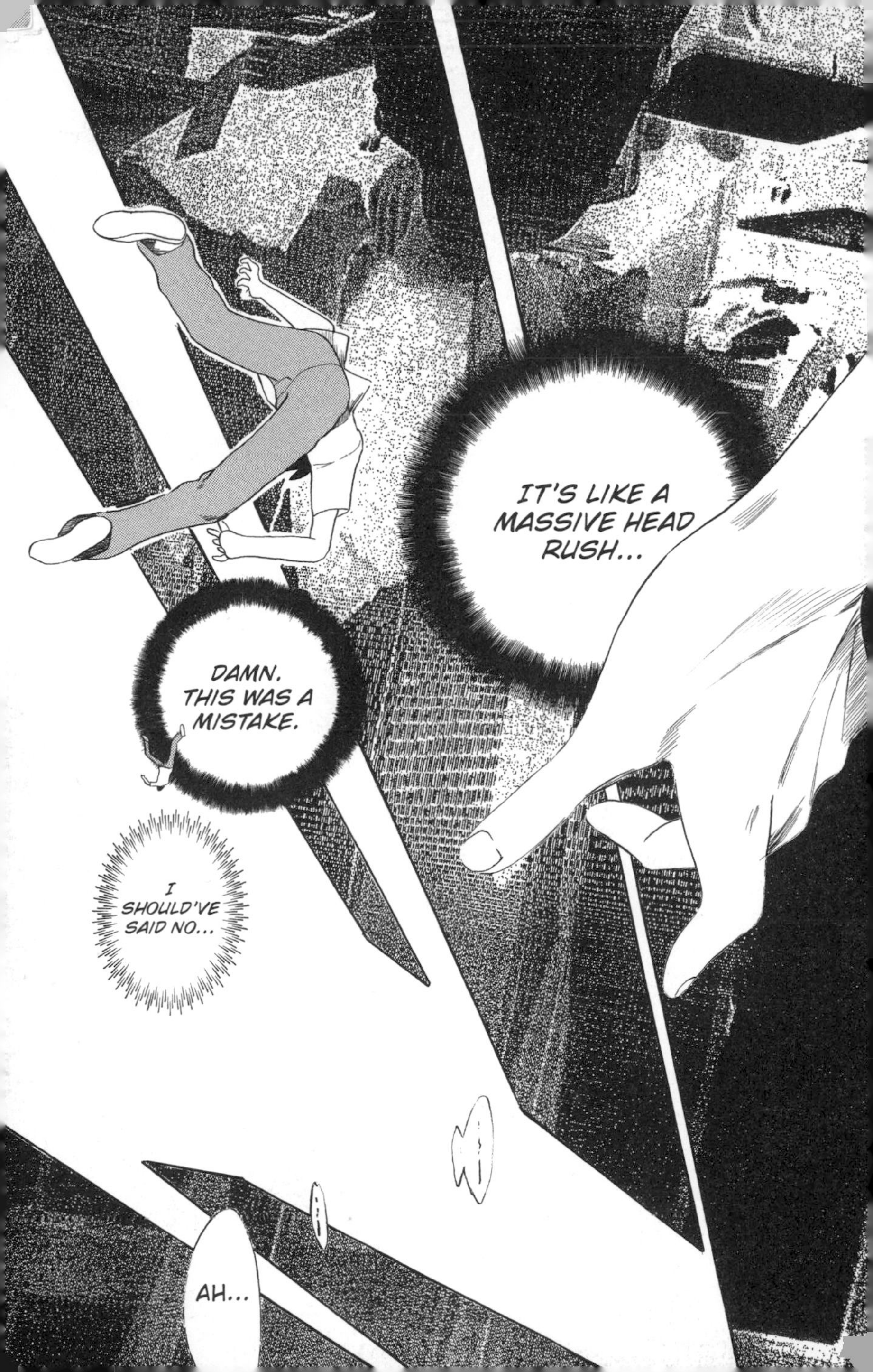
IT'S LIKE A MASSIVE HEAD RUSH...
DAMN. THIS WAS A MISTAKE.
I SHOULD'VE SAID NO...
AH...

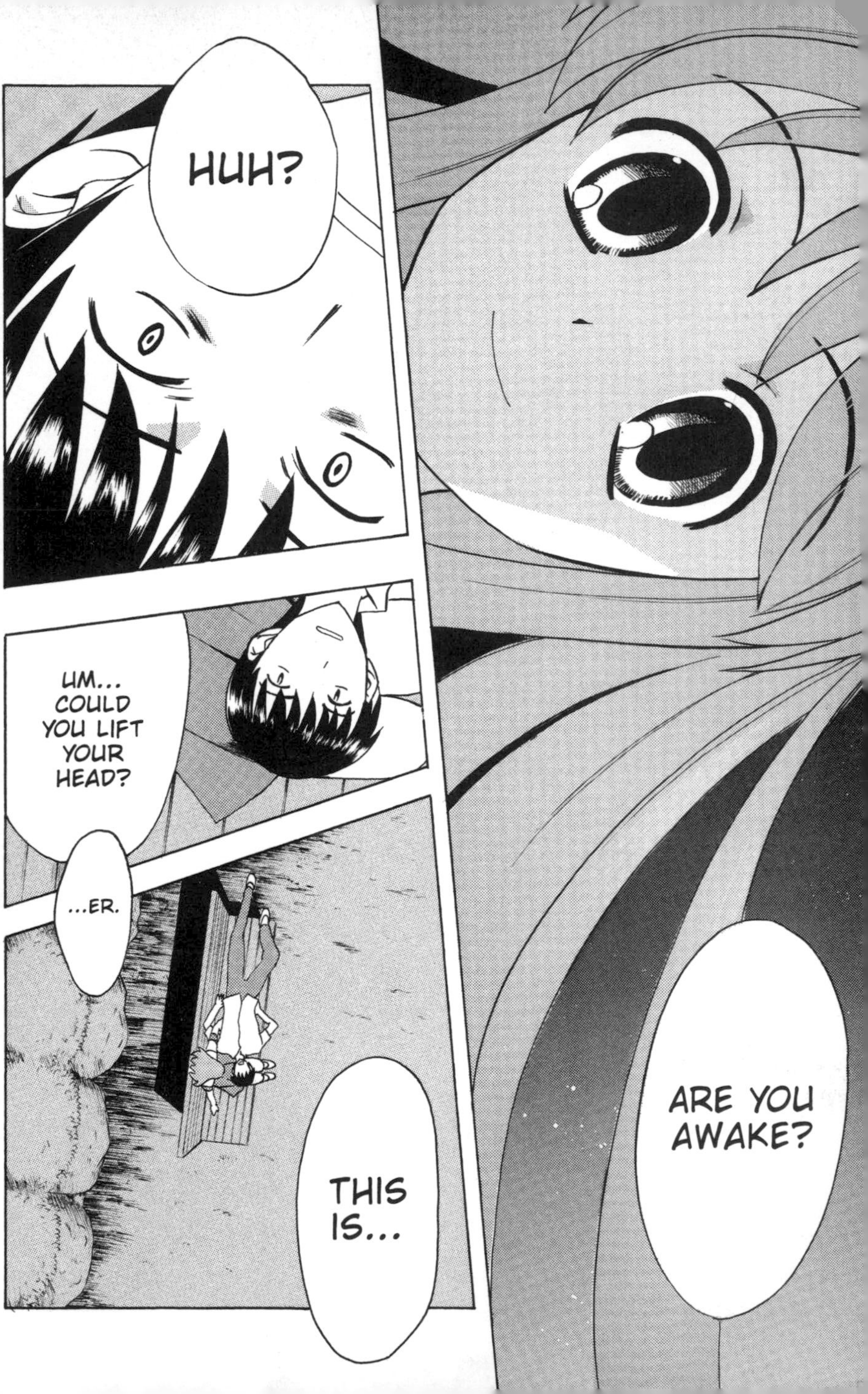
ARE YOU AWAKE?
HUH?
UM... COULD YOU LIFT YOUR HEAD?
...ER.
THIS IS...

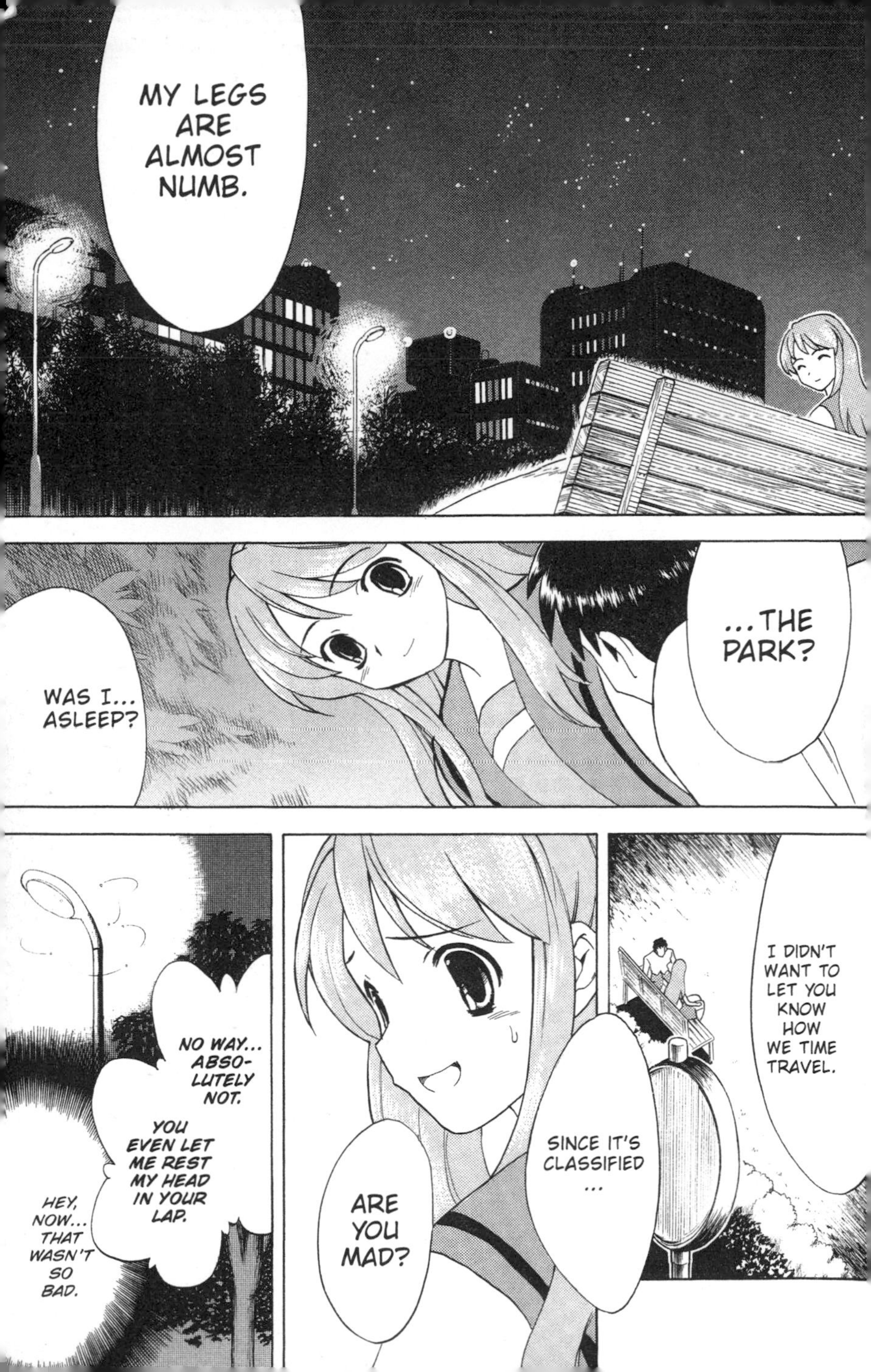
MY LEGS ARE ALMOST NUMB.
...THE PARK?
WAS I... ASLEEP?
I DIDN'T WANT TO LET YOU KNOW HOW WE TIME TRAVEL.
SINCE IT'S CLASSIFIED ...
ARE YOU MAD?
NO WAY... ABSO-LUTELY NOT.
YOU EVEN LET ME REST MY HEAD IN YOUR LAP.
HEY, NOW... THAT WASN'T SO BAD.

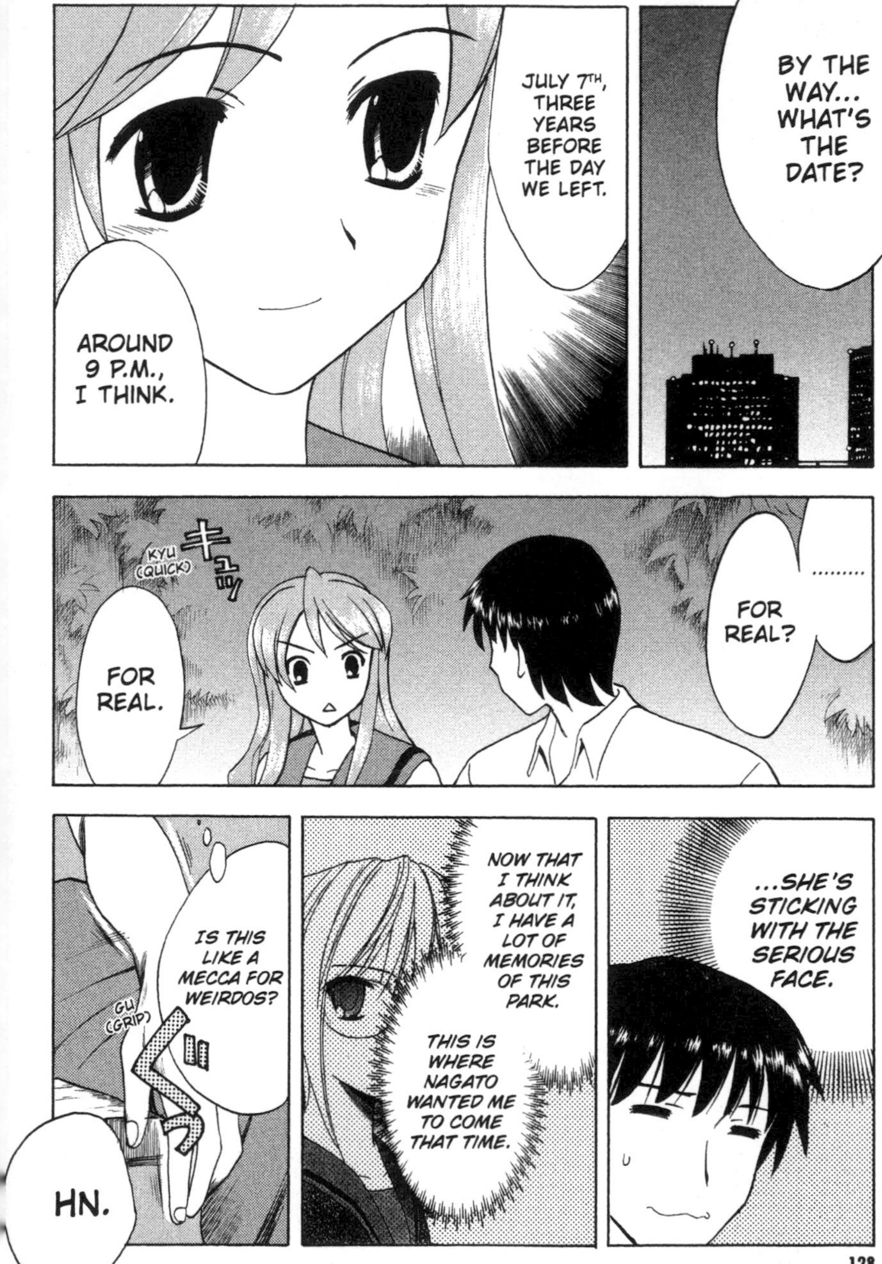
BY THE WAY... WHAT'S THE DATE?
JULY 7TH, THREE YEARS BEFORE THE DAY WE LEFT.
AROUND 9 P.M., I THINK.
....
FOR REAL?
KYU (QUICK)
FOR REAL.
...SHE'S STICKING WITH THE SERIOUS FACE.
NOW THAT I THINK ABOUT IT, I HAVE A LOT OF MEMORIES OF THIS PARK.
THIS IS WHERE NAGATO WANTED ME TO COME THAT TIME.
IS THIS LIKE A MECCA FOR WEIRDOS?
GU (GRIP)
HN.

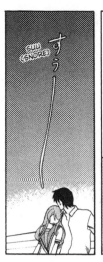

SUU
(SNORE)

HUH
...?
HOLD
ON!

WHAT
IS...

FUWA
(FLOP)

SUU

SHE'S
ASLEEP!?

AH,
GOOD
EVENING.

IS SHE
SLEEP-
ING
SOUND-
LY?

GASA
(RUSTLE)

BIKU
(FLINCH)

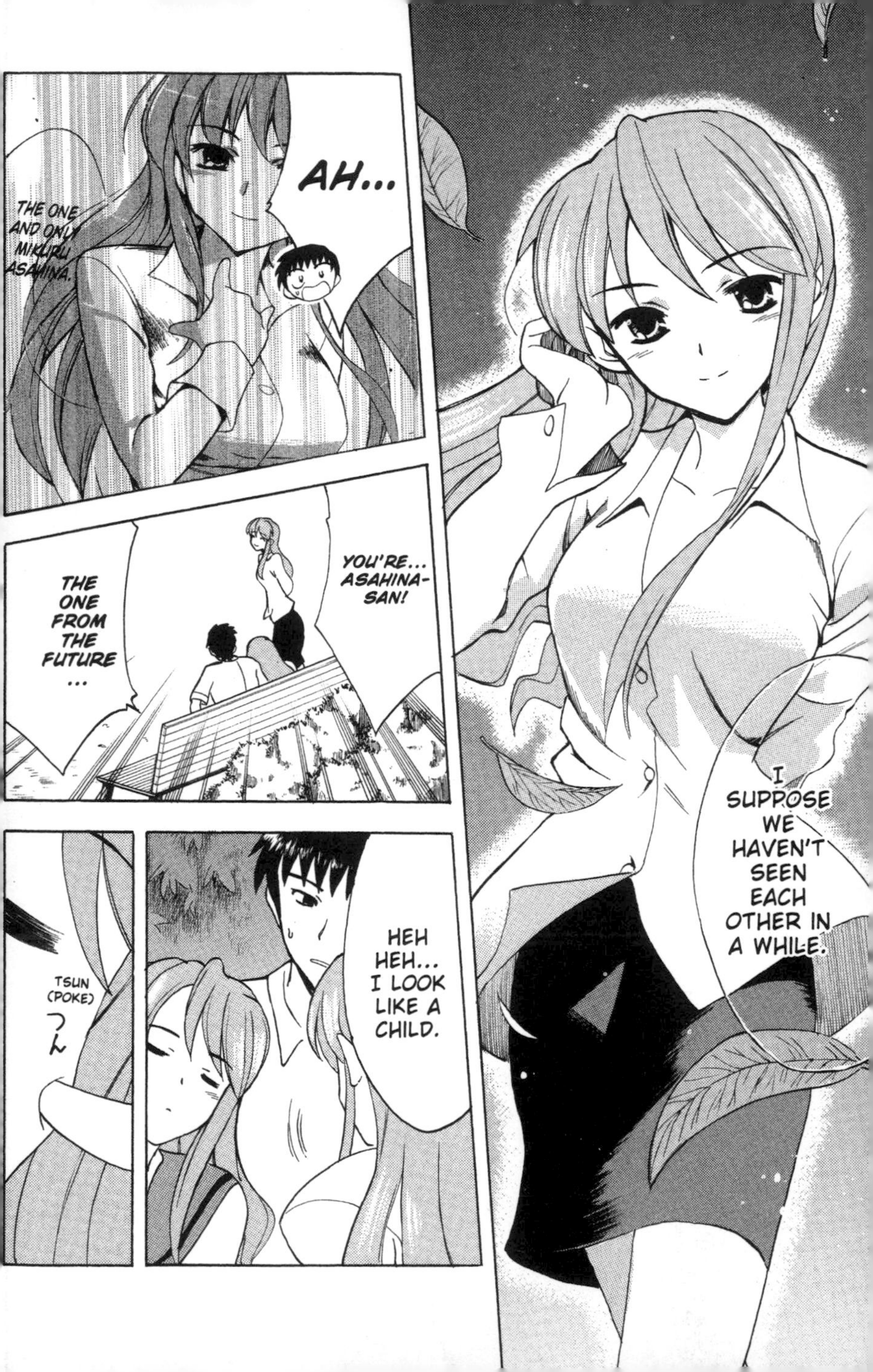
I SUPPOSE WE HAVEN'T SEEN EACH OTHER IN A WHILE.
AH...
THE ONE AND ONLY MIKURU ASAHINA.
YOU'RE... ASAHINA-SAN!
THE ONE FROM THE FUTURE ...
HEH HEH... I LOOK LIKE A CHILD.
TSUN (POKE)
つん

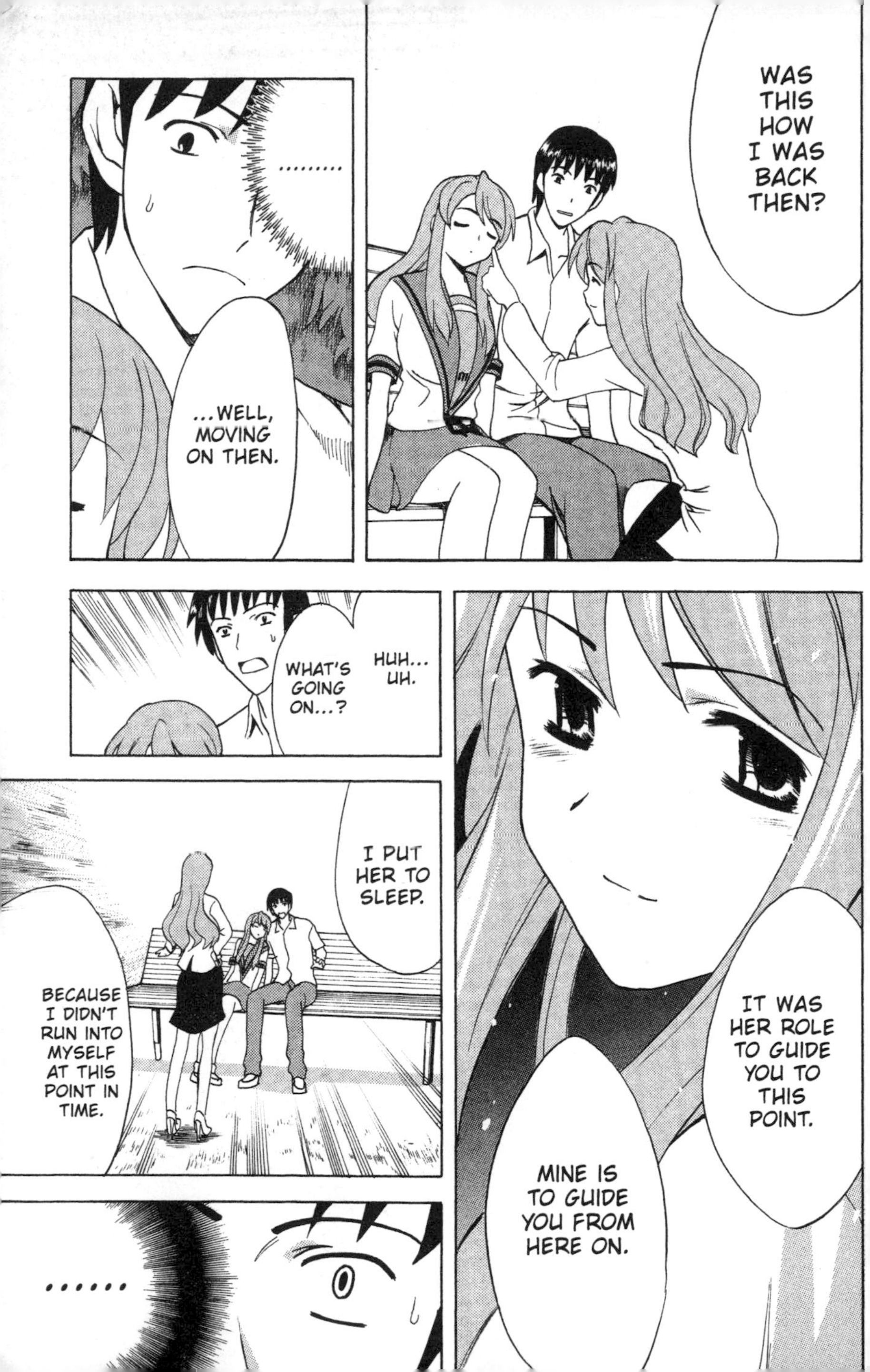
WAS THIS HOW I WAS BACK THEN?
....
...WELL, MOVING ON THEN.
IT WAS HER ROLE TO GUIDE YOU TO THIS POINT.
MINE IS TO GUIDE YOU FROM HERE ON.
HUH... UH.
WHAT'S GOING ON...?
I PUT HER TO SLEEP.
BECAUSE I DIDN'T RUN INTO MYSELF AT THIS POINT IN TIME.
......

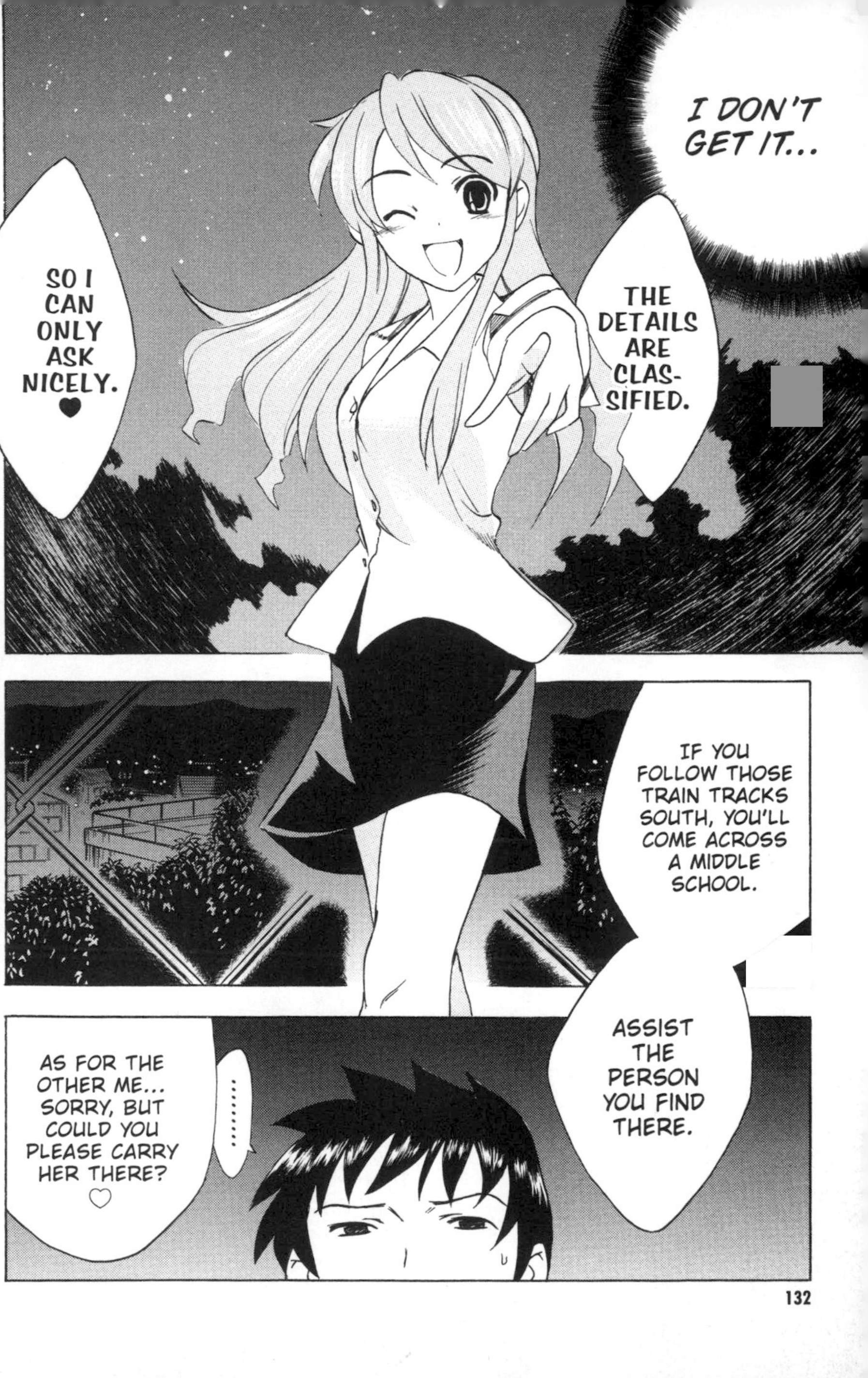
I DON'T GET IT...
THE DETAILS ARE CLAS-SIFIED.
SO I CAN ONLY ASK NICELY. ♥
IF YOU FOLLOW THOSE TRAIN TRACKS SOUTH, YOU'LL COME ACROSS A MIDDLE SCHOOL.
ASSIST THE PERSON YOU FIND THERE.
....
AS FOR THE OTHER ME... SORRY, BUT COULD YOU PLEASE CARRY HER THERE? ♡

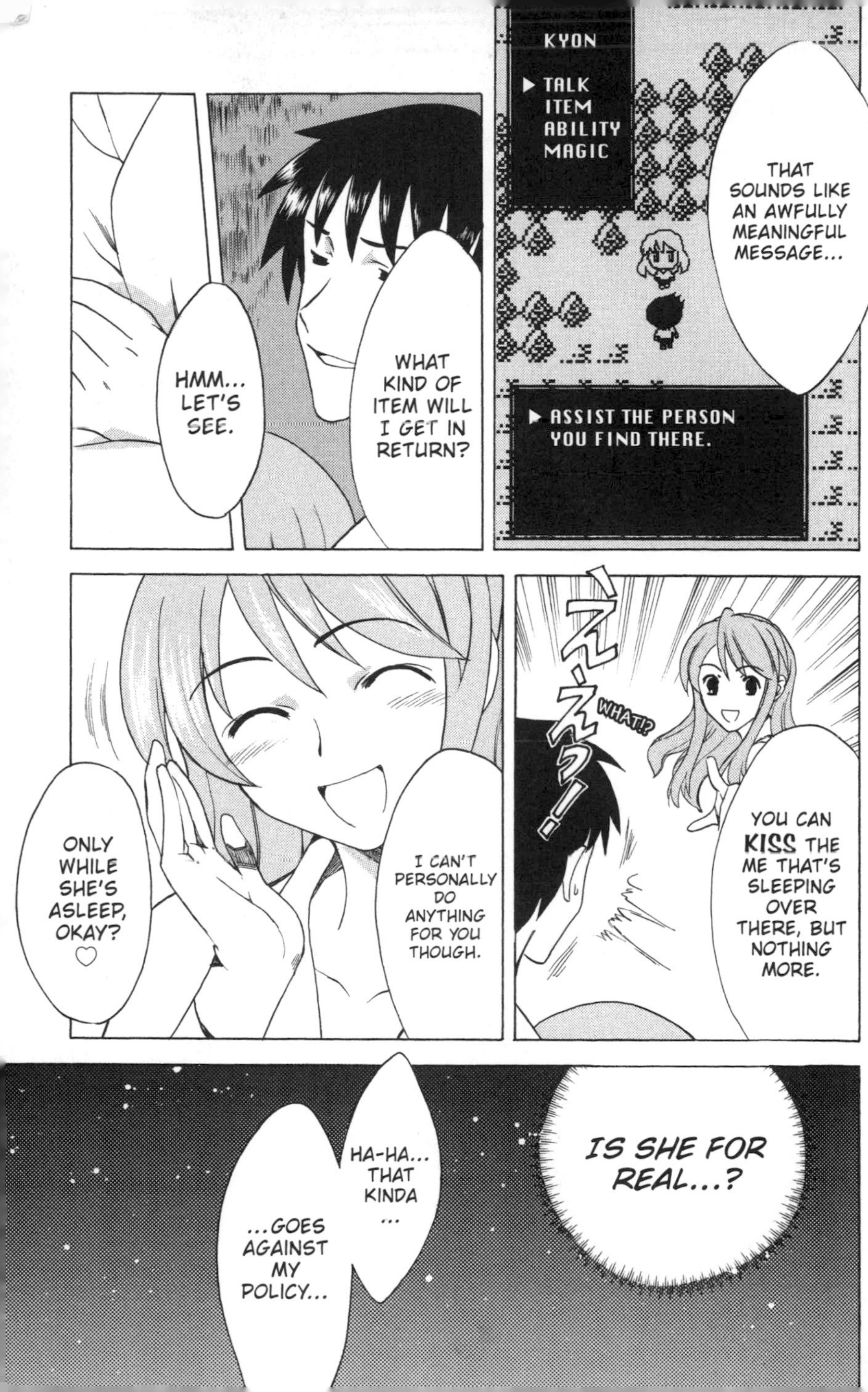
KYON
▶ TALK
ITEM
ABILITY
MAGIC
▶ ASSIST THE PERSON YOU FIND THERE.
THAT SOUNDS LIKE AN AWFULLY MEANINGFUL MESSAGE...
WHAT KIND OF ITEM WILL I GET IN RETURN?
HMM... LET'S SEE.
WHAT!?
YOU CAN KISS THE ME THAT'S SLEEPING OVER THERE, BUT NOTHING MORE.
I CAN'T PERSONALLY DO ANYTHING FOR YOU THOUGH.
ONLY WHILE SHE'S ASLEEP, OKAY? ♡
IS SHE FOR REAL...?
HA-HA... THAT KINDA ...
...GOES AGAINST MY POLICY...

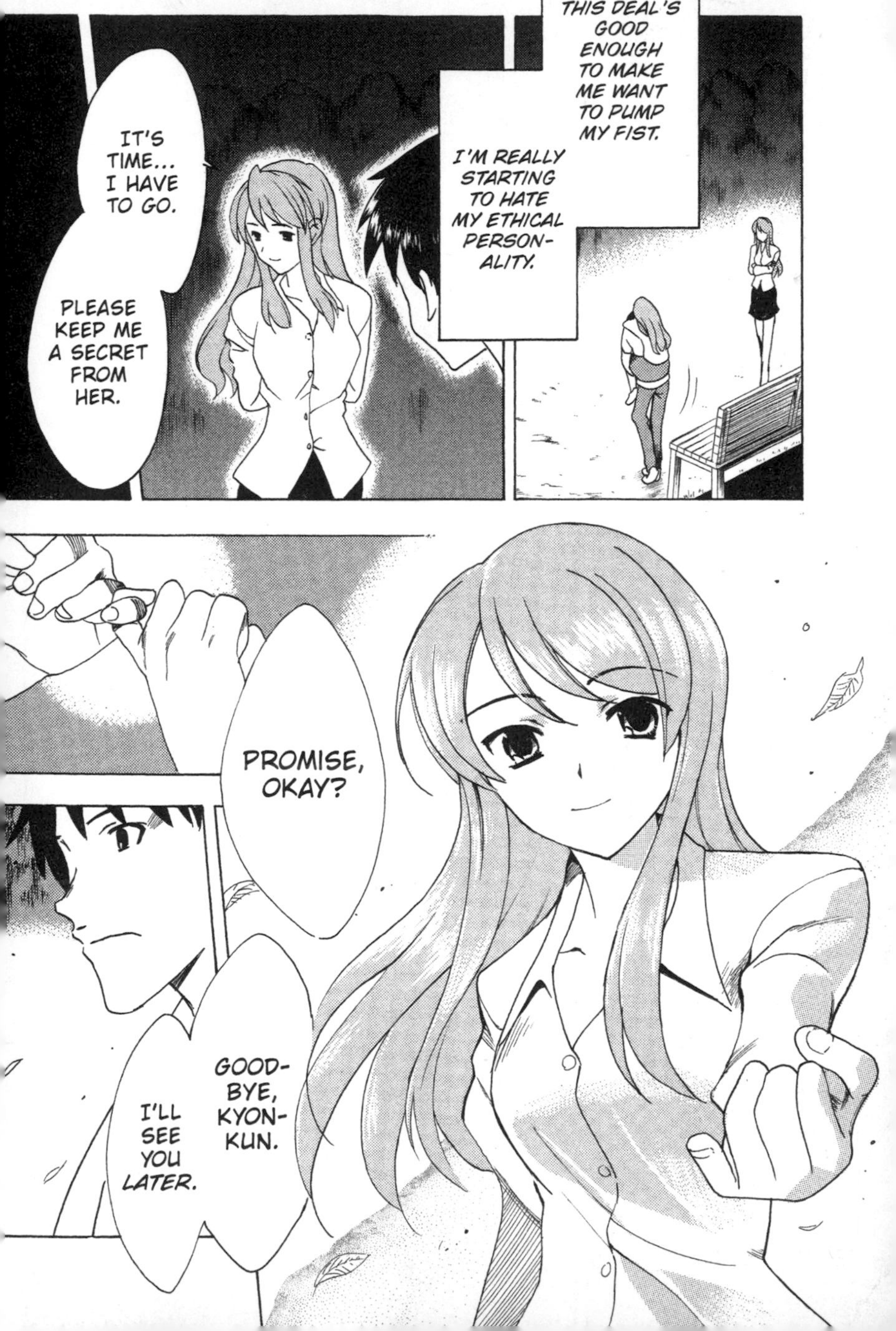
THIS DEAL'S GOOD ENOUGH TO MAKE ME WANT TO PUMP MY FIST.
I'M REALLY STARTING TO HATE MY ETHICAL PERSON-ALITY.
IT'S TIME... I HAVE TO GO.
PLEASE KEEP ME A SECRET FROM HER.
PROMISE, OKAY?
GOOD-BYE, KYON-KUN.
I'LL SEE YOU LATER.

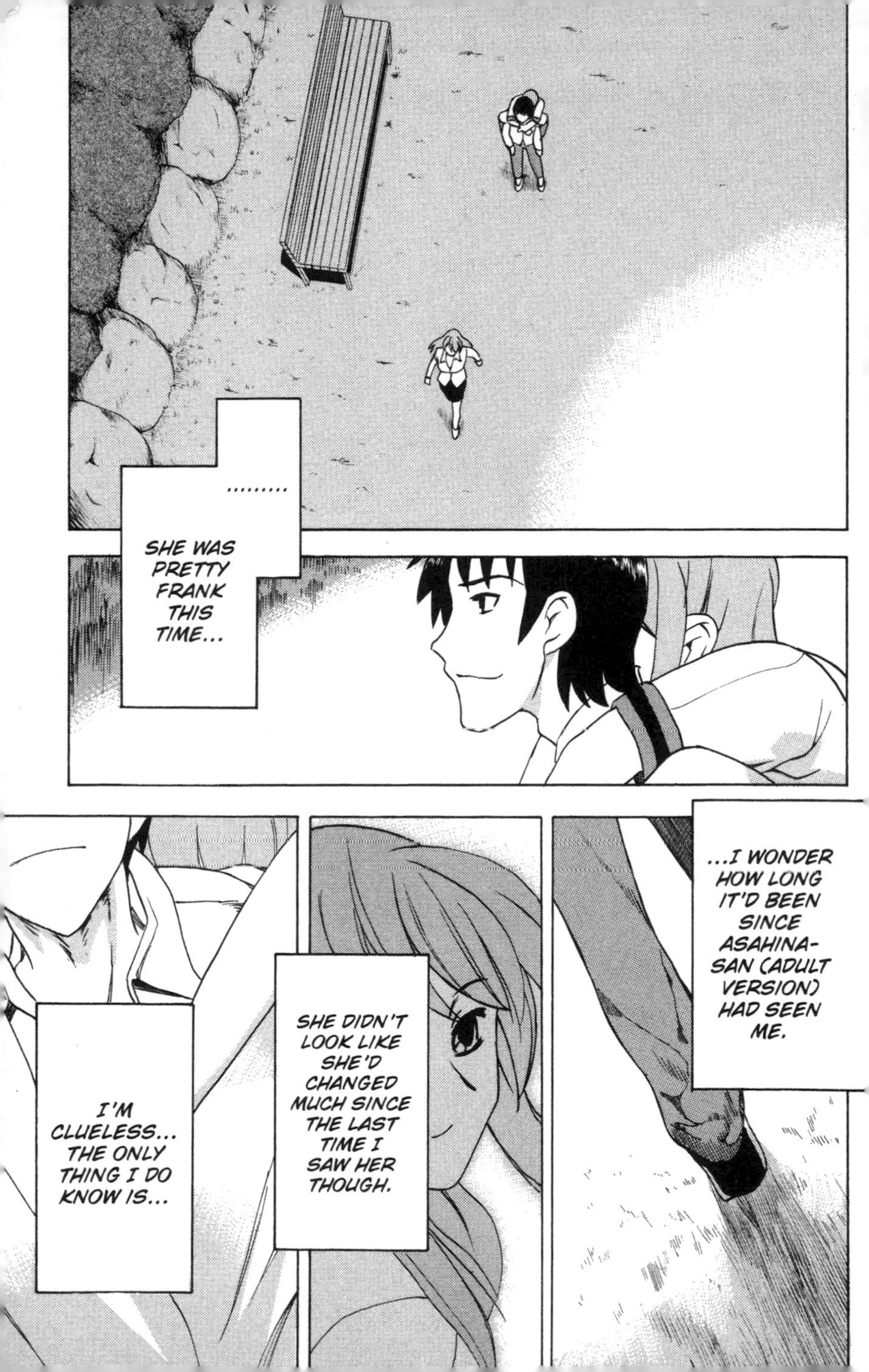
....
SHE WAS PRETTY FRANK THIS TIME...
...I WONDER HOW LONG IT'D BEEN SINCE ASAHINA-SAN (ADULT VERSION) HAD SEEN ME.
SHE DIDN'T LOOK LIKE SHE'D CHANGED MUCH SINCE THE LAST TIME I SAW HER THOUGH.
I'M CLUELESS... THE ONLY THING I DO KNOW IS...

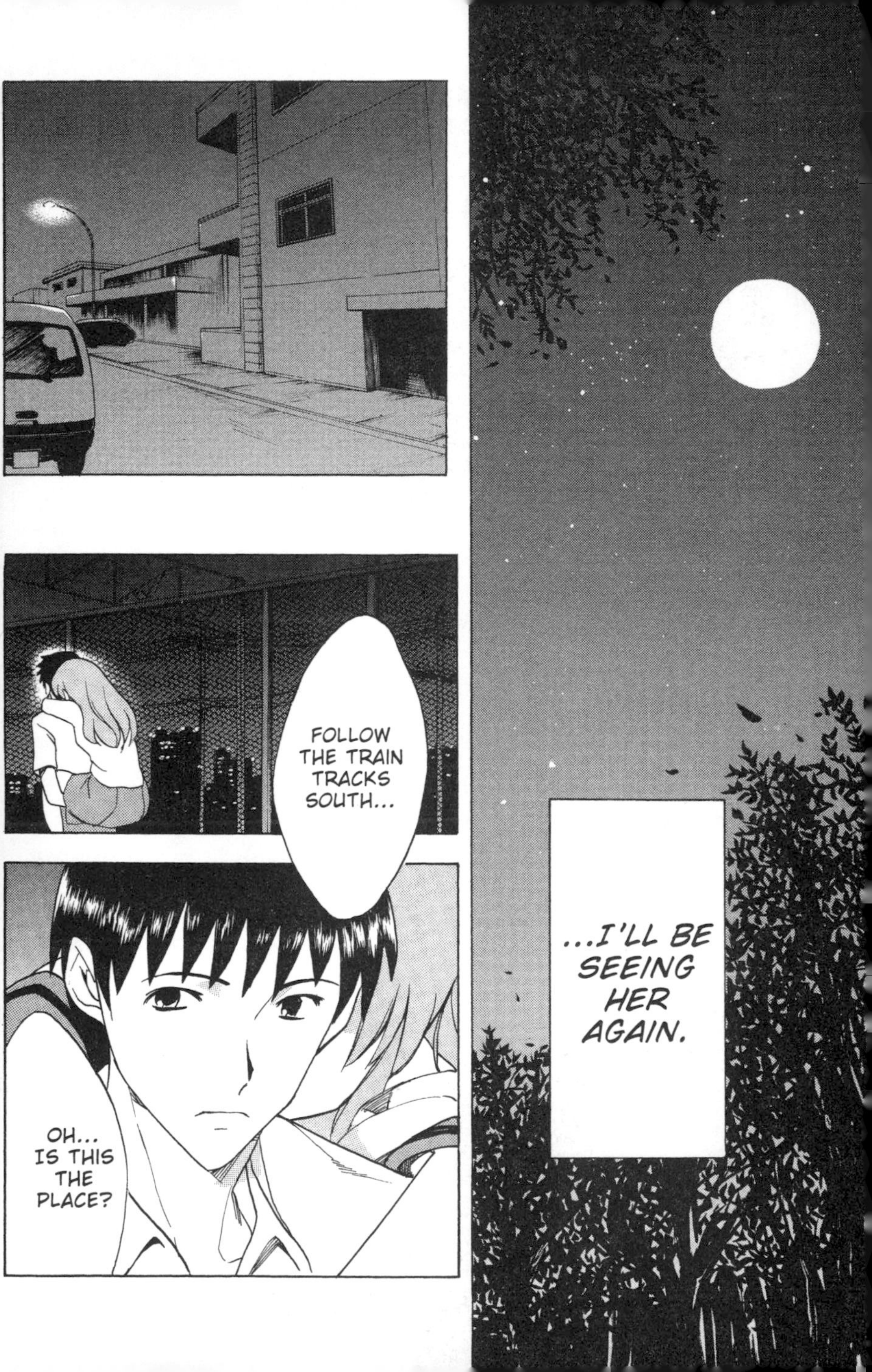
...I'LL BE SEEING HER AGAIN.
FOLLOW THE TRAIN TRACKS SOUTH...
OH... IS THIS THE PLACE?

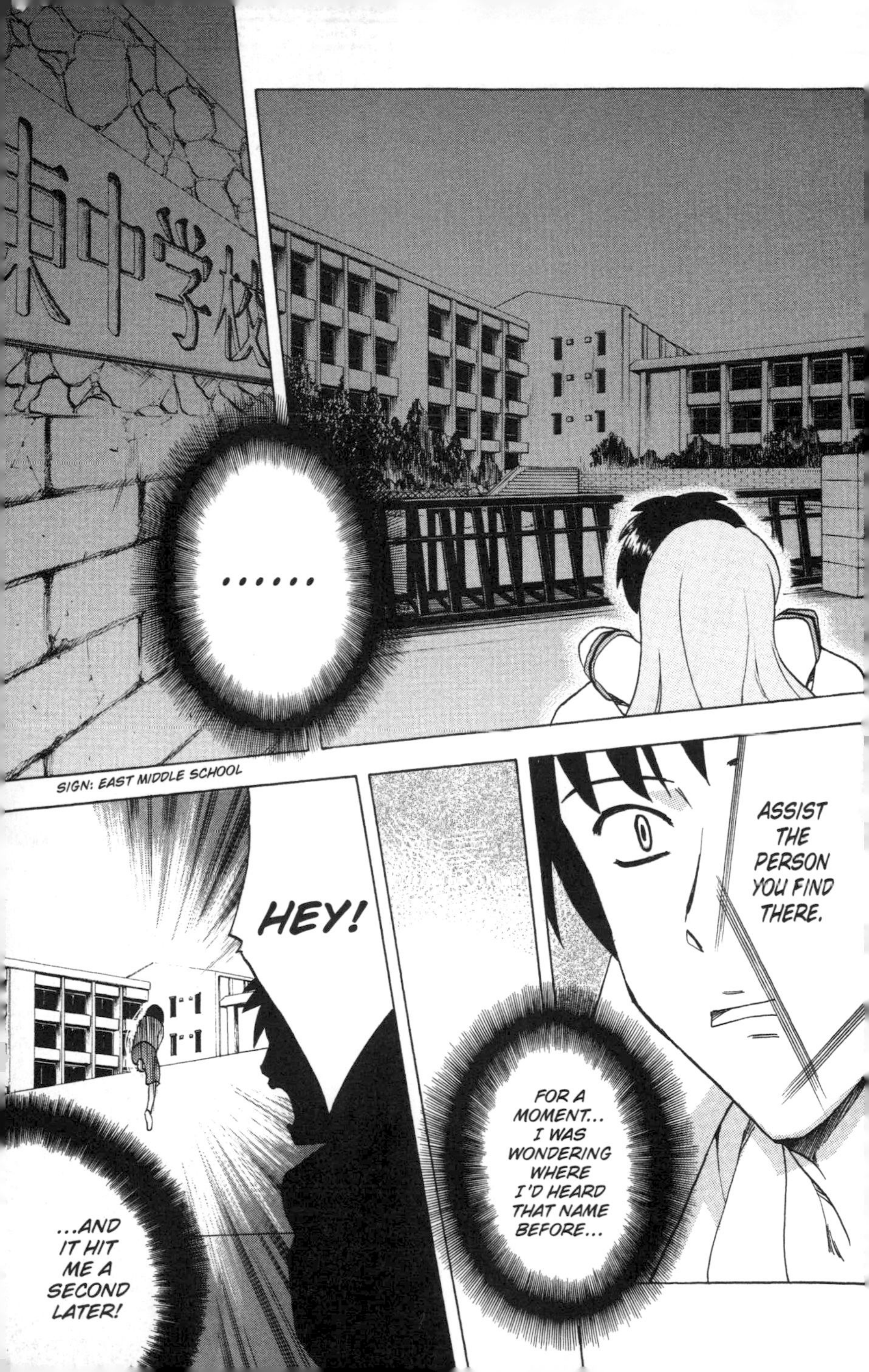
......
SIGN: EAST MIDDLE SCHOOL
ASSIST THE PERSON YOU FIND THERE.
FOR A MOMENT... I WAS WONDERING WHERE I'D HEARD THAT NAME BEFORE...
HEY!
...AND IT HIT ME A SECOND LATER!

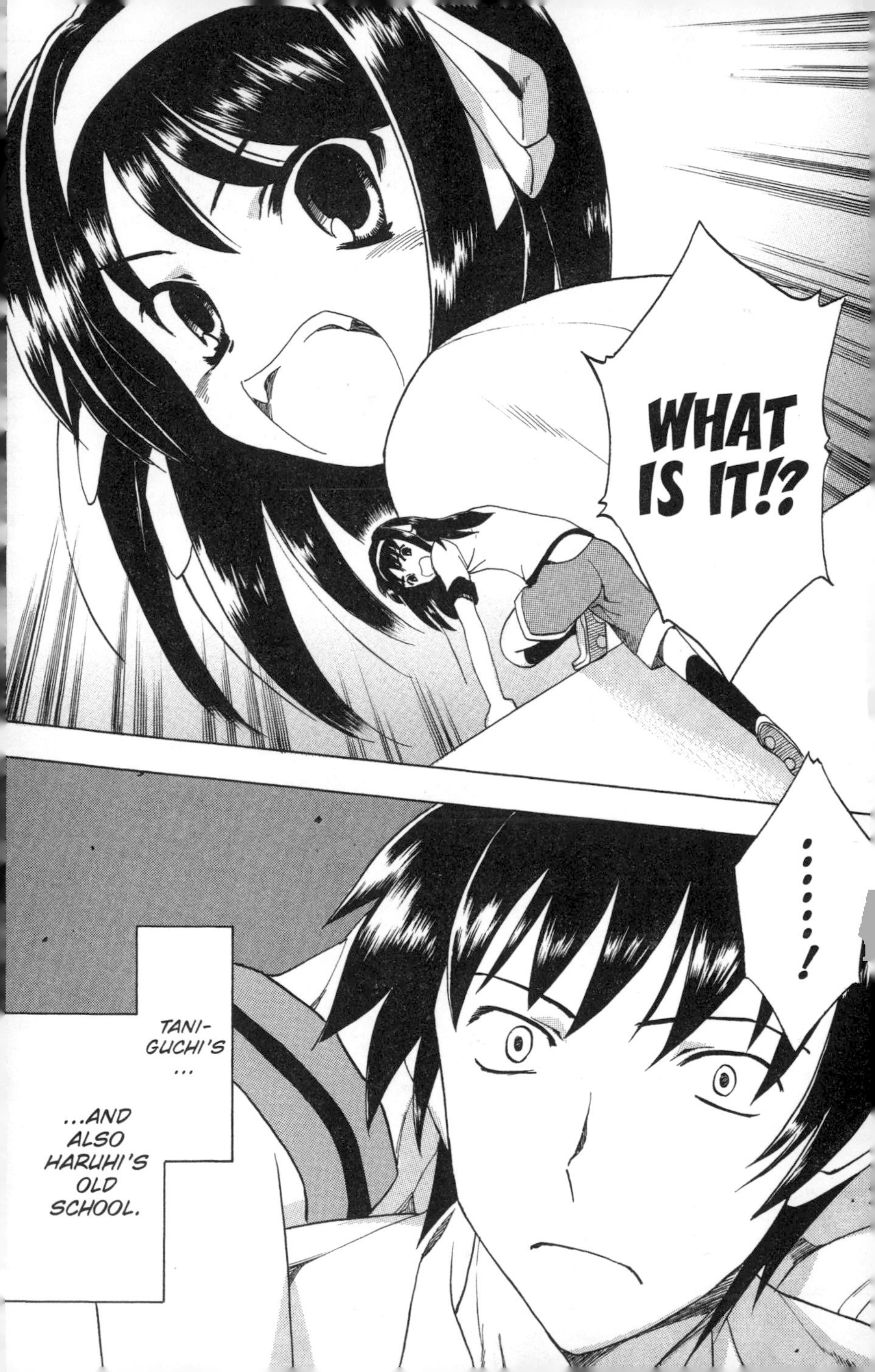
WHAT IS IT!?
......!
TANI-GUCHI'S ...
...AND ALSO HARUHI'S OLD SCHOOL.

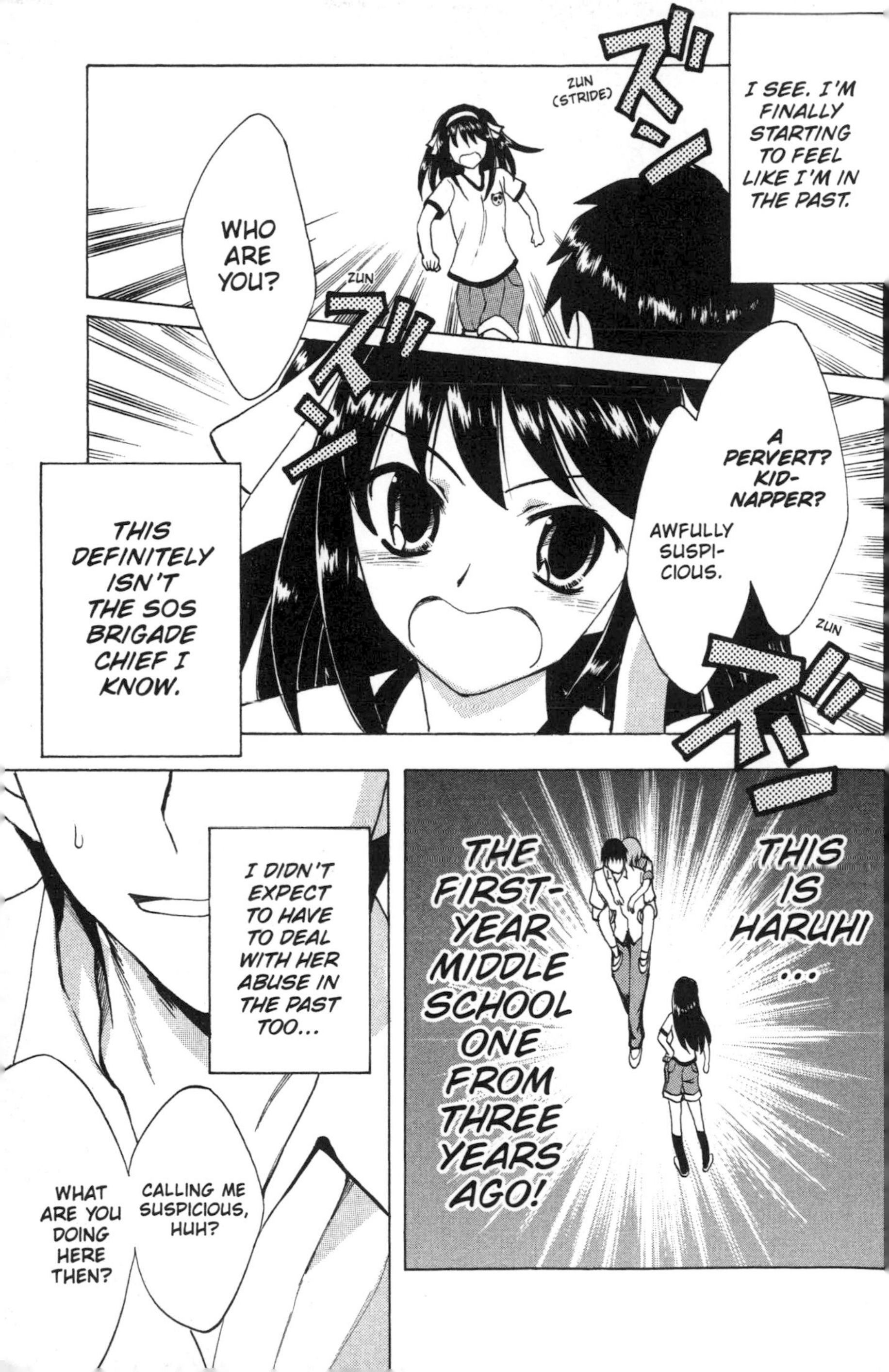
I SEE. I'M FINALLY STARTING TO FEEL LIKE I'M IN THE PAST.
ZUN (STRIDE)
WHO ARE YOU?
ZUN
A PERVERT? KIDNAPPER?
AWFULLY SUSPICIOUS.
ZUN
THIS DEFINITELY ISN'T THE SOS BRIGADE CHIEF I KNOW.
THIS IS HARUHI...
THE FIRST-YEAR MIDDLE SCHOOL ONE FROM THREE YEARS AGO!
I DIDN'T EXPECT TO HAVE TO DEAL WITH HER ABUSE IN THE PAST TOO...
CALLING ME SUSPICIOUS, HUH?
WHAT ARE YOU DOING HERE THEN?

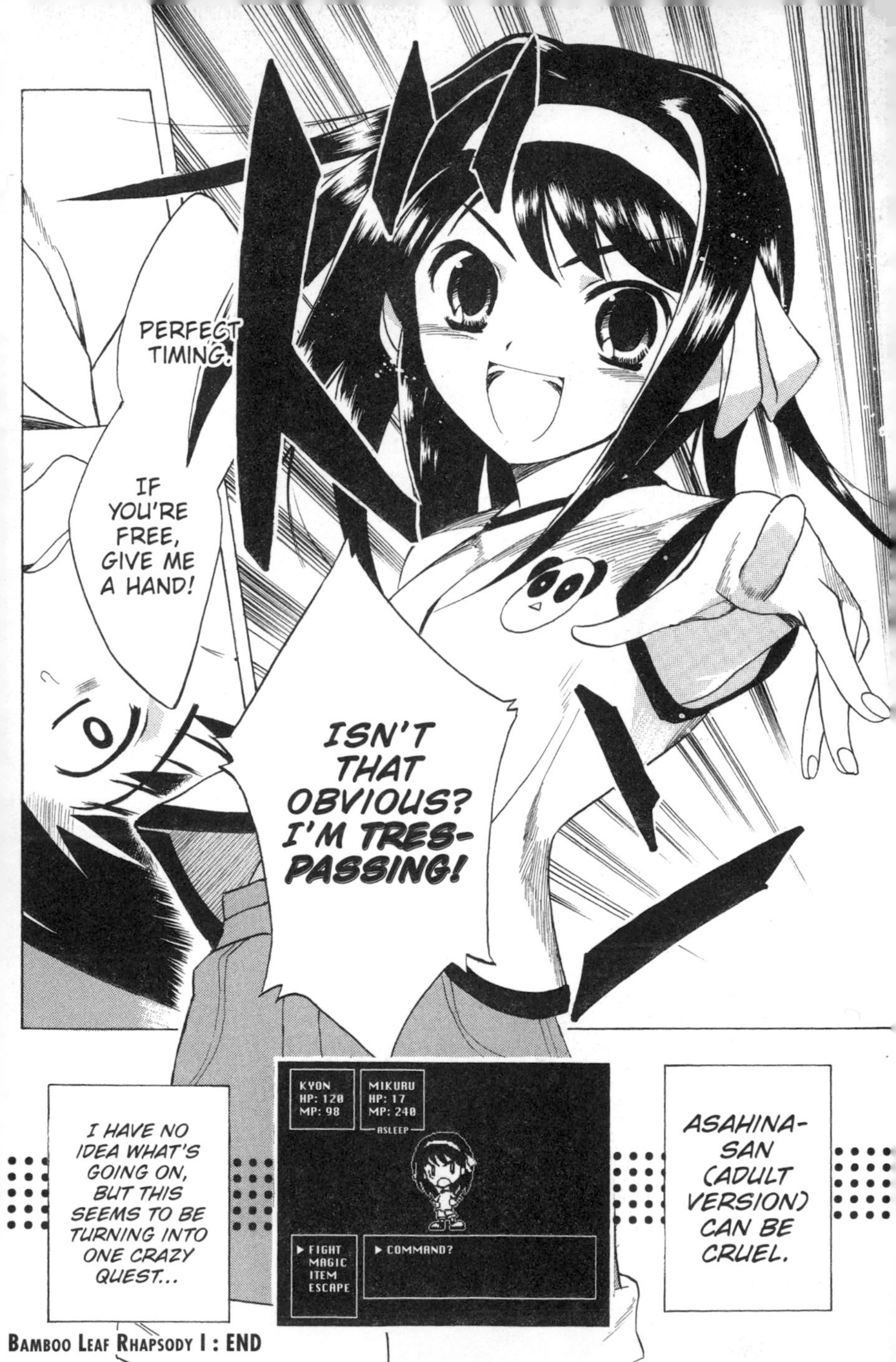
ISN'T THAT OBVIOUS? I'M TRES-PASSING!
PERFECT TIMING.
IF YOU'RE FREE, GIVE ME A HAND!
ASAHINA-SAN (ADULT VERSION) CAN BE CRUEL.
KYON HP: 120 MP: 98
MIKURU HP: 17 MP: 240 ASLEEP
▶ FIGHT MAGIC ITEM ESCAPE
▶ COMMAND?
I HAVE NO IDEA WHAT'S GOING ON, BUT THIS SEEMS TO BE TURNING INTO ONE CRAZY QUEST...

BAMBOO LEAF RHAPSODY I : END

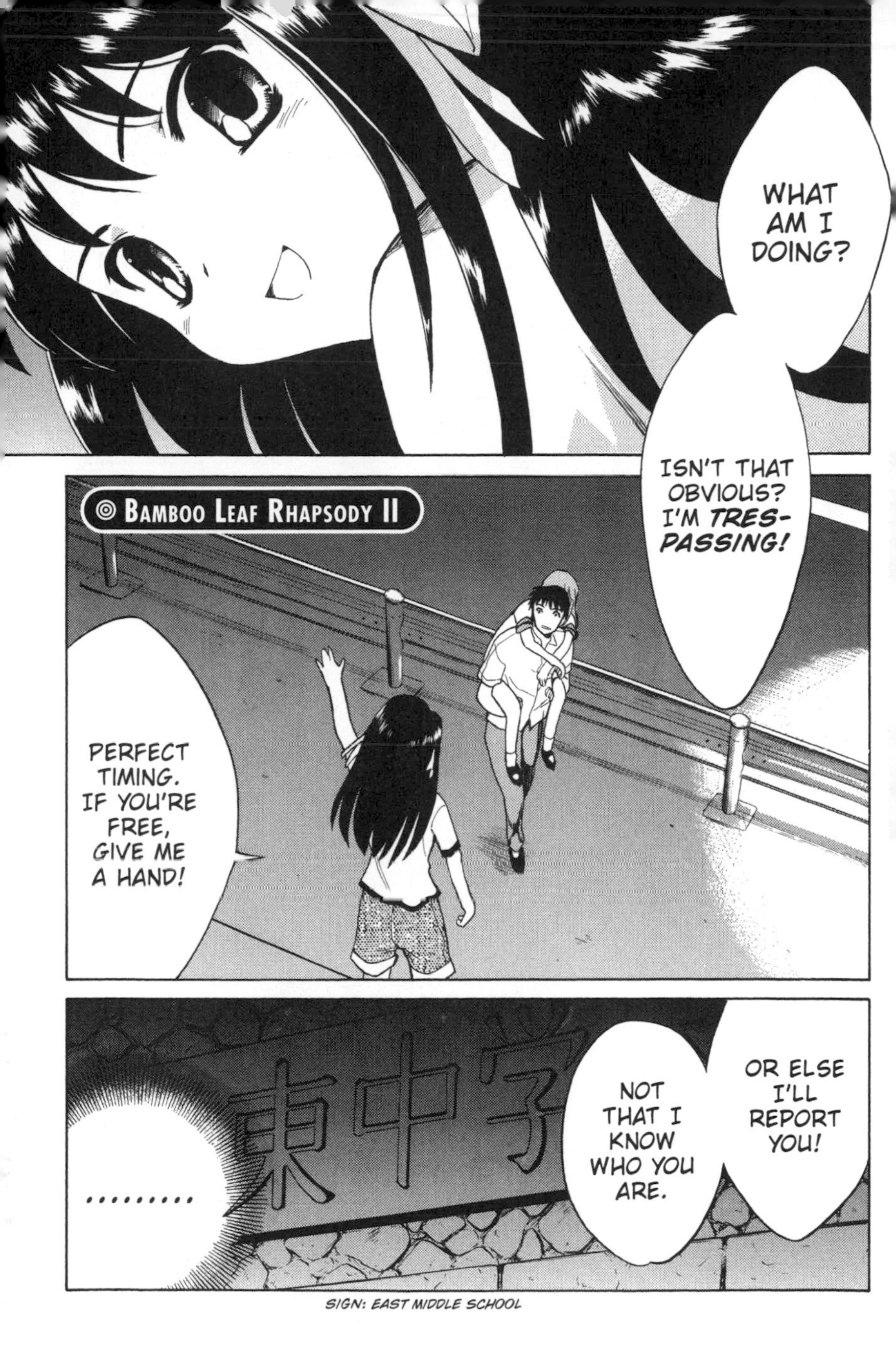
WHAT AM I DOING?
BAMBOO LEAF RHAPSODY II
ISN'T THAT OBVIOUS? I'M *TRES-PASSING!*
PERFECT TIMING. IF YOU'RE FREE, GIVE ME A HAND!
OR ELSE I'LL REPORT YOU!
NOT THAT I KNOW WHO YOU ARE.
....
SIGN: EAST MIDDLE SCHOOL

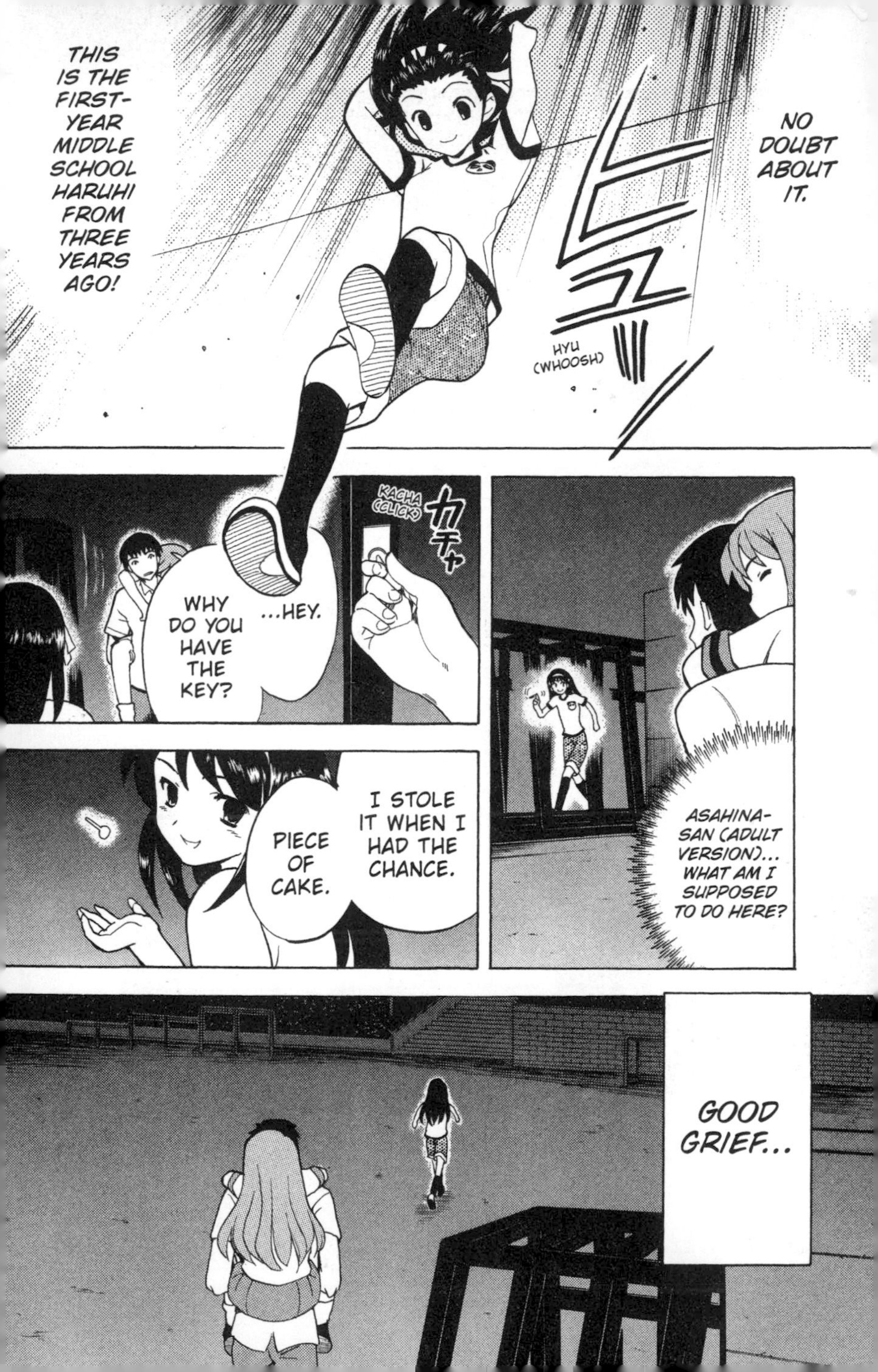
NO DOUBT ABOUT IT.
THIS IS THE FIRST-YEAR MIDDLE SCHOOL HARUHI FROM THREE YEARS AGO!
HYU (WHOOSH)
ASAHINA-SAN (ADULT VERSION)... WHAT AM I SUPPOSED TO DO HERE?
KACHA (CLICK)
...HEY.
WHY DO YOU HAVE THE KEY?
I STOLE IT WHEN I HAD THE CHANCE.
PIECE OF CAKE.
GOOD GRIEF...

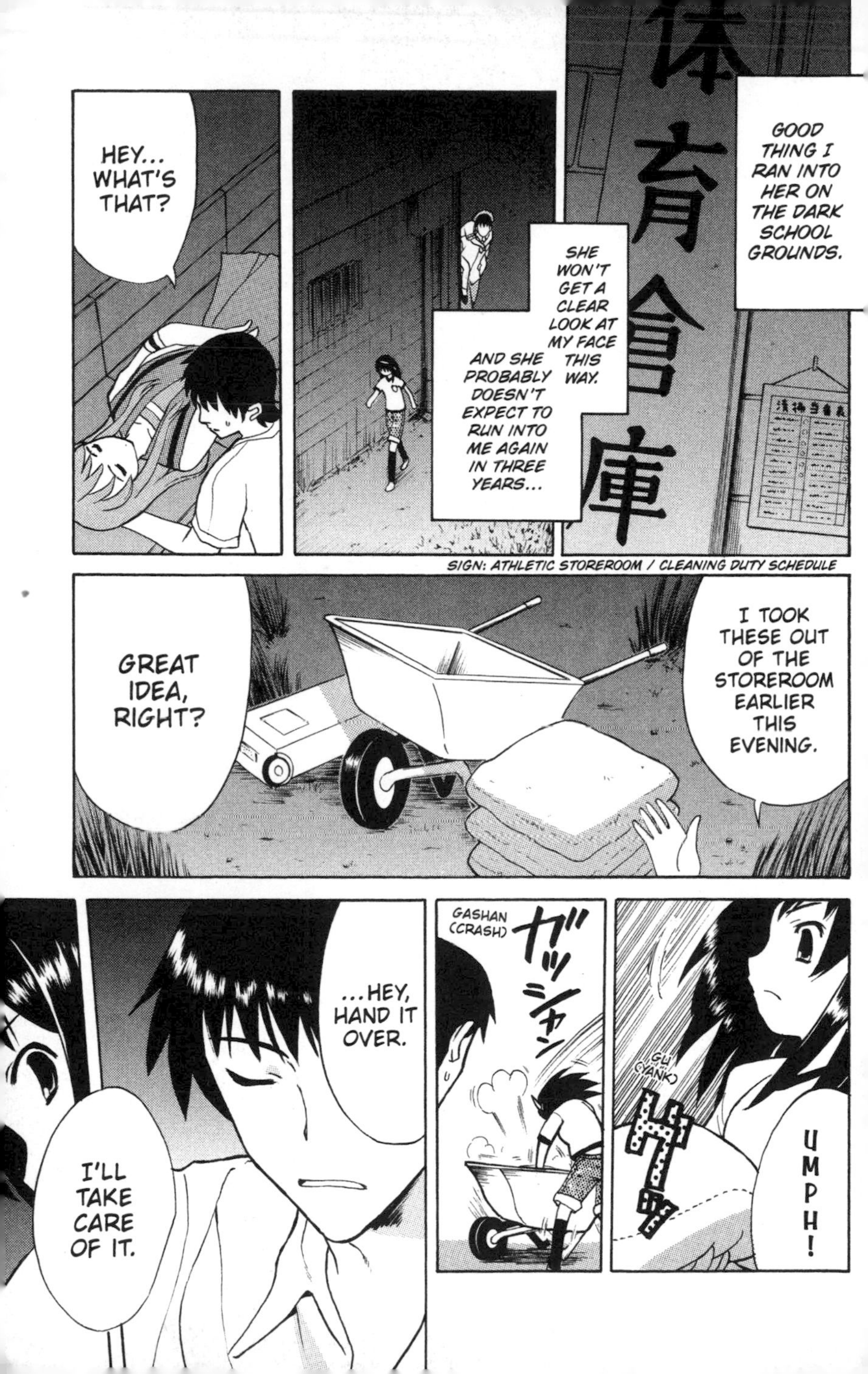GOOD THING I RAN INTO HER ON THE DARK SCHOOL GROUNDS.
体育倉庫
SHE WON'T GET A CLEAR LOOK AT MY FACE THIS WAY.
AND SHE PROBABLY DOESN'T EXPECT TO RUN INTO ME AGAIN IN THREE YEARS...
HEY... WHAT'S THAT?
SIGN: ATHLETIC STOREROOM / CLEANING DUTY SCHEDULE
I TOOK THESE OUT OF THE STOREROOM EARLIER THIS EVENING.
GREAT IDEA, RIGHT?
GU (YANK)
UMPH!
GASHAN (CRASH)
ガッシャン
...HEY, HAND IT OVER.
I'LL TAKE CARE OF IT.

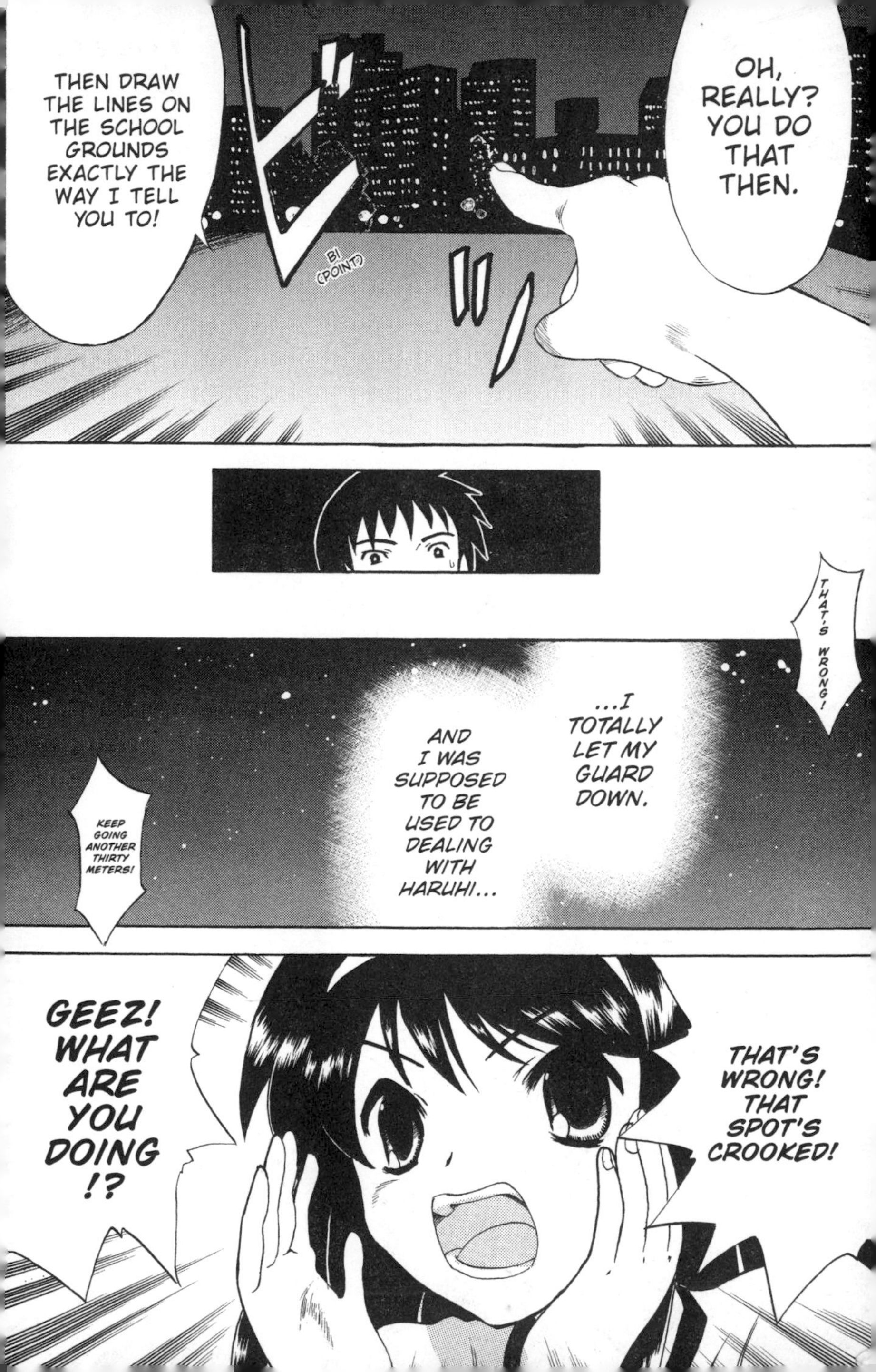
OH, REALLY? YOU DO THAT THEN.
BI (POINT)
THEN DRAW THE LINES ON THE SCHOOL GROUNDS EXACTLY THE WAY I TELL YOU TO!
THAT'S WRONG!
...I TOTALLY LET MY GUARD DOWN.
AND I WAS SUPPOSED TO BE USED TO DEALING WITH HARUHI...
KEEP GOING ANOTHER THIRTY METERS!
THAT'S WRONG! THAT SPOT'S CROOKED!
GEEZ! WHAT ARE YOU DOING !?

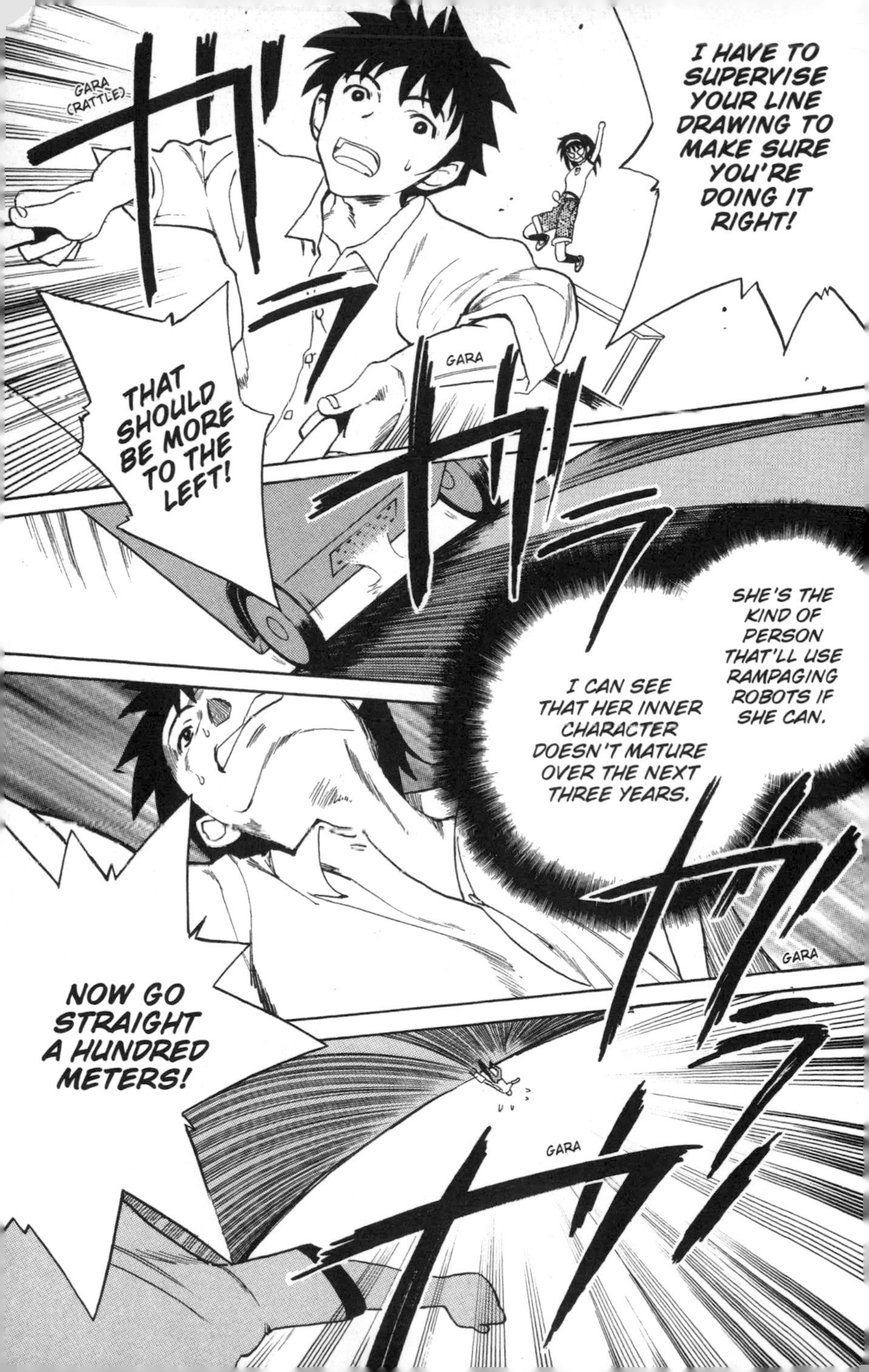
I HAVE TO SUPERVISE YOUR LINE DRAWING TO MAKE SURE YOU'RE DOING IT RIGHT!
GARA (RATTLE)
THAT SHOULD BE MORE TO THE LEFT!
GARA
SHE'S THE KIND OF PERSON THAT'LL USE RAMPAGING ROBOTS IF SHE CAN.
I CAN SEE THAT HER INNER CHARACTER DOESN'T MATURE OVER THE NEXT THREE YEARS.
GARA
NOW GO STRAIGHT A HUNDRED METERS!
GARA

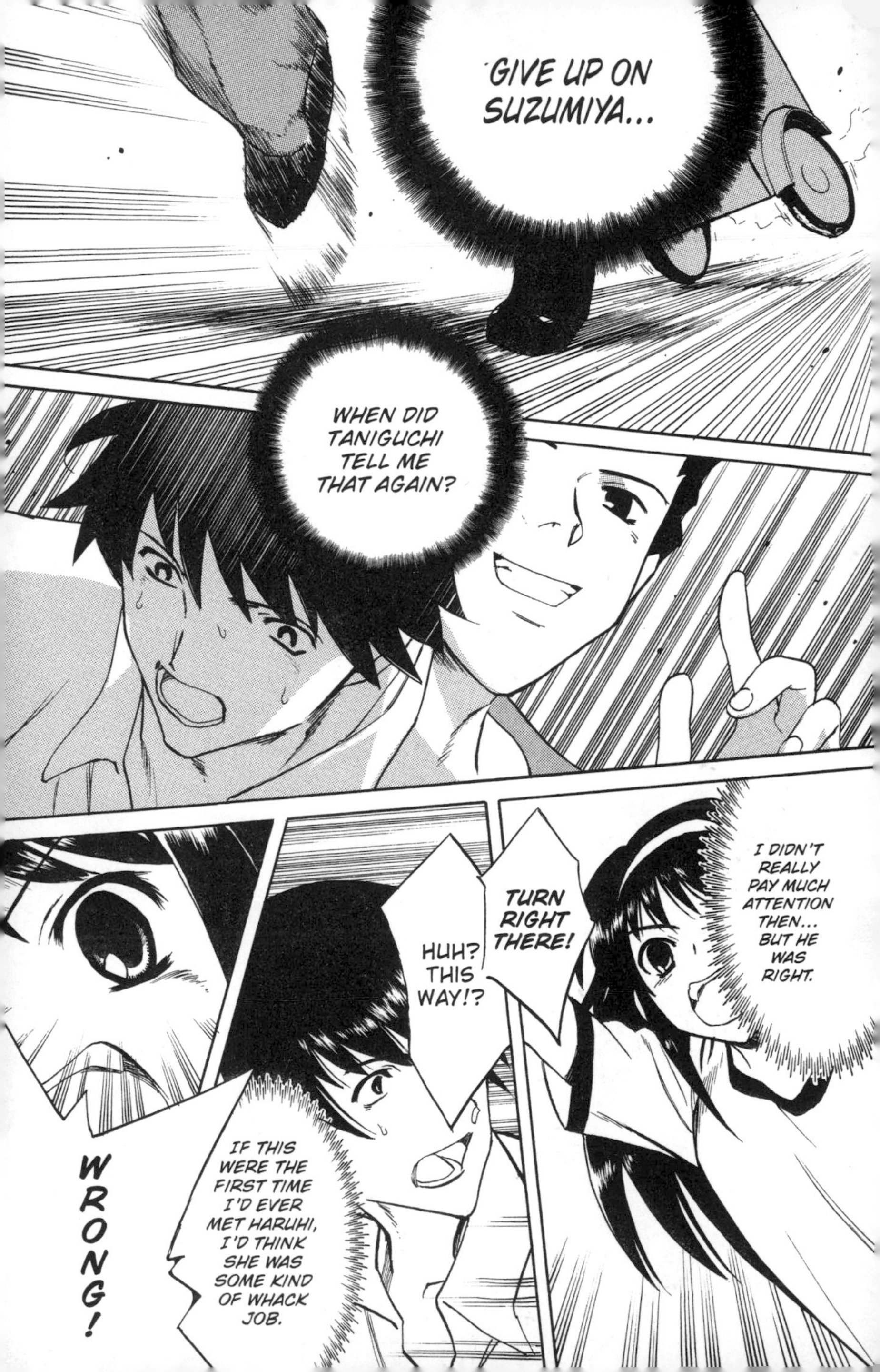
GIVE UP ON SUZUMIYA...
WHEN DID TANIGUCHI TELL ME THAT AGAIN?
I DIDN'T REALLY PAY MUCH ATTENTION THEN... BUT HE WAS RIGHT.
TURN RIGHT THERE!
HUH? THIS WAY!?
IF THIS WERE THE FIRST TIME I'D EVER MET HARUHI, I'D THINK SHE WAS SOME KIND OF WHACK JOB.
WRONG!

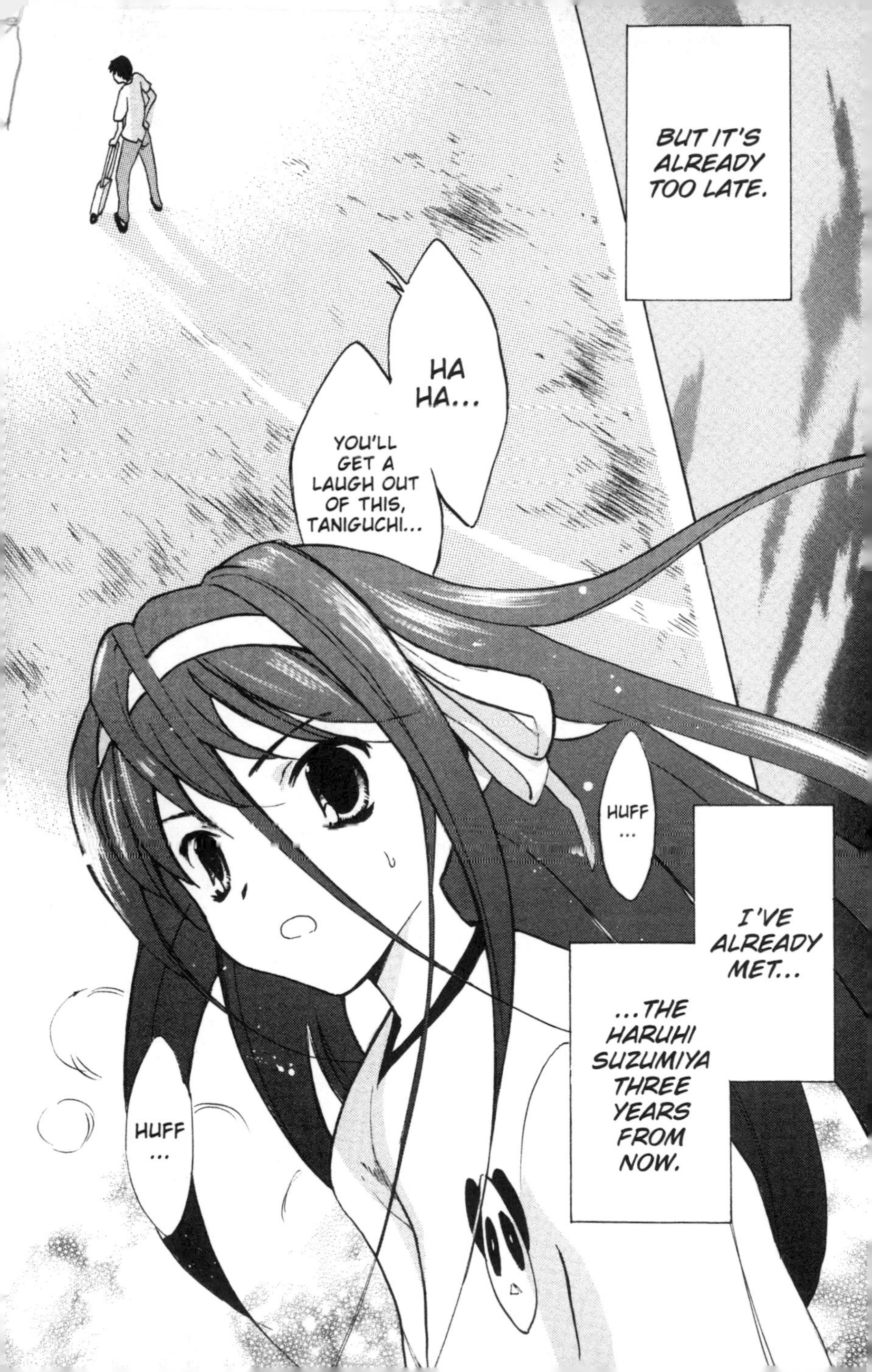
BUT IT'S ALREADY TOO LATE.
HA HA...
YOU'LL GET A LAUGH OUT OF THIS, TANIGUCHI...
HUFF...
I'VE ALREADY MET...
...THE HARUHI SUZUMIYA THREE YEARS FROM NOW.
HUFF...

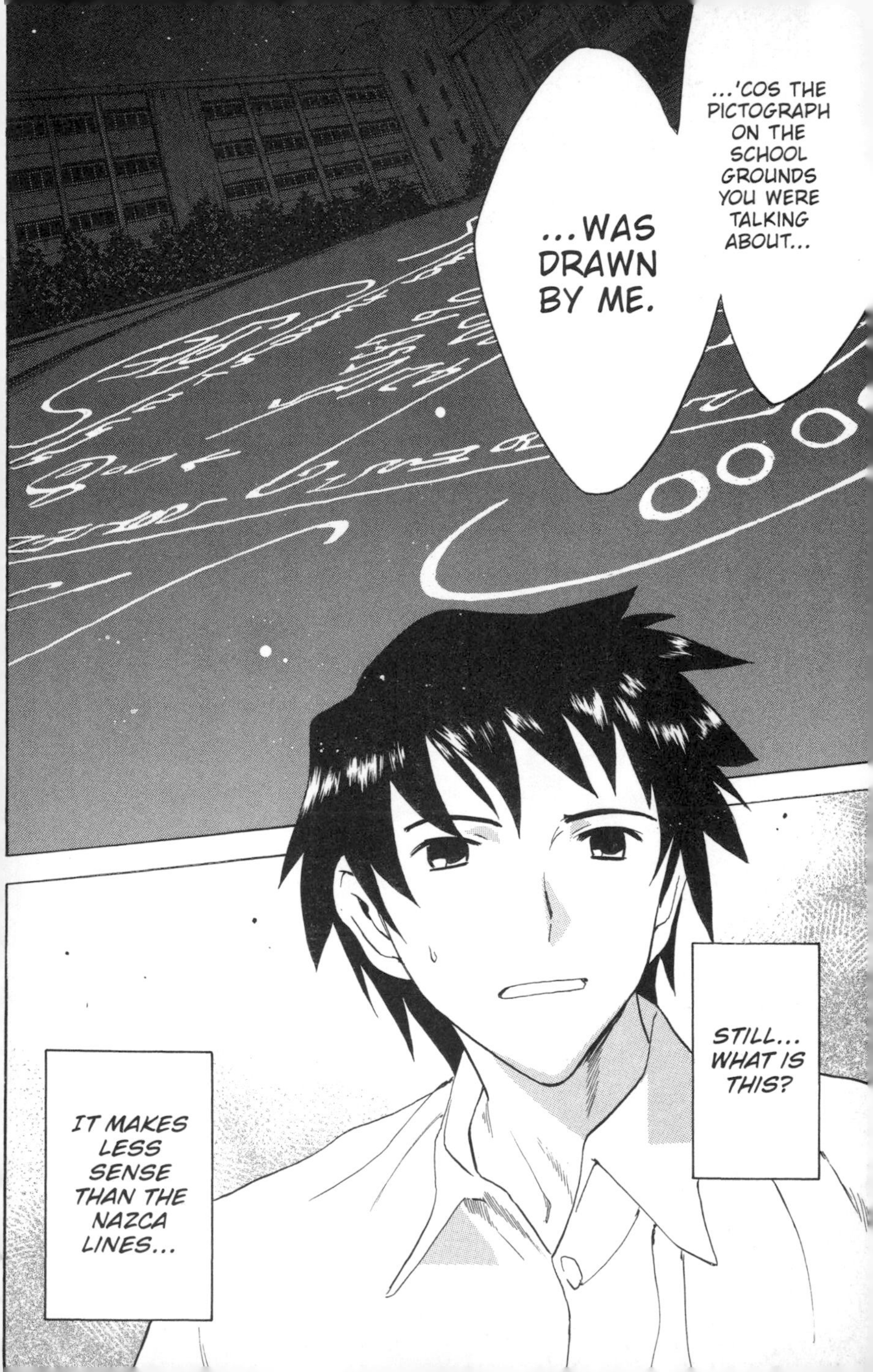
...'COS THE PICTOGRAPH ON THE SCHOOL GROUNDS YOU WERE TALKING ABOUT...
...WAS DRAWN BY ME.
STILL... WHAT IS THIS?
IT MAKES LESS SENSE THAN THE NAZCA LINES...

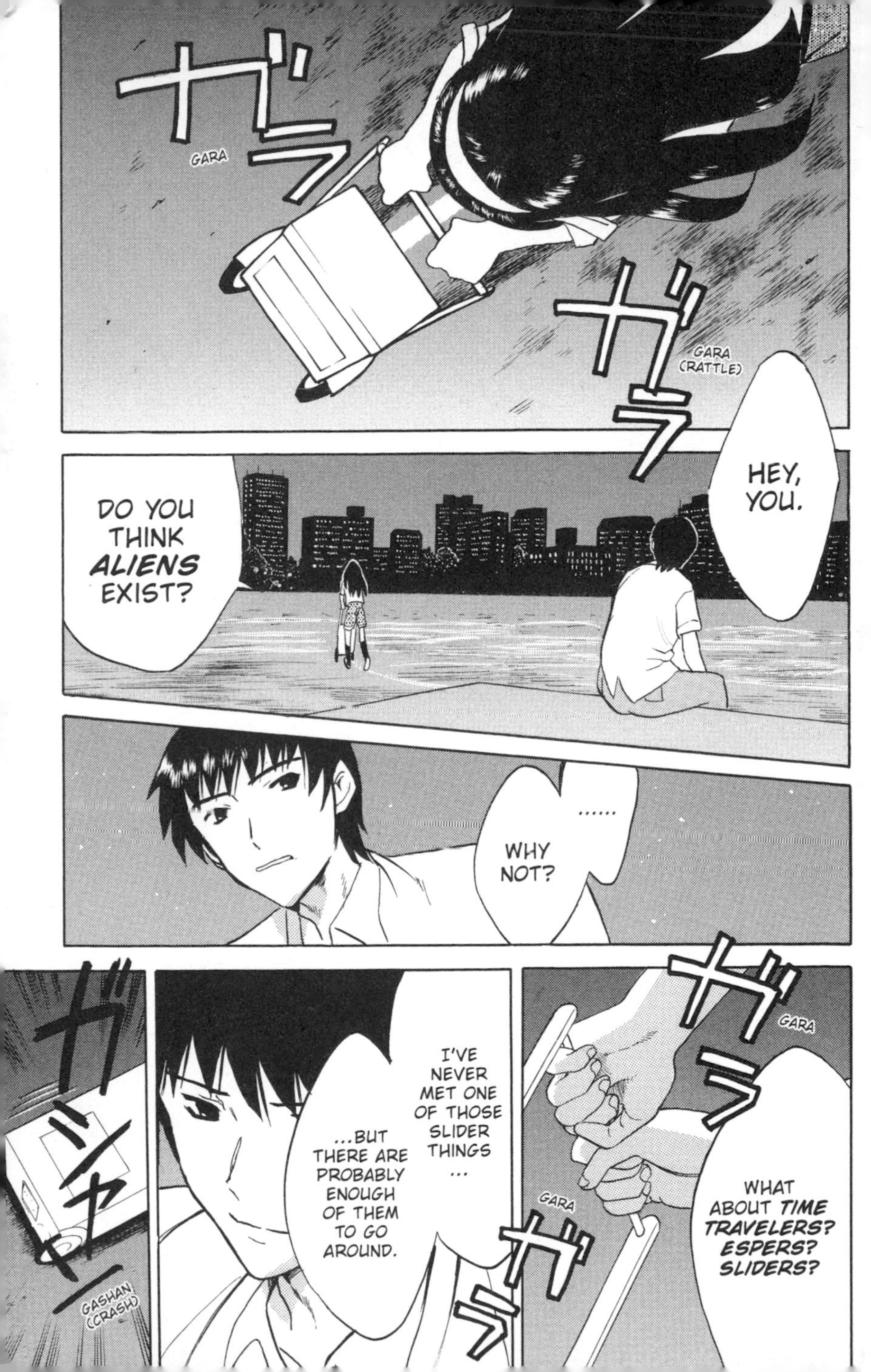
GARA
GARA (RATTLE)
HEY, YOU.
DO YOU THINK ALIENS EXIST?
......
WHY NOT?
GARA
GARA
WHAT ABOUT TIME TRAVELERS? ESPERS? SLIDERS?
I'VE NEVER MET ONE OF THOSE SLIDER THINGS ...
...BUT THERE ARE PROBABLY ENOUGH OF THEM TO GO AROUND.
GASHAN (CRASH)

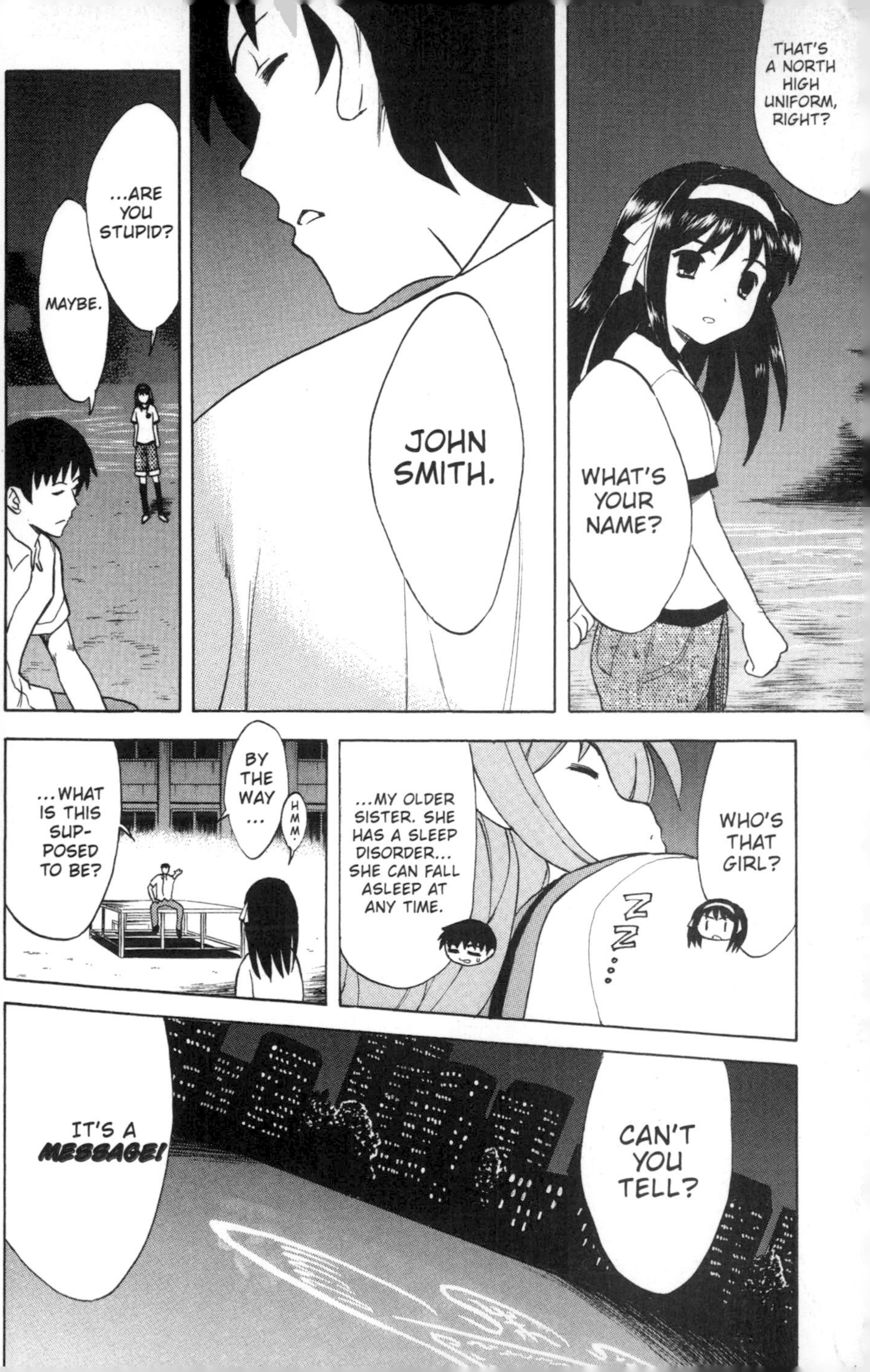
THAT'S A NORTH HIGH UNIFORM, RIGHT?
WHAT'S YOUR NAME?
JOHN SMITH.
...ARE YOU STUPID?
MAYBE.
WHO'S THAT GIRL?
Z Z
...MY OLDER SISTER. SHE HAS A SLEEP DISORDER... SHE CAN FALL ASLEEP AT ANY TIME.
HMM.
BY THE WAY...
...WHAT IS THIS SUP-POSED TO BE?
CAN'T YOU TELL?
IT'S A MESSAGE!

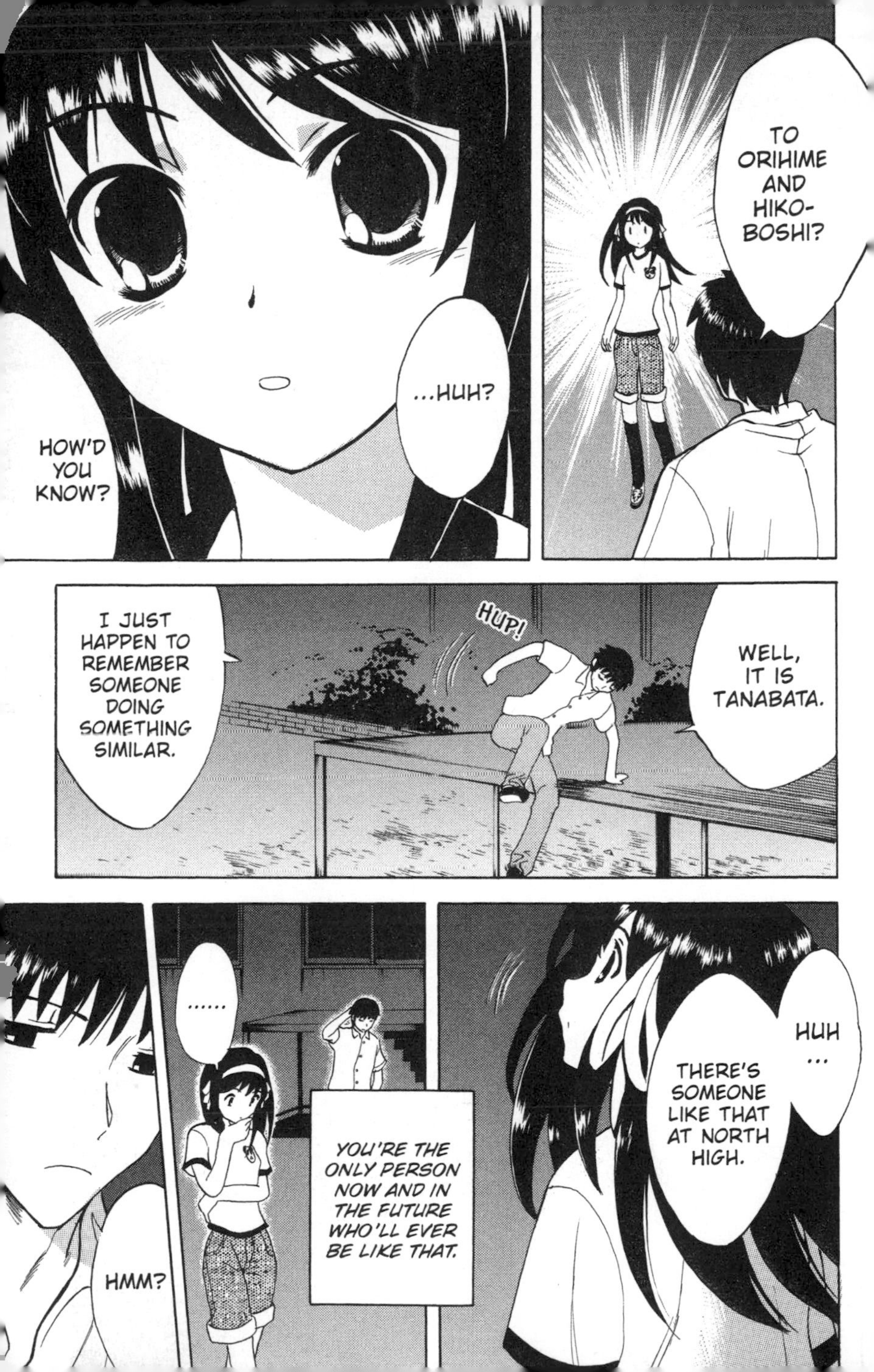
TO ORIHIME AND HIKO-BOSHI?
...HUH?
HOW'D YOU KNOW?
WELL, IT IS TANABATA.
HUP!
I JUST HAPPEN TO REMEMBER SOMEONE DOING SOMETHING SIMILAR.
HUH ...
THERE'S SOMEONE LIKE THAT AT NORTH HIGH.
......
YOU'RE THE ONLY PERSON NOW AND IN THE FUTURE WHO'LL EVER BE LIKE THAT.
HMM?

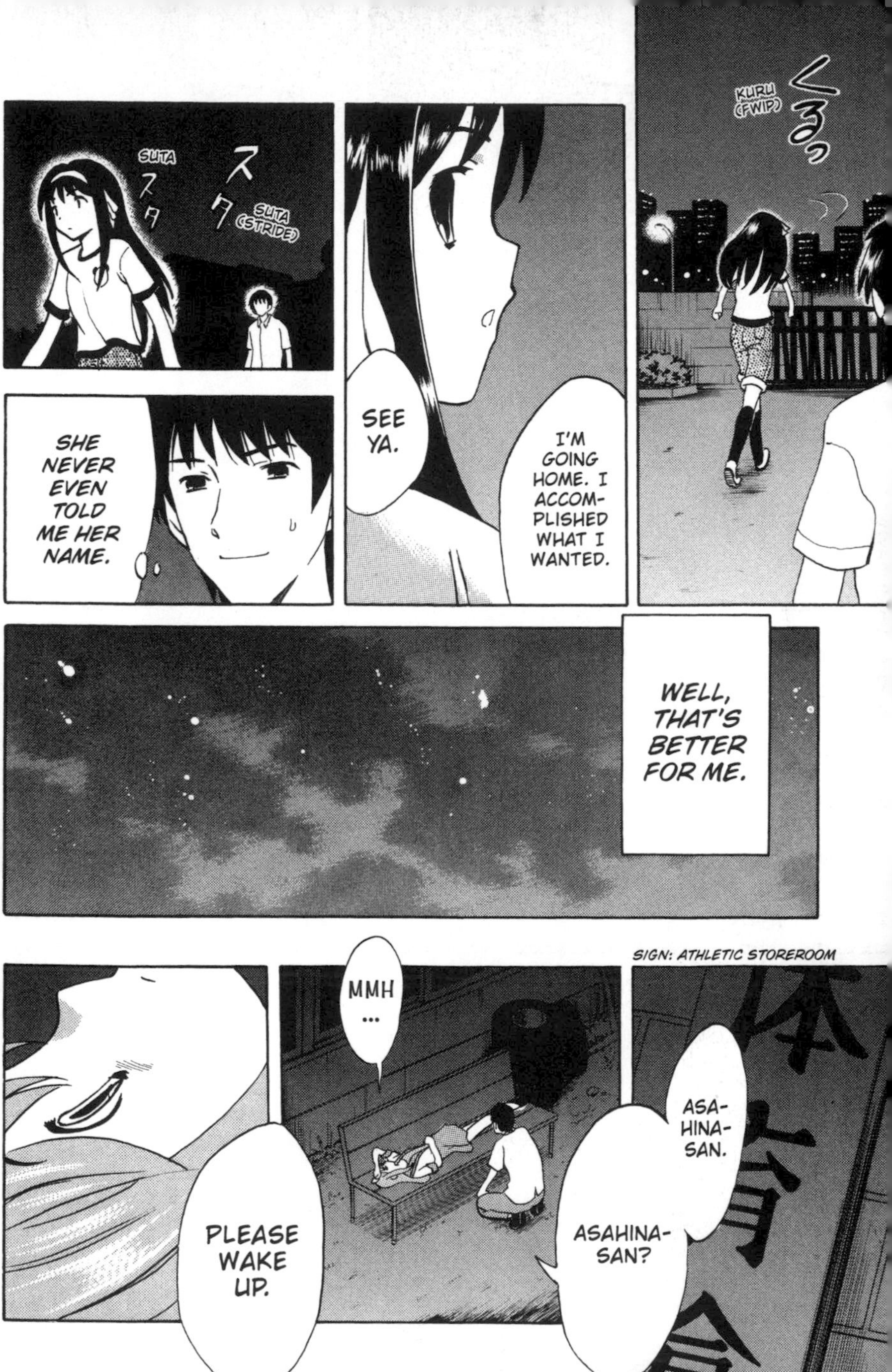
くるっ
KURU (FWIP)
I'M GOING HOME. I ACCOMPLISHED WHAT I WANTED.
SEE YA.
スタスタ
SUTA
SUTA (STRIDE)
SHE NEVER EVEN TOLD ME HER NAME.
WELL, THAT'S BETTER FOR ME.
SIGN: ATHLETIC STOREROOM
ASA-HINA-SAN.
ASAHINA-SAN?
MMH...
PLEASE WAKE UP.

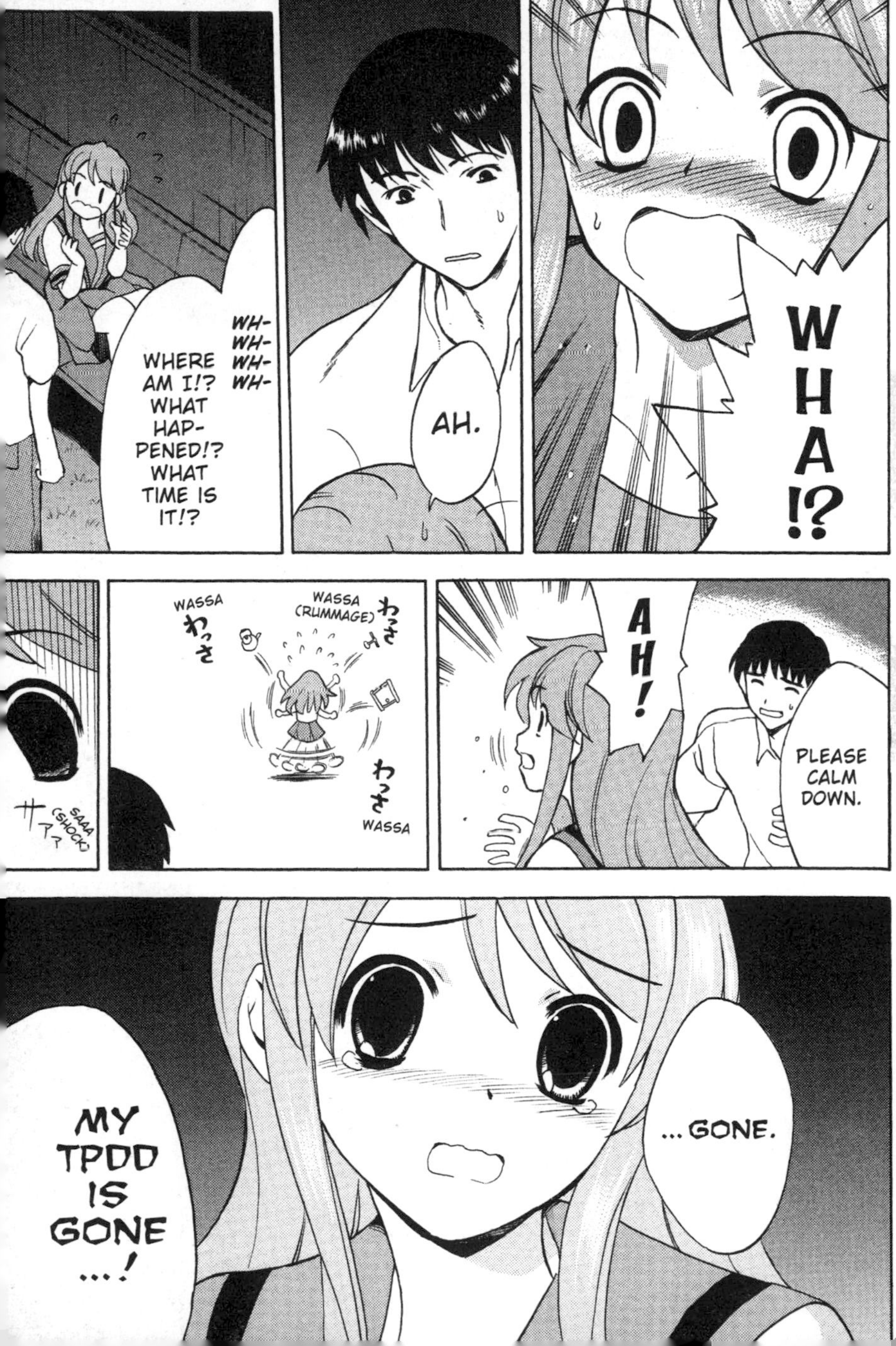
WHA!?
AH.
WH- WH- WH- WH-
WHERE AM I!? WHAT HAPPENED!? WHAT TIME IS IT!?
AH!
PLEASE CALM DOWN.
WASSA わっさ (RUMMAGE)
WASSA わっさ
わっさ WASSA
サァァ SAAA (SHOCK)
...GONE.
MY TPDD IS GONE...!

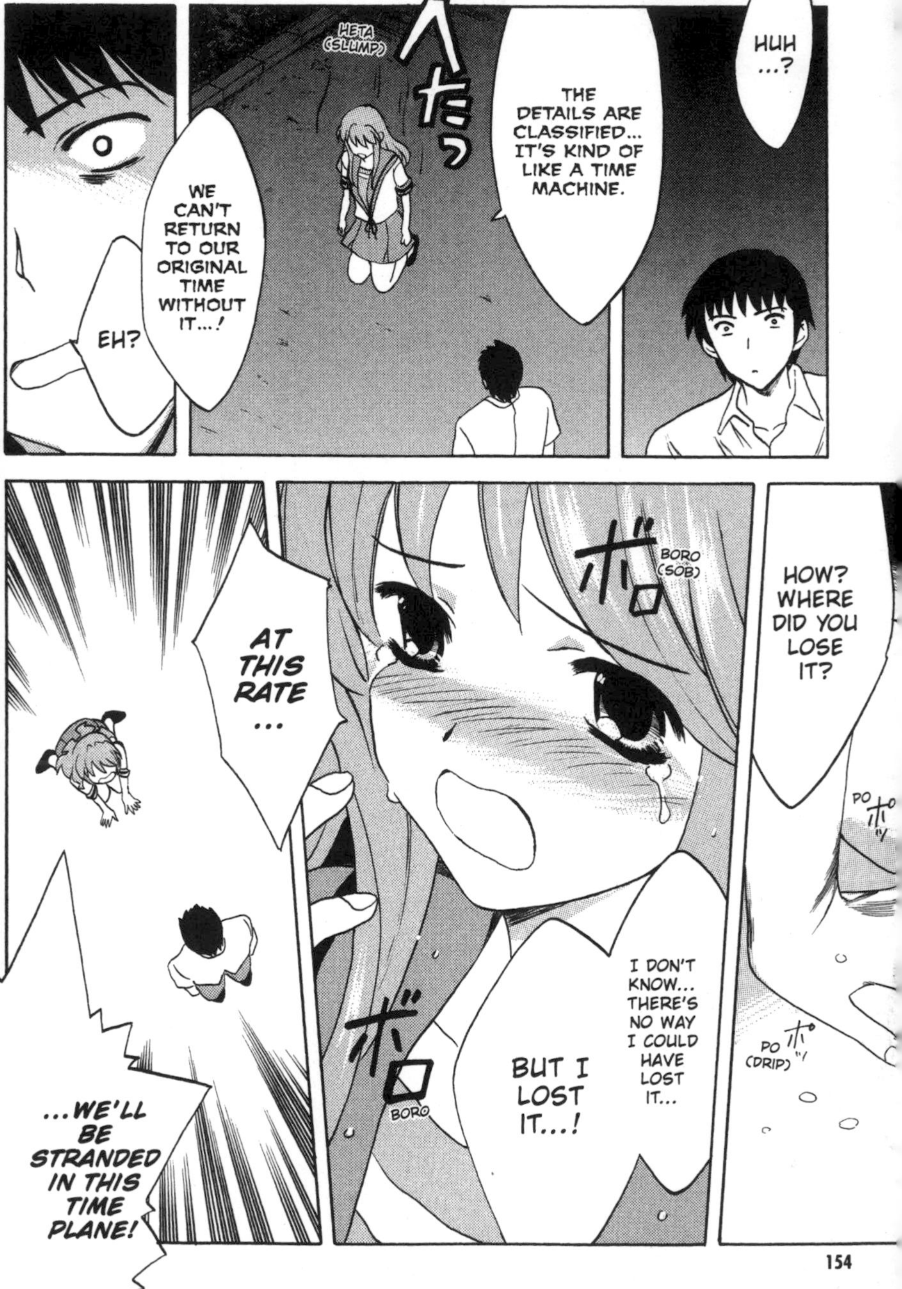
HUH ...?
THE DETAILS ARE CLASSIFIED... IT'S KIND OF LIKE A TIME MACHINE.
HETA (SLUMP)
WE CAN'T RETURN TO OUR ORIGINAL TIME WITHOUT IT...!
EH?
HOW? WHERE DID YOU LOSE IT?
PO
PO (DRIP)
BORO (SOB)
I DON'T KNOW... THERE'S NO WAY I COULD HAVE LOST IT...
BUT I LOST IT...!
BORO
AT THIS RATE ...
...WE'LL BE STRANDED IN THIS TIME PLANE!

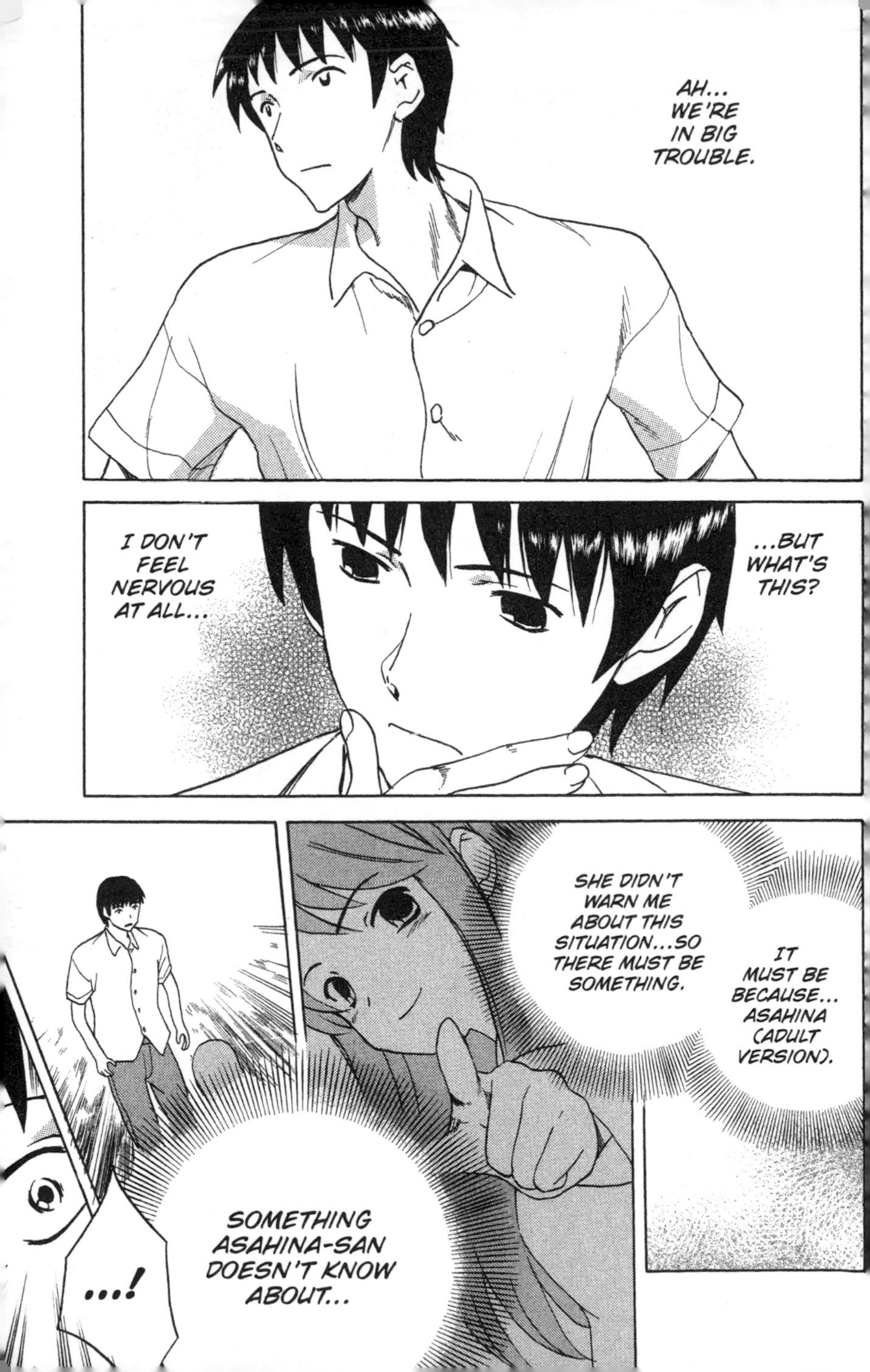
AH... WE'RE IN BIG TROUBLE.
...BUT WHAT'S THIS?
I DON'T FEEL NERVOUS AT ALL...
IT MUST BE BECAUSE... ASAHINA (ADULT VERSION).
SHE DIDN'T WARN ME ABOUT THIS SITUATION...SO THERE MUST BE SOMETHING.
SOMETHING ASAHINA-SAN DOESN'T KNOW ABOUT...
...!

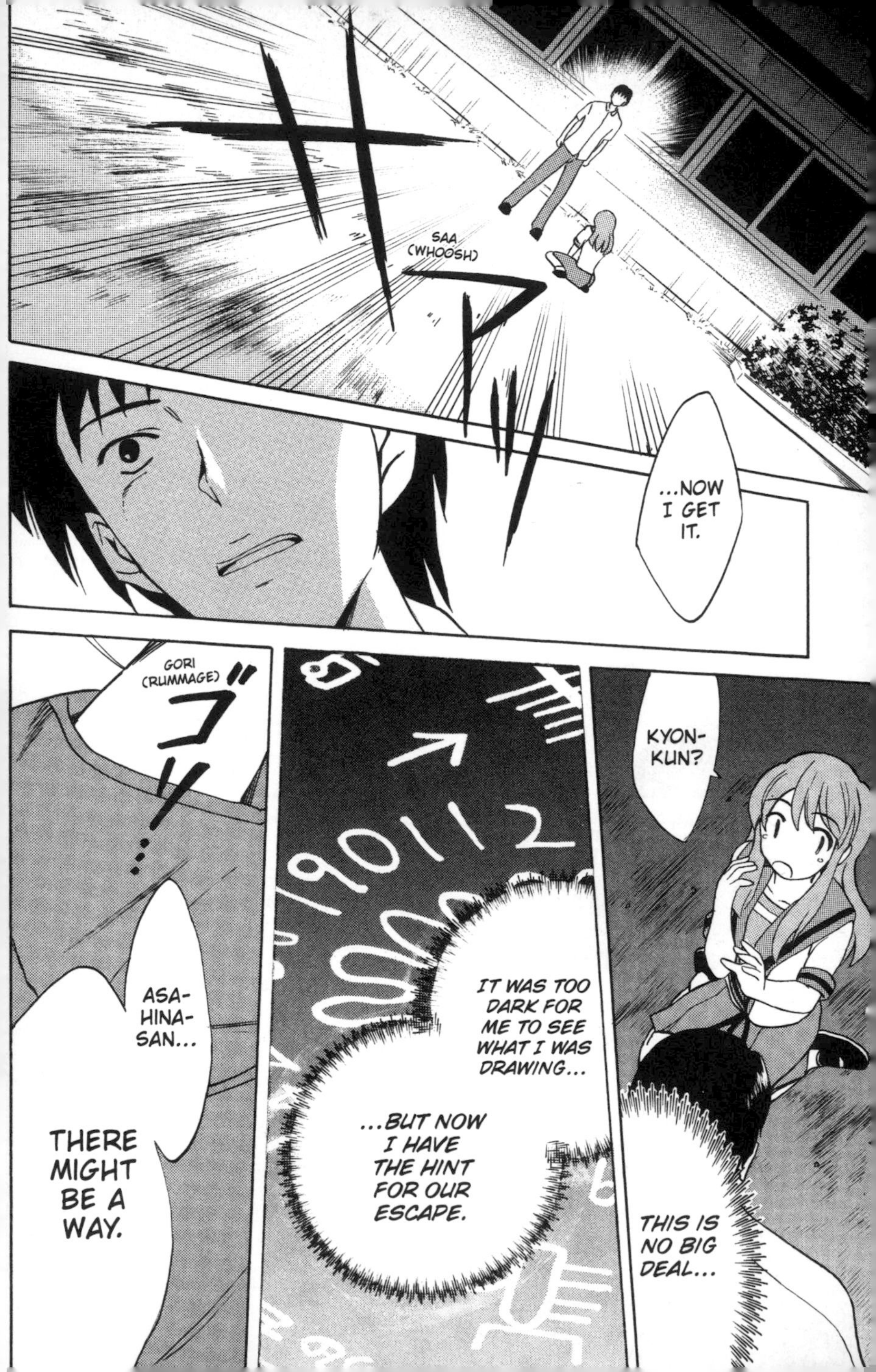
SAA (WHOOSH)
...NOW I GET IT.
KYON-KUN?
THIS IS NO BIG DEAL...
IT WAS TOO DARK FOR ME TO SEE WHAT I WAS DRAWING...
...BUT NOW I HAVE THE HINT FOR OUR ESCAPE.
GORI (RUMMAGE)
ASA-HINA-SAN...
THERE MIGHT BE A WAY.

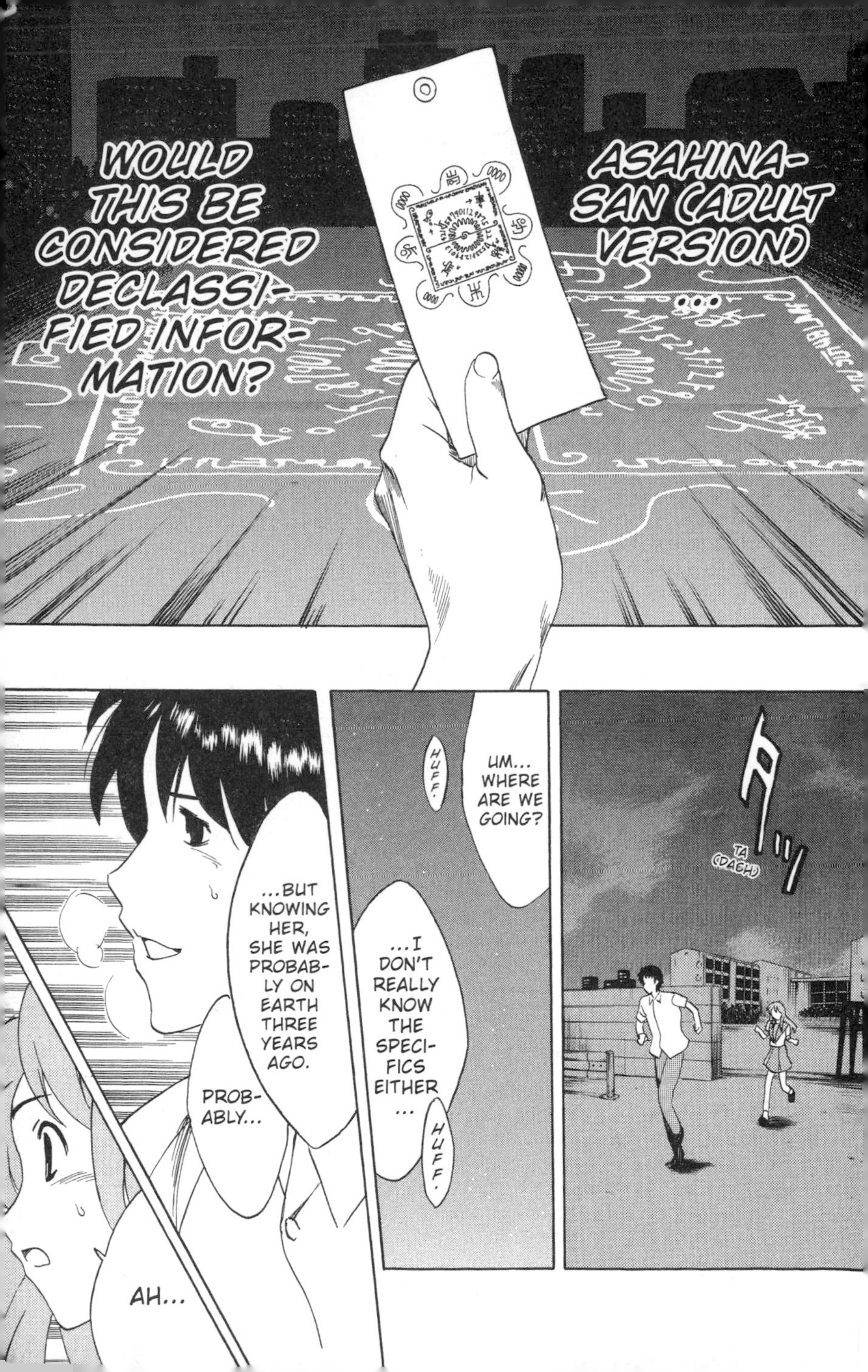
ASAHINA-SAN (ADULT VERSION)
WOULD THIS BE CONSIDERED DECLASSI-FIED INFOR-MATION?
TA (DASH)
UM... WHERE ARE WE GOING?
HUFF.
...I DON'T REALLY KNOW THE SPECI-FICS EITHER...
HUFF.
...BUT KNOWING HER, SHE WAS PROBAB-LY ON EARTH THREE YEARS AGO.
PROB-ABLY...
AH...

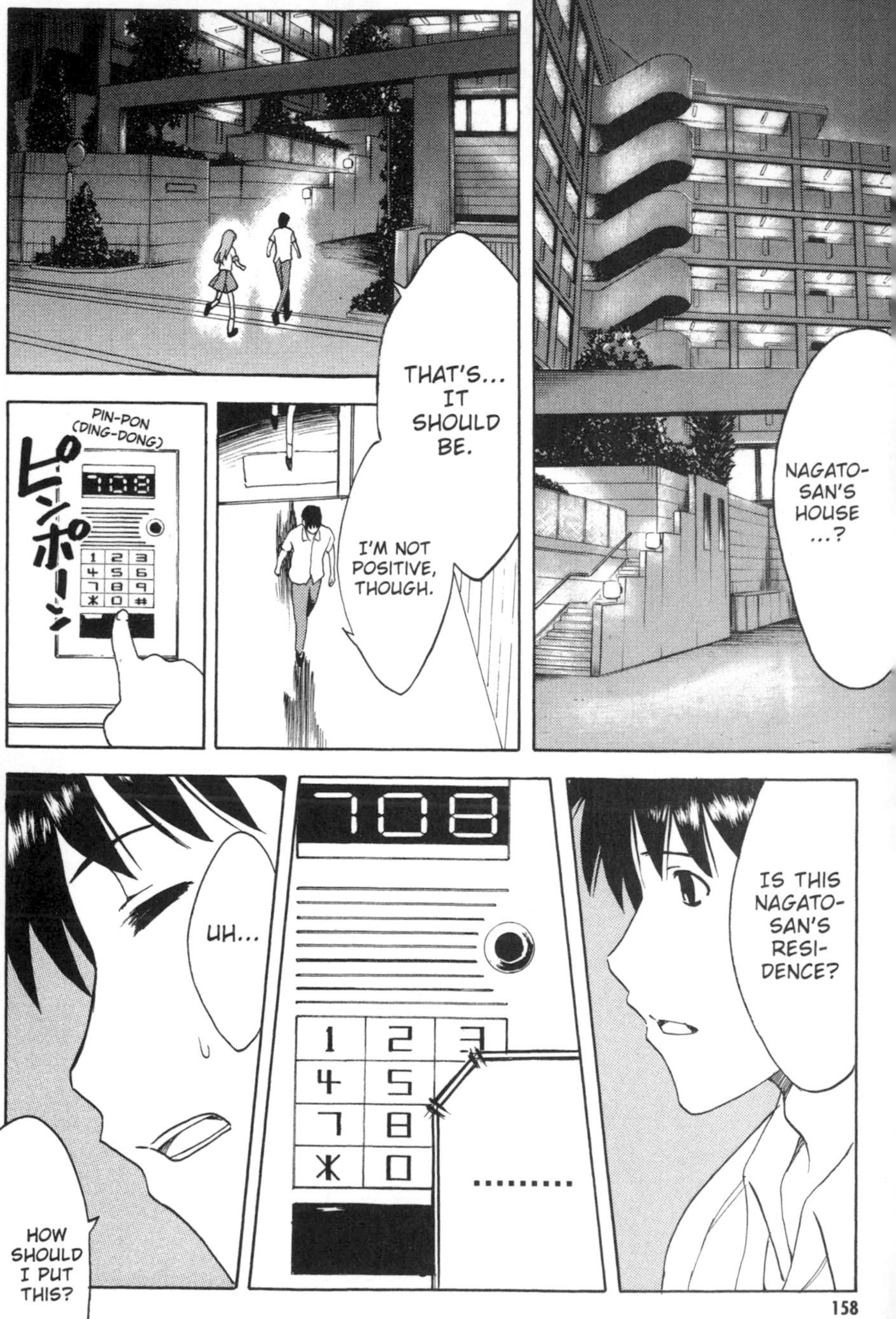
NAGATO-SAN'S HOUSE ...?
THAT'S... IT SHOULD BE.
I'M NOT POSITIVE, THOUGH.
PIN-PON (DING-DONG)
ピンポーン
708
IS THIS NAGATO-SAN'S RESIDENCE?
....
UH...
HOW SHOULD I PUT THIS?

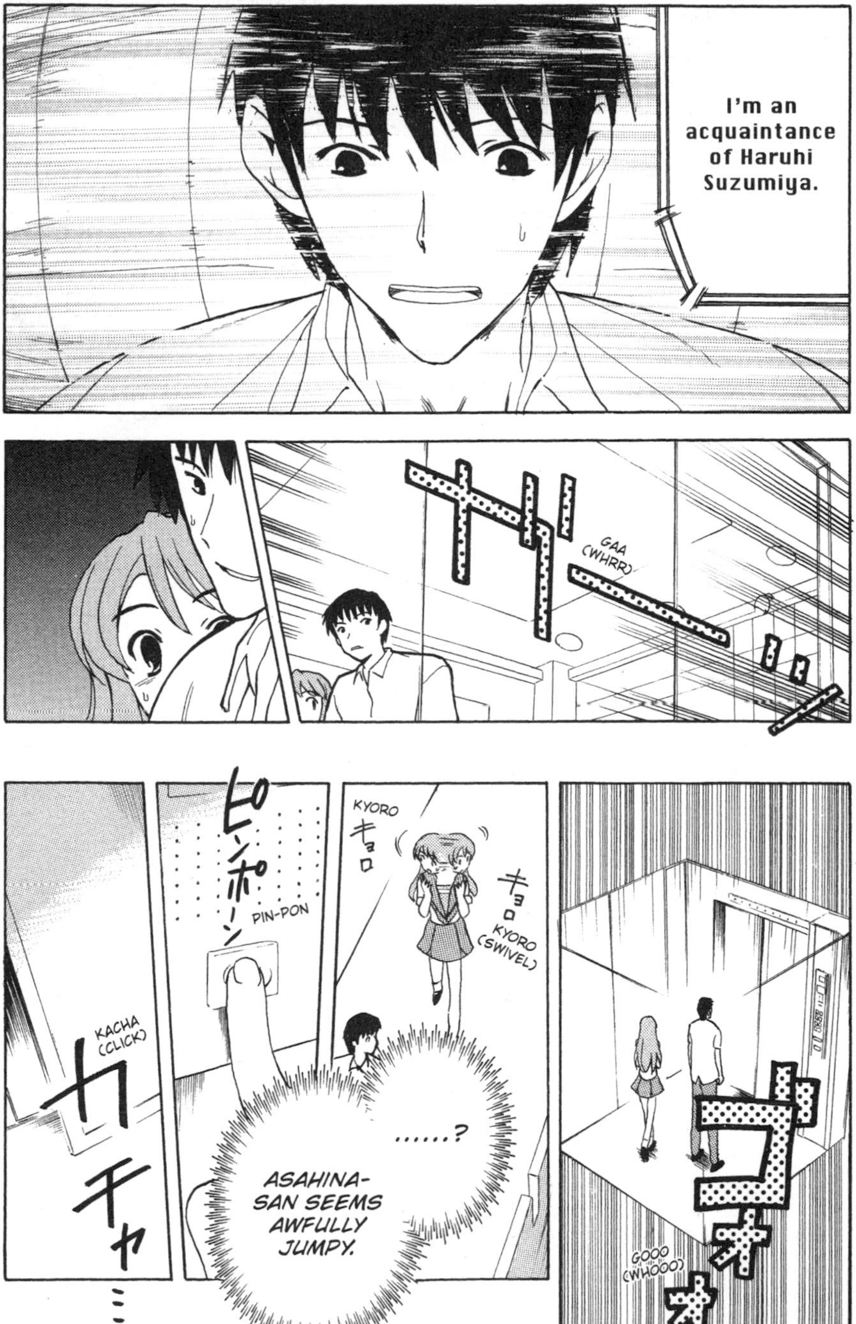
I'm an acquaintance of Haruhi Suzumiya.
ザーッ
GAA (WHRR)
ゴォォ
GOOO (WHOOO)
キョロ
KYORO
キョロ
KYORO (SWIVEL)
......?
ASAHINA-SAN SEEMS AWFULLY JUMPY.
ピンポーン
PIN-PON
カチャ
KACHA (CLICK)

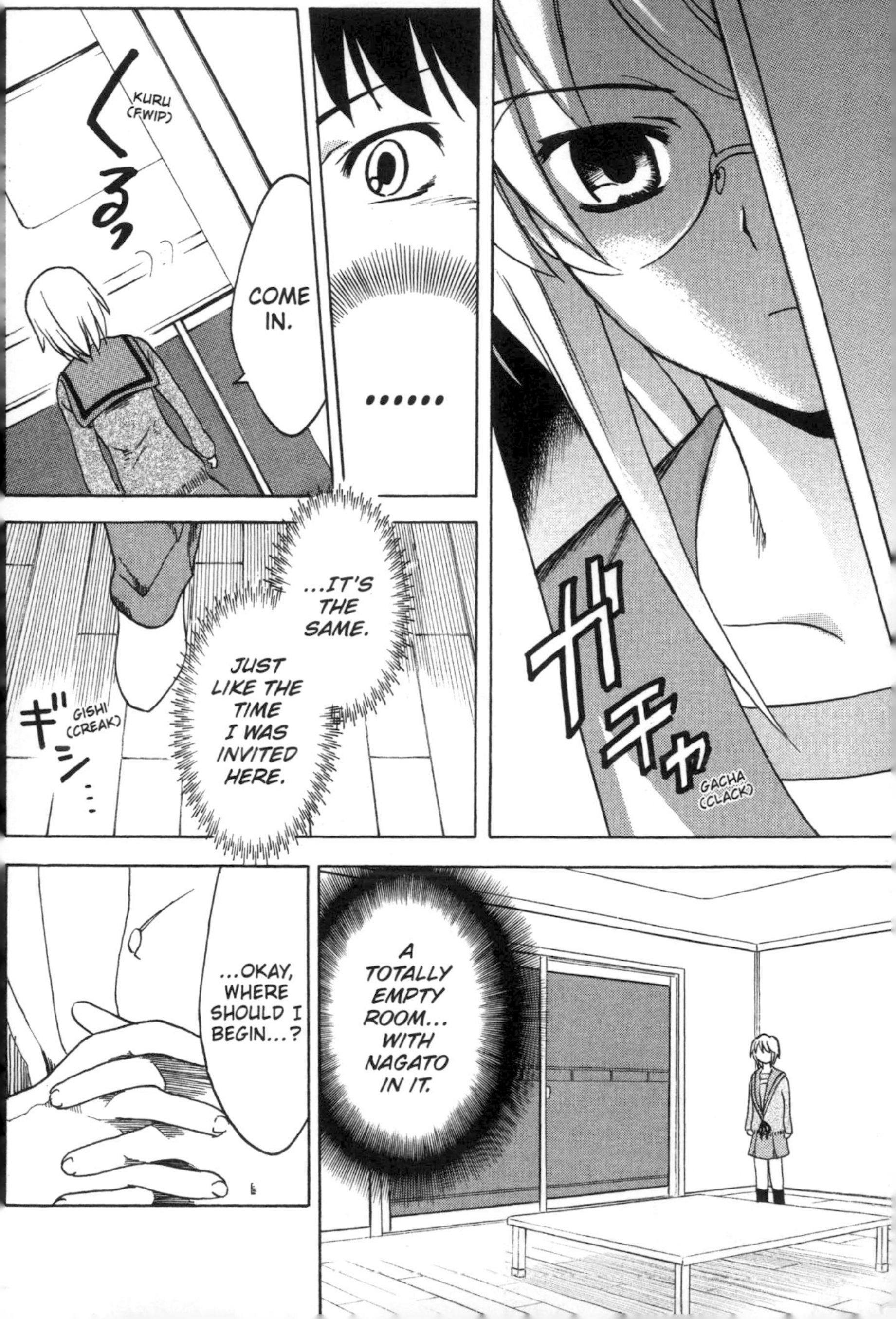
ガチャ
GACHA (CLACK)
......
くるっ
KURU (FWIP)
COME IN.
ギシ…
GISHI (CREAK)
...IT'S THE SAME.
JUST LIKE THE TIME I WAS INVITED HERE.
A TOTALLY EMPTY ROOM... WITH NAGATO IN IT.
...OKAY, WHERE SHOULD I BEGIN...?

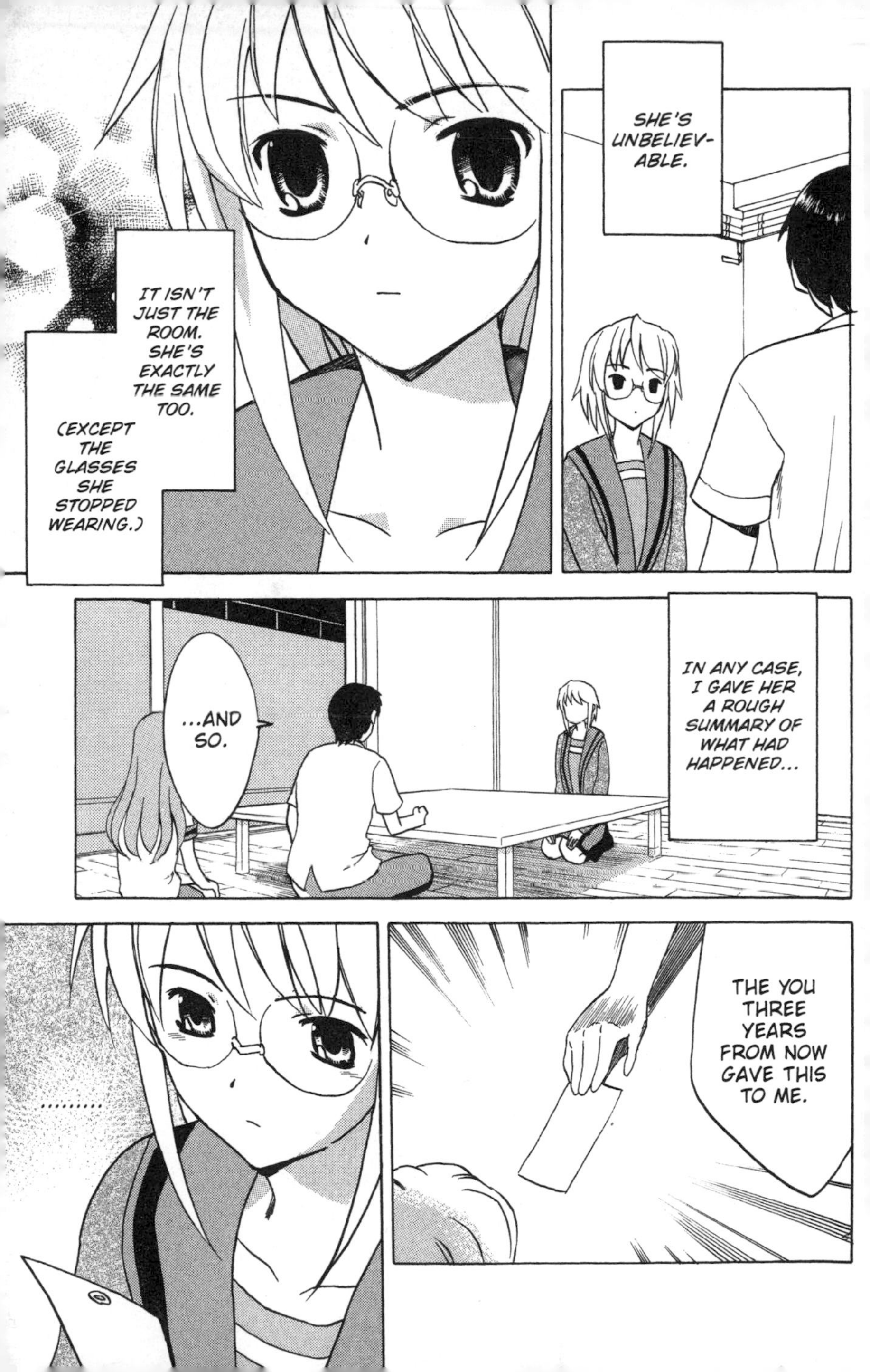
SHE'S UNBELIEV-ABLE.
IT ISN'T JUST THE ROOM. SHE'S EXACTLY THE SAME TOO.
(EXCEPT THE GLASSES SHE STOPPED WEARING.)
IN ANY CASE, I GAVE HER A ROUGH SUMMARY OF WHAT HAD HAPPENED...
...AND SO.
THE YOU THREE YEARS FROM NOW GAVE THIS TO ME.
....

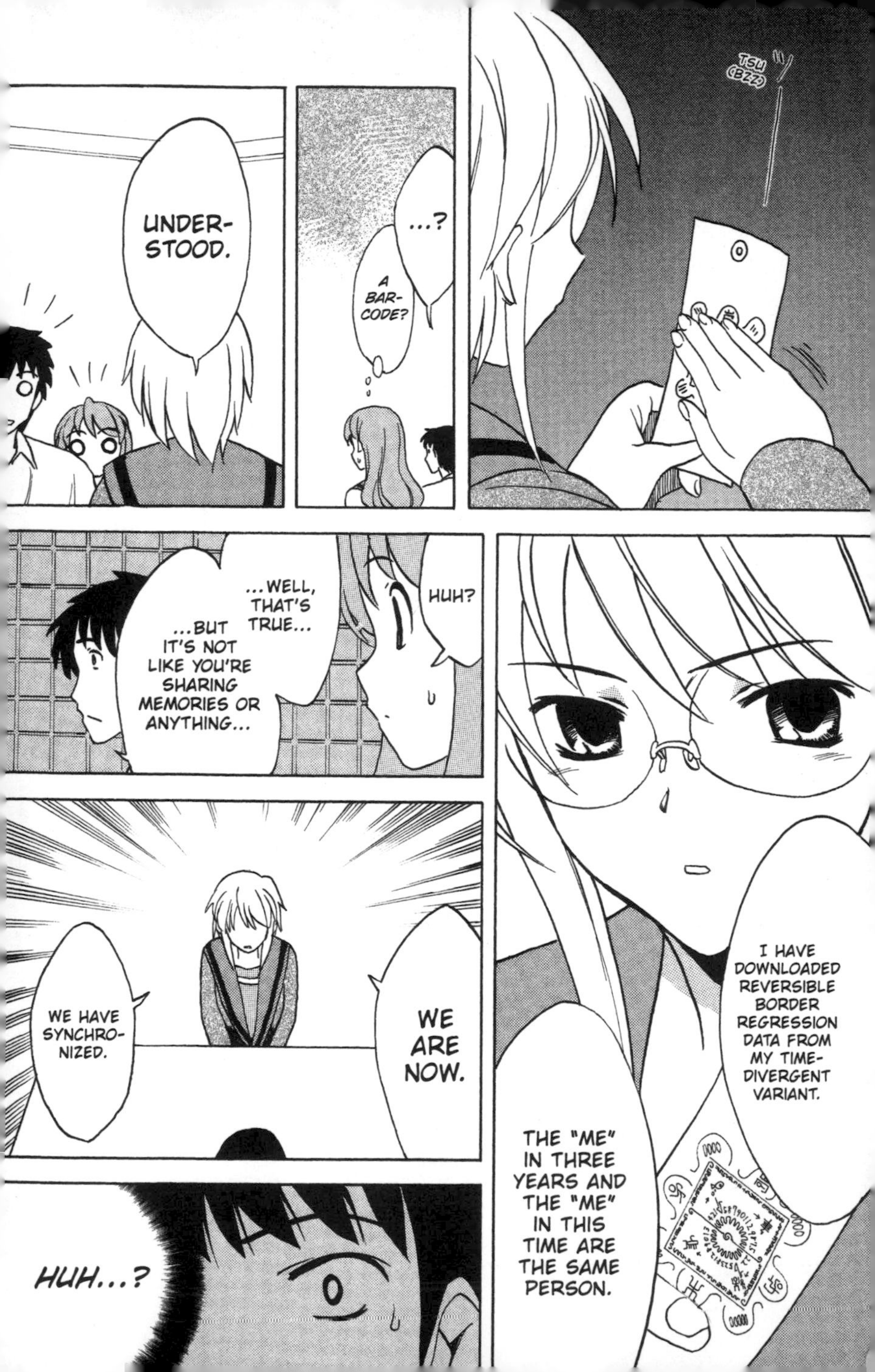
TSU (BZZ)
...?
A BAR-CODE?
UNDER-STOOD.
I HAVE DOWNLOADED REVERSIBLE BORDER REGRESSION DATA FROM MY TIME-DIVERGENT VARIANT.
THE "ME" IN THREE YEARS AND THE "ME" IN THIS TIME ARE THE SAME PERSON.
HUH?
...WELL, THAT'S TRUE...
...BUT IT'S NOT LIKE YOU'RE SHARING MEMORIES OR ANYTHING...
WE ARE NOW.
WE HAVE SYNCHRO-NIZED.
HUH...?

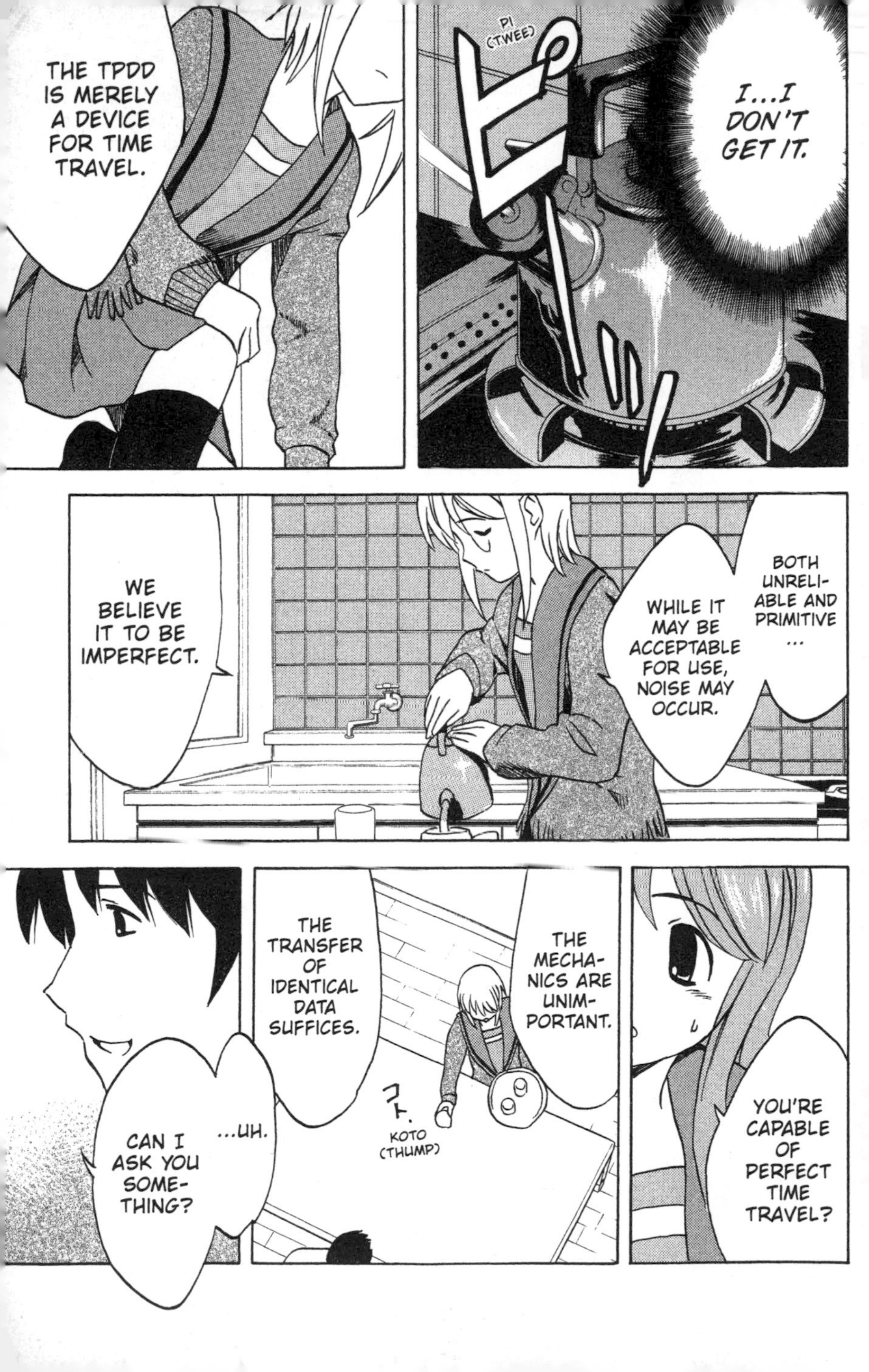
PI (TWEE)
I...I DON'T GET IT.
THE TPDD IS MERELY A DEVICE FOR TIME TRAVEL.
BOTH UNRELIABLE AND PRIMITIVE ...
WHILE IT MAY BE ACCEPTABLE FOR USE, NOISE MAY OCCUR.
WE BELIEVE IT TO BE IMPERFECT.
YOU'RE CAPABLE OF PERFECT TIME TRAVEL?
THE MECHANICS ARE UNIMPORTANT.
THE TRANSFER OF IDENTICAL DATA SUFFICES.
コト.
KOTO (THUMP)
...UH.
CAN I ASK YOU SOMETHING?

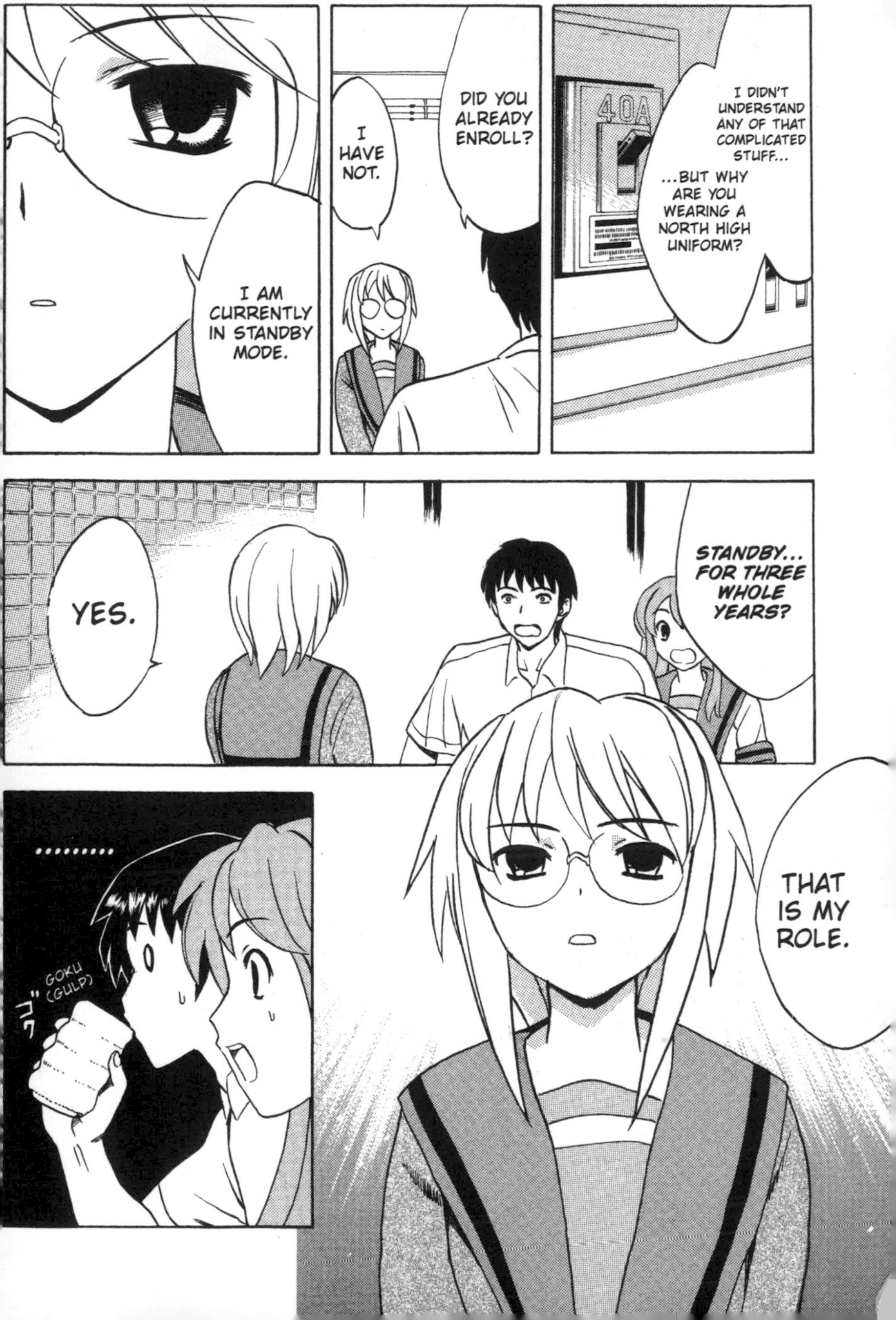
I DIDN'T UNDERSTAND ANY OF THAT COMPLICATED STUFF...
...BUT WHY ARE YOU WEARING A NORTH HIGH UNIFORM?
DID YOU ALREADY ENROLL?
I HAVE NOT.
I AM CURRENTLY IN STANDBY MODE.
STANDBY... FOR THREE WHOLE YEARS?
YES.
THAT IS MY ROLE.
....
GOKU (GULP)
ゴク

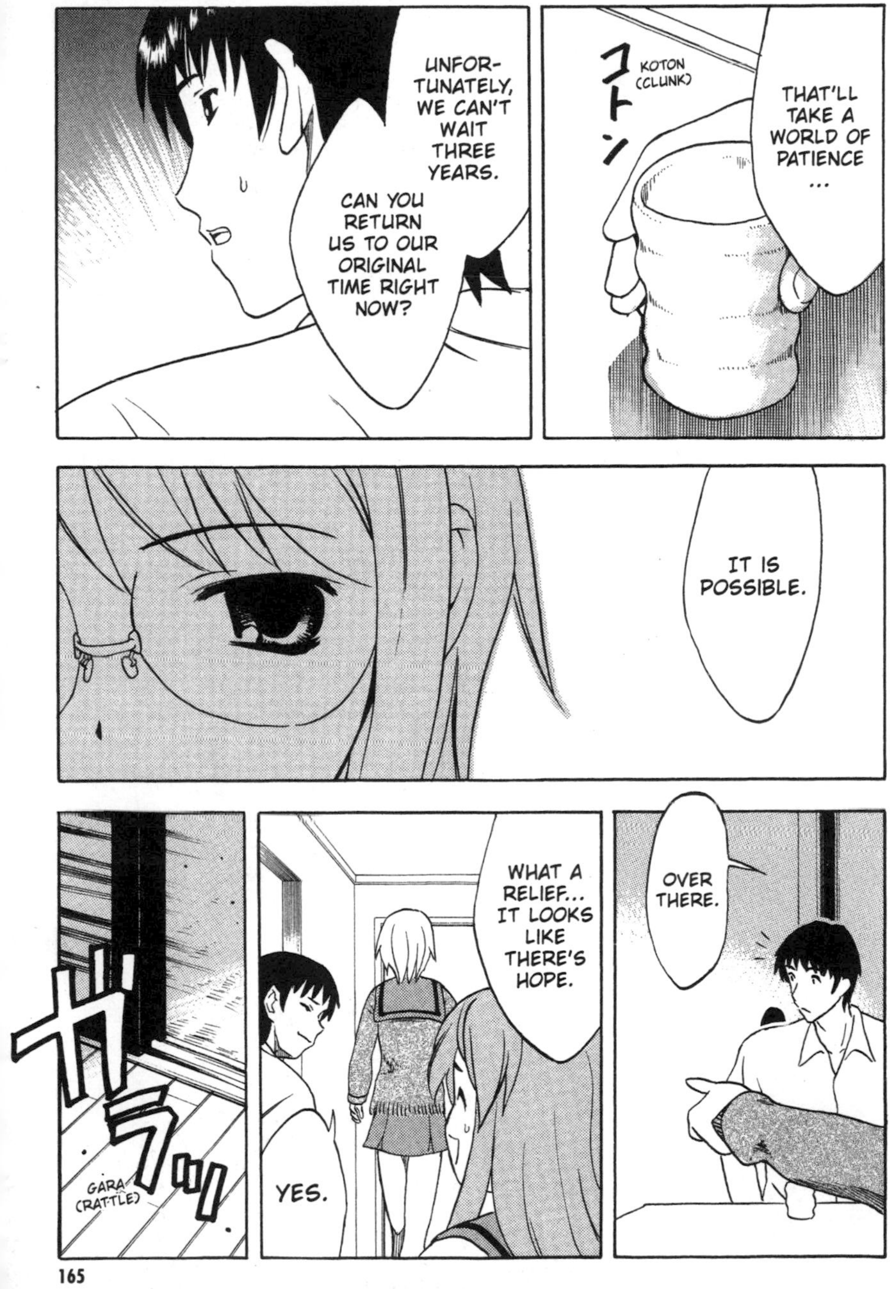
THAT'LL TAKE A WORLD OF PATIENCE ...
コトン
KOTON (CLUNK)
UNFORTUNATELY, WE CAN'T WAIT THREE YEARS.
CAN YOU RETURN US TO OUR ORIGINAL TIME RIGHT NOW?
IT IS POSSIBLE.
OVER THERE.
WHAT A RELIEF... IT LOOKS LIKE THERE'S HOPE.
YES.
ガラッ
GARA (RATTLE)

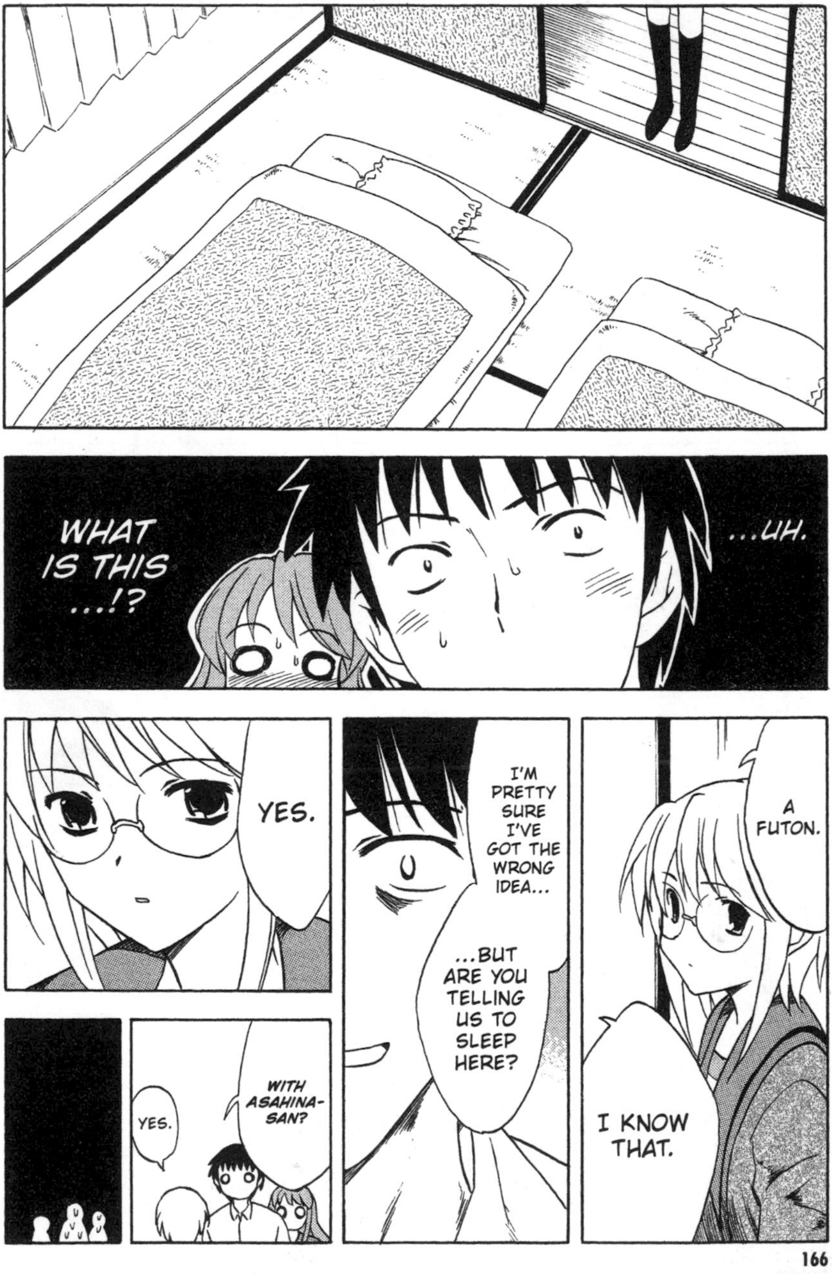
...UH.
WHAT IS THIS ...!?
A FUTON.
I KNOW THAT.
I'M PRETTY SURE I'VE GOT THE WRONG IDEA...
...BUT ARE YOU TELLING US TO SLEEP HERE?
YES.
WITH ASAHINA-SAN?
YES.

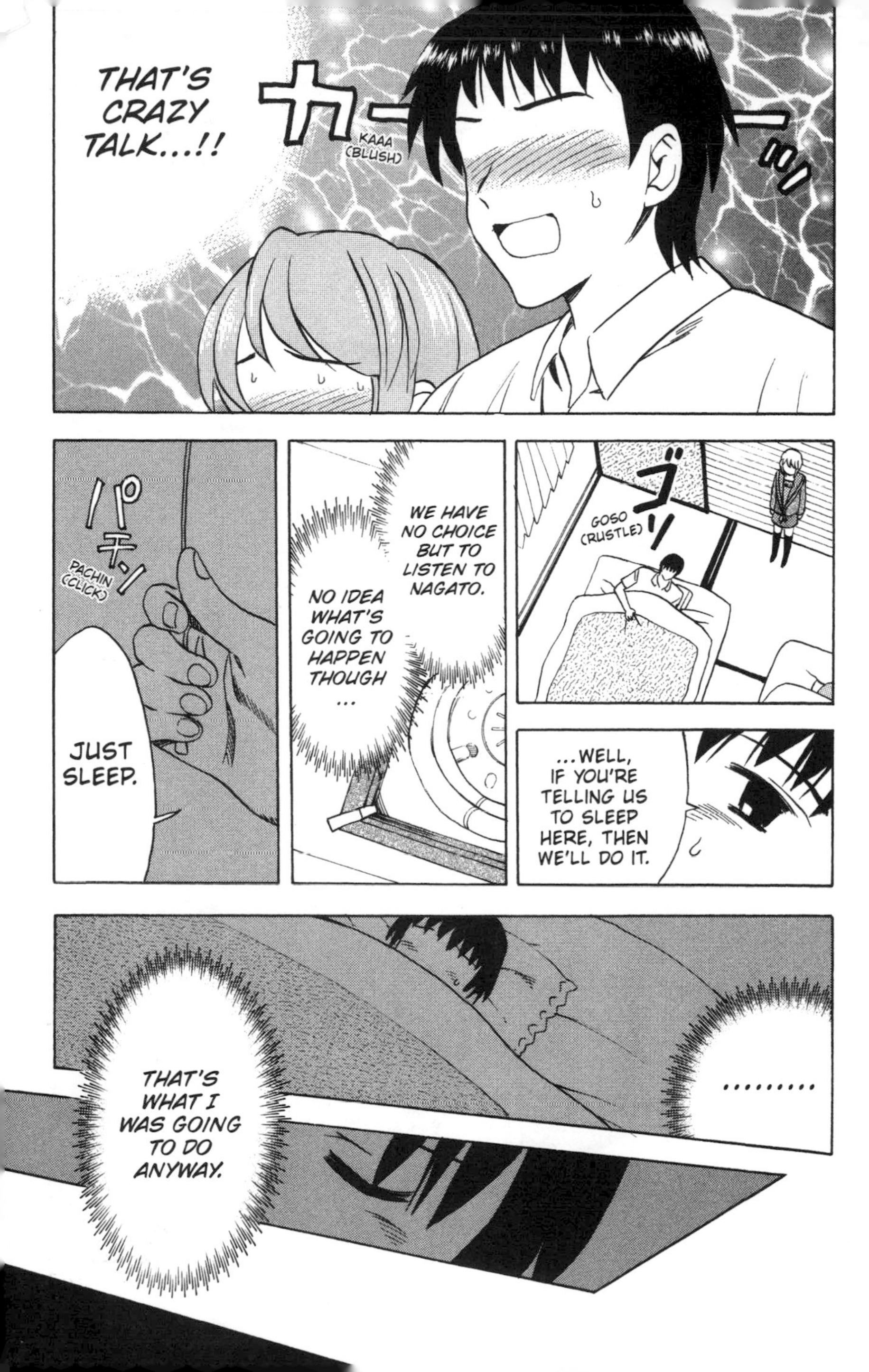
THAT'S CRAZY TALK...!!
KAAA (BLUSH)
GOSO (RUSTLE)
...WELL, IF YOU'RE TELLING US TO SLEEP HERE, THEN WE'LL DO IT.
WE HAVE NO CHOICE BUT TO LISTEN TO NAGATO.
NO IDEA WHAT'S GOING TO HAPPEN THOUGH ...
PACHIN (CLICK)
JUST SLEEP.
....
THAT'S WHAT I WAS GOING TO DO ANYWAY.

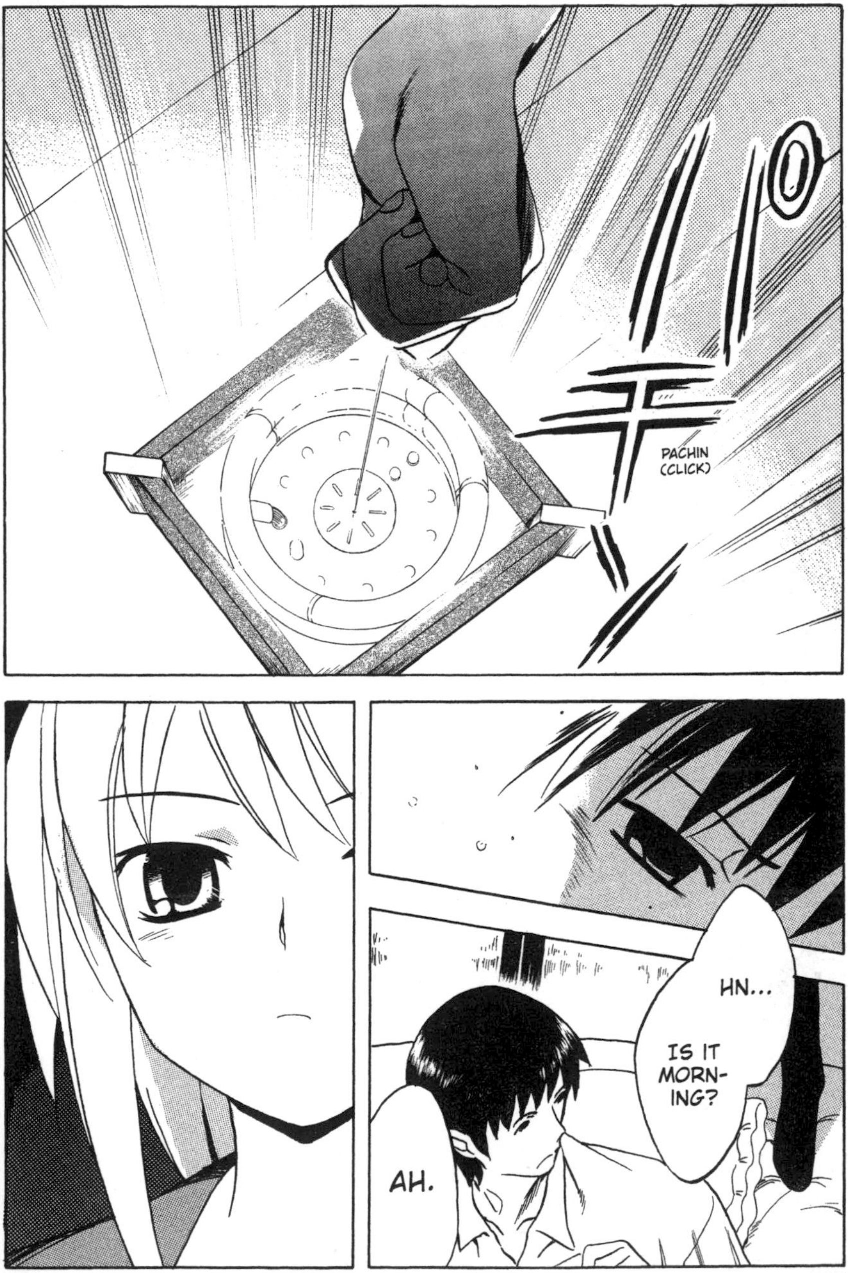
PACHIN (CLICK)
HN...
IS IT MORNING?
AH.

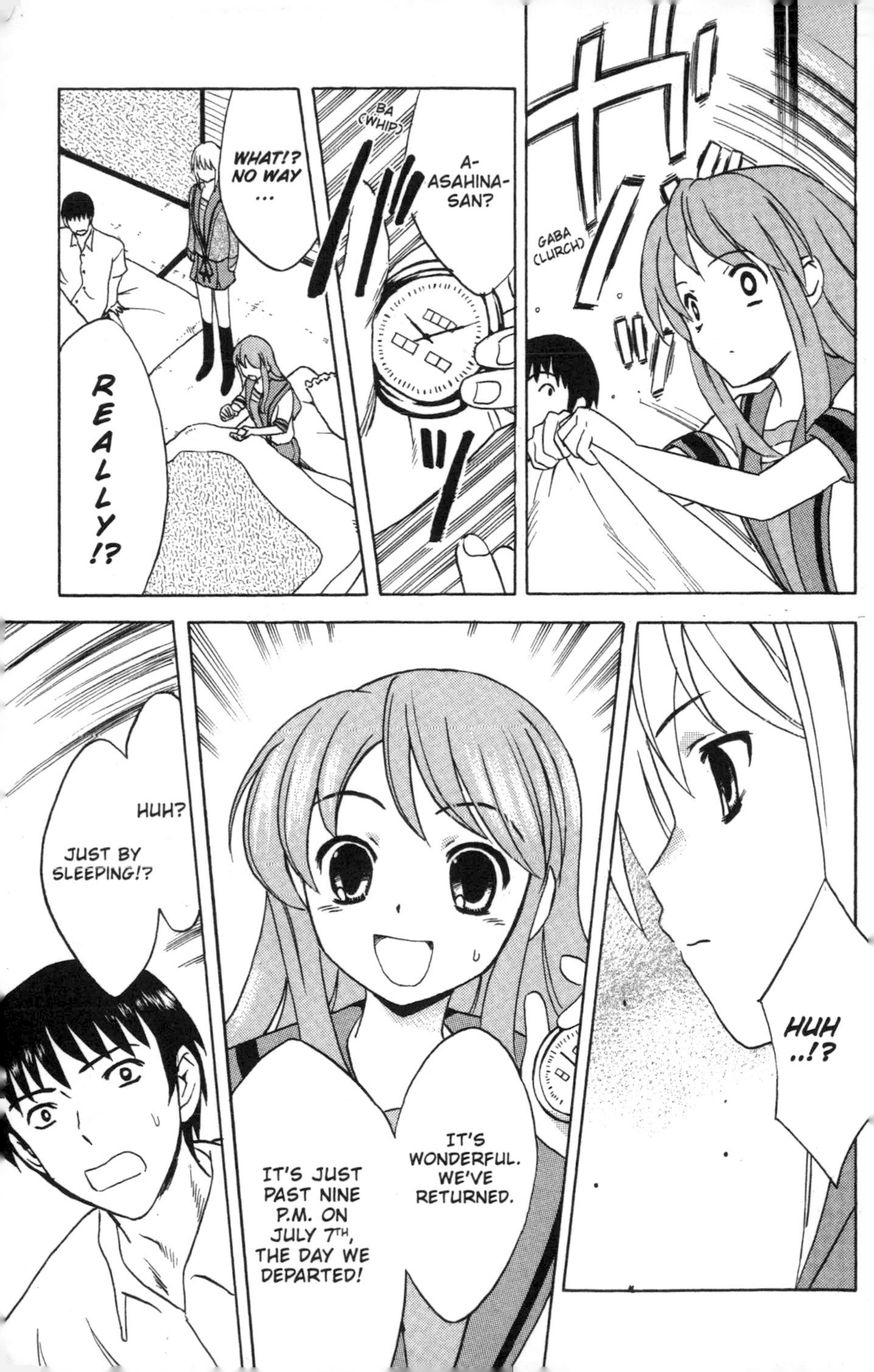
GABA (LURCH)
BA (WHIP)
A- ASAHINA- SAN?
WHAT!? NO WAY ...
REALLY!?
HUH ..!?
IT'S WONDERFUL. WE'VE RETURNED.
IT'S JUST PAST NINE P.M. ON JULY 7TH, THE DAY WE DEPARTED!
HUH?
JUST BY SLEEPING!?

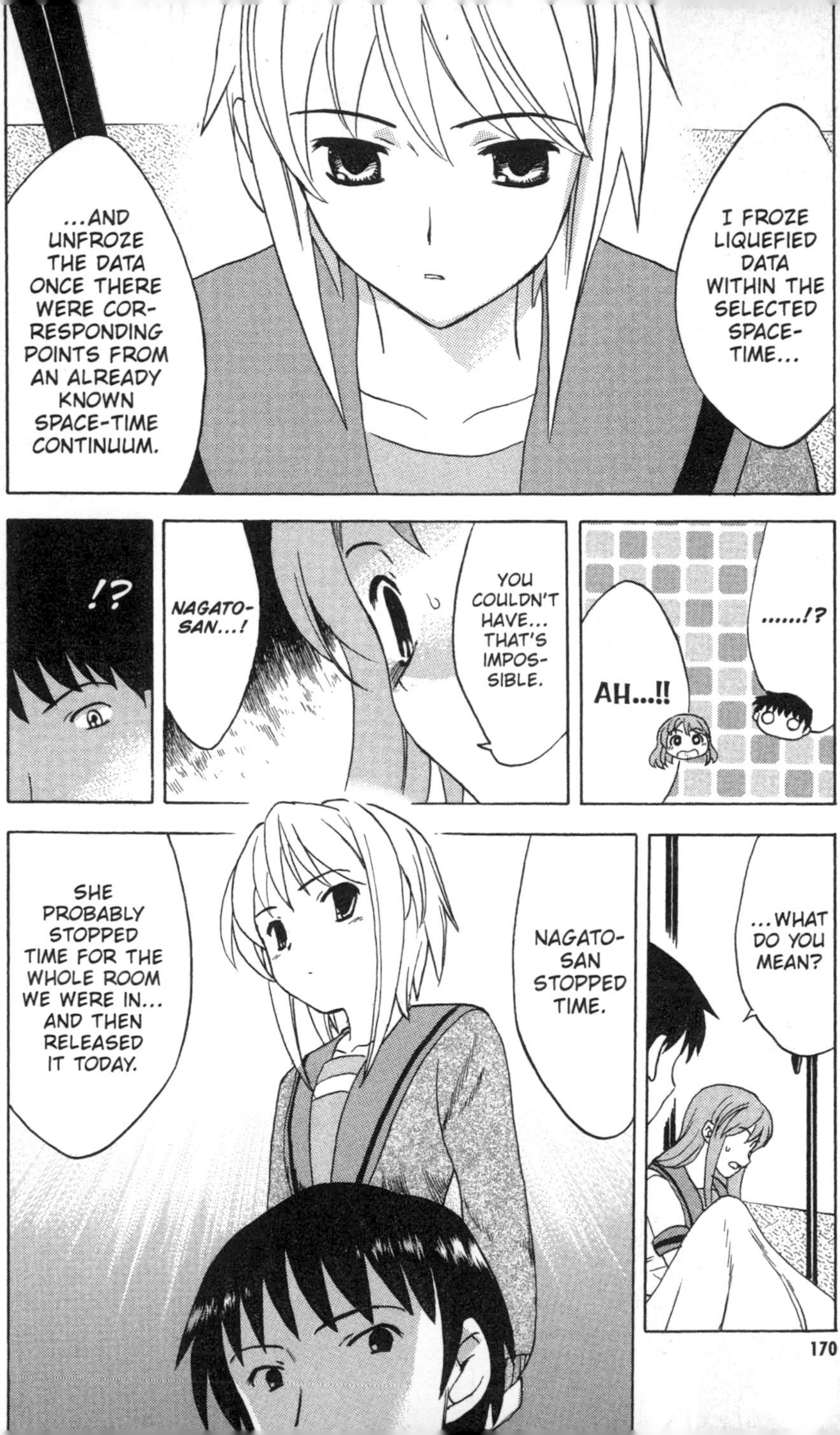
I FROZE LIQUEFIED DATA WITHIN THE SELECTED SPACE-TIME...
...AND UNFROZE THE DATA ONCE THERE WERE COR-RESPONDING POINTS FROM AN ALREADY KNOWN SPACE-TIME CONTINUUM.
......!?
AH...!!
YOU COULDN'T HAVE... THAT'S IMPOS-SIBLE.
NAGATO-SAN...!
!?
...WHAT DO YOU MEAN?
NAGATO-SAN STOPPED TIME.
SHE PROBABLY STOPPED TIME FOR THE WHOLE ROOM WE WERE IN... AND THEN RELEASED IT TODAY.

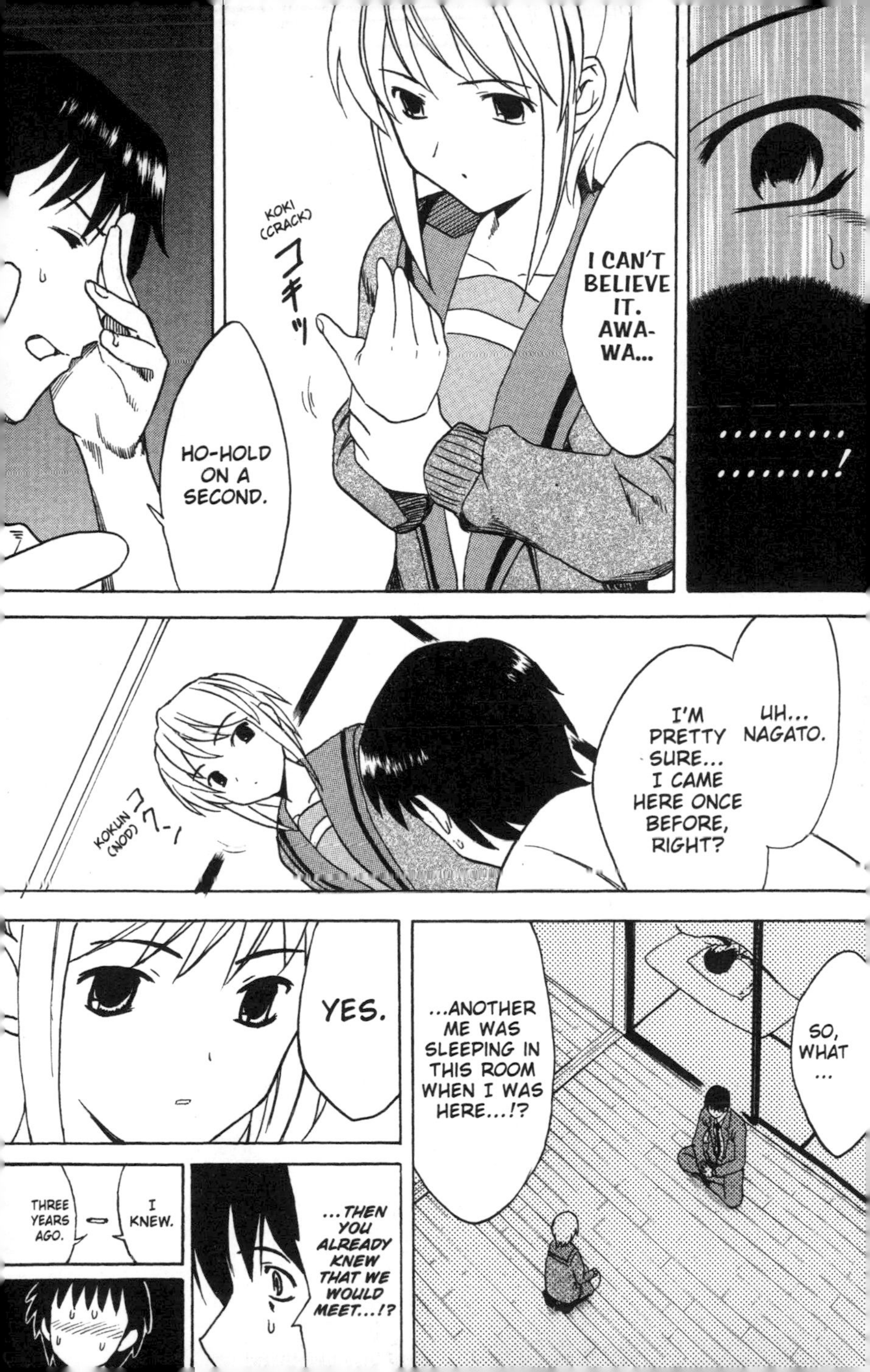
....
........!
I CAN'T BELIEVE IT. AWA-WA...
KOKI (CRACK)
HO-HOLD ON A SECOND.
UH... NAGATO.
I'M PRETTY SURE... I CAME HERE ONCE BEFORE, RIGHT?
KOKUN (NOD)
SO, WHAT ...
...ANOTHER ME WAS SLEEPING IN THIS ROOM WHEN I WAS HERE...!?
YES.
...THEN YOU ALREADY KNEW THAT WE WOULD MEET...!?
I KNEW.
THREE YEARS AGO.

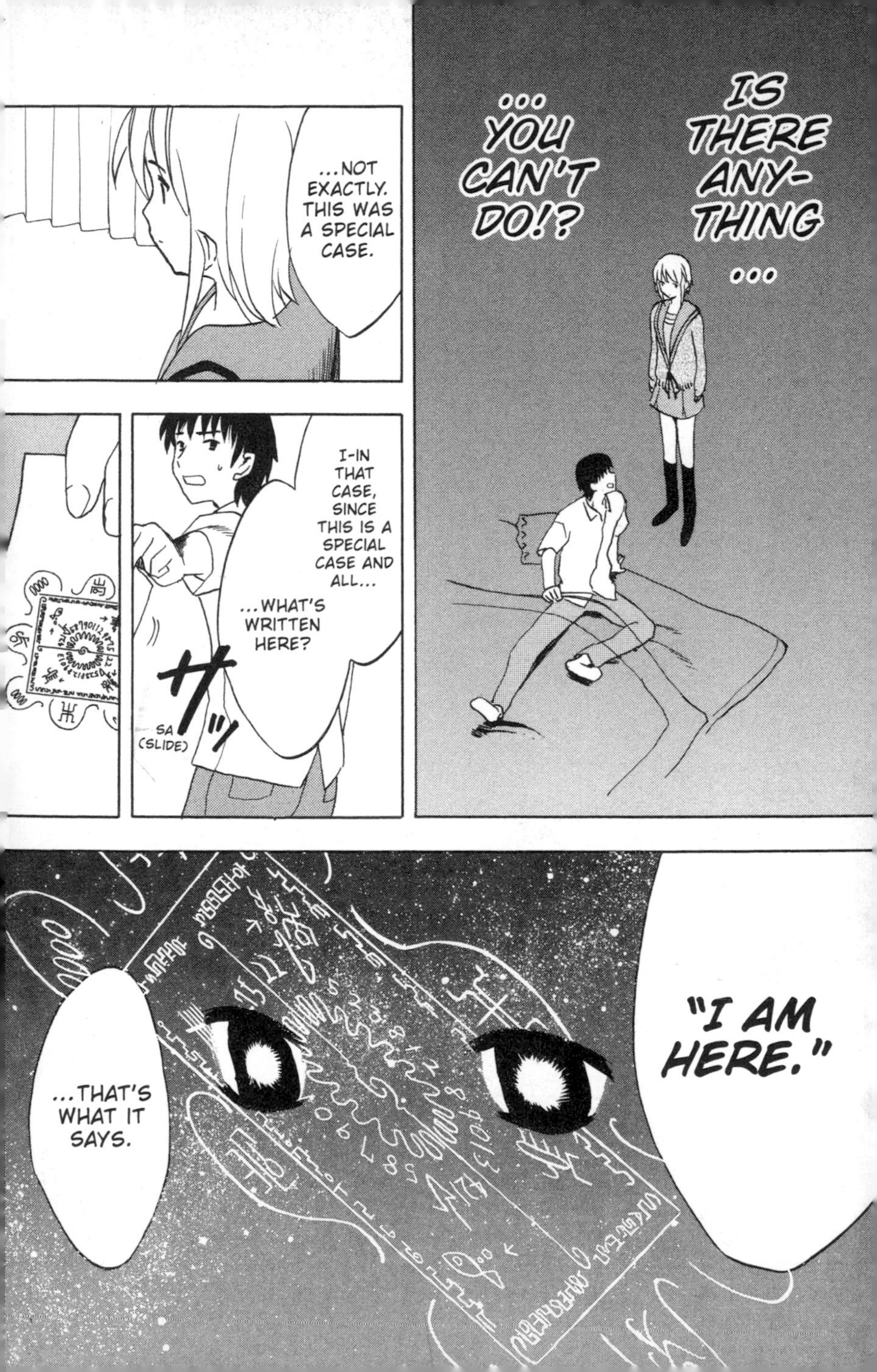

IS THERE ANYTHING...
...YOU CAN'T DO!?
...NOT EXACTLY. THIS WAS A SPECIAL CASE.
I-IN THAT CASE, SINCE THIS IS A SPECIAL CASE AND ALL...
...WHAT'S WRITTEN HERE?
SA (SLIDE)
"I AM HERE."
...THAT'S WHAT IT SAYS.

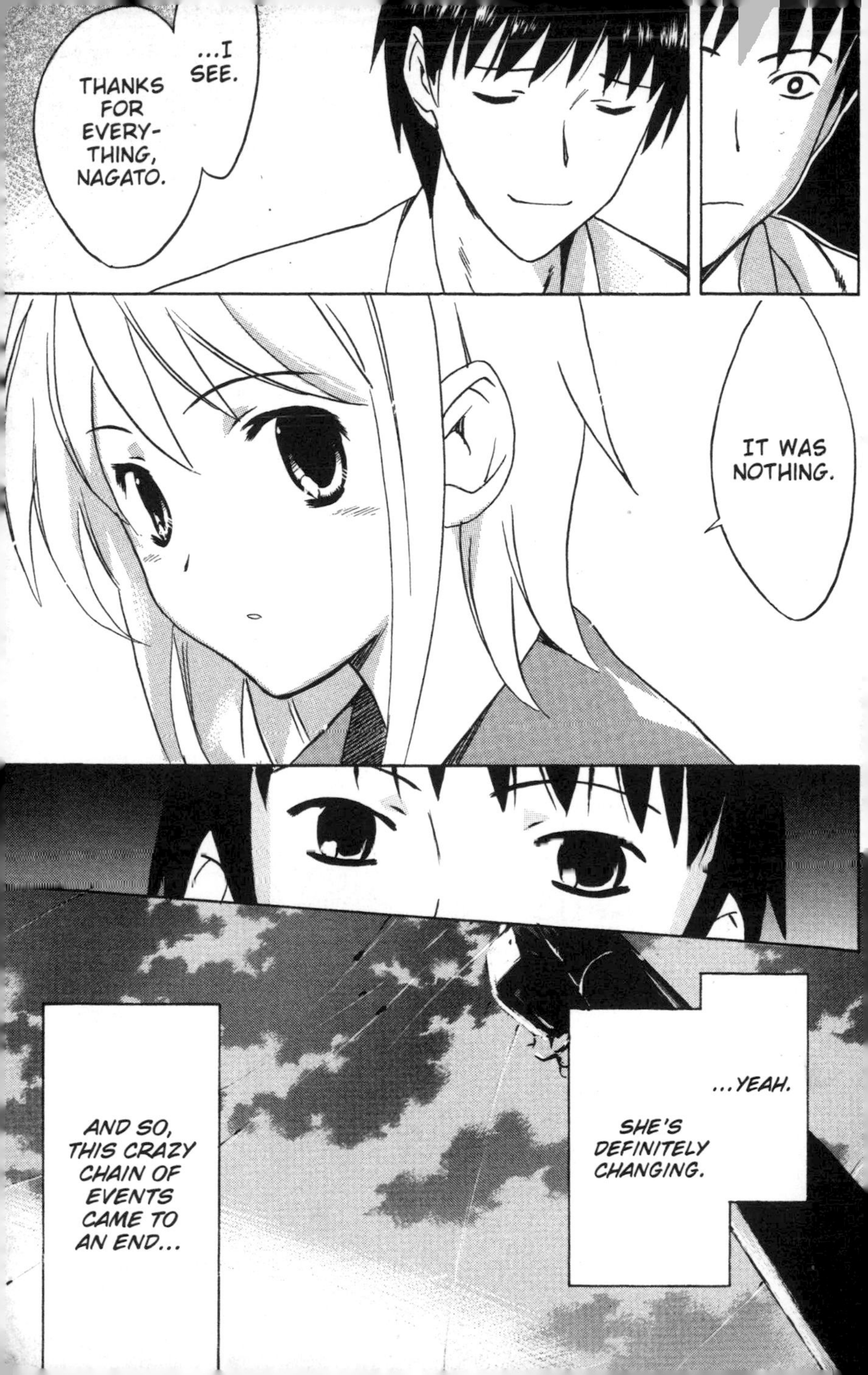
...I SEE.
THANKS FOR EVERY-THING, NAGATO.
IT WAS NOTHING.
...YEAH.
SHE'S DEFINITELY CHANGING.
AND SO, THIS CRAZY CHAIN OF EVENTS CAME TO AN END...

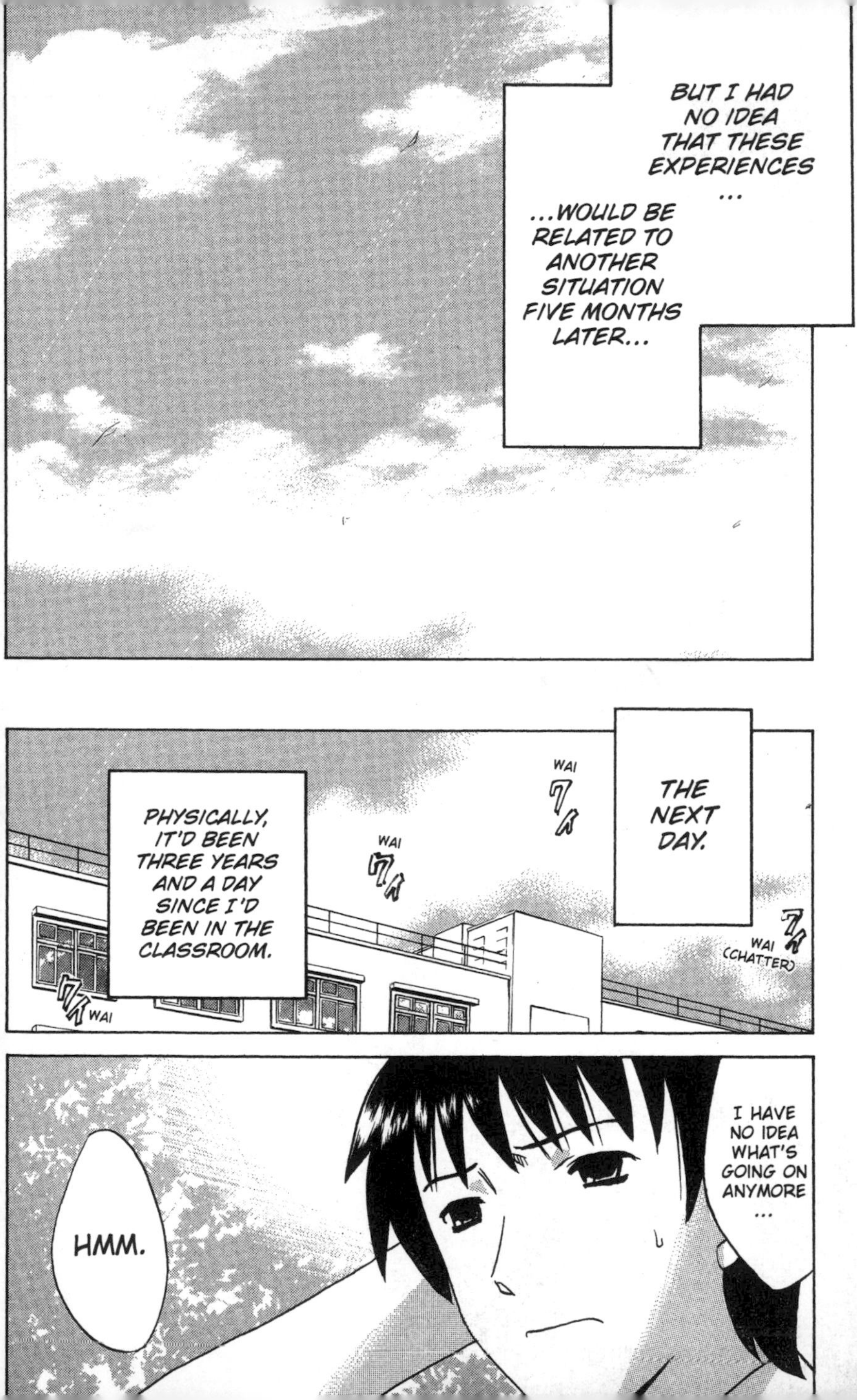

BUT I HAD NO IDEA THAT THESE EXPERIENCES ...
...WOULD BE RELATED TO ANOTHER SITUATION FIVE MONTHS LATER...
THE NEXT DAY.
WAI
WAI (CHATTER)
WAI
PHYSICALLY, IT'D BEEN THREE YEARS AND A DAY SINCE I'D BEEN IN THE CLASSROOM.
WAI
I HAVE NO IDEA WHAT'S GOING ON ANYMORE ...
HMM.

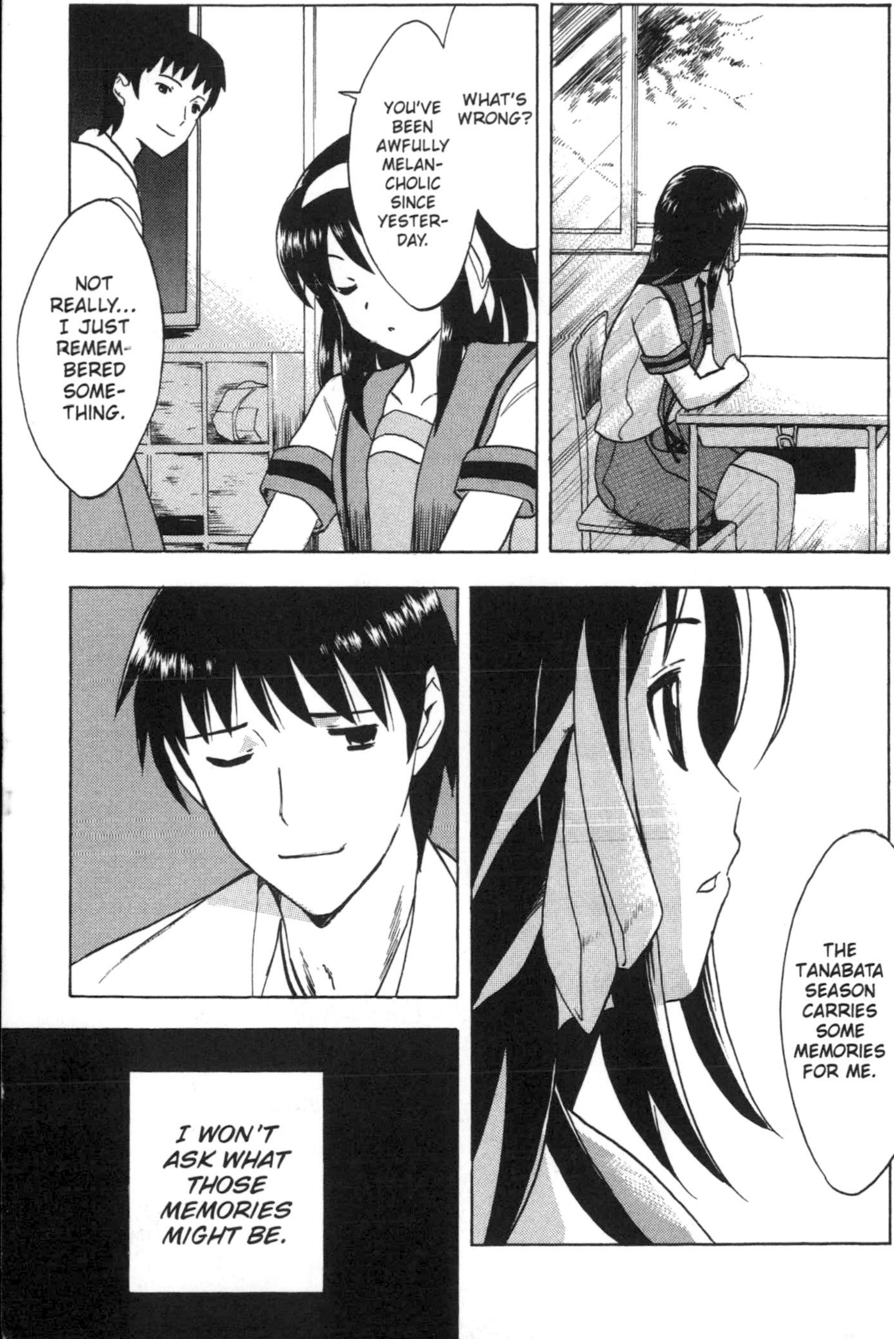
WHAT'S WRONG?
YOU'VE BEEN AWFULLY MELAN-CHOLIC SINCE YESTER-DAY.
NOT REALLY... I JUST REMEM-BERED SOME-THING.
THE TANABATA SEASON CARRIES SOME MEMORIES FOR ME.
I WON'T ASK WHAT THOSE MEMORIES MIGHT BE.

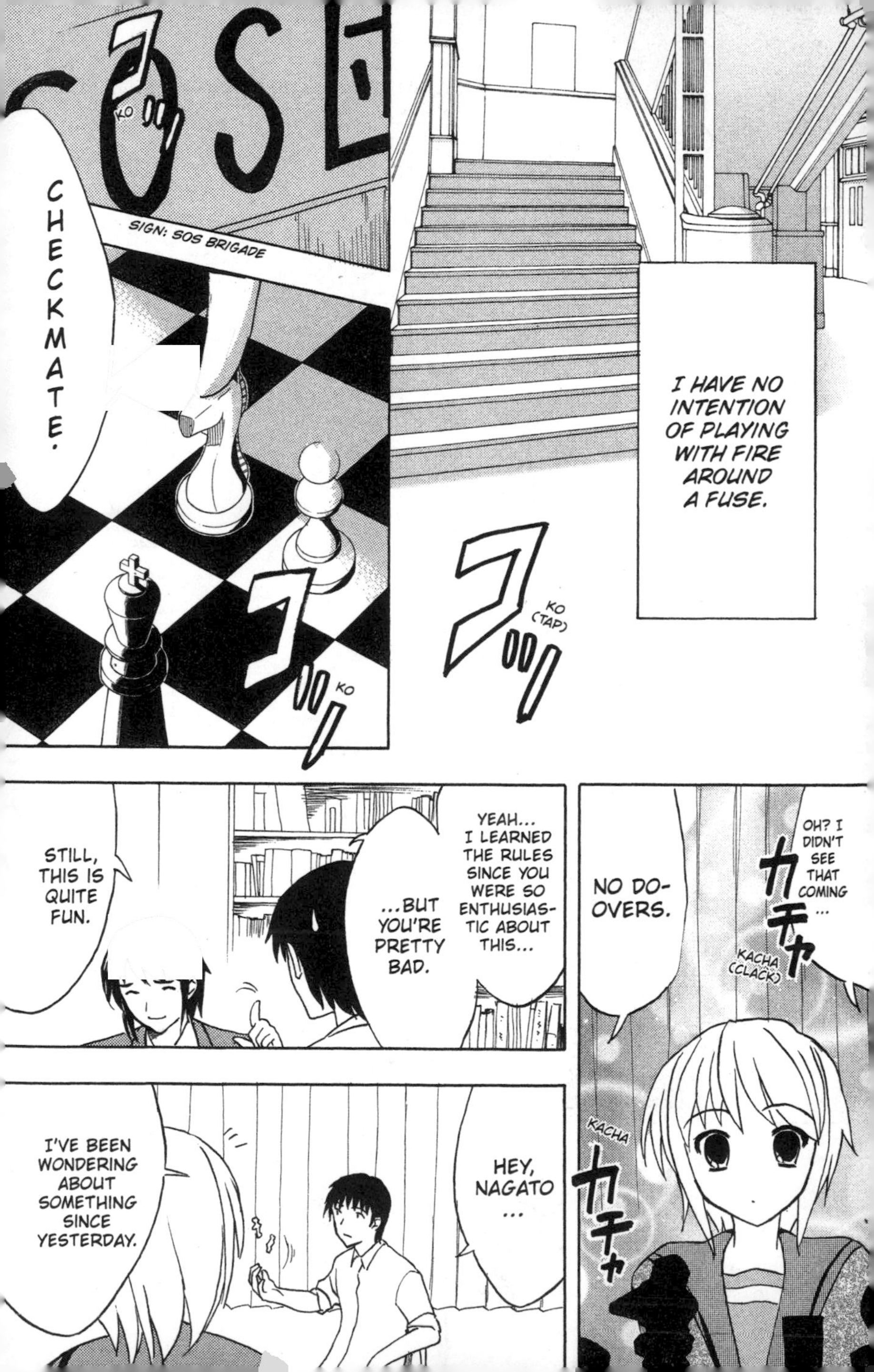
I HAVE NO INTENTION OF PLAYING WITH FIRE AROUND A FUSE.
KO (TAP)
KO
KO
SIGN: SOS BRIGADE
CHECKMATE.
OH? I DIDN'T SEE THAT COMING...
KACHA (CLACK)
NO DO-OVERS.
KACHA
YEAH... I LEARNED THE RULES SINCE YOU WERE SO ENTHUSIAS-TIC ABOUT THIS...
...BUT YOU'RE PRETTY BAD.
STILL, THIS IS QUITE FUN.
HEY, NAGATO...
I'VE BEEN WONDERING ABOUT SOMETHING SINCE YESTERDAY.

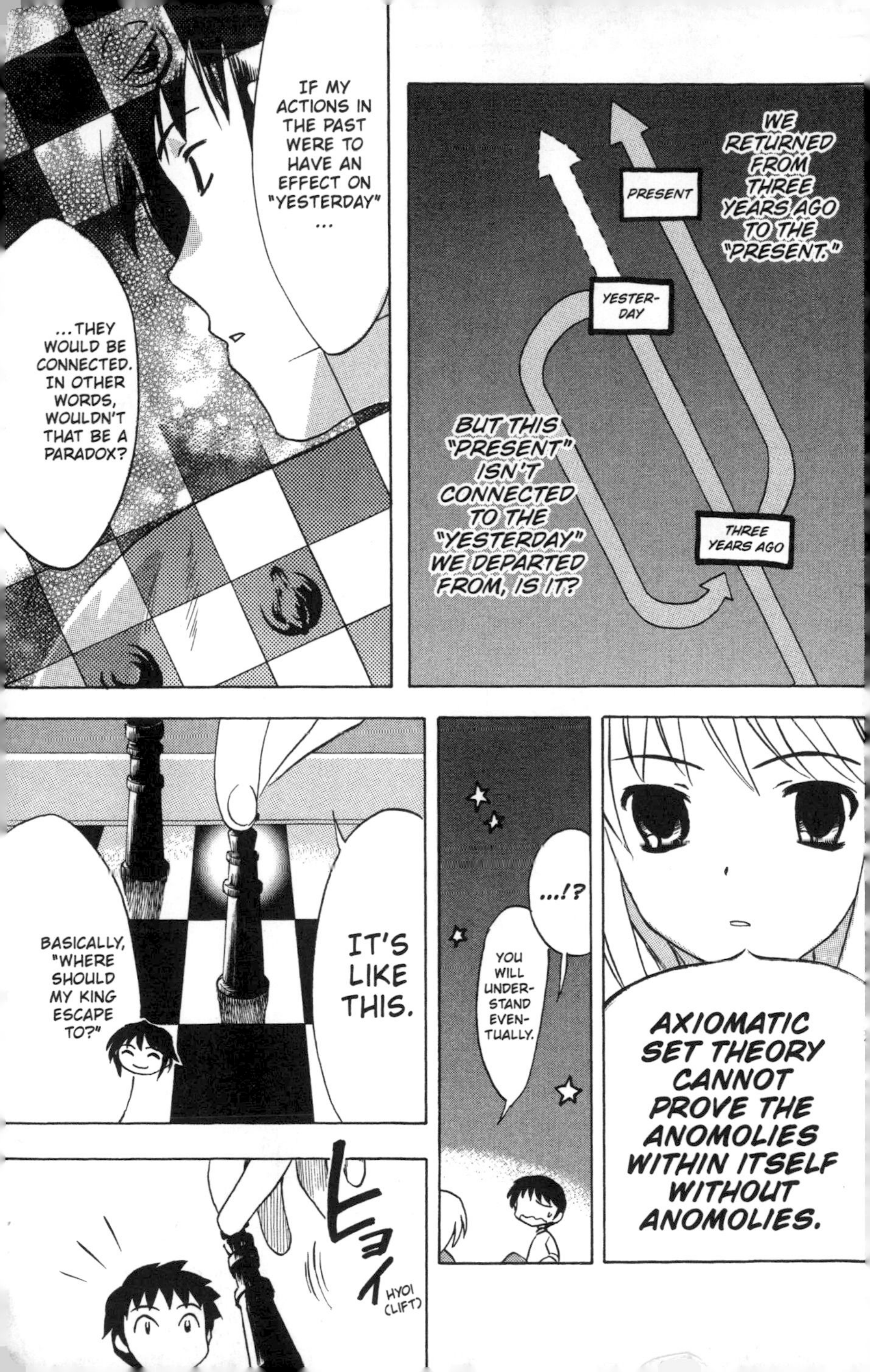
WE RETURNED FROM THREE YEARS AGO TO THE "PRESENT."
PRESENT
YESTER-DAY
THREE YEARS AGO
BUT THIS "PRESENT" ISN'T CONNECTED TO THE "YESTERDAY" WE DEPARTED FROM, IS IT?
IF MY ACTIONS IN THE PAST WERE TO HAVE AN EFFECT ON "YESTERDAY" ...
...THEY WOULD BE CONNECTED. IN OTHER WORDS, WOULDN'T THAT BE A PARADOX?
AXIOMATIC SET THEORY CANNOT PROVE THE ANOMOLIES WITHIN ITSELF WITHOUT ANOMOLIES.
...!?
YOU WILL UNDER-STAND EVEN-TUALLY.
IT'S LIKE THIS.
BASICALLY, "WHERE SHOULD MY KING ESCAPE TO?"
ヒョイ
HYOI (LIFT)

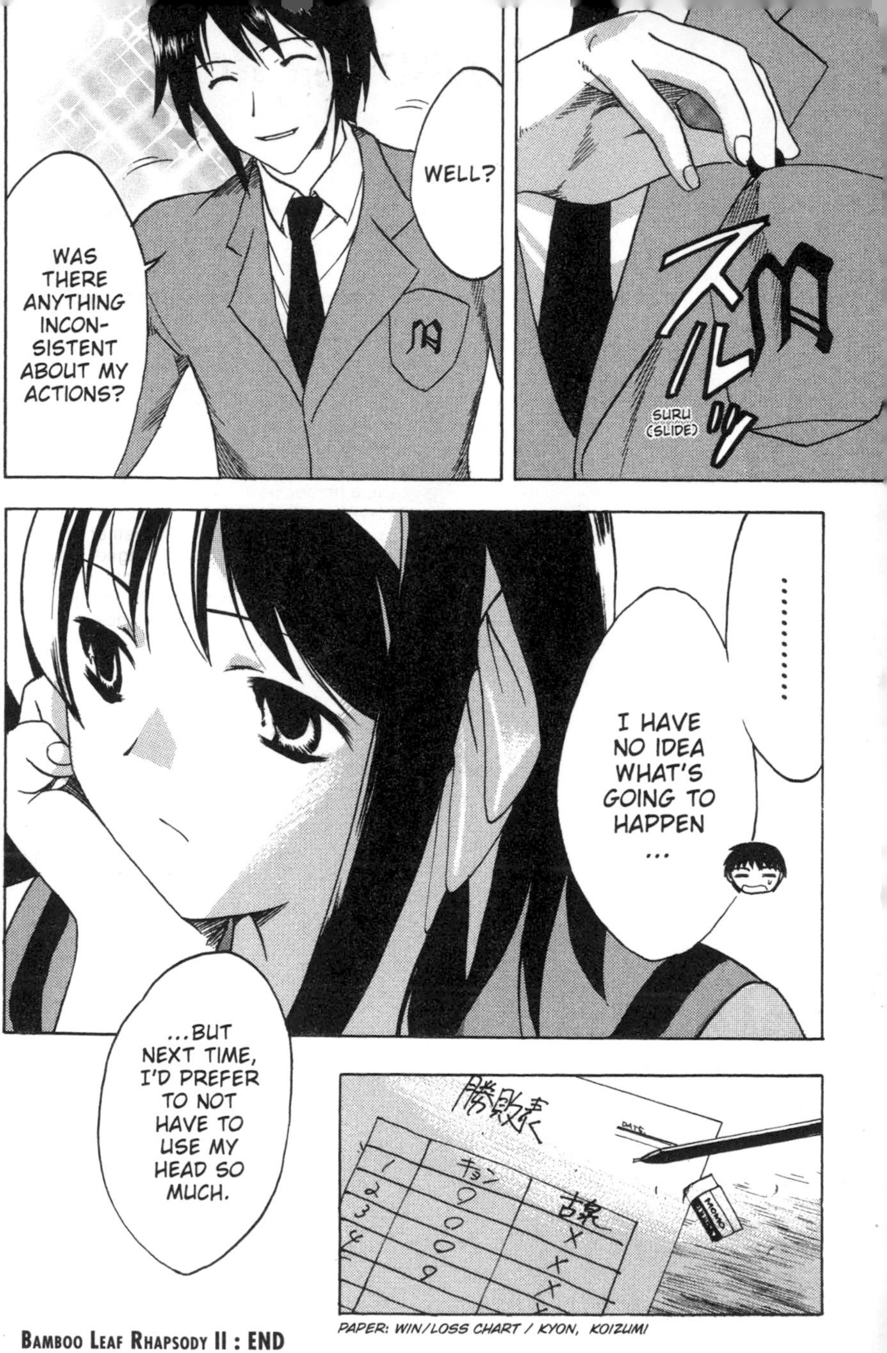
SURU (SLIDE)
WELL?
WAS THERE ANYTHING INCON-SISTENT ABOUT MY ACTIONS?
......
I HAVE NO IDEA WHAT'S GOING TO HAPPEN ...
...BUT NEXT TIME, I'D PREFER TO NOT HAVE TO USE MY HEAD SO MUCH.

PAPER: WIN/LOSS CHART / KYON, KOIZUMI

BAMBOO LEAF RHAPSODY II : END

TRANSLATION NOTES

Page 55
Battery is a collective term for the pitcher and catcher in a baseball game.

Page 71
Tanabata is the Japanese star festival which takes place on the evening of July 7th. It celebrates the meeting of *Orihime* (the star Vega) and *Hikoboshi* (Altair). The story of Orihime and Hikoboshi comes from Chinese folklore. Orihime was the daughter of the king of the sky. Every day she worked hard weaving beautiful cloth on the banks of the Milky Way, but she was so busy weaving that she didn't have time to look for a husband. So the sky king arranged a meeting with Hikoboshi, a herder who worked on the other side of the Milky Way. The two fell in love at first sight and were married, but their happiness together drew them from their weaving and herding. Enraged, the sky king forbade them from seeing one another. But his daughter's weeping softened his heart, and the sky king decided to allow the couple to meet once a year on the seventh day of the seventh month, as long as Orihime promised to keep up her weaving.

Page 105
The prayer cards on this page read:
I wish for the world to revolve around me.
I wish for the Earth to rotate in the other direction.
I wish to get better at cooking.

TO BE CONTINUED

THE MELANCHOLY OF HARUHI SUZUMIYA

Original Story: Nagaru Tanigawa
Manga: Gaku Tsugano
Character Design: Noizi Ito

Translation: Chris Pai for MX Media LLC
Lettering: Alexis Eckerman

SUZUMIYA HARUHI NO YUUTSU Volume 3 © Nagaru TANIGAWA • Noizi ITO
2006 © Gaku TSUGANO 2006. First published in Japan in 2006 by KADOKAWA
SHOTEN PUBLISHING CO., LTD., Tokyo. English translation rights arranged
with KADOKAWA SHOTEN PUBLISHING CO., LTD., Tokyo through TUTTLE-
MORI AGENCY, INC., Tokyo.

Yen Press
Hachette Book Group
237 Park Avenue, New York, NY 10017

Visit our Web sites at www.HachetteBookGroup.com and
www.YenPress.com.

Yen Press is an imprint of Hachette Book Group, Inc. The Yen Press name and
logo are trademarks of Hachette Book Group, Inc.

First Yen Press Edition: June 2009

ISBN: 978-0-7595-2946-5

10 9 8 7 6 5 4 3

BVG

Printed in the United States of America